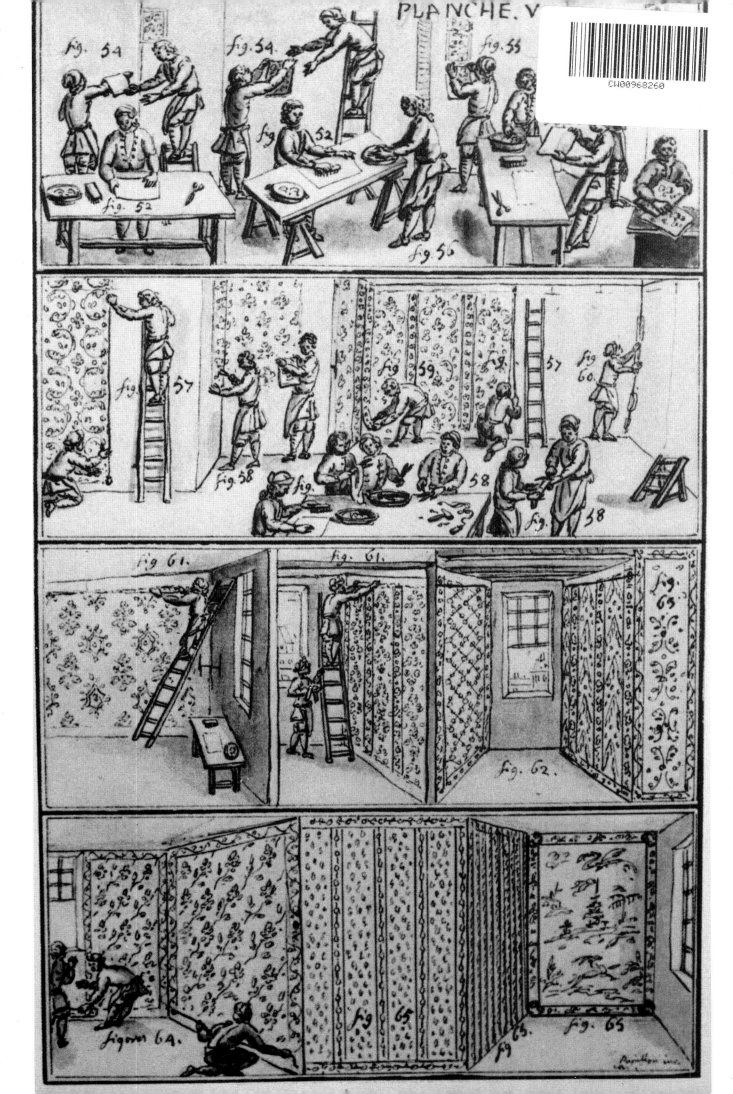

Edited by LESLEY HOSKINS

THE PAPERED WALL

The History, Patterns and Techniques of Wallpaper
New and Expanded Edition

Ill. p. 1: A drawing by J. M. Papillon shows mid-18th-century methods of paper-hanging and a variety of pattern types. The single sheets (not yet in rolls) are pasted and positioned on the wall, which has been prepared by means of a plumb line and, in the corners, filler strips. Paper borders are then used to finish the edges – either around continuous fields or between individual widths. At bottom right is a landscape paper in Chinese style.

Ills pp. 2-3: top French *décor, c.* 1815–20 (see ill. 121); *centre* English flock paper, *c.* 1825 (ill. 40); *left, above* Chinese paper of *c.*1800, with Audubon birds (ill. 65); *left, below* dado by Arthur Silver, *c.* 1885 (ill. 219); *below, left* paper by Réveillon, *c.* 1780 (ill. 107); *below, right* panel by Arthur & Grenard, *c.* 1785 (ill. 108); *right* paper from Boston (?), *c.* 1790–1810.

First published in the United Kingdom in 1994 by
Thames & Hudson Ltd, 181A High Holborn, London WC1V 7QX

www.thamesandhudson.com

© 1994 and 2005 Thames & Hudson Ltd, London

New and expanded edition 2005

British Library Cataloguing-in-Publication Data
A catalogue record for this book is available from the British Library

ISBN-13: 978-0-500-28568-8
ISBN-10: 0-500-28568-3

Printed and bound in Singapore by C.S. Graphics

(The FRANCE difference in style.)

Contents

Introduction

LESLEY HOSKINS

Ever since wallpaper first became widely available its status has been questioned: is it background or foreground, art or decoration, vulgar or respectable, a substitute or the real thing? As long as hand-production and expense confined its use, the nature of the product was less of a problem. It was possible to enjoy unashamedly, if not unselfconsciously, 18th-century hand-painted Chinese panels or English flocks which rivalled silk damasks in their style and grandeur. Similarly, when French manufacturers of the late 18th and earlier 19th centuries developed techniques to achieve extraordinary illusionistic and imitative effects, the resulting panoramas, *trompe l'oeil* draperies, lusciously super-real flowers and complex panel decorations went far beyond what we expect of wallpapers today. But as mechanization increased availability it also increased anxieties about taste. Doubts often took a moral form: *Should* wallpaper imitate other materials? *Should* it be noticeable? *Should* it use three-dimensional effects? The negative responses of many design commentators over the last 150 years have tended to push decorative wallcoverings into the background except when the involvement of artists and famous designers has offered an obvious association with higher culture.

Whether such worries have impinged much on the consumer is another matter. But the low ranking of wallpaper compared with other decorative arts has certainly affected the study of its history, which did not develop as a serious subject until the 20th century. The general surveys written in the 1920s and 1930s were the first to gather together much of the basic material. *A History of English Wallpaper* by A. V. Sugden and J. L. Edmondson (1926), Henri Clouzot and Charles Follot's *Histoire du papier peint en France* (1935) and the American Nancy McClelland's *Historic Wallpapers from their Inception to the Introduction of Machinery* (1924) remain important reference sources today.

This relatively late interest has meant the loss of evidence. The use of printed or patterned papers as wall or ceiling decorations is thought to have started at the end of the 15th century, but samples from the first two centuries are extremely rare and *in situ* finds are rarer. Although the incidence of examples increases from the 18th century onwards, paper is a fragile substance, easily damaged; styles and patterns go out of fashion and are deliberately obliterated; if older schemes have been preserved in redecoration it is not usually out of forethought for history. This is especially true of work a day papers. Types that were highly valued when new have fared somewhat better; there are more schemes of 18th-century hand-painted Chinese papers still hanging on the original walls than there are of 19th-century cheap papers. While the lack of available archaeological evidence is undoubtedly frustrating, current research is uncovering further material and, in such a previously understudied area, any discovery can add significantly to our knowledge.

Nor is new and exciting work confined to finds of actual samples. The field of interest has widened in recent years as the attitudes and approaches of design history and cultural studies have had an increasing influence on the study of wallpapers, extending the more traditional emphasis on stylistic development and technological determination. Certain commercially successful types of paper, such as the 'sanitaries' of the late 19th century or the vast output of orangey-brown patterns and flamboyant borders in the 1930s, were derided by the design establishment when current and have been largely ignored in the histories. Now, as 'popular culture', they are as legitimate and interesting a subject as beautifully crafted panels of the late 18th century, artist-designed prints of the 1950s or any of the other highly regarded kinds produced for a cultivated minority. Moving out from the product itself, other questions are raised: What were the mechanics of design? How did the industry function and what effect did its structure have? How have wallpapers been marketed and sold? Who bought what types and why? How did they use them? Wallpaper, like clothing, is a very expressive and often very public form of communication. We can read the messages of our own time without too much difficulty but need some help in deciphering those of the past.

Eric Entwisle's writings in the 1950s, 1960s and 1970s, Heinrich Olligs' three-volume *Tapeten* (1969–70) and Catherine Lynn's immensely scholarly *Wallpaper in America* (1980) had already expanded coverage of the subject. Since the early 1980s this has been further broadened by a burst of exhibitions and publications which have also had the effect of popularizing the history of wallpaper as part of a widespread and increasingly informed taste for historic interior decoration. The fifteen authors of this book, drawn from Belgium, France, Germany, Great Britain and the United States of America, are all wallpaper historians who have played their part in the recent activities. Their contributions here present the most recent research in their chosen areas.

In outline, the book follows technical developments, focusing on important changes and their impact on the nature of the finished product. The early wallpapers made in Europe were offshoots of the juvenile papermaking and printing crafts. They were wallpapers in so far as they were used to decorate walls or ceilings, but the same papers also ornamented furniture, boxes and books. They were printed on small single sheets which, if they were to make a repeating or large pattern, had to be pasted together on the wall. It was the apparently simple step, taken in the late 17th century, of joining the small sheets together *before* printing that laid the ground for an independent wallpaper industry and made possible some virtuoso feats of decoration, as well as the eventual proliferation of patterns for more modest situations. The introduction of machine-printing increased production and brought down prices. In the 19th century technical inventiveness put new kinds of wallcoverings and a vast choice of designs before enthusiastic and receptive markets. In the 20th century output continued to rise, and the last thirty years have seen major technical and commercial innovations.

Other themes are traced as well. The most obvious function of a wallpaper is decorative, and we find a vivid visual record of designs for different markets and tastes. We glimpse some of the wider preoccupations of the users: keeping up appearances; concern for health; control over their surroundings, however symbolic. More concrete is the story of international competition which, after the establishment of coherent national wallpaper industries, dominates the history of the 18th and 19th centuries, with Britain and France struggling for commercial, aesthetic and technical superiority. America joined the race rather late but had her own vast market to satisfy. The 20th century, with the rapid diffusion of technical invention and improvements in transport and communication, has seen the growing internationalization of products and producers.

But if wallpaper itself is now more international, the study of it is not homogeneous. Terminology varies from country to country, depending largely on the particular incidence of paper or pattern types. Even the most basic words – wallpaper, *Tapeten, papier peint* – have different connotations. National interests and approaches to the subject have determined the body of available evidence. France has excellent collections of the high-quality luxury products at which that country so excelled, but the study of them *in situ* is limited compared with the United States of America where the use of such material, in combination with documentary sources, has resulted in a rich industrial and sociological history. In Britain, the longstanding bias towards technical determination is now joined by an interest in wallpaper as used and sold. Germany is fortunate in having the oldest museum dedicated solely to wallpaper. The individual contributions to this book show a diversity which has the value of emphasizing the width of the subject while, taken together, they provide a current survey of the history of wallpaper in Western Europe and America from its 15th-century origins up to that most neglected period, the late 20th century.

1 Manifold Beginnings:
Single-Sheet Papers

GEERT WISSE

The great diversity in design, use and quality of the early wallpapers makes it hard to give a simple overview.[1] Appearing for the first time at the end of the 15th century, papers used ornamentally on walls and ceilings did not form a class of their own. Patterned papers had a wide variety of possible uses and the same, or similar, designs have been found decorating all manner of household objects as well as walls. One common factor, however, of all the earliest decorated papers was that they were produced as small single sheets. Some were intended to be used alone. Others made a continuous design when joined together. As a method of producing repeating patterns in large quantities for treating expanses of wall surface the technique had clear limitations. Even so, by the 18th century a substantial and successful trade in papers designed specifically and solely as wall-hangings had grown up. These wallpapers were of a sufficiently high standard that single-sheet printing continued to be used, in France at least, through to the latter part of the 18th and even, in a limited way, into the 19th century. The situation was different in England, where the invention of a more appropriate technique by 1700 led to the earlier abandonment of single sheets and the development of an independent trade and pattern types which will be the focus of the next chapter.

Early printed papers have been the subject of much research and surprising 'interior-archaeological' discoveries have been made regarding their use in 16th-century rooms, giving the impression that paper, though an expensive commodity, must have been popular as a decorative finish. Interestingly, France at that time played only a minor role, the first instances of such uses being found in Germany, northern Italy and the Netherlands. It was of course in these countries that the graphic arts were most prominent.

Developments in the art of papermaking and printmaking were significant. From the 15th century onwards they were seen as an important medium for the diffusion not only of texts but also of all kinds of images and ornaments. The 'paste-on ornaments' intended as cut-outs for use on frames and the like, which were already circulating in Italy, are a good example of the spread of visual ideas. Pattern books with ornamental motifs were very popular and reflected changes in decorative taste from the Gothic of the northern countries to the Classical ornamentation of the Renaissance and the more refined styles of Mannerism in the south. During the late Renaissance fortified castles became superfluous, and the nobility began to build palaces where much thought was given to interior decoration and furnishings. At the same time, the Church remained an important patron of works of art. Wealthy citizens, too, built imposing dwellings, and commissioned local craftsmen to make artefacts which conformed to the new taste. It was almost inevitable that the painters, goldsmiths, woodcarvers, sculptors, stucco workers and other craftsmen would turn for inspiration to the numerous pattern books of ornamental prints.

Ceiling papers

A number of Renaissance interiors of the second half of the 16th century have ceilings covered with decorated papers which are of particular interest: less subject to damp and wear, they have survived more frequently than contemporary papers on walls. Simple ceilings consisted of plain beams and the exposed wooden boards forming the underside of the floor above, while more luxurious versions had carved panelling or coffers. Most of the papers found in such situations were printed in imitation of wood grain or woodcarving.

A wooden ceiling of about 1563, from the most important room in the Winckelriedhaus at Stans (Tyrol), has a pattern of coffers that seems to have been based on a design published in 1537 by the Italian architect Sebastiano Serlio in Book IV of his *Treatise*. The polygonal compartments are covered with

1 Detail of a ceiling formerly in the Winckelriedhaus at Stans (Tyrol), *c.* 1563. The coffers and boards are covered with paper block-printed to look like figured ash, and a separate woodcut in the centre imitates ebony inlay. The 'carved' border at the top is similarly of paper.

remarkable grained papers (known in German as *Fladerpapiere*) which imitate figured ash wood. In the centre of each coffer is a cut-out printed rosette in moresque style which looks like intarsia or inlay-work of costly ebony. A similar coffered ceiling dating from about 1587 survives in the abbess's cell in the convent at Wienhausen, near Celle in Germany. The surfaces are again covered with paper that imitates figured wood, but instead of intarsia motifs the central coffers contain vignetted woodcuts depicting God the Father, two angel heads and ornamental foliage. Finally, a ceiling of this type has been reconstructed in the castle of Rodewisch, also in Germany. Here in the centre of each of the square coffers there is a woodcut of an angel's head encircled by sun rays, which with its imitation of wood grain and of three-dimensional carving was clearly designed for the purpose.

In addition to these ornately patterned ceilings, woodcuts were also used on ceilings of simpler construction. Only a very few examples are still intact. In the castle at Annaburg in eastern Germany enough fragments survived to enable a faithful reconstruction of a ceiling which was completely covered in paper giving the illusion of rectangular coffers. In these coffers, the outer areas imitate figured wood while the centres have two alternating kinds of ornament: circular intarsia motifs taken from *Imperatorum Romanorum . . . Imagines* (1559) attributed to Peter Flötner, and strapwork cartouches containing Christian symbols or heraldry.

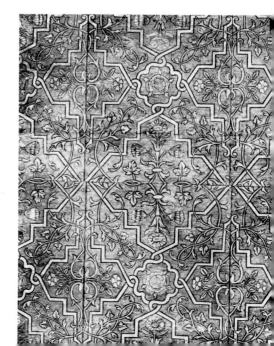

Ceilings decorated with printed papers which create the illusion of carved wood are known in Switzerland (at Bern, Chur, Zurich and Basel), Holland (Middelburg) and Poland (Cracow). Antwerp, in what is now Belgium, was a very prosperous city in the 16th century and, although paper was still costly, ceilings decorated with printed and coloured papers, some of them suggesting relief and simple strapwork, have been found in five relatively modest houses. This is not surprising, since it appears from a document of 1582 that a certain

Anthony de Leest of that city, described as a 'cutter of figures and printer', amongst other things also sold ceiling papers.[2] The fashion seems to have disappeared gradually in favour of plaster decoration.

Another important class of ceiling papers comprises those based on, or imitating, fabric patterns. Some fragments found in 1911 on a ceiling in Christ's College, Cambridge, fall into this category: the reconstructed design shows an imitation velvet or damask. This paper, traditionally assigned to about 1509, is known as the earliest example of wallpaper, but the dating should as yet be regarded as uncertain. It has been suggested that the end of the 16th century would be more appropriate, on the grounds of both archaeological evidence and design type.[3] At the convent at Wienhausen there is another ceiling, in addition to the one already mentioned, where the paper, dated 1564, has a repetitive design related to textiles. It shows some scattered remnants of colouring. Examples of the same pattern, also coloured, were found at Malmö in Sweden and at Antwerp.

At this time + wallpaper was not the height of fashion.

Early papers on walls

The remains of early printed papers on walls are very sporadic. The most prized wallcoverings were tapestries and other textiles, mural paintings, gilt leather, wainscot, and sometimes stucco. There are documentary records and extremely fragmentary finds of paper decorations with painted scenes dated to the end of the 15th and the beginning of the 16th century. The evidence suggests that those on walls displayed a wider variety of styles and motifs than those used on ceilings.

For some years various prints by, amongst others, Albrecht Dürer, Hans Sebald Beham and Albrecht Altdorfer have been classed as wallcoverings of paper.[4] Dürer's *Satyr Family* of 1505 is particularly attractive: the pattern is built up by a left-to-right mirror-image repetition of the design, and the

opposite
2 The ceiling of an upper-floor room in the castle of Annaburg, near Torgau (Saxony), covered with block-printed paper imitating wood-graining and alternating circular and rectangular woodcuts: reconstruction of the original ensemble of *c*. 1570–75.

3 One of the coffers of a ceiling from the castle of Niederrödern, re-erected in the castle at Rodewisch (Saxony). In the reconstructed ceiling, surviving fragments of the mid-16th-century two-colour woodcuts were supplemented by exact copies, of which this is one.

4 Detail of a paper on the ceiling of a nun's cell in the convent at Wienhausen (Lower Saxony); block-printed, with scattered remains of colouring, 1564.

this page
5 A reconstruction of the overall pattern created by Albrecht's Dürer's *Satyr Family* of 1505. Two woodblocks supply the mirror-image pattern, which is also linked vertically.

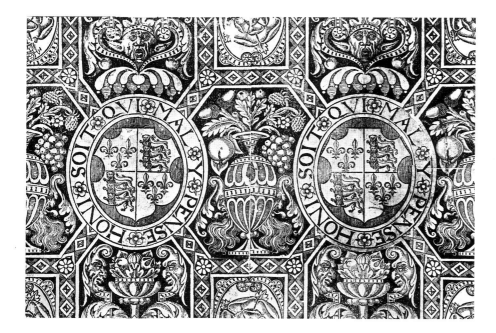

background of scrolling vines runs across from sheet to sheet, both horizontally and vertically. There are also woodcuts with floral motifs which use the mirror-image principle to produce frieze-like designs. Sometimes known as 'ornament prints', they could be used as a surface decoration on wainscot. Particularly popular for vertical elements were candelabra motifs. A simpler variant consisted of narrow borders, often in the form of garlands.

Imitations of intarsia work and wood grain on ceilings have already been mentioned; in a house in Basel the same papers that were used on the ceiling were also used on the walls, where they would have simulated wainscot.

Representations of coats-of-arms were popular up to the mid-17th century. Many fragmentary examples of this type, making up repeating patterns, have been found in England. A paper from Besford Court (Worcestershire), dating from about 1550–70, has a design of panels containing the arms of England, Tudor roses, masks and vases of flowers. The latter motif also appears in a paper found in narrow strips around a door in Howbridge Hall at Witham (Essex), which was possibly intended to imitate plasterwork. The heraldry in this case has not yet been identified, but other fragments include the arms of Mary Tudor, Elizabeth I, and Prince Henry, the son of James I.

These early papers have several current names: 'black-and-white' because they were printed in carbon ink (colours were added after printing, with a brush or stencil), and 'lining papers' because they have often been found pasted to the inside of cases, charter-boxes and deed-boxes. Included among them are the many so-called 'black-stitch' papers which were used in England throughout the 17th century. Their main motifs are flowers (carnation, fleur-de-lys, rose, pansy), leaves and fruit (strawberry, pomegranate, acorn). They originated as printed designs meant for multi-coloured needlework on table- and bedlinen, or, very rarely, for luxurious silk, and were spread via numerous Italian pattern books (from Venice, Milan and Florence) in the late 16th and the beginning of the 17th century. As well as repeating patterns, they provided simple designs for edgings. All are clearly recognizable by the characteristic indications of the various stitches. Once their function had changed to that of decorative papers, they could be coloured in.

Printed paper was also used on furniture and other objects in the 16th and 17th centuries, usually imitating wood grain and marquetry. Choir stalls and pulpits decorated in this way have survived in northern Italy and in Germany,

6 Detail of a paper from Besford Court (Worcestershire), incorporating the royal arms of England and motto of the order of the Garter; block-printed, c. 1550–75.

7 Black-stitch paper used to line a charter box at Corpus Christi College, Oxford; block-printed, early 17th century.

especially in Saxony where wood-grain papers were used on a large scale well into the 17th century. The paper on a pulpit from St Bartholomew's church in Dresden, of about 1570, is the finest example. In a domestic setting, harpsichords were often decorated with strips of printed paper.

From *domino* to *papier de tapisserie*

In the Baroque 17th century, papers simulating wood grain gradually went out of use, and their place was taken by papers with patterns based on flower motifs, both stylized and more naturalistic. An important impetus came from the world of textiles (see below, pp.22–24). Many printmakers followed this trend, and sought with the means at their disposal to enter into competition, with very variable results. Sadly, almost no examples survive *in situ*; but a late 17th-century north Italian doll's house offers an interesting possible use of paper in the room of a well-to-do family: while the walls are covered in costly fabrics, the window surrounds are faced with colourful printed paper, suggesting its use in this position in real houses, where it could be easily and cheaply replaced when damaged by light and damp.[5]

The late 17th and 18th centuries saw the emergence of a variety of types of printed and coloured paper.[6] A vigorous papermaking industry and flourishing international trade enabled the heavy demand to be met. In town and country alike fine houses were springing up, and great importance was attached to style, which was reflected not only in architecture but also in the refinements of interior decoration: textile workshops of all kinds were working to capacity, and the quality of furniture reached new heights. It was in this context that the production of papers intended specifically for walls, as distinct from printed papers of a more general use, developed into a substantial trade. There were significant technical differences between England and France at this time, and the internationally acknowledged superiority of certain types of English paper which resulted will be discussed in the following chapter. What we will be concerned with here is the single-sheet papers which, during the late 17th and 18th centuries, were gradually superseded at different times throughout Europe by wallpapers printed on a number of sheets pasted together into rolls and finally, from the 1830s onwards, on continuous rolls.

In France, wallpaper is considered to be a descendant of the so-called *domino*. The etymology of this word is obscure. *Dominos* were small printed or hand-painted sheets portraying religious scenes. Because disputes regularly occurred amongst guilds and printers, their artistic merits are mentioned in royal documents from the second half of the 16th century on into the 18th century. As the demand for religious images decreased, more and more secular themes were used. The craftsmen combined to form the guild of *Feuilletiers, Cartonniers, Fabricants d'Images et Cartes à Jouer* (makers of paper and card, manufacturers of images and playing cards) – a gathering that makes their diversity apparent.[7] Various illustrations give us some insight into the craft. Around 1735–40 Martin Engelbrecht immortalized the *dominotiers* in two fanciful figures of a man and a woman, clothed in colourful sheets of patterned paper, accompanied by the tools of their trade and brief explanatory captions. The most important centres of production in France were Chartres, Le Mans, Orleans, Paris and Rouen, but there was also a thriving industry in Germany, Italy and the Netherlands.

But, although there were similarities, the term *domino* should not be used indiscriminately for all 18th-century single-sheet patterned paper production. It was joined in about 1700 by what were known as *'papiers de tapisserie'*, which were superior in quality and design and were used by a class further up the social scale. In the *Dictionnaire universel du commerce* by Jacques Savary des Bruslons (completed in 1713 and published in 1723) we read:

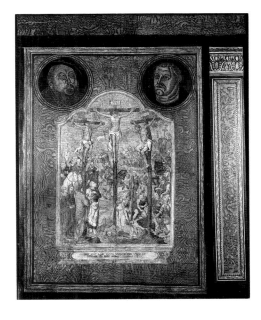

8 Side view of the pulpit from St Bartholomew's church in Dresden. Separate elements of block-printed paper are used for the portraits of the Elector John Frederick the Magnanimous and Martin Luther, the Crucifixion scene, the inscription, the wood-grained panels, their frames, and the capital. The inscription is in Old Dutch, not German. A poem on the front of the pulpit is dated 1569.

Fashion was 'leading' the way even then and fabric patterns were influencing paper design.

this kind of paper hanging . . . had long been used only by country folk and the lower classes in Paris to decorate and, so to speak, 'hang' certain parts of their huts, shops and rooms; but at the end of the 17th century [it] was raised to such a peak of perfection and attractiveness that, apart from the large consignments sent to foreign lands and to all the principal cities of the kingdom, there was not a house in Paris, however magnificent, that did not have somewhere, be it in a dressing room or an even more secret place, which was not hung with paper and quite pleasantly decorated.

This text, which reflects the rising popularity of paper for walls, is supplemented by the publications of Jean Michel Papillon (1698–1776). A woodcut printer himself, he was commissioned by Diderot and D'Alembert to write on the subject in their great *Encyclopédie*. His entry headed '*Domino*' was published in 1755:

9 Fragment of a *papier de tapisserie* produced by the Papillon workshop in the rue St-Jacques, Paris, and hung in the château of Bercy near Paris: block-printing, counterproof and hand-colouring, *c.* 1710. The pattern is built up symmetrically in both directions on the basis of four sheets, which meet at the darker rosette: the upper left and lower right sheets are prints taken directly from the same block; the two other sheets are counterproofs.

10 A *dominotière*, or 'maker of brocade papers and all kinds of coloured and printed papers'; hand-coloured engraving by Martin Engelbrecht, *c.* 1735–40. This fanciful image shows her in a skirt decked with different types of single-sheet decorative papers.

Une Dominotiere. Eine Gold u: allerley gefärbtes u: geprägtes Papier macherin.
1. *Godet pour les couleurs.* 1. das Farb Tiegel.
2. *une brosse* 2. die Bürste. 3. *la crosse.* 3. die Krucken. 4. *auge au papier marbré.* 4. der Trog zum Türckhisch Papier

a kind of paper on which the lines, patterns and figures are printed from roughly cut wood blocks, then coloured by stencil, as is done with playing cards. This *domino* is made especially in Rouen and in other provincial cities. It can only be of use to peasants, who buy it to ornament their overmantels. All *dominos* are without taste, poorly drawn, even worse coloured, and stencilled with harsh colours.[8]

It is not surprising that he was so denigratory. Jean Michel Papillon was a renowned printmaker, the descendant of a family of printmakers. His father, Jean Papillon II (1661–1723), was a wallpaper maker: indeed, the younger Papillon, in his erudite *Traité historique et pratique de la gravure en bois* (begun in 1734 and published in 1766), wrote that wallpaper, which he called '*tapisserie de papier*', was invented by his father in 1688. It is rather curious that he gives the exact year. It could be that Papillon senior put a new wallcov-

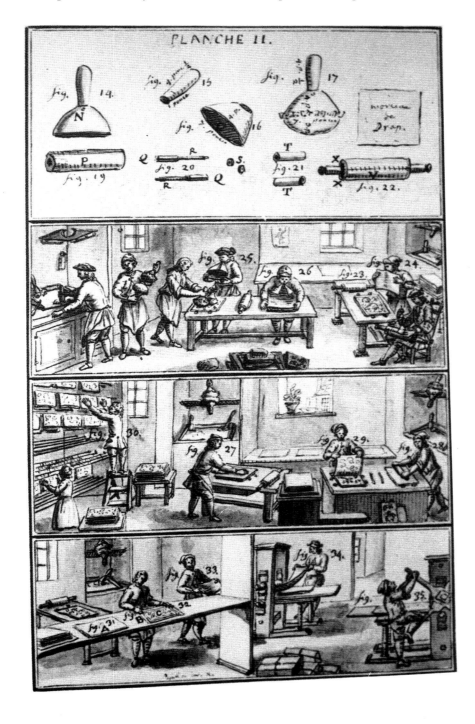

11 A drawing by J. M. Papillon showing processes in the workshop. *Top row*: elements of the dabber (used to apply colour – ink, not yet distemper – to the block) and of the roller (used to press the paper down on the block); the blanket (*drap*) on the roller protects the paper from too much pressure. *Second row*: at the left, workmen are mixing the colours, preparing the dabbers, and applying colour to the block, which is held in place on the table by screws; centre and right, three men hold sheets of paper in their hands and teeth, in the process of applying it to the block; far right, a man sews a blanket on a roller *Third row*: the sheets are printed, and hung up to dry. *Fourth row*: left, the flattened papers are sorted; right, rolling presses are used to produce counterproofs by pressing clean paper against still-wet block-prints.

12 Two borders imitating egg-and-dart moulding and drapery, probably by Remondini of Bassano (Italy), early 19th century; printed in colours on a single sheet of paper, perhaps *c.* 1900, from the original blocks.

13, 14 A child's bedroom in the Hôtel de Groesbeeck-de Croix in Namur (Belgium). The room was papered in the 1930s with single-sheet reprints of a pattern originally dating from *c.* 1760–70.

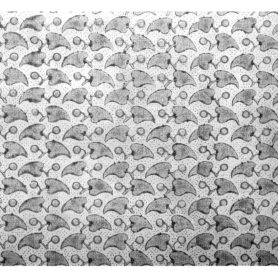

ering on the market based on the counterproof technique, which had the advantage over other papers that the motif could continue on several sheets.

Of great historical interest in the study of wallpapers are a number of illustrations by the younger Papillon showing the production processes in detail. In the simplest printing method, a woodblock was screwed down to a table, cut surface uppermost, and the colouring was applied to it. At the beginning, only printer's ink with a base of walnut oil and turpentine was used, but later distemper paints with a base of lime and gum became common. A sheet of paper was placed on the block, and the design was transferred under the pressure of a roller. (Early English and American trade-cards show the block lowered onto the paper and struck with a mallet, but the principle is the same.) When the sheet was dry it was coloured with a fine brush or stencil. Another technique used was the counterproof, in which a mirror-image print is made by pressing a damp sheet of paper against a freshly printed proof. This method allowed continuous patterns to be produced, as the contours of the design continue on to the next sheet. A fine example of this type of paper survives from the workshop of Papillon senior, where it was printed about 1710.

J. M. Papillon's illustrations also show methods of hanging. Before the paper is fixed to the wall, it is smoothed. After that small marks are made on the wall with the aid of a plumb line and square, to ensure that the pattern will be straight. Then one by one the sheets are fixed to the wall. When the wall is covered, the edges are finished off with a paper border. This was, not surprisingly, popular, since inaccuracies at the edges could thus be concealed. Two borders – most commonly flowers and foliage scrolls, supplemented later in the century by fictive drapery and plasterwork – were printed together on a single sheet, which was then cut by the paper-hanger. Another way of hanging paper was to fix it to a loosely woven canvas support stretched across the wall, often attached to a wooden framework made to measure for the purpose.

The papers were sold in small shops, which frequently sold other articles as well, such as music manuscript paper and writing paper and materials. Ordinary people chose the wallpaper themselves. Those who could afford to left the task to professionals who might decorate a room as a complete ensemble, providing chairs in matching upholstery, hanging the right curtains, etc.

Types of stained or patterned papers

In spite of the fact that the *papiers de tapisserie* were so popular, none has been found *in situ*. However, a reproduction of the 1930s in the Hôtel de Groesbeeck-de Croix at Namur in Belgium shows how they were used. The motif is particularly simple, consisting of a stylized flower or fruit on a speckled background. One would expect to see such paper on the binding of a book rather than on a wall. Papillon's illustrations reveal a large range of patterns. In the commoner types, such as that just described, all the sheets are printed with the same motifs. There was also a better class of work where a number of sheets were required to complete the design. This was the case with architectural motifs, imitations of Chinese papers, and imitation tapestries such as that found in France in the tiny village church of Guibertes, near Monêtier-les-Bains (Hautes-Alpes). In this case the careful observer will see that the 'tapestry' consists of two identical scenes, each printed on a number of small sheets and hand-coloured. The depiction could be infinitely enlarged by adding more and more scenes. Another landscape paper of the same date – the mid-18th century – was found in Switzerland in a manor-house in the village of Léchelles, in the canton of Fribourg: here the subject, a hunting scene, is a single image made up of eight separate sheets. Such imitation tapestries can be seen as the precursors of some of the panels and panoramic papers which came on the market around 1800 and which will be discussed in subsequent chapters.

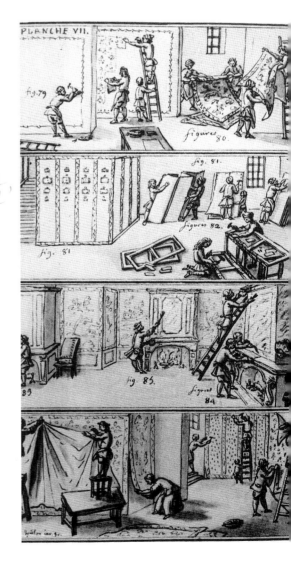

15 Detail of a drawing by J. M. Papillon showing some of the less common and more difficult operations in paper-hanging. *Top row:* delicate papers such as flocks and distemper prints could be transformed into 'ready-made' hangings by pasting them to canvas nailed temporarily to the wall and then taken down. *Second row:* the manufacture of draught-excluding screens. *Third row:* different ways of decorating chimneybreasts with marbled papers; the panels on the flanking walls have landscape scenes. *Fourth row:* in background, a large panel is nailed to the wall; on the right, paste is brushed on the back of a sheet; centre, a woman finishes hanging a long panel; left, a fragile flock paper is protected by a cloth. Note, throughout, the use of borders as edgings and vertical divisions.

A great variety of multi-purpose papers continued to be produced, and though so far we have no clear idea of the full extent of their diversity, there are a number of recognized types. Marbled papers were used in large-scale decoration as well as for the more modest ornamental purposes they serve today. They have their origins in China during the Ming dynasty (1368–1644). The first examples were already being imported into Europe at the end of the 16th century, under the name of 'Turkish papers'. The production process is quite different from that of printed papers, and was long regarded as mysterious. The most common technique involves the use of a trough filled with liquid on which colours mixed with ox-gall are floated: the sheet of paper is then laid on the surface, and picks up the colours. Described by various European observers, the process spread fairly rapidly, and from about 1620 marbled papers were being made in Germany, followed some years later by France. As one of Papillon's illustrations shows, marbled papers were regarded as suitable for use on walls and overmantels. In Germany, the small late 18th-century private theatre in the castle of Kochberg is completely covered with marbled papers, supplemented by painted *trompe-l'oeil* drapery and paper cut-out flower garlands.

Another category of paper used on walls is known as 'cotton papers', because the sheets were printed from blocks made to print cotton textiles (although there is no known example of a paper and a textile bearing the same motif). The effect is distinctive, since on the wooden blocks the designs cut in relief from the wood were supplemented with metal strips and pins. The motifs – which are, of course, those of textiles – consist of realistic or stylized flowers. These are shown loose, entwined, or tied together in a bouquet, against a neutral speckled or striped background. Sometimes there are also miniature scenes containing figures. Other papers derived their patterns from chintz, known in Dutch as *sits* and in French as *indienne*. Chintz was originally imported from India. A long ban on its importation stimulated European imitations, and it seems that in times of hardship the European manufacturers printed their designs on paper instead of cotton. It is also not improbable that the blocks for patterns that had ceased to be fashionable were sold off to small *dominotier* workshops.

Paste papers, like marbled papers, represent a special technical genre. The earliest examples date from the 17th century. A thin layer of paste is applied to two sheets of paper of the same size, together with an image in one or more colours. The two treated sides are then pressed face-to-face and separated. The technique made possible special effects of colours merging into one another. *Papiers brillants* with flowers and figures are more sophisticated relatives of paste papers. Jean Michel Papillon in the *Encyclopédie* attributed their invention to his father, and described the production process: the design (transferred by pouncing through a pricked drawing or template) is painted in a mixture of fish-glue and starch, and then sprinkled with glittering powder which adheres to the glue. Further colours could be added by repeating the process with different templates.[9] Brocade papers originated in Germany at the end of the 17th century and were later produced in other European countries as well. In France they were known as *papier doré* and *papier argenté*.[10] Metal foil is stamped onto the paper by means of an engraved plate cut out in the required pattern and a press. The most common motifs are flowers and scrolling foliage. Although such papers were probably too fragile for use on walls, an example of about 1730, produced in the workshop of J. M. Schwibecher of Augsburg, bears a close resemblance to an 'Irish stitch' wallpaper pattern illustrated on a trade card of about 1720 for Abraham Price's Blue-Paper Warehouse in London.

It will be evident from the above that wallpaper as we know it was by no means a single, isolated invention. It was rather the result of several different developments taking place at the same time in various countries. The practical

16 A 'tapestry' of paper which hangs above the pulpit of the church in the hamlet of Guibertes, near Monêtier-les-Bains (Hautes-Alpes); block-printed in black and hand-coloured, *c*. 1760. The design consists of two identical scenes, each made up of six sheets (printed as usual in upright format), and a surrounding border printed separately.

17 A 'tapestry' of paper from the manor-house of Gottrau at Léchelles (Fribourg); block-printed in black and hand-coloured, 1742–43. The pattern is incomplete.

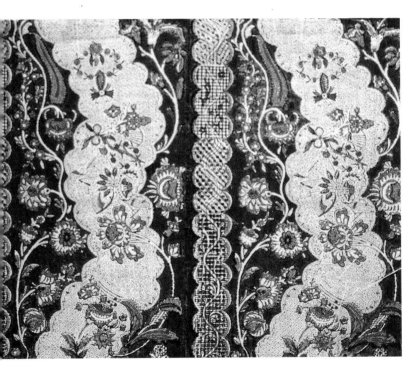

influence of the few German Renaissance artists who designed for the genre was slight, compared to the enormous production of the small craftsmen. Furthermore, the latter guaranteed a certain continuity, and met the demand of the different classes of society for a cheaper imitation of luxury wall-hangings. Another important factor, with regard both to motifs and to production processes, was the continuous interaction with textiles.

19   There was a wide range on offer: imitations of marble, of wood and of architectural details, of drapery and tapestries, and even of Oriental vases sitting on a shelf. These may have been imitations, but many of them are unquestionably creative in their own right.

   The great variety of technique and motif in these early papers paved the way for the emergence of an enormous and homogeneous trade with its own specialist methods and workforce and for the development of wallpaper (*papier peint*) as we know it today.

opposite
18 The private theatre of the castle of Kochberg near Weimar, late 1790s. The main surfaces are covered with two different kinds of marbled paper, the floral borders were block-printed in colours and then cut out, and the bands of imitation drapery on the columns were also block-printed in colours. The ensemble is a fine reconstruction based on the original papers.

this page, clockwise from upper left
19 A *papier de tapisserie* with Chinoiserie motifs; block-printed and hand-coloured, *c.* 1785. In the lower margin is the maker's mark, 'A ORLÉANS CHEZ LETOURMI'.

20 A *papier de tapisserie* with an Orientalizing design; coloured by stencil and block-printed, *c.* 1760. The paper does not form a repeating pattern, and was probably used as a decorative panel.

21 A 'cotton paper', German, *c.* 1770. The characteristic fine dots on the pale ground were produced by metal pins inserted in the woodblock, a common technique in textile printing. Characteristic too is the use of paste colours.

2 Flocks, Florals and Fancies: English Manufacture 1680–1830

ANTHONY WELLS-COLE

Dramatic developments in the manufacturing technique – and consequently the design – of paper hangings took place in England during the second half of the 17th century. These developments laid the foundation for the domination of the European, and consequently the world, market for paper hangings which lasted at least until the 1770s. For much of the 17th century, decorative papers were produced in England by stationers using single sheets of paper on which the pattern, complete within the size of the sheet and generally enclosed within rudimentary borders, was printed in carbon-black printing ink. Even before the end of the reign of Charles II in 1685, colours were being added as a matter of course by brushing coloured inks – blue, orange, pink, green are known – through stencils to cater for a demand for less austere products. The trade card of the London stationer George Minnikin (printed about 1680) mentions 'all kinds of Japan & other paper hangings both in sheets & Yards'[1] and provides valuable evidence that rolls of paper were being produced by pasting individual sheets together, although whether this was done before or after they were printed is not specified.

The simple technical expedient of joining up the sheets, together with the late 17th-century improvements in the manufacture of paper, was crucial for the development of paper hangings in England to their refined mid-Georgian character. Both types were recorded in 1699 by John Houghton:

> a great deal of Paper is now a-days so printed to be pasted on Walls, to serve instead of Hangings; and truly if all Parts of the Sheet be well and close pasted on, it is very pritty, clean, and will last with tolerable Care a great while; but there are some other done by Rolls in long Sheets of a thick Paper made for the Purpose, whose Sheets are pasted together to be so long as the Height of a Room; and they are managed like woollen Hangings; and there is a great Variety with curious Cuts which are cheap and if kept from Wet, very lasting.[2]

Many examples of these early papers have been found at Epsom in Surrey, which was not only a spa town but was a place where wealthy merchants from London liked to live. The papers could even have been made there. The patterns were imitative, using for inspiration textiles mostly – embroideries, printed fabrics and lace – but also adapting designs from contemporary plasterwork or wood-carving.[3] The best evidence for their variety comes from contemporary trade-cards or advertisements. That of Edward Butling, for instance, 'At the Old Knave of Clubs at the Bridge-foot in Southwark', London, of c. 1690, specifies that he 'Maketh and Selleth all sorts of Hangings for Rooms, in Lengths or in Sheets, Frosted [with isinglass] or Plain: Also a sort of Paper in imitation of Irish Stich [or flame stitch],[4] of the newest Fashion, and several other sorts, viz.

left
22 Fragment of a single-sheet decorative paper, stencilled in colours and block-printed with a narrative design of a stag hunt, probably based on painted cloth hangings and ultimately on a woodcut, hung in The Shrubbery, Epsom (Surrey) during the late 17th century.

above
23 Detail of a fine early wallpaper made from pre-joined sheets, grounded in yellow and stencilled and block-printed in various colours with the addition of isinglass to give lustre, hung in a house in Epsom *c.* 1710. The angular pattern is of 'Irish stitch' type.

23

Flock-work, Wainscot, Marble, Damask, Turkey-Work. . .'[5] Similar products are listed in a notice of *c.* 1700 for the 'Blew Paper Warehouse' in Aldermanbury, London, where 'Are sold the true sorts of Figured Paper Hangings in pieces of twelve yards long and others after the mode of real Tapistry, and in imitation of Irish Stich, and flowered damask and also of marble & other Coloured Wainscot, fitt for the hanging of rooms, and stair-Cases. . .'[6] The length of 12 yards (approximately 10 m) remains standard today for a 'piece' or roll of wallpaper, whilst the commonest width, 21 inches (56.5 cm), was that of the silks they aped. The advertisement illustrates a Chinese-style paper in the process of being hung and incidentally proves that this firm was already printing the main decorative papers and the border designs on separate rolls. In order to produce a room imitating the fashionable 'paned' arrangement, in which a main textile was framed into panels with a contrasting textile or border,[7] lengths of the decorative paper had to be hung with gaps between them, and the borders applied later.

Surviving papers from the beginning of the 18th century are difficult to date precisely without corroborative evidence, either from the architectural context in which they were found or from the type of Excise duty stamp on the back of the paper. The interest in historic paper hangings during the past decade has resulted in the recovery of many previously unknown designs and these appear to prove that rolls were already being produced by pasting constituent sheets of paper together before printing.[8] This was the crucial development, for it released the designer from the tyranny of the paper size, allowing patterns of a repeat far exceeding the 18 or 20 inches (46 or 51 cm) of a single sheet. Of the two grand-est surviving examples of a large-scale printed pattern one is at Erddig (Powys); the other is a magnificent paper rescued from a builder's skip in Epsom during the 1980s. This is constructed from individual sheets of paper prejoined to form the roll: that was then grounded in yellow and printed, using a combination of stencils and wood blocks, in at least three shades of blue with orange and pink which includes talc or isinglass to give a truly lustrous effect.

With the manufacture of pre-joined paper rolls, fashionable luxury textiles came within reach of imitation by the paper-stainers, and the first third of the 18th century saw moves to develop convincing versions. The demand for Oriental chintzes was partly satisfied by imitations in the form of stencilled and block-printed wallpapers, while cut velvets, damasks, brocades and brocatelles began to be copied in flocked paper hangings.

Manufacturing techniques and the taxation of wallpapers

The methods of manufacture were described by Robert Dossie, whose compre-hensive book *The Handmaid to the Arts* was first published in London in 1758,[9] and they did not change much until the application of machines to papermaking and printing in the early 19th century. In the case of the stencilled and block-printed papers, first the lengths were brushed with a distemper ground

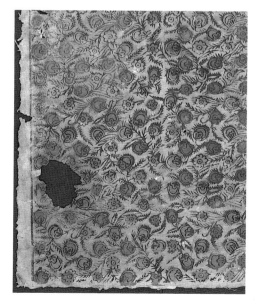

> made by mixing whiting [with water and] with the size and laying it on the paper with a proper [specially designed] brush in the most even manner. This is all that is required, where the ground is to be left white; and the paper being then hung on a proper frame, till it be dry, is fit to be painted [decorated].

For coloured grounds, pigment was mixed into the distemper or, for greater intensity, a second, coloured ground was laid over the first.

> There are three methods, by which paper hangings are painted: the first by printing on the colours: the second by using the stencil and the third by laying them on with a pencil [brush], as in other kinds of painting.

Patterned wallpapers were rarely hand-painted in England.[10] They were usually stencilled or block-printed, or both. Stencils, in which all the elements of a design that are to be a particular colour are 'cut out, in a piece of thin leather, or oil cloth', were mostly used to apply broad areas of colour beneath block-printed outlines.

When the colours are laid on by printing, the impression is made by wooden prints [blocks]; which are cut in such manner, that the figure [design] to be expressed is made to project from the surface by cutting away all the other part: and this, being charged with the colours . . . by letting it gently down on a block [tray] on which the colour is previously spread, conveys it from thence to the ground of the paper, on which it is made to fall more forcibly by means of its weight, and the effort of the arm of the person who uses the print [block].

Dossie called the technique of flocking the 'raising a kind of coloured emboss-ment by chopt cloth. This embossed sort is called *flock-paper*: the art of making which is of very late invention, and is a great improvement of the manufacture of paper hangings, both with regard to the beauty and durableness.' Flock papers were made in much the same way as papers printed in colours except that the paper was often

prepared with a varnish ground; for as the flock itself requires to be laid on with varnish [adhesive, sometimes found to be animal glue], the other kind of [distemper] ground would prevent it from taking on the paper; and render the cohesion so imperfect, that the flock would peel off with the least violence.

Actually distemper grounds *were* used as well, sometimes with a transparent varnish ground over them, for maximum brilliance of colour. The paper was then ready to be printed and instead of printing colours, the block was used

to lay the varnish on all the parts where the flock is to be fixed. The sheet, thus prepared by the varnished impression, is then to be removed to another block or table; and to be strewed over with flock; which is afterwards to be gently compressed by a board, or some other flat body, to make the varnish take the better hold of it; then the sheet is to be hung on a frame until the varnish be perfectly dry: at which time the superfluous part of the flock is to be brushed off by a soft camel's hair brush; and the proper flock will be found to adhere in a very strong manner.

Wallpapers began to be taxed in 1712 along with other luxury goods, in the Whig government's attempt to recoup some of the cost of the country's involve-ment in the War of the Spanish Succession (1702–13). Duty was levied on all paper 'Printed, Painted, or Stained in Great Britain to serve for Hangings and other Uses . . . (over and above the Duties payable for such Paper before the Printing, Painting, or Staining thereof)'[11] at the rate of 1*d*. per square yard, raised to 1½*d*. in 1714 and to 1¾*d*. in 1787. The duty on the decoration by whatever means could be reclaimed if the wallpaper was exported, a useful incentive. The duty stamp bearing the Stuart arms, used in the last years of the reign of Queen Anne between 1712 and 1714, is very rarely found, as is what may be its early Georgian successor which reads GR OWING DUTY.[12] From 1715, Excise Officers had to 'mark or stamp every Sheet and Piece' with a stamp (the FIRST ACCOUNT TAKEN stamp) and, after it was decorated, with another, the charge stamp, consisting of the crowned GR cipher with paper number, which

Single-sheet decorative papers hung in houses in Epsom during the late 17th century

24 Block-printed with a pattern based on plasterwork. An identical paper was hung in a house in Chichester (Sussex).

25 Block-printed with a pattern resembling lacework. This example was hung *c*. 1680 in The Shrubbery, where the 'Stag Hunt' paper (Ill. 22) was also found.

26 Grounded in grey-blue, stencilled in colours and block-printed with a pattern of flowers and leaves. The edges of the individual sheet are visible at left and bottom.

showed that duty had been charged on the stainer. The latter mark was used, with the addition of GR III, until 1830 and it is the most commonly found Excise duty stamp. Imported 'painted paper' had from 1712 been subject to a duty of 8*s*. per ream, but competition, particularly from France, led to the imposition in 1773 of duty at the same rate as English-made papers, although Chinese papers imported by the East India Company remained exempt until 1792. In order to avoid at least part of the duty, wallpapers were often painted a plain colour *in situ*, generally in the blue or green verditer shades derived from copper which were popular as a background for pictures in gilt frames. Excise Officers were instructed in 1764 to 'use every likely and legal means to discover where rooms have been hung with plain Paper, and afterwards Stained or Painted'.[13] Other evasions were countered in 1778 when each sheet had to be stamped twice. None of these duty stamps bore the date (so wallpapers still have to be dated using stylistic, architectural or documentary evidence) but from 1786 the so-called 'frame mark', bearing the year as well as other information, was stamped at both ends of a piece of wallpaper. The measures were repealed in 1836 although imported products continued to be taxed until 1861.

27 Detail of an advertisement sheet for Abraham Price's Blue-Paper Warehouse in London. *c.* 1720. Samples of paper-hanging are displayed on boards outside the premises: of the long panels, the two outer samples are typically Baroque and Continental in style, and the second from the left is 'in Imitation of Irish Stitch'; flanking the door are samples of 'Flower'd Sprigs'. The shop is visible through the open door. Inset top left is a depiction of the workshop: on the right, a workman applies the ground with a brush, while on the left his colleague has placed a woodblock on the paper and prepares to strike it with a mallet. Both are assisted by boys.

Flock papers

Early 18th-century flock papers may all have had a somewhat linear character, perhaps inspired by the flocked canvas hangings popular in Holland. One excellent example, with a pattern of oak stems and lattice, was hung at Welwick House, South Lynn (Norfolk), around 1715–20. It is probably significant that the house belonged to a member of the wealthy merchant community (King's Lynn was for several centuries one of the principal ports in England, with an extensive trade with northern Europe) rather than to a member of the aristocracy. The survival of paper hangings here and in other ports and towns popular with merchants in the late 17th and early 18th centuries suggests that it was at this social level that the fashion was introduced generally into English houses. In great country houses, paper hangings may first have been hung in the rooms occupied by servants, and only after their gradual improvement did they become an acceptable alternative to textiles for the parade or family rooms.

The repertoire of pre-1730s large-scale patterns, if we can judge by those that survive, seems to have been somewhat limited. Two grand Continental-style paper hangings are depicted in Abraham Price's advertisement, but no known example is very close to them in pattern. A superb Chinoiserie flock paper hung *c.* 1720 imitates contemporary Chinese-style silk damasks.[14]

The first wholly satisfactory imitations of damask, with the most magnificent Baroque designs, appeared in a rush in the 1730s. Unquestionably the most popular was the pattern which was hung in the offices of His Majesty's Privy Council in Whitehall, London, *c.* 1735: it was also used in the Queen's Drawing Room at Hampton Court Palace and in several town and country houses, such as Christchurch Mansion at Ipswich (Suffolk) and Clandon Park (Surrey) – both in the 1730s – and, in green flock, in the great Picture Gallery at Temple Newsam near Leeds (Yorkshire) in 1745.[15] These are even now sumptuous papers, just as magnificent as the damasks or velvets they imitated,[16] particularly when areas of the pattern were enhanced by a stencilled colour underlying the flock, which may have been a sophistication introduced during the 1740s.[17] The novelty of flock papers led the compiler of an inventory of Temple Newsam in 1740 to search for an appropriate word to describe them: he chose *postick*, a now archaic term meaning counterfeit or imitation. Their popularity was no doubt enhanced by their astonishing durability. Those at Clandon and Christchurch Mansion are still intact more than 250 years after they were hung; few damasks have proved so long-lasting. Another factor was expense. In the 1740s green cut velvet for the Drawing Room at Longford Castle (Wiltshire) cost 25*s.* a yard and green silk damask for the Gallery 12*s.* By comparison, a flock paper supplied to the Duke of Bedford in 1754 cost only 4*s.* (These prices may not be truly comparable, however, for there were several qualities of flock.)

The grandest flock papers have a pattern repeat of 6 or 7 feet (1.83 or 2.2 m), requiring three or four woodblocks to complete the pattern, and have usually been found in the most formal of interiors. It is probable that by printing adjacent blocks further apart the pattern could be extended perhaps by as much as 10 per cent to fit the wall height without undue and costly waste.[18] Sometimes the pattern spread across two widths, as in a great mid-18th-century paper found in All Souls' College, Oxford.[19] Occasionally papers were flocked in more than one colour, to give an effect of still greater luxury.[20]

Large-scale Baroque designs symmetrical about a vertical axis may have been appropriate in saloons or galleries but would have overpowered more intimate interiors. For these rooms there were available a number of more informal patterns relying not on symmetry but on movement and colour for their appeal, which inherit the Baroque tradition of asymmetrical patterns known from silks.[21] They are exemplified by a paper which was hung in dressing rooms at Christchurch Mansion and Clandon.

28 Green flock wallpaper hung at Welwick House, South Lynn (Norfolk) *c.* 1715–20.

Flock papers great and small

29 *left, top* In the grand crimson flock paper hung in All Souls' College, Oxford, *c.* 1735, two widths are required to complete the design (which has been partly reconstructed).

30 *above* Another great large-scale flock paper was hung at Clandon Park (Surrey) *c.* 1735. The deep pink ground colour has completely faded, intensifying the contrast with the crimson-flocked pattern. This popular design was also hung in the offices of His Majesty's Privy Council in London, at Hampton Court, and elsewhere.

31 *left, centre* Also at Clandon, a small-scale flock paper with an asymmetrical pattern was chosen at the same time for a dressing room. It is grounded in yellow, stencilled in mid-blue, and flocked in darker blue.

32 *left, bottom* One of the 'papiers bleus d'Angleterre' sought-after in France in the mid-18th century was hung in the Château of the Bishops of Dax at St-Pandelon in the mid-1770s. The pattern is stencilled, printed and flocked on blue paper stock. The flocking stands out against a small 'mosaic' motif in a style typical of the 1750s and 1760s.

From such designs there seems to be a natural line of development to the fine-quality informal patterns in the French Rococo manner which was becoming popular in England from the 1740s onwards. Several distinct but related examples survive and they date probably from the 1750s and 1760s.[22] Typically, against a small background pattern in white, stems sprouting a variety of flowers and leaves wind their serpentine way up and across the surface. A handsome blue flock paper of this kind was hung in a bedroom in the Château of the Bishops of Dax at St-Pandelon, about 90 miles (145 km) from Bordeaux, as late as the mid-1770s, along with other English papers (see below, p. 37).[23] They were also exported to America. One was hung in the Governor John Wentworth House in Portsmouth (New Hampshire) about 1769 and another, probably the most luxurious of its kind to survive, in the parlour chamber of the Sarah Orne Jewitt House in South Berwick (Maine).[24]

All these paper hangings are characterized by background patterns introduced around this time in response to the popularity of lace-pattern silks. Dossie called them 'some mosaic, or other small running figure in colours',[25] and they usually take the form of areas of grey brushed through a stencil, with small-scale diaper-work (recalling that of contemporary Sèvres and other porcelain) block-printed in white over them; in the spaces left blank, the main pattern was finally block-printed. The same sort of design was also produced as a 'mock-flock', the main pattern being printed in adhesive and then dusted with dry pigment. Dossie calls the technique 'counterfeit flock' and describes it: 'instead of the flock, some pigment, or dry colour, of the same hue with the flock required by the design, but somewhat of a darker shade, being well-powdered, is strewed on the printed varnish; and produces greatly the same appearance.'[26] The varnish grounds mentioned by Dossie impart great lustre and are a feature of many mid-18th-century English flocks.

The small background diaper pattern was also used in new formal flock paper designs introduced during the 1760s, one of which seems to have been particularly popular. This is a 6-foot (1.84 m) symmetrical pattern of superimposed floral elements. An example was hung, in a blue flock, in the first-floor drawing room at Doddington Hall near Lincoln, for Sir John Hussey Delaval, between 1760 and 1765. A two-colour version of the same pattern was hung in the first-floor front room of Sir William Robinson's house in Soho Square, London, by Thomas Chippendale in 1760. His version is probably identifiable with the '414 yds Crimson Emboss'd paper £15 10 6' (i.e., 9s. per 12-yard piece) specified in Chippendale's account, although it is actually flocked in yellow as well as red.[27]

Another handsome formal damask pattern was surprisingly hung in a second-floor bedroom of a London town house, which it must have dominated,[28] and a further pattern of the same type survives at Ormesby Hall near Middlesbrough (Yorkshire).[29]

this page
33 A sumptuous wallpaper grounded in crimson, block-printed in white with mica, and flocked in crimson. (The colours have now faded.) This English paper was hung in the parlour chamber of the Sarah Orne Jewitt House in South Berwick (Maine) *c.* 1775–80.

opposite
34 A popular formal pattern, seen here in a version with a blue ground, block-printed and flocked in blue, which was hung in the drawing room at Doddington Hall near Lincoln between 1760 and 1765.

35 A pink-ground wallpaper, block-printed in grey and white, and flocked in crimson, hung in a first-floor front room at 6 St James's Place, London, in the 1760s.

36 A pink-ground wallpaper flocked in crimson, hung in a second-floor bedroom at Temple Newsam (Yorkshire) in 1766. The abstracted design is similar to one in a pattern-book of 1615.

37 A blue-ground paper, stencilled, block-printed and flocked in dark blue, hung in a first-floor room at 80 St John's Street, Islington, London, *c.* 1760.

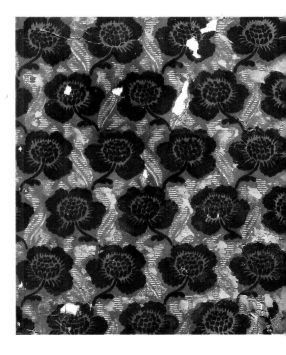

Again, for bedrooms and dressing rooms smaller, less overpowering designs were available. Technically similar to the grandest lace-pattern flock papers (with background diapering and the principal design rendered in flock), these papers differ dramatically in scale, repeats sometimes being no more than 2½ inches (64 mm). Some are amongst the most attractive of 18th-century English papers, and three patterns can be dated with some confidence to the 1760s. One, 35 grounded in deep pink, printed in grey and white, then flocked in crimson, was hung in a first-floor front room of an early 18th-century house at 6 St James's Place in London; it is very similar in character to a flock which seems to have been supplied for the Red Dressing Room at Temple Newsam in 1766.[30] A 36 second flock at Temple Newsam probably supplied at the same time is simpler but equally distinctive: here the design is a diaper type familiar from a pattern-book compiled more than a century earlier – in 1615 – *A Booke of Sundry Draughtes*, by the glazier Walter Gedde.[31] This paper too hung in a smallish 37 room. The third paper, blue-grounded and flocked in dark blue, was hung in London at 80 St John's Street, Islington, a house probably complete by the mid-1750s. This is likely to have been the kind of paper described by Mrs Kenyon in association with her new house at 18 Lincoln's Inn Fields in London: 'The entrance is a broad lobby well lighted by a window over the door . . . it is wainscot painted white. The dining room is 21' × 17' wide [6.4 × 5.2 m] and is to be new papered this week. The paper is to be a blue small-patterned flock. I will send you a bit of it.'[32] This letter shows, incidentally, a nice appreciation of the relationship between the pattern size of her chosen paper hangings and the dimensions of the room.

Changing fashions in textiles probably accounted for the appearance in the 1760s and 1770s of papers incorporating backgrounds organized in vertical bands or stripes. This pattern type is more common in printed papers, as we shall see, but is also found in flocks. One, with a background which convincingly 38 imitates the figuring of lace-pattern silk, was hung at Campsall Hall near Doncaster (Yorkshire) shortly after the house was completed by John Carr *c.* 1770. A simpler flock paper of this kind was exported to America and hung in the Philosophy Chamber in Harvard Hall between 1764 and 1766.[33] In both examples, the serpentine line of the superimposed floral trail mimics Rococo textile patterns. The vertical bands were to be a feature of Neoclassical textiles and paper hangings and they were much in vogue during the early 19th century.

Before we leave the subject of flock papers it is worth reminding ourselves that formal flock papers imitating damasks remained in demand despite changes in architectural styles, from the formality of the Palladian through the frivolity of the Rococo to the elegance of the Neoclassical, and beyond. Some of the most splendid formal patterns we have today first appeared during the 1820s. Two are quite well known already (although both have been dated incorrectly in the past to the mid-18th century) but are of particular interest because they appear 39, 40 to have a double layer of flock. The first is a crimson paper in a handsome pomegranate design which survives in two state rooms at Lydiard Park (Wiltshire), and once graced a Regency bedchamber and dressing room at Temple Newsam; the second is a magnificent formal pattern, again in crimson flock and again formerly at Temple Newsam, which was hung by Lady Hertford in 1826 or 1827 in the great mid-18th-century Picture Gallery where it remained until 1940.[34] Their double-flocked appearance was actually achieved by a development of the technique described by Dossie in which the flock, after being strewn on the varnished impression, 'is gently compressed by a board, or some other flat body'. The blocks used to compress the flock on these 1820s papers were carved with a detailed pattern which gave them an embossed finish that made them convincing substitutes for cut velvet. This blind-stamped technique is very apparent on Victorian flock papers.[35]

38 A green-ground wallpaper, stencilled, block-printed and flocked in green, hung at Campsall Hall near Doncaster (Yorkshire) *c.* 1770–75.

39, 40 A pink-ground wallpaper flocked in crimson, hung in the drawing-room at Lydiard Park (Wiltshire) *c.* 1825. The flocked areas were blind-stamped to give the relief effect of cut velvet. On each strip the pattern extends out to the edge. to join the next strip – either as a straight match (seen here) or as a half-drop (in the adjoining state bedroom). This differs from the self-contained arrangement of earlier patterns (see Ill. 30).

Floral and small-scale printed papers

The imitative nature of paper hangings at the beginning of the 18th century was specified unashamedly in the early Georgian trade-card of Abraham Price's Blue-Paper Warehouse, already mentioned: in it he advertised not only 'a Curious Sort of Imboss'd Work Resembling Caffaws, and Bed Damasks' (which was his description of the flock papers we have just been examining) and 'Others Yard-wide in Imitation of Marble, and other colour'd Wainscots [panelling], fit for the Hangings of Parlours, Dining-Rooms, and Staircases', but also imitations of 'Irish Stitch, Flower'd Sprigs and Branches'. By the mid-18th century, the advertisement for James Wheeley's Paper Hanging Warehouse merely distinguished between 'Embossed Chints' (presumably flocks) and 'Common Papers' (all the rest). Matthias Darly was somewhat more specific: papers could be had in the 'Modern [i.e., Rococo], Gothic or Chinese Tastes'.[36] A provincial supplier, William Armitage of Leeds, advertised in 1773 that he had 'just returned from London where he has laid in an elegant assortment of the following articles, which are of the newest construction and the genteelest Taste, viz India [i.e., Chinese], Mock India, Imboss'd and Common Paper Hangings &c.'[37]

Early 18th-century floral papers usually present a distinct character deriving from their somewhat primitive manufacturing technique. A fine yellow-ground floral paper, stencilled in red, green and blue and printed in black against a pattern of dots diaper-wise, was hung in the Ancient High House in Stafford, probably during the first decade of the century: the ground colour is thin and the stencilled colours are transparent. It has a matching border and it is worth pointing out that throughout the 18th century in England borders were made *en suite* with the decorative paper, the taste for borders of contrasting colour and pattern becoming established only at the beginning of the following century.

Another yellow-ground paper, hung in a house in the prosperous market town of Burford (Oxfordshire), probably around 1715–20, represents a technical advance, for the stencilled pink is made opaque with white and the outlines are printed not in black but in a deep puce. This technique of stencilling and printing continued up to the middle of the century and beyond. Dossie explains: 'In common paper of low price it is usual . . . to print only the outlines, and lay on the rest of the colours by stencilling; which both saves the expense of cutting more prints [woodblocks]; and can be practised by common workmen, not requiring the great care and dexterity necessary to the using prints.'[38]

By improving the carving of the blocks, controlling their registration and adding further colours, English paper-stainers were able during the second quarter of the century to achieve very satisfactory imitations of Oriental chintzes[39] and Chinese painted wallpapers. The latter were becoming fashionable for bedrooms and dressing rooms during the 1740s and English manufacturers seem to have been quick to imitate them.

Textiles remained a potent source of inspiration, and by the middle of the century floral patterns had been adapted to the Rococo style which had become all the rage in the decoration of interiors: in one of the best designs of the period, naturalistic polychrome flowers are combined with Rococo-style vases and scrollwork and more abstract floral decoration in white to produce a paper which has much of the richness of contemporary brocaded damasks – at a fraction of the cost.

We have already seen how flock papers of the 1750s, 1760s and 1770s mimicked luxurious lace-pattern silks by introducing a background figure before the adhesive was printed and strewn with flock. These designs were available in unflocked versions, too, and fine examples survive from houses as far apart geographically as St James's Place in London and Northgate in Wakefield (Yorkshire).[40]

42

43

41
156

44

159

below
41 Fragment of wallpaper stencilled and block-printed in imitation of an Oriental chintz, *c*. 1725–40.

opposite
42 An early yellow-ground wallpaper, stencilled in red, green and blue, and block-printed in black, hung in the Ancient House in Stafford, *c*. 1700–1710.

43 A yellow-ground wallpaper, stencilled in pink and block-printed in puce, hung in a first-floor front room of a house in Burford (Oxfordshire), *c*. 1715–20.

44 A blue-ground wallpaper, stencilled and block-printed in a floral design with Rococo vases, from a house in High Street, Brentford (Middlesex), *c*. 1755–60. An ornamental border is pasted at the bottom.

45, 46 Two papers hung one on top of the other at 51 Northgate, Wakefield (Yorkshire), perhaps in the 1760s (*top*) and 1790s (*above*). Both have blue grounds; the earlier one is stencilled and block-printed, the later one block-printed with a floral pattern. Both retain fragments of border.

47 A block-printed floral paper from Ashburnham Park (Sussex). This bears a frame mark on the back dated 1815.

48 A white-ground wallpaper block-printed with pink stripes and patterned bands, hung in a house in Maddox Street, Mayfair, London, *c.* 1830.

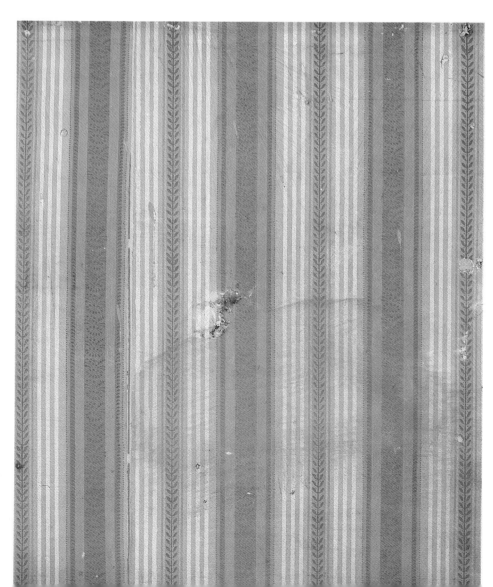

Small-scale diaper patterns had been extremely popular during the 17th century for the decorative papers used to line deed-boxes and the drawers in chests, but re-emerged during the first half of the 18th century with renewed
49 vigour. A notable paper of this kind, grounded in grey, stencilled in blue and block-printed in black and white, was hung (with a similarly coloured border) in a house known as Whitehall in Cheam (Surrey), perhaps soon after 1741 following a change of tenant.[41] The particular character of this paper, in which the block-printed white was very imperfectly registered over the stencilled blue and black, helps to date it; but small-pattern papers can be notoriously difficult to
36 place, as the red flock with a diaper design hung in a bedroom at Temple Newsam in 1766 demonstrates very clearly.[42] The house in Northgate, Wakefield, mentioned earlier, is particularly interesting for having been the premises occupied by the cabinet-makers and furnishers Wright & Elwick, provincial rivals of Thomas Chippendale, and the many layers recovered from the building may represent showroom patterns. These include two handsome blue-ground papers (with borders) hung in an upstairs room perhaps during the
45 1760s and the 1790s: the earlier has a stylized floral design formed by the
46 juxtaposition of two elements repeated, while the later has vertical bands of floral motifs. Other popular ground colours in England during the last quarter of the 18th century, in addition to blue, were French grey, pea-green and blue and green verditer.

Some floral papers from the 1760s and 1770s onwards have background pat-
38 terns arranged in vertical bands; and as we noted, more printed than flocked versions have survived. Thomas Chippendale supplied one to Sir Ninian Home at Paxton House (Berwickshire) in 1774: '[bedchamber] 13 pieces of Blue stripe and Sprig paper @ 6/-'.[43] The most remarkable group – no fewer than three different designs survive – was hung in the Château of the Bishops of Dax during the 1770s. Some were made by an Irishman, Edward Duras, who set up business in Bordeaux in 1772, while others may have been English papers supplied by him.[44]

The taste for stripes was long-lived and there was a huge vogue for them in the 1820s. A securely datable example will demonstrate their character. This is
48 a pink stripe design hung in a house in Maddox Street, Mayfair, London. It is identical to a blue paper hung in 1829 in a first-floor bedroom and dressing room at Temple Newsam, where a second example of the same date adorned a
50 ground-floor dressing room. This is more elaborate, the green bands consisting of numerous parallel stripes overlaid by a honeycomb pattern printed in buff.

47, By this date there was an enormous choice of floral paper hangings available.
158 Some were entirely naturalistic, while others were highly stylized, with 'hatched' shadows and highlights and richly coloured grounds.

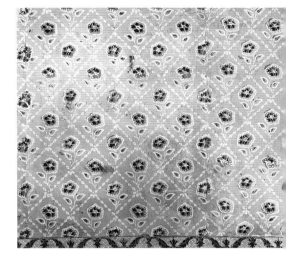

49 A grey-ground wallpaper and border, stencilled and block-printed, hung at Whitehall, Cheam (Surrey), c. 1740–45.

50 A buff-ground wallpaper, block-printed in buff and green with patterned bands in cream, hung in a ground-floor dressing room at Temple Newsam (Yorkshire), c. 1829.

'Modern' and 'Gothic' papers

In the years around the middle of the 18th century a demand for paper hangings appropriate to the current architectural and decorative fashions was met by the production of handsome papers in what Matthias Darly described in his trade-card as the 'Modern' or Rococo and 'Gothic' styles. Paper-stainers produced hangings imitating the effect of print rooms, following the taste described in 1753 by Horace Walpole, who in Strawberry Hill, his house near London, had rooms hung with yellow or red paper and prints, 'framed in a new manner invented by Lord Cardigan; that is, with black and white borders printed.'[45] No fewer than three papers of this kind were supplied to Doddington Hall near Lincoln in the 1760s, where they were pasted onto the walls of small closets and passages: all give the impression of a wall hung with engraved landscape scenes in variously shaped frames set either between vertical bands including baskets, musical and military trophies, or alternatively amongst scatterings of flower sprigs.[46] Like all mid-18th-century English wallpapers these were printed in distemper colours. Attempts were also made by John Baptist Jackson during the period c. 1752–55 to print similar patterns in oil colours to give a chiaroscuro effect. Panels printed by Jackson survive in museums,[47] but no wallpaper securely attributable to him has been found *in situ* and the experiment seems to have had little if any effect on the development of English papers.

The use of paper hangings to mimic designs in plasterwork had been pioneered in England no later than the last quarter of the 17th century. They became popular again in the mid-18th century, Dossie mentioning papers 'made in representation of stucco work, for the covering of ceilings, or the sides of halls, stair-cases, passages, &c.'[48] Some were Classical, while others were in the Gothic style revived under the championship of individuals like Horace Walpole, who described two of his paper hangings at Strawberry Hill:

> The bow-window below leads into a little parlour hung with a stone-colour Gothic paper . . . From hence under two gloomy arches you come to the hall and staircase . . . Imagine the walls covered with (I call it paper, but it is really paper painted in perspective to represent) Gothic fretwork.[49]

Surviving papers fall into two classes. Some closely imitate contemporary Gothic-style plasterwork and, although not actually based on medieval examples, are architectural in character. Their scale is bold, the drawing simple: no pastoral scenes, vases or figures offset their severity. Their colouring is austere, too, grey grounds often stencilled in ochre and printed only in black and white. A paper of this type was hung on the staircase of the Minster House in Ripon (Yorkshire) probably during the 1760s,[50] and whoever designed and made it was almost certainly responsible for other, similar papers that are known. It was probably a severe design of this kind that Thomas Chippendale described as '30 Pieces of Cathedral Gothic paper £5 5 0 [3s. 6d. per piece]' in his 1760 invoice to Sir William Robinson for his Soho Square house in London.

The second type of Gothic paper hangings, though no less austere in colouring, managed to combine fanciful medieval architecture with scenes and other decoration in the Rococo manner, resulting in a much more light-hearted and romantic appearance. One of the best examples was hung in a downstairs front parlour of 1 Amen Court, London, probably in the 1760s. This consists of ogee Gothic arches and clustered piers enclosing alternately large and small compartments in which appear a vase and a pastoral scene of figures and a cottage amongst trees. Even the architectural elements are embellished with Rococo scrollwork. Similar papers, perhaps even made by the same paper-stainer, were hung around the same time on the staircase of the Ancient High House in Stafford (a remarkable method of bringing a timber-framed Elizabethan house

51

52

53

51 A 'print-room' wallpaper, block-printed on a blue ground, from Doddington Hall near Lincoln, c. 1760–65. Two unused strips are shown juxtaposed, with the selvedge of one visible in the middle.

into the current decorative fashion), and in a first-floor Rococo-style bedroom at Temple Newsam shortly after 1759.[51]

All these are, in fact, Gothic versions of the so-called 'pillar-and-arch' papers which are more familiar in later, Classical guise. Finest of all is the design which survives as an end-roll, left over from the decoration in 1769 of the Old Manor, Bourton-on-the-Water (Gloucestershire), but others were used in the decoration of houses in Ireland and America (see below, pp.115–16).[52]

154, 155

In world markets, English wallpapers seem to have maintained their popularity into the 1770s, with exports to Northern Europe (except France, in the later years), Spain and Portugal, the British West Indies, the American colonies and Canada being particularly strong. However, from 1776, the American War of Independence, if it did not completely close the door to imports from England, must have restricted English suppliers' access while positively favouring French manufacturers and home-grown American products. Increased competition from France contributed to a decline in the importance of English wallpapers in world markets. The home market became increasingly inward-looking after the imposition of higher taxes on imported wallpapers in 1773. English taste, more-over, seems to have stagnated: there was a perceptible attachment to grey-ground papers, often printed in drab-looking grisaille colourings of umber, black and white, which must have proved fatal in terms of exports. Numerous examples survive today. No artists of the calibre of those employed by Jean-

52 A grey-ground wallpaper, stencilled and block-printed with a Gothic design, hung in the Minster House, Ripon (Yorkshire), probably in the 1760s.

Baptiste Réveillon worked for English paper-stainers, so that when Edwin Lascelles required paper hangings for his Neoclassical Picture Gallery at Harewood House (Yorkshire), Thomas Chippendale had to design them himself – or so, at least, his account, dated 4 September 1776, suggests:

> 41 Pieces of Paper of the Antique Ornament with Palms &c on a fine paper with a pink Ground. The pattern Cut on purpose and printed in various Colours – @ 30/- [per piece] [£]61 10 0
>
> 3 piece Borders to do [ditto] the pattern Cut on purpose 4 10 0
>
> Designing and making a Drawing at Large with the proper Colours for the paper Maker 3 3 0[53]

It would be surprising, however, if Chippendale had been able to produce the design himself, for this was a very specialized task, when an easier solution would have been to purchase and copy a French paper. It is, therefore, interesting to remind ourselves that Glamorgan Street House in Monmouth was hung in the late 18th century with a reversed copy of Réveillon's 'Les Deux Pigeons' design.[54]

Whatever the truth, it was not long before French manufacturers were producing not just the Neoclassical wallpapers for grand interiors but a variety of beautifully designed, naturalistic floral papers which English makers would have had a hard job in matching.

3 The China Trade: Oriental Painted Panels

GILL SAUNDERS

In the late 17th century, while European craftsmen were still struggling to achieve a coherent approach to the wall surface, the first specimens of Chinese hand-painted wallpapers arrived in England.[1] Very different from their Western counterparts in technique, scale and aesthetic conception, with their rich colours and exquisite draughtsmanship they were unequalled by anything produced in Europe at the time. Such were their beauty and sophistication that they were considered appropriate for the best interiors: in Austria at Schlosshof auf dem March in the 1750s, and in England at Nostell Priory (Yorkshire) in the late 1760s, Chinese papers were chosen for the state bedrooms; later, a Chinese paper presented around 1792 to Lord Macartney, British ambassador to Peking, was hung in the boardroom of Coutts Bank in the Strand, London, where it survives to this day.

The vogue for these decorative wallpapers was at its height between 1740 and 1790, when they were being imported in large numbers and almost every great house and many smaller ones boasted a room furnished, as Madame du Bocage noted in 1750, with 'painted Paper of Pekin . . . and choicest moveables of China'.[2] Many contemporary letters and journals testify to the popularity of these papers, which was part of the taste for all things Chinese that followed the foundation of the British East India Company in 1599, and its Dutch and French equivalents in 1602 and 1664 respectively. The East India companies enjoyed a virtual monopoly of the Oriental trade, importing artefacts whose precise origins were not always of great concern in the West (Chinese wallpapers were also known as Japan or India papers). The trade, centred on London and Paris, was substantial and profoundly influenced European styles of decoration in the 17th and 18th centuries. Papers imported into London were sent on all over Europe and to America. Most American customers purchased papers through friends or agents abroad, but after the Revolution Americans entered the China trade directly, and wallpapers were imported in quantity by firms such as A. A. Low of New York. Although much is known of their importation, very few Chinese wallpapers exist in American houses today;[3] by far the largest number to survive are in England, Germany, Holland and Belgium, with scattered examples elsewhere across the Continent.[4] Because of the rich combination of documentary evidence and existing examples of all types, this survey will concentrate on Britain.

Little is known of the precise origins of the trade in Chinese papers, though various theories have been advanced. It is generally thought that they were initially given as gifts to European merchants to secure a contract or to mark the conclusion of a sale. They were then imported, in increasingly large quantities; demand soon outstripped supply, leading to exorbitant prices. In the 1760s, for instance, when a good flock paper cost 9s. a roll, a fine Chinese paper cost 63s. – £3 3s. – a panel, or twenty times as much; at around the same time, the

54 Chinese wallpaper of the figure
type in the hunting lodge at
Stupinigi, Piedmont, *c.* 1730.

parson in Oliver Goldsmith's *Deserted Village* lived on £40 a year.[5] Wallpapers were classed as a minor product and thus carried as 'private trade', not separately recorded in inventories and bills of shipment.

The Chinese themselves did not use elaborately decorated papers of this kind, except as funerary or festival decorations. In the 1690s Father Louis Le Comte, a Jesuit missionary in China, recorded the use of silk hangings by the wealthy, though he added that 'others only whiten the Chamber or glew Paper upon it'.[6] Later, the future architect William Chambers (in 1757) and Lord Macartney, the British ambassador (in 1794), both noted that plain papers – usually white, crimson or gold – were preferred as wallcoverings. It was however a Chinese practice to paste paper over the windows, and in the regions around Macao and Canton, both centres of the export trade, such papers were often painted with pictorial decorations. Perhaps the admiration of European visitors encouraged the Chinese to produce similar articles for export.

In both motifs and use, Chinese wallpapers had a precursor in another decorative material imported by the East India companies: this was chintz, a hand-painted or printed cotton cloth produced in India to designs influenced by European taste. The relationship is particularly clear between chintzes with the 'flowering tree' pattern, 'bird and flower' Chinese wallpapers and English 17th-century embroideries. The motif of a sinuous asymmetrical flowering tree growing from schematized rocks is a version of the Eastern 'tree of life', a complex amalgam of various influences – Persian, Indian and Chinese; when Britain, Holland and France became involved in the chintz trade in the third quarter of the 17th century, they supplied their own modified patterns for what were then described as 'branched hangings'.[7] As that phrase indicates, these painted cloths, or 'pintados', soon came to be used as wall-hangings. Samuel Pepys recorded in his diary for 5 September 1663 that he had bought his wife 'a chinte . . . that is paynted Indian callico for to line her new study, which is very pretty', and in 1665 John Evelyn – like Pepys, in London – saw 'a room hung with Pintado full of figures great and small, prettily representing Sundry Trades and occupations of the Indians with their habits &c: very extraordinarie'.[8] As we shall see, similar figure scenes provided the subject-matter for the earliest Chinese papers exported to Europe.

Manufacture and hanging

Wallpaper, since its inception, has most commonly been decorated with repeating or repeatable patterns applied by printing. Neither feature is characteristic of Chinese papers. Though printing had been known in China for centuries, the papers were almost always painted by hand throughout, in gouache or tempera, on a white mulberry-fibre paper called '*mien lien*'.[9] Wallpapers were produced by workshops, and what little we know of the practices there is based largely on evidence of other export wares. It is possible to distinguish the hands of different artists, but the individuals remain anonymous. Some papers bear Chinese characters to indicate which colours the painter should use to fill in areas of the design. Recently a paper at Penrhyn Castle in North Wales was found to be inscribed with the name of the workshop which produced it. The paintings were normally lined with a stouter bamboo paper, and a stamp on the back of Oriental lining paper at Ightham Mote (Kent) is almost certainly the name of the factory which supplied it rather than the workshop which painted the wallpaper that it supports.[10]

Despite the production in workshops, it is unusual to find the same pattern used in two different schemes. A rare example of two papers painted by the same hand or sharing a common model is provided by the correspondences in design between three panels with figure subjects in the Victoria and Albert Museum, London, and a paper hung in Oud-Amelisweerd at Utrecht, in Holland.[11]

55
56

55 One of three panels in the Victoria and Albert Museum, London, showing hunting, boating and festival scenes; second half of the 18th century. The compositions resemble those of a paper at Oud-Amelisweerd, Utrecht (*right*).

Chinese papers were supplied in sets of 25 or 40 panels, usually 12 feet (3.65 m) long and 3 or 4 feet (0.91 or 1.22 m) wide. This length suited most European interiors, but the sheets were designed so that they might be trimmed at the top edge without losing any vital part of the pattern. They were usually hung to form a continuous panoramic decoration around the room. Unused and untrimmed rolls found at Penrhyn Castle are marked with Chinese numbers (in the centre of the lower edge at the front) to indicate the sequence in which they should be hung to achieve a flowing design. Less commonly, the papers were framed as individual panels, as at Bowood House (Wiltshire). The records of the decorating firm Cowtan and Sons[12] include an order in 1838 for the drawing and dining rooms at Bletchley Rectory. Fenny Stratford (Buckinghamshire), which specifies that the paper was to be 'put up in pannels with pearl coloured . . . narrow bamboo satin border round pannels' and that ceilings and cornices were to be painted plain green to match the paper.[13] Another unusual method of display is to be found in the private apartments at Saltram (Devon), where in the

56 A detail from the wallpaper at Oud-Amelisweerd. Utrecht, showing a party of hunters spearing their quarry; second half of the 18th century.

58 1760s disparate panels in various styles and sizes were hung contiguously in a patchwork arrangement, the joins concealed by a narrow key-pattern border of
57 English manufacture. At Sünching in Bavaria a delightfully eccentric collage of *c.* 1765 combines Chinese papers of various dates and styles with European chinoiserie panels.

The Chinese papers were considered so valuable that they were rarely if ever pasted directly to the wall. The best way of hanging them was to mount them on canvas or on a thicker paper support which was then stretched on wooden battens to be fixed to the wall. The procedure is referred to in the accounts of Chippendale Haig & Co. for the furnishing of the house of the actor David Garrick in Adelphi Terrace, London, in 1772:

> Back room . . . Battens, nails & preparing the Room with proper fastenings for Hangings; 72 yds. [66 m] Canvas to hang the Room; 7 Quires cartridge paper; hanging the canvas & paper, Tacks, Paste etc. included; ditto [i.e., hanging] the Room with your own India paper, paste etc.
> April 1st, 1772: scrapeing the paint of the Walls in passage; hanging the Canvas & paper & afterwards the India . . .[14]

This method had the advantage of making the hangings portable: they could be moved to another room, or even to another house. It also protected them to some

extent from damp and decay. Since they were readily movable, they were rarely pasted over at a later date. All this helps to explain why so many fine well-preserved papers survive today.

Pattern types

With a few exceptions, Chinese papers can be divided into three classes according to their design. The first has figure scenes showing life and occupations in China; this was the earliest to appear in Europe, at the end of the 17th century. The second is the 'bird and flower' pattern, based on the motif of a flowering tree. The third category combines figures and trees. The rare papers which conform to none of these types will be considered at the end of this section.

54   The papers with figure subjects had a precedent in chintz wall-hangings of the kind observed by John Evelyn in 1665, which represented 'Sundry Trades and occupations of the Indians with their habits &c.' Typical examples of these
61   papers are those in the Mirror Room at Saltram and in Coutts Bank, where vignettes of daily life and industry in China are interspersed with mountainous landscape elements. Industrial and agricultural activities are commonly depicted, such as the throwing and firing of pots, silk-making and dyeing, the
60   growing and curing of tea, and harvesting rice. Festivals, theatrical performances, and hunting scenes were also popular. A particularly fine early paper
59   can be seen, again at Saltram, in the Chinese Dressing Room: here the figures

opposite
57 Detail of a wall in the Levée Room at Sünching (Bavaria). *c.* 1765. The main element is a Chinese paper showing figures and flowering trees. Below this is a European Chinoiserie design.

58 The south-west bedroom at Saltram (Devon). The larger panels are of landscape or architectural subjects employing the single-point perspective of Western art. In style and subject they closely resemble Chinese export watercolours of *c.* 1770–90. The scheme is completed by smaller studies, mostly of single figures.

below
59 The Chinese Dressing Room at Saltram is hung with a late 17th- or early 18th-century paper in which figures are arranged in repeating groups. Extra birds, flowers, rocks and figures are pasted on to disguise the joins and the repetitive effect.

are on a larger scale than usual, being about 2 feet (61 cm) high, and arranged in repeating groups rather than forming a changing panorama. They are boldly drawn and finely coloured in the formal manner of the groups we find on vases of the contemporaneous Kang-Hsi period (1662–1722), and are quite distinct from the more naturalistic figures in later papers.

The second category of Chinese wallpaper is the 'bird and flower' type, to which most surviving examples belong. Here, the central element is a flowering tree which grows from a stylized base of rocks to climb the height of the paper. As we have seen, this too was a pattern used for chintz. The branches of the tree are interspersed with birds, butterflies and other insects, and a variety of flowering plants grow around the base – bamboo, chrysanthemums, prunus, paeonies and lotus. These motifs are set against a plain-coloured ground, usually buff or pale green, occasionally deep blue or pink.[15] (Early papers tend to be neutral in colour; blues, greens, etc. appear from the mid-18th century onwards.) A rare yellow-ground paper, purchased by the Prince Regent from Crace & Sons in 1802, was installed in the Royal Pavilion, Brighton, where it was replaced by a similar paper given by Queen Victoria in 1856.

Individual artists introduced slight variations to this standard design: sometimes birdcages hang from the branches of the trees, and ornamental balustrades and shrubs in pots may enliven the 'foreground'. Usually the busier and more crowded the design, the later the date of the paper. This development was a response to changing demand from European customers, as the spare and elegant designs of the earliest papers were no longer entirely to their tastes.

With their studied attention to market demands, the Chinese provided extra sheets with each set of papers. Birds and branches could be cut from these and pasted over damaged or discoloured areas, used to fill awkward corners, or simply to embellish the overall effect. Lady Mary Coke recorded in her journal in 1772: 'I called on the Duchess of Norfolk and found her sorting butterflies cut out of India paper for the room she is going to furnish.'[16] Lady Hertford hung a Chinese paper (a gift from the Prince Regent in 1806) at Temple Newsam near Leeds in the 1820s and proceeded to impose a degree of symmetry on the designs by the addition of vases, birds, insects, foliage and flowers. But it seems that the spare sheets did not yield sufficient material for her embellishments, and she hit upon a novel way of further elaborating the designs: she added twenty-five birds cut from ten plates in the first volume of J. J. Audubon's *Birds of America* (1827–38). These impostors married well with their setting, and their ultimate source was not identified until 1968.[17]

It is no surprise that these ornithological illustrations worked so well in their new context: though the 'bird and flower' papers were rather formal in style, with the additional artifice of black outlines, they nevertheless exhibit a remarkable degree of realism. When William Whitehead, writing in the London *World* in 1753, described 'the richest China and India paper where all the flowers of fancy were exhausted in a thousand fantastic figures of birds, beasts and fishes which never had existence', he seems to have been confusing fanciful European imitations with the genuine Chinese papers. Although the flora and fauna depicted would have been exotic and unfamiliar to a European audience – for example the lemur that appears in a paper at Abbotsford in Scotland (home of Sir Walter Scott) – in all but the latest papers they are existing species rather than fantastic inventions. No less an authority than the botanist Sir Joseph Banks noted in his journal in 1771 that 'Some of the plants which are common to China and Java [such] as Bamboo, are better figured there than by the best botanical authors that I have seen.'[18]

This intense realism had its origins in the 'academic' tradition of Chinese painting, and specifically the bird and flower studies of the Song dynasty in the 12th and 13th centuries. In this period Chinese artists were perfecting a style

60 A figure paper with scenes of rice-growing and processing. This is a part of a set of three papers depicting the rice, tea and porcelain industries that were brought back on the 'Empress of China', the first American ship to sail to China. The receipt-book of the voyage records their purchase from the Canton merchant Eshing: 'recd at Canton Decr 2nd 1784 of S. Molineux for accot. Capt. Green One Hundred dollars for Paper Hangings for Robt Morris Esq.' Morris, of Philadelphia, had a half-interest in the ship. The papers were never hung, and were discovered in the early 20th century in a house at Marblehead (Massachusetts), apparently in their original crates – hence their pristine freshness.

61 Detail of another figure paper, typically dense with incident. Here we see a procession to a shrine or temple, and labourers working in fields in the background. This forms part of a set acquired by Lord Macartney, British ambassador to Peking, and presented by him in 1794 to Coutts Bank in the Strand, London. It has since been rehung after each of several rebuildings, most recently in 1978 – illustrating the mobility of prized Chinese papers.

Variations on the 'bird and flower' theme

62 A panel showing two birds on a rock, late 17th century. This early piece in the style of Song dynasty painting exhibits the traditional naturalism which is such a significant feature of the 'bird and flower' wallpapers.

63 In the Saloon of the Brighton Pavilion (Sussex) individual panels are hung like framed pictures. The paper, of *c.* 1800, is rare in having a yellow ground. In style it is very similar to the Temple Newsam pattern (*opposite, top right*) with its potted shrubs and foreground balustrade.

opposite
64 Fragmentary panel, mid-18th century, one of a set of eight in which the predominant motif is the bamboo. The botanical accuracy is of a high order, with details such as the markings on the bamboo stems and the mossy growths on the prunus branches clearly and accurately painted. On the birds, too, each feather is separately drawn.

65 A panel in the Chinese Drawing Room at Temple Newsam (Yorkshire). The paper dates from *c.* 1800. When it was hung, in the late 1820s, the two larger birds on the left (and the branch they sit on) were supplied by Lady Hertford from a plate in Audubon's *Birds of America*. In colour and in scale they are so well matched to their new setting that they remained undetected until 1968. It is some credit to the Chinese artists' high standards of 'truth to nature' that their decorative work should stand comparison with some of the finest natural history illustrations ever produced.

66 A lemur appears in the paper in the Chinese Drawing Room at Abbotsford (Scotland), hung in 1824. Though Europeans, unfamiliar with the animals and birds depicted in Chinese papers, found them fantastic and exaggerated, they were almost always fully identifiable species, and seem to have been drawn from direct observation.

which was characterized by a close and exact observation of nature. They also established the technique of working with ink outlines filled in with colour, which remained a standard convention of botanical drawing in China, as in Europe, India and Western Asia. The clear continuities of practice between Song dynasty painting and the wallpaper workshops of the 17th and 18th centuries are evident in the rich colours, fine details and predominant naturalism. The styles and subjects found in wallpapers are repeated in the Chinese export watercolours produced for the same market.[19] The artists successfully combined scientific accuracy with decorative purpose, and their realism seems to have been fostered by European tastes: John Barrow noted in his *Travels in China* (1804) that 'the Chinese, having found that the representation of natural objects are [*sic*] more in request among foreigners, they pay strict attention to the subject that may be required.'

Some of the later papers, however, eschewed a strict naturalism in favour of more whimsical designs: one example shows at least four different flowers, none of them precisely identifiable, growing from a single stem.[20]

A third distinct group of Chinese papers combines flowering trees with figures. All these papers can be dated after 1755, and it seems that the combination of elements was devised as a further response to specific demands from Europe for variety. Typically, the standard flowering tree fills the top three-quarters of the sheet, forming a backdrop to a frieze of lively figure groups below, as at the Old

67 One of two panels from the Old Brewery House, Watford (Hertfordshire), second half of the 18th century. This is typical of the third class of Chinese wallpapers, where figures in the 'foreground' are united with a backdrop of flowering trees.

opposite
68 A panel from Hampden House, Great Missenden (Buckinghamshire), *c.* 1800. This paper is so far unique, but it has a close precedent in the design of two painted silk panels of *c.* 1740 with which it shares the trellis pattern of twisted ribbons framed with flowering plants (just visible at the left-hand side). The motifs of flowers, fruit and musical instruments are, however, slightly different from those in the silk.

69 A fragment of Chinese wallpaper, also from Hampden House. This Cantonese panel, of *c.* 1730–40, shows a Chinese garden scene set in a decorative cartouche derived from a design by Watteau of *c.* 1710–20, engraved by Gabriel Huquier and published *c.* 1730.

67 Brewery House, Watford (Hertfordshire). An example at Powis Castle in North Wales shows flowering trees and bamboo screening landscape and figures. The landscape element is unusual and suggests that this is a late paper, because the Chinese artist has assimilated the European conventions of perspective to depict recession. Some of the panels in the private apartments at Saltram are also composed according to European rules and bear strong similarities to Chinese export watercolours produced after 1770.

Finally, a few rare papers have patterns that conform to none of these types. In some later examples the flowering tree motif is adapted to a repeating pattern, and may echo the curves of Rococo-style ornament.[21] A paper from Hampden
68 House in Great Missenden (Buckinghamshire), dated to *c.* 1800, is patterned with a trellis-work of ribbons enclosing Oriental motifs – flowers, fruit, insects, ceremonial pots, a mask, a fan, musical instruments. No comparable wallpaper is known but a pair of painted silk panels dated to *c.* 1740, almost identical in design, recently appeared on the market.[22] Hampden House also yielded a frag-
69 ment of a Cantonese paper that shows conclusive evidence of a direct stylistic influence from Europe: the decorative cartouche which the painter used to frame a Chinese garden scene was taken from a design by Watteau, engraved by Gabriel Huquier around 1730. European engravings were commonly used as source material by porcelain painters, but this is the only documented example of such influence on wallpaper design.[23]

Western imitations

The popularity of Chinese wallpapers, combined with their expense and lengthy delivery times – up to eighteen months – prompted English and French manufacturers to produce imitations. As early as 1680, the London stationer George Minnikin of St Martin's-le-Grand was advertising his own 'Japan' paper hangings for sale. The results of copying and imitation were often beautiful but can rarely be mistaken for the authentic Chinese product. Some, such as a paper of about 1700 from Ord House, Berwick-on-Tweed, in which a Chinese figure is dwarfed by exotic birds and an English red squirrel, all set haphazardly in the branches of a crudely drawn flowering tree, reveal a very incomplete understanding of the standard conventions of Chinese landscape painting. John Baptist Jackson, in an advertisement for his own papers dated 1758, complained that Chinese wallpapers showed 'Lions leaping from bough to bough like Cats, Houses in the Air, Clouds and Sky upon the Ground, a thorough confusion of all the Elements; nor Men and Women, with every other

70 View of a set of paper-hangings in a room from Berkeley House, Wotton-under-Edge (Gloucestershire), c. 1740. This is an English paper attempting a direct pastiche of the Chinese 'bird and flower' style, hand-painted in tempera throughout. The European colours have sadly faded compared with those of real Chinese papers.

71 An early attempt at Chinoiserie, from Ord House, Berwick-on-Tweed (Northumberland); block-printed, stencilled and varnished. c. 1700.

Animal turn'd Monsters'.[24] The 'faults' of design that he perceived in the Chinese papers were perpetuated, indeed exacerbated, in many European exercises in the genre. Another fundamental problem was that, as the painter Eugène Delacroix observed in 1847, 'we have nothing to equal their skill in producing fast colours'.[25] One of the best attempts at copying the Chinese style

70 can be seen in a paper of *c.* 1740 from a house at Wotton-under-Edge (Gloucestershire), which mimics the 'bird and flower' pattern; but though hand-painted, delicate and beautifully executed, it betrays its origins in the dull faded colours, a certain naivety in the drawing, and the crude simplicity of the botanical details.

72   Mid-18th-century panels with etched outlines and hand-colouring, produced in both France and England, are not convincing imitations, largely because of their awkward mix of Chinese and European styles. But perhaps they would be better judged as early examples of the recurrent fashion for using adaptations of Oriental motifs in essentially Western wallpapers.

Orders in the Cowtan pattern books from the 1830s and 1840s attest to the remarkable longevity in England of the taste for genuine Chinese papers. In part the 19th-century revival was fostered by that Chinoiserie extravaganza, the

63 Royal Pavilion, Brighton, with its mix of the genuinely Chinese and exuberant pastiche. But by the 1880s the fashion was well and truly dead. Mrs Haweis, in *Beautiful Homes* (1882), described the decoration of the drawing room at Ashley Park, Walton-on-Thames (Surrey), as being 'papered with such vast branches and birds of paradise, in harsh colours, which though interesting as a relic of Queen Anne taste, are scarcely more pleasing on walls than on dresses. . .'

72 Panel showing a man on a camel in a landscape of flowering trees; hand-coloured etching, *c.* 1769. A valiant attempt at the Chinese style, this panel fails as a convincing pastiche: the Oriental elements are combined in a composition based on Western perspective which has the effect of emphasizing the disparities of scale. The camel is a fantastic creature, and the plants are not identifiable.

4 Luxury Perfected:
The Ascendancy of French Wallpaper 1770–1870

BERNARD JACQUÉ

The late 18th and early 19th centuries were the golden age of French wallpaper. Not only the more spectacular papers – arabesque panels, draperies and scenic papers – but even those with ordinary repeating patterns were of a quality that has never been surpassed. There seems to have been a perfect match between the technique (block-printing), the clientèle (which in France was the rising bourgeoisie, rather than the aristocracy), and the patterns suited to that clientèle.[1]

But wallpaper proper, *papier peint* – that is to say a roll of paper with a pattern printed in distemper colours using engraved wooden blocks – came relatively late to France. Single-sheet *dominos* and *papiers de tapisserie* continued in use right into the 1760s. In England, by contrast, the practice of joining sheets of paper to form rolls prior to printing had been customary since the beginning of the century and distemper colours had been introduced by the 1740s.[2]

Such papers had been imported into France since the 1750s. First came flocks, then distemper-printed patterns. Jean Michel Papillon describes the latter clearly in the 'Additions historiques et importantes' to his enormous *Historique et pratique de la gravure sur bois* (1766):

> Other papers from England of a new type known as painted are made like the flocks in pieces nine ells [*c.* 12 yards] long; the grounds are first laid in evenly with a brush or with woodblocks in thick and pasty colours; over that several woodblocks, in the same sort of colours, print coloured designs, some like a sort of cameo [i.e., in shades of a single colour], others with flowers, damask patterns, ornaments, etc. in different colours, all in distemper and absolutely matt, like stage scenery.

Although Papillon expressed major doubts about the efficacy of this technique (the colours, he said, were susceptible to damp and came off on the hands during hanging), the time was ripe for *papier peint*. In the course of the 18th century the population of France doubled, and the number of people living in cities quadrupled. With growing prosperity, more and better houses were built; stone replaced wood, and the drier, warmer plastered walls were suited to paper. In addition, the desirability of hand-painted hangings from China and flocks from London gave the new form of wall decoration its *imprimatur*.

During the Seven Years' War (1757–63) commercial transactions with London were interrupted, giving an impetus to the establishment of French production. The technical problems of printing in distemper were soon overcome and by 1770 *papier peint* had definitively replaced *papier de tapisserie*, particularly in the areas of innovative design and luxury products. Even common kinds of paper express the '*douceur de vivre*' associated with the Ancien Régime.

In the last decade of the 18th century, French society changed profoundly, with the rise of the energetic, inventive, financially alert bourgeoisie. Anxious to establish their status, they wanted show without going to aristocratic lengths. The new houses had a variety of rooms with specially designated functions, and wallpaper offered an unrivalled variety of types, from plain colours through small figured patterns for bedrooms to grand architectural panels for the *salon*. Its twin attractions, compared with other decorative media, were its delightful designs and its relatively reasonable cost. In 1795 the *Journal du Lycée des Arts* gave its blessing: 'For appearance, cleanliness, freshness and elegance, these papers are to be preferred to the rich textiles of yesteryear.' French products achieved a supremacy which was not challenged until the second half of the 19th century, and then only slowly, by the English Design Reformers; and even when

73, 74 Panels designed by Joseph Laurent Malaine, attributed to the manufacturer Hartmann Risler of Mulhouse, *c.* 1795. These block-printed vases of flowers could be used as overdoors or as chimneyboards, or they could be combined with a dado counterfeiting a balustrade to create the effect of a garden, which is delicately suggested in the background of the paper. The popularity of flowers in decoration at the time is reflected in the fact that these impressions were printed after 1830.

the creative torch had passed back across the Channel, market inertia was such that French or French-inspired designs continued to dominate the international scene until the turn of the century or after.[3]

The wallpaper industry was concentrated in Paris – in the Faubourg St-Antoine, in the heart of the luxury furniture and furnishings district, and on the Boulevard, the best showcase in the city – and in Lyons, the capital of silk-weaving. The one notable exception was at Rixheim, near Mulhouse in Alsace (a free city), where Jean Zuber & Cie had similar links with the printed textile industry. In all those areas, the wallpaper manufacturers could draw on a highly skilled workforce which was cheaper than that in London. The patterns were provided by a large pool of decorative artists and specialized designers who were keenly aware of the slightest change in taste. The market was demanding and in the forefront of fashion, and it imposed its vision on the rest of the Western world – both by word of mouth and by means of the exhibitions of manufactures that were held regularly in Paris from 1798 onwards.

The most famous French manufacturer of the later 18th century is undoubtedly Jean-Baptiste Réveillon, whose firm in Paris became a *manufacture royale* and produced papers of superb quality. In a document drawn up in 1789 (after his works had been attacked and looted by rioters at the end of April on the eve of the Revolution), he gives an illuminating account of his staff:

> More than 300 workers (the others are occupied in town) are present in my workshops every day, and receive salaries that are more or less substantial.
>
> I have four classes of workers.
>
> The first is that of the Designers and Engravers, who are really my collaborators rather than my employees. They earn 50–100 *sous* a day.
>
> The second class, comprising the Printers, Grounders and Carpenters, receive 30–50 *sous*. . . .
>
> The third class consists of the Porters, Colour-Grinders, Packers and Sweepers, who earn 25–30 *sous*.
>
> The fourth class is the children, aged from 12 to 15. For I wanted to find a way of using their services as well, so as to help out their fathers and mothers. They earn 8, 10, 12 and 15 *sous*. . . .
>
> Finally, the Painters form a separate class of piece-workers, who may earn 6–9 *livres* a day.
>
> There is yet another category of workman, the paper-hangers; there are three Heads in this class, each of whom employs eight to ten workers a day in Paris, and those workers earn 40 or 50 *sous*, sometimes 3 *livres*.
>
> A very distinguished artist agreed to become associated with my manufactory and to receive annually, for his skills, 10,000 *livres* in fees, as well as other advantages. I also employ a designer who gets 3,000 *livres* and lodging; another who receives 2,000 *livres*, and three others who each receive 1,200 *livres* as a basic salary, not counting gratuities. Finally, some of my five salesmen receive one hundred *louis*.[4]

For information about manufacturers we have to rely on contemporary newspapers and almanachs and on a few archival documents. Much more documentary material survives for Réveillon than for his competitors, and this has contributed to the giant shadow that he casts over the period. From the *Almanach de Paris*, for instance, we learn that in 1788 there were in the capital forty-eight merchants and manufacturers of *papier peint*, but we know little or nothing about them beyond their names. Lyons must have been in the first rank not only in the quality but also in the quantity of wallpapers produced; yet the industry there is shrouded in almost total darkness. Many papers of the period survive – in manufacturers' albums, taken down from walls, or still *in situ* – but most remain anonymous. Frustratingly, producers and products cannot be linked up. According to the *Journal du Lycée des Arts, Inventions et Découvertes*, in 1795 the Parisian firm of Robert & Cie (the successors of Arthur & Robert[5]) employed 400 workers, more than Réveillon's successors Jacquemart & Bénard, and produced papers 'worthy of the same esteem' – but of those papers we know with certainty today no more than half a dozen. What is definite is that by the end of the 18th century the industry was large, and that the quality of its products was unrivalled.

The first decades of the 19th century saw an unprecedented increase in production. Study of the available evidence shows that French manufacturers were extremely inventive not only in design but in the improvement of manual techniques, reflected in forty-seven patents applied for by 1844. In 1847, 3,300 workers were employed in more than 140 manufactories printing some 2,000,000 rolls of wallpaper, most of it intended for the top end of the market.

Conditions in the late 18th and early 19th centuries were very different in London, which was the main centre for English wallpaper production until the rise of mechanization in the 1840s. Labour was expensive; heavy stamp duties, not repealed until 1836, added to the cost of the finished product whatever its quality; and the existence of a middle class that was larger and extended further down the social scale than in France meant that manufacturers could thrive by producing papers of indifferent quality, boring designs and poor colouring – the latter especially unattractive to international taste, formed as it was by French standards. Protectionist duties, moreover, limited the import of foreign papers which might have provided stimulating competition.

In the German-speaking lands, production centres were extremely scattered, and design was very much under French influence. Until the introduction of a ban in 1846, the best wallpapers were imported from France. In the United States, where labour was expensive and there was a large middle class, ordinary papers were manufactured locally but fine papers were imported from France: indeed, Americans were the principal foreign customers for French papers. With the exception of Belgium, other countries produced little and were heavily dependent on France.

153

This chapter will attempt to set out the main types of luxury wallpapers through an examination of the decorative motifs. The two chapters that follow will look in greater detail at specialized forms of wallpaper – decorative panels of the late 18th and early 19th centuries and scenic papers.

Floral papers

The most striking feature of late 18th-century design is the emergence of flowers as a decorative motif; it is also the least studied, probably because it has been regarded as banal, and unamenable to historical analysis. Flowers had, of course, been widely used in decoration before then: they had garlanded woodwork or bloomed in vases on overdoor panels. But around 1780 they took on a new importance which they have maintained to this day.

103–
105

Most spectacular are the large vases of flowers incorporated in the design of the arabesque wallpapers to be discussed further in the next chapter. These brilliantly coloured bouquets of garden flowers such as lilac, narcissus and poppies, arranged in Antique vases, also lived an independent life as overdoors and chimneyboards right up to the 1840s. Sometimes they were incorporated into more complex decorative schemes: in a wing of the palace of Nymphenburg, outside Munich, a wallpaper ensemble of about 1826 shows Medici Vases crammed with flowers alternating with statues against a background of acacia branches. Endless variants of this type of decoration appear in the engraved or litho-

73.
74.
83

graphed plates of French manufacturers' catalogues as late as the 1860s. the most splendid and successful of all is the 'Jardin d'Armide', created by the Parisian firm of Jules Desfossé in 1854.

Flowers also came in much simpler forms, notably in the printed borders that were an indispensable accompaniment to any wallpaper. The 1780s saw the appearance of naturalistic blossoms, of which the best-known are those produced by Réveillon. Light, graceful, deliciously fresh everyday species, edged by a simple multicoloured twist or geometrical band, twine together realistically in borders whose printing might require twenty-four colours or more. The earliest designs commissioned by Nicolas Dollfus & Cie of Mulhouse, in 1790, included 'Two wide borders with naturalistic flowers, one life-size, 8 inches [20.3 cm] wide, the other 6 inches [15.2 cm] wide.' These borders could be used in a variety of ways: they could frame areas of plain grass-green or royal blue paper, as can be seen (much restored) in a room in Schloss Favorite at Ludwigsburg, near Stuttgart, and they could also be used around arabesque panels, like the roses border at Moccas Court, Herefordshire.

In patterns intended for the wall as a whole, naturalistic flowers tended to displace the stylized versions derived from chintz or from silk damask or velvet. The arrangement is less dense here than in the borders: the blooms are disposed on a plain ground, or occasionally combined with ribbons, stripes or trellis, in designs characterized by their lightness and their fluid, elegant lines. Many examples survive, some combining several species while others concentrate on a single type.

A revealing story emerges from the discovery of two wallpapers, one on top of the other, in a house in the Quai Voltaire in Paris. The outer layer, a pattern of bright red nasturtiums on a pale blue ground, was made in 1795–96 by Jacquemart & Bénard. The paper underneath, printed in 1784, has roses in medallions in white on a crimson ground, imitating silk damask. Perhaps we have here a partial explanation of the success of the new floral papers: damask, with its aristocratic connotations, yields to the more democratic simplicity and naturalism celebrated by Jean Jacques Rousseau.

What was happening in fact was a profound change in attitude, which went beyond the Revolutionary reaction against sophistication. In late 18th-century France flowers occupied a special place, and particular success attended a group of Flemish flower-painters: Gerardis van Spaendonck and his brother Cornelis, Jan Frans van Daël, Pierre Joseph Redouté (1759–1840) and Joseph Laurent Malaine (1745–1809).[6] The latter is particularly interesting for us because he was employed until 1792 at the Gobelins factory, supplying designs for upholstery, while at the same time he provided designs for wallpaper to Arthur & Grenard in Paris and to Nicolas Dollfus & Cie and their successors in Mulhouse and Rixheim. The type of flower painting created by these Flemish artists was realistic and sumptuous but at the same time delicate and light, with a hint of porcelain about it, in the tradition of Jan van Huysum (think of Redouté's roses). In the order of 1790 referred to above, Dollfus commissioned from Malaine 'A *parterre* [flower border] . . . made up of all sorts of flowers, but always very delicate . . . avoid using too many colours: 20 to 24 are the limit in this instance.'[7] The popular appeal of these floral patterns is clear from the success of the wallpapers, which were frequently reprinted after selling out.

At the beginning of the 19th century there was a short interruption in the development of naturalistic floral patterns. Realistic flowers continued to be used in interior decoration (they even figure, surprisingly, in Percier and Fontaine's *Recueil de décorations intérieures* of 1801, which so strongly influenced international Neoclassicism), but another type also appeared, especially in Paris: this was something far more stylized, drawn in a more austere way, and tinted in virulent, sharp, thoroughly artificial colours.

Another break came around 1810:[8] from then on, for many years, wallpaper designs resumed the trend of 18th-century naturalism, expressing it in sumptuous borders often enriched with flock where flowers displayed their varied shapes and colours in ways that echoed the newly popular plantings introduced into French gardens under English influence. New species, too, made their appearance, especially dahlias and hydrangeas. The *irisé* or rainbow technique,[9] perfected in Rixheim in 1819 by Jean Zuber's brother-in-law Jean Spoerlin, himself a wallpaper manufacturer in Vienna, introduced new aesthetic opportunities: effects of shading in a single colour, and of subtle transitions from one colour to another, were achieved by means of a special brushing of the ground or of the colours in the tray before printing. It became possible to create stylized flowers with uncannily transparent petals, which were combined with architectural elements in borders that were used with papers imitating in *irisé* the large-scale woven silks of Lyons, or rich damask-patterned flocks. When the main wallpaper itself had a floral pattern, the blossoms in it were delicate and usually stylized, with a preference for light colours. The result, first exported and then imitated, conquered Europe and North America.

The 1840s saw the appearance of a type of floral design that was immensely popular right to the end of the century and indeed even beyond:[10] it is still produced and sought-after in England today, a proof that its appeal was not merely Victorian. It was expressed not so much in borders as in entire walls, covered

75 Wallpaper with a pattern of roses imitating damask, by Réveillon of Paris (no. 508); block-printed in two colours on a satin ground, 1784. This was found in a house in the Quai Voltaire, Paris, underneath the paper shown to the right.

76 Wallpaper with a pattern of nasturtiums, by Jacquemart & Bénard of Paris (no. 1245) block-printed in six colours, 1795–96.

Around 1780 flowers took on a
new importance in decoration.
Naturalistic or stylized, in borders
or covering the wall, they spread
from France to conquer the
Western world.

77 Naturalistic flower borders of
exceptionally fresh design mark the
last years of the 18th century. This
example, including narcissus and
peonies, is a Jacquemart & Bénard
design (no. 1072) block-printed in
colours in 1792.

78 The Empire period saw a mode
that was harder in both design and
colouring, as in this Jacquemart &
Bénard border (no. 1992) block-
printed in colours, c. 1805–14.

79 Detail of a wallpaper with a
pattern of roses and clematis,
designed by Louis Marie Lemaire for
Zuber of Rixheim; block-printed in
colours, 1856. Such all-over patterns
of flowers on a pale satin ground are
very characteristic of French taste in
the mid-19th century. Highly
popular in England at the time, the
style is so established across the
Channel today that in France,
paradoxically, such designs are
thought to be English.

with flowers treated naturalistically both in scale and in colour. The effect was enhanced by the use of a white satin ground, created by polishing with talc to make the surface shine in contrast to the matt distemper. The papers represent the culmination of artistic experiments begun in the late 18th century: in them we find very precise, almost scientific depiction in the tradition of Redouté and the series of botanical illustrations executed in gouache on vellum for the Natural History Museum in Paris; a great range of colours used also to enhance painterly effects of depth and modelling; sumptuousness and elegance of the flowers, which are depicted in full bloom, at the height of their perfection; and a seductive style of presentation that emphasizes the fleshly, sensuous quality of the blooms. The varieties selected are the sophisticated products of the horticulture of the day, rich in new introductions and hybrids.

As the 1840s drew to a close, roses were in the ascendant, roses in all the new hybrid varieties developed since the turn of the century thanks to plants brought in from the East. The rendering might be straightforwardly botanical, though the naturalism of the colours might be slightly adjusted to the range of wallpaper pigments; or roses might be mixed with other plants, creating a garden-like effect; or they might be combined with motifs drawn from published grammars of ornament; or they might be rendered in monochrome – usually in grey – to provide a wonderful foil for richly coloured velvet upholstery.

Who designed all these flowers? It cannot have been 'fine' artists. Wallpaper designs are executed in gouache, not oil, and it is hard to imagine a painter agreeing to work in that way; furthermore, the 19th century saw an almost complete break, based on misunderstanding and contempt, between the world of the fine arts and that of industry. It is true that we have lists of names of designers,[11] sometimes with addresses, but we know virtually nothing about the individuals. Some heads of studios had studied at the Ecole des Beaux-Arts in Paris (where still-life was not considered worthy to be taught) and completed their training with eminent flower painters or at the Natural History Museum; humbler workers learned on the job and perhaps in evening classes at one of the new schools of industrial design that were being set up in many manufacturing towns. How was the commissioning done? In the case of Jean Zuber & Cie, contracts were drawn up with designers requiring them to submit every year a certain quantity of designs for *fleurs riches* using a strictly stipulated number of colours – twelve, sixteen, or frequently more. Many of the studios were in Paris and Lyons, but from the 1840s until the end of the century Mulhouse was the base from which hundreds of designers supplied orders that came from the whole of the Western world.

In these designs, 18th-century freshness has given way to a somewhat heavier, agreeably sensuous hothouse atmosphere: the multiplicity of the blooms, the richness of the colours, and the fact that not a single leaf or petal is in less than perfect condition combine to create a slightly artificial atmosphere, like the immaculately tended world of a conservatory, with the same hint of airlessness. In a word, these flowers are too beautiful to be true.

But that they responded to expectations, even to a need, is proved by their commercial success. Hand-block-printed and therefore expensive, these papers were aimed at a well-to-do bourgeois clientèle whose prosperity they proclaimed, creating a quasi-narcissistic setting for lives that were, if not happy, certainly self-satisfied. Utterly devoid of intellectual content, they could appeal directly to the newly rich; flowers at the peak of perfection, neither growing nor fading, made nostalgia impossible, and formed the ideal background for a young, dynamic, upwardly mobile class. Finally, dare one suggest that the 'charm', in the literal sense of the word, exerted by these flowers might be due to their pregnant sensuality, indirectly responding to the pent-up emotions of a corseted society?

80 The salon of the Princesse Mathilde, cousin of Napoleon III, in her château of St-Gratien near Paris (detail of a painting by Sébastien Charles Giraud). The whole setting, including the ceiling – perhaps covered with a coordinated fabric – is transformed into a sumptuous hothouse filled with *fleurs riches*.

Decoration derived from textiles[12]

Stretched smooth or softly draped, textiles were the most common decorative element in bourgeois houses. This was a new development, dependent on the fact that many of them could be mass-produced industrially. Some however remained expensive, and their luxury status led to them being copied in wallpaper: this was the case with silk, velvet, tapestry and toile de Jouy in the 18th century, and glazed chintz in the 19th century. (These imitations should not be confused with wallpapers designed to coordinate with fabrics – a common practice in the 19th century, and known earlier.[13])

The tradition of imitation goes a long way back to the early 18th-century English flock wallpapers. Réveillon produced similar designs at the outset of his career, though with smaller repeats; and then, in the 1770s, he devised a very different sort of flock paper, which was still based on classic Lyons silks but was now multi-coloured, and used the techniques both of superimposed layers of flock (perhaps to suggest brocade) and of *repiquage* or overprinting with distemper colour. The result was something both refined and sumptuous, and more in tune with the taste of the time than the English flocks, which had remained virtually monochrome.

In the 19th century, manufacturers of flock papers turned again to traditional patterns derived from damask and brocade, reproduced either in a single colour or in grisaille. In the first half of the century, for instance, the walls of a dining room had to be covered with red velvet – or with an imitation of red velvet. Flock was also popular for borders: in red overprinted with vermilion, it edged papers with drapery and *irisé* patterns, taking its ornamental vocabulary from the world of braid, whose substance and material it imitated.

81 Detail of a flock wallpaper by Réveillon (no. 372), 1776. The pattern of flowers and ribbons is based on a Rococo silk, and achieves its effect by means of five different colours of flock, overprinted in black. This highly refined and complicated way of reproducing silks in flock, so different from the large-scale English patterns, is seen in other Réveillon papers of the time, such as the flocked version of 'Les Deux Pigeons' hung in England at Clandon Park (Surrey) in the 1780s.

65

It was not only in flock that Réveillon copied silks: among his distemper-printed papers of the years 1770–90 there are line-for-line replicas of known Lyons designs, on crimson, blue or yellow grounds. Parallel white lines overprinted on the pale grey pattern suggested the floating threads in brocade, and the use of a colour to which varnish had been added gave the paper a silken gleam.

In 1811, when the Lyons silk industry was in the doldrums, Napoleon issued commissions that were remarkable both for their scope and for their exceptionally high quality. The resulting silks were used in the redecoration of French palaces throughout the 19th century, and their designs provided patterns for wallpapers right up to the mid-century, in France and beyond, as long as the Empire style held sway. The shimmer of light on silk was not easy to render in flat distemper, but with the development of the *irisé* process the problem was solved, and many of the Napoleonic damasks appeared in the form of *irisé* papers, produced throughout the 1820s and early 1830s by Zuber in Rixheim and Dufour & Leroy in Paris. Their influence can also be seen in the products of Spoerlin & Rahn in Vienna and Arnold in Kassel.

Spectacularly illusionistic papers imitating drapery were expressions of a taste which emerged at the end of the 18th century and lasted until the 1830s. However one explains it – as a manifestation of Neoclassicism, as a sign of *nouveau riche* flashiness, as an antidote to the stiffness of contemporary furniture – it was extremely widespread, and a plethora of wallpaper designs vied with each other in the ingenuity of their fictive three-dimensional compositions.

Walls were covered with *trompe-l'oeil* panels in which silk, velvet or satin appeared pleated, in vertical folds, gathered up at the sides and held in place by gold braid or tie-backs, creased with sharp folds as if freshly ironed, or encrusted with embroidery. The 'drapery' may have been merely flat sheets of paper printed by woodblocks, but it looked astonishingly real. A remarkable set of designs by Dufour preserved in the Bibliothèque Forney in Paris shows the range of possibilities, from the simplest to the most sumptuous.

The panels were completed by borders modelled on the complex pelmets of the time or suggesting bunched velvet, perhaps incorporating ostrich plumes or rich braids. Some manufacturers placed an extreme emphasis on realism – especially in the 1820s, when heavy shadows stressed the soft fullness of the fabrics – while others preferred a graphic treatment in keeping with the more austere doctrines of Neoclassicism.

The illusion was so perfect that, faced with one of the meticulous watercolours of the time recording interiors, one cannot always be certain whether one is looking at textiles or paper on the walls. The only sure indication is the way in which the pattern turns a corner.

Drapery in the form of panels and borders went out of fashion in the 1830s, to be replaced by all-over effects. Special favourites were tulle and lace, which could be rendered with uncanny realism thanks to the perfection by Zuber in 1826 of the intaglio printing technique, which used engraved copper cylinders or rollers capable of producing finer lines: against a cylinder-printed honeycomb background counterfeiting net, a pattern of embroidery or a suggestion of gathered folds was created by block-printing. This type of paper stayed in production until the end of the century, a favourite pattern being lace flounces arranged in lozenge shapes and embellished with garlands of flowers and braid.

The 1830s saw the appearance of wallpapers giving an effect of padding like that of the buttoned upholstery which came into fashion at the same time. More or less realistic depending on the design, some were printed in a quasi-monochrome grey and soft blue, while others were a sensuous pink, all held in position by buttons or masses of ribbons. The same principle was used to create the effect of a textile alternately stretched taut and bunched up, held in place by ornamental nails arranged in a lozenge pattern.

82 A French flock paper of c. 1820–25, inspired by Neoclassical Lyons silks of the previous decade.

opposite (upper row and below left)
83 Detail of the Blue Saloon of Selso Castle, Denmark. The overdoor panel was designed by Pierre Antoine Mongin for Zuber (no. 609) and first produced in 1803, block-printed in colours. The wallpaper, emulating woven silk, is a Zuber pattern designed by Kupfer (no. 2308), of 1826. Its graduated effects of colour are obtained by the *irisé* or rainbow technique, which had been developed at Rixheim in 1819 by Michel Spoerlin, Jean Zuber's brother-in-law. (Spoerlin had his own wallpaper manufactory in Vienna, and sometimes produced Zuber patterns there.)

84 A wallpaper imitating silk in which *irisé* is used both for the ground and for the block-printed impression, by Zuber, 1832. The two borders would edge the paper above the dado and below the cornice; flocking gives the naturalistic flowers a three-dimensional effect.

85 An *irisé* and block-printed paper by Arnold of Kassel, Germany, c. 1825.

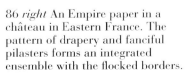

86 *right* An Empire paper in a château in Eastern France. The pattern of drapery and fanciful pilasters forms an integrated ensemble with the flocked borders.

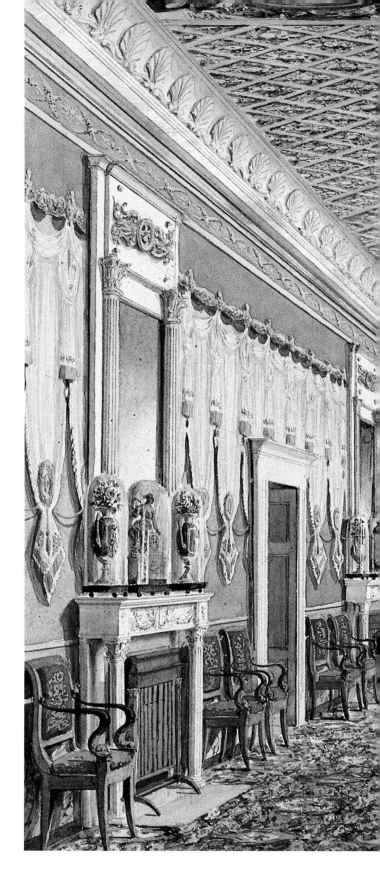

87, 88 A watercolour of a drawing room at Nice – then Nizza, part of Savoy – painted *c*. 1830 records walls hung with elaborately gathered and trimmed drapery that echoes the muslin curtains. The 'drapery' bends at the corner, however, indicating that it is really wallpaper. A sample of the same pattern (though with a dark, rather than red, ground) survives: it is by Dufour & Leroy of Paris (no. 1852), block-printed in colours in 1825–26.

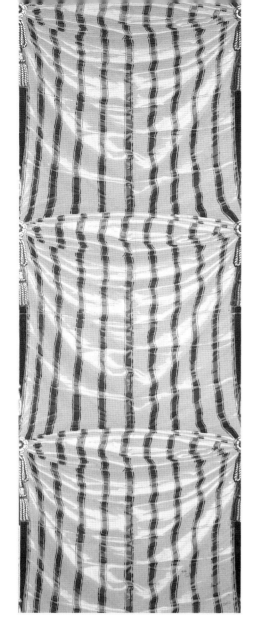

above left

89 Wallpaper imitating drapery, probably one of the earliest papers manufactured by Dufour after the firm's move to Paris; block-printed in thirteen colours, 1808. Glossy satin, gold braid. even ironing creases, would have been exposed as sham on the wall only by their too perfect repetition.

above right

90 Wallpaper patterned with 'drapery and a rising flounce of embroidered net', by Zuber, designed and engraved by Koechlin-Ziegler. 1831. This astonishing effect was made possible by printing with an engraved copper cylinder, a technique perfected by Zuber in 1826. The ground is *irisé*. The piece was awarded gold medals by the Société d'Encouragement pour l'Industrie Nationale in 1832 and the Exposition des Produits de l'Industrie in 1834.

below and right
The 1830s saw the appearance of
wallpaper patterned to look like soft
buttoned upholstery, offering a
unique sense of comfort.

91 A watercolour by Mary Ellen Best
of her room in the new hotel in the
Boomtjes, Rotterdam, 1835.

92 Wallpaper designed by Wagner
for Zuber, 1856. Twelve blocks, for
twelve colours, were needed to create
this cosy, Victorian effect.

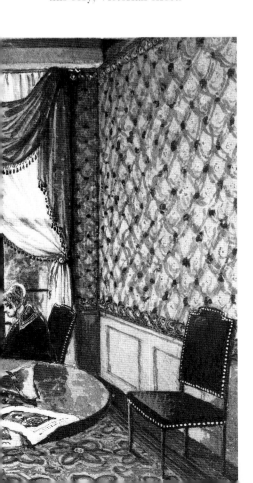

The world of ornament[14]

Another source of inspiration was ornament. Different countries had different favourites in the international vocabulary or grammar of forms: the Pompeian or Etruscan manner, for instance, was particularly popular in late 18th-century Germany, and Neo-Gothic had much more appeal in England, where it made its appearance in the mid-18th century, than in France. The bourgeoisie of all countries were agreed on one thing, however, and that was the need for show, for a display that manifested their social status. What could be better than wall-paper at suggesting their wealth while respecting their sense of thrift?

The most 'logical' ornaments are those with an architectural character.[15] As the building industry became more and more rationalized, rooms were produced as bare cubes without panelling or mouldings, and the whole ensemble of dado, framed panels, mouldings, and even perhaps the ceiling decoration had to be created in *trompe-l'oeil*.

128 To this end, in the late 18th century ornaments began to be produced in sheet form (*'en feuille'*),[16] to be cut out and pasted on the wall piece by piece. In 1789 the Parisian manufacturer Durolin (to whom nothing can so far be attributed) offered for sale

> architectural ornaments in grisaille and highlighted with gold, papers imi-tating Brazil wood and book spines of all sizes, grillework imitating that of bookcases, open as well as closed, trellising, brickwork, stonework, ashlar, marbles, granites, columns, pilasters, margents, balusters, cornices, archi-traves, statues, swags, *parterres*, corners, borders, panelling and overdoors of all kinds.

73, 74 In the inventory of Hartmann Risler of Mulhouse, drawn up in 1797–98, one finds *camées* (scenes), statues, landscapes, pedestals, frames, rosettes, batswings in three different sizes, margents of flowers and fruit, spandrels and overdoors. Other manufacturers' inventories show a similar range of items. With these ornaments and a plain-coloured background paper it was possible to create highly sophisticated interiors with a Pompeian flavour. The Schloss at Guntersblum (Rhineland-Palatinate) in Germany has four notable examples of this type of ornament dating from the 1790s – part of a remarkable suite of nine rooms with both *en feuille* and arabesque panel decoration – and a store-room in the aristocratic Hôtel d'Ursel in Brussels yielded some three hundred separate pieces of ornament cut from sheets.[17]

Alongside these decorative elements printed *en feuille*, manufacturers also produced dados, uprights, borders and friezes in roll form. The motifs were derived from copies of the paintings at Herculaneum and from numerous collec-tions of engravings of Greek and Roman monuments, but they were rendered in a sketchy way – a simple line of ochre suggesting shadow and thereby volume – which made them evocations rather than recreations of their models.

113–119, 127 Decorative elements in sheet form disappeared shortly after 1800, but orna-ments such as columns, dados, friezes, trophies and statues, conceived as part of more organized schemes, maintained their popularity right up to the 1870s.

94 In the early years of the 19th century the style of drawing became rather more rigid and the shadows, while still coloured, were strengthened to increase the effect of three-dimensionality. This can be seen in dados and friezes where, against an imitation marble ground, cherubs apparently of white marble carved in high relief are combined with Neoclassical ornaments rendered in shades of ochre to suggest gilding. These papers were produced by several manufacturers, but the finest are those of Dufour, designed by Xavier Mader, whose firm draughtsmanship gives them an unrivalled vigour. By 1820, shades of chrome yellow (by then inexpensive) heightened with vermilion and sometimes with

gold dust produced spectacular effects. and combined with a more elaborate. heavier style of drawing to create astonishing illusions of perspective. for instance in the ornate entablatures which came onto the market around this time. Dados and friezes were of course used in conjunction with much lighter patterns based on textiles. or with plain paper.

In the early 1830s, as pure Neoclassicism passed out of fashion (though Classical references survived). it was succeeded by an explosion of motifs of all kinds. prompting Alfred de Musset to exclaim in 1836: 'The apartments of the rich have become cabinets of curiosities: Antique. Gothic. Renaissance. Louis XIII. everything is jumbled up together. We have something from every century but our own – a situation never seen before in any age. Eclecticism is our style . . .' These motifs drawn from all periods and all lands – or more precisely. it was fondly believed. from the aristocratic class of all periods and lands – were

93 Border imitating a cornice. possibly German; block-printed in colours. *c.* 1810–20.

94 Border with putti designed by Xavier Mader for Dufour; block-printed in colours. 1831–32. This paper. so Neoclassical in both design and colouring. could be used at dado level or as a frieze below the cornice.

perfectly tailored to the needs of a bourgeoisie uncertain of its taste, who could turn to a past that was tried and true, redolent of an aristocracy which might be politically less and less significant but which had lost none of its glamour. Wallpaper also appealed to those who believed in the progress of Art and its diffusion through industry to a wider audience, since interior decoration worthy of a palace could be created at a fraction of the cost. It is an attitude that we find hard to understand, as we sit surrounded by bare walls after decades of war on ornament. But let us be responsive at least to the perfection of the craft itself, and avoid facile accusations of plagiarism. What we are seeing is not slavish copying but imitation, rich with the spirit of its own age: who could mistake a Neo-Rococo decorative scheme of the 1840s, with its bold line and outrageous colours so characteristic of its time (those intense ultramarine blues of the 1830s and 1840s!), for a section of panelling from an 18th-century *hôtel*?

The 1840s witnessed the systematic development of a type of wallpaper that had made its appearance at the end of the 18th century (see below, p.87). Known in France as *décor*[18] (less often as *décoration, boiserie* or *encadrement*), in England as pilaster-and-panel decoration, and in the United States as fresco paper, this consists of an integrated scheme organized around a panel in the manner of wooden wall-panelling. Publicity lithographs of the time commonly show a panel, a narrower intermediate panel, a pilaster, a border, corners, a frieze and a cornice, and for the lower part of the wall a dado. The design ingeniously made it possible for these decorations to fit any size of room, by allowing in each element the possibility of extension or contraction.

Relief was accentuated by very heavy shadows and by touches of gold, which not only flattered the client but by providing highlights increased the sense of depth – a further manifestation of the designers' skill. As the years went by, forms became complex to the point of fussiness, but the strength of the design, the density of the colours, and the underlying rhythm perfectly expressed a society capable of transforming the world.

Pilaster-and-panel sets of the 1840s drew with varying degrees of success, but always with vigour, on the most diverse styles, far removed now from Neoclassical sobriety. Rococo returned, with *décors* entitled 'Watteau', 'Louis XV' and 'Rocaille'; the 16th century was reflected in patterns called 'Florentine' and 'Renaissance'; Neo-Gothic was rare, despite the lure of the English market; the Orient was reflected chiefly in Moorish-style designs (e.g., a decoration called 'Alhambra'), with nothing at all from the Far East. In the 1850s and 1860s designers produced flowers in profusion, often combined with ornamental motifs, and turned again to historic styles – first, around 1850, to Louis XIV, and then to Louis XVI.

Throughout their existence, pilaster-and-panel decorations remained an almost exclusively French area of wallpaper manufacture. Few British firms attempted the genre; the only one to obtain a medal at the Great Exhibition of 1851, Townsend, Parker & Co., did so with a work of this type. In the German-speaking lands, the only manufacturers of *décors* were Engelhard of Mannheim, who were keen followers of French styles, and Spoerlin & Rahn in Vienna, closely linked to Rixheim.

In addition to *décors*, there was an abundant production of repetitive ornaments, as immense skill went into effects aimed at disguising the flatness of the wall. One device was to hollow it out into deeply shadowed coffers; another was to suggest that there was something a little distance away casting light shadows, such as an interlaced grille.

The development of embossing techniques in the 1840s made it possible to increase these effects of depth, and encouraged the realistic imitation of other substances, notably stamped leather, which satisfied the market's craving for almost tactile richness.

Far Eastern motifs gained currency through wallpapers imitating lacquer. Designs for these papers, in which a black ground is overprinted and then varnished, were supplied to several manufacturers from 1840 onwards by Victor Poterlet (1811–89). The illusion was so convincing that they were used to decorate folding screens.

Designs for the papers based on ornament emanated from studios in Paris and Mulhouse working for a variety of companies. Most frequently mentioned of the *ornemanistes* is Wagner, though we do not even know his first name; others are Georges Zipélius (1808–90) and Victor Poterlet, referred to above.[19] They worked on a mass-production system, and were capable of taking a basic scheme and devising endless variations to suit different sizes of repeat and different numbers of colours. Their skill was such, however, that once the paper was on the wall the magic started to work. The humble materials and pigments were forgotten, and you were in the presence of a grand interior.[20]

95 Part of the *décor* known as 'Chasse et Pêche', designed by Wagner for Lapeyre & Cie of Paris; block-printed in colours, 1839. Motifs alluding to hunting and fishing are combined with fictive statuary and much else, in an ornate, free Northern Renaissance style.

92,
95
146

75

5 Arabesques and Allegories: French Decorative Panels

VÉRONIQUE DE BRUIGNAC-LA HOUGUE

In the course of the 18th century, and especially at the beginning of the 19th century, wallpaper in France literally came out of the closet. Hitherto confined to areas of secondary importance, it now blossomed in the public rooms of newly appointed houses in both town and country. The explanation lies chiefly in the development of the decorative panel: devised by the best designers, it was accepted as a worthy rival of the panelling, stamped leather, textiles or tapestries which had hitherto been the only possible ways of ornamenting a reception room. In choosing this type of paper, the newly rich set themselves off both from those lower down the social scale who used more modest wallpapers and from the high dignitaries of the realm, who remained faithful to the traditional luxury materials. Madame de Genlis, writing in 1802, was expressing criticism already current in the reign of Louis XVI when she lamented that 'in furnishing their houses people choose not masterpieces from the Gobelins but printed papers, or even plain ones, which have constantly to be replaced.'[1]

Origins

Nothing comes out of nothing: certain existing tastes and traditions prepared the way for the new fashion. In the realm of furnishing and mural decoration, the wallpaper panel seems to have had two precedents – woodblock prints and copperplate engravings.

Surviving landscape papers printed by woodblock are rare. Two notable ones, as we have seen (above, p.17), are those from the manor-house of Gottrau at Léchelles in Switzerland (1742–43) and a church near Monêtier-les-Bains in France (c. 1760). In the case of the former, the quality of the printed line and of the stencilled colouring, together with the skilful composition, suggest that the paper came from a first-class workshop in Paris – perhaps even from that of Jean Michel Papillon. Together, the two papers show that from an early stage block-printed decorative hangings could be large, could be printed on several sheets and joined up to form a single image as was to be done later with scenic papers, and could serve as substitutes for paintings or tapestries in interior decoration.

Copperplate engravings, mounted as single panels but conceived as sets, are the other pictorial precedent for decorative panels in wallpaper. One example is a group of five mid-18th-century scenes produced by Daumont in Paris, with Chinese subjects probably taken directly from the illustrations of Jean-Baptiste Pillement. (Pillement's *Oeuvres*, published in 1769, included '130 Chinese subjects, figures and ornaments, as well as several flowers', and provided a rich source of models in the vogue for Chinoiserie, which affected wallpaper as well as other decorative arts.) As in the case of the woodcut *dominos*, the line is printed and the colours are then brushed or stencilled on. The same technique was used for another set, this time of *scènes galantes* or amorous adventures,

96 Five panels mounted as a folding screen: hand-coloured copperplate engravings, mid-18th century. At the bottom of each panel is the inscription: 'Lyon chez Pariset avec privilège du Roy'.

97–101 Five panels in Chinoiserie style: hand-coloured copperplate engravings, mid-18th century. Each panel bears the inscription 'à Paris chez Daumont', and a number handwritten in India ink.

printed by Pariset in Lyons. The five compositions are mounted as a folding screen, a very popular item of furniture in the draughty interiors of the time, which was often covered with woodcuts or wallpaper. Surprisingly, this genre of engraved panel was not really developed further in France. In Britain and America, however, prints were used for walls in various ways: pasted directly on the wall with surrounding ornaments in the classic 'print room' arrangement; as 'print room papers', simulating that arrangement; or faithfully translated into large monochrome paintings by skilled artists.

32 A craze for English wallpapers, especially the famous 'blue papers' or flocks, developed in mid-18th-century France; faced with this new fashion, French manufacturers were spurred to imitate their neighbours across the Channel, and they soon achieved a quality of execution that left nothing to fear from foreign competition. Papers like those produced by the great Parisian firm of Jean-Baptiste Réveillon (see above, p.58) in the 1780s, printed in distemper and gold leaf and brushed with diluted ink or varnished, are genuine masterpieces.

105, 106

A final element that lay behind the creation of the new wallpaper was the fashionable taste of the day for gardens and grottoes and everything connected with Italy, an interest further stimulated by the discovery of Herculaneum and Pompeii.

Large mural panels

In France, and particularly in Paris, the passion for arabesque or grotesque patterns was reflected in the 1770s in the growing popularity of papers decorated in this way. The compositions, which were fitted into wood panelling, placed above dados and surrounded by mouldings and cornices, are over 6 feet (2 m or more) in height, and though they were often conceived as part of a series each is self-contained and could stand on its own. Their decoration is developed symmetrically around a central axis, and comprises scrolling leaves, flowers, branches and palm-fronds, lambrequins, animals, human figures, vases, fragments of architecture, landscapes, and ornamental cartouches. Their ultimate source is the decorative schemes of the Roman world – the Golden House of Nero, Hadrian's Villa at Tivoli, the more recently discovered remains at Herculaneum and Pompeii – and Renaissance versions of those schemes such as the Logge in the Vatican, completed by Raphael and his assistants in 1519. All these works were widely known through engravings and travel, so it is not surprising to find them reflected in the new industry of wallpaper manufacture, as they were in wall-painting and especially in the genre of painted *boiseries*. The patterns were devised by talented French designers specializing in ornament, whose work was exported or copied throughout Europe and even in North America in the second half of the 18th century.

102–105

A number of arabesque panels can be securely attributed to Réveillon. Madame de Genlis herself was impressed by their production:

> To make arabesque papers, you need as many blocks as there are colours. . . . Those that have twenty or thirty are very expensive, particularly since the figures are painted by hand. At M. Réveillon's manufactory I saw a paper that had required eighty blocks, and which in consequence cost as much as a tapestry from the Gobelins.[2]

These panels of wallpaper are original creations and not mere imitations, even where their sources are clearly identifiable.

Other products of the Réveillon factory include a set of panels where allegorical male and female figures representing the five senses stand in identical aedicules garlanded with roses and crowned by vases of wheat. The design is printed in grisaille on a green or else on a blue ground.[3]

Réveillon's output was extremely prolific and diverse. In the panels of the senses, there was relatively little room for variation beyond the details of the figures and their relation to one another. In other designs, however, single panels or pairs of panels are made up of a number of interchangeable elements, such

102 as a roundel containing a winged putto riding on a lion, a statue under a canopy, or an octagonal medallion with a Classical seated figure – each of which occurs in several papers. What matters in the design is the balanced disposition of the larger decorative elements, not a straightforward repetition of the ornamental details.

103 The paper hangings in the château of Frucourt (Somme) show every possible combination, both in their placing in the room and in the variety of the elements that make up the individual compositions. The panels are set within a wooden framework of dado, mouldings and cornice. they consist of wider pieces which are identical in general design but differ in every detail, and, flanking these on each wall, pairs of narrower pieces, which match each other but again differ from wall to wall. The decorated papers are framed and linked by wide borders of plain coloured paper.

The sphinxes, lions, pheasants, vases, foliage scrolls and medallions seen at Frucourt appear, with variations, in two other surviving interiors. At St-Jean-de-Losne (Côte-d'Or), the Town Hall's Salle des Mariages presents a similar arrangement of panels with some additional decorative elements absent at Frucourt. And motifs from both the Frucourt and St-Jean-de-Losne papers

104 occur in England in the Round Room at Moccas Court (Herefordshire).

This last example is a reminder of the international trade in wallpapers throughout the West. Like England, France exported its products as far afield as Russia and the New World. Britons who had made the Grand Tour surrounded themselves at home with souvenirs of their travels; and cultivated people felt bound to keep up-to-date with the latest literature and the latest scientific and technological developments, including the latest wallpapers, with which it became fashionable to decorate one's house. It was a matter of taste and of style, but politics also entered in. First, the American Revolution led to French manufactured goods being preferred over British ones in the United States; then the French Revolution forced many well-to-do French people to emigrate, taking with them, whenever possible, portable goods which they were happy to convert into currency in the countries that took them in; and finally, later still, the Napoleonic armies played a part in the commercial development of French wallpapers across the Continent.

In addition to these decorative panels, Réveillon also devised wallpapers with a repeating pattern in which full- or half-width arabesque compositions are arranged in a half-drop rhythm. They could be framed and used in the same way as the individual panels, or used to paper the whole wall area above a

107 dado. One of these papers survives *in situ* in two French houses – the château of Cardet (Gard), and the Château du Plessis at Casson (Loire-Atlantique). It is interesting to note that while neither example hangs in a major reception room, in both cases the paper is treated as panels in the usual way, surrounded by printed borders and placed above a wooden dado. The pattern is known as 'L'Eau et le Feu' (Water and Fire), because of the ewer and brazier flanking figures under the triple arcades. Another sample of what at first appears to be the same paper is known, but there, curiously, ewer and brazier are transposed, and no smoke emerges from the latter.[4] It may be a contemporary or slightly later copy.

A pattern might also be used in a way that combines the classic formula of single-width panel and narrower strips with wider panels in which the single arabesque is tripled or flanked by two half-arabesques: this is the scheme in the dining room of Le Chalumet, a house near St-Germain Laval (Loire).

102 An arabesque panel by Réveillon of Paris; block-printed in colours, *c.* 1780.

103, 104 Decorative panels by Réveillon with the same basic scheme, block-printed in colours *c.* 1780, appear in France in the château of Frucourt (Somme), *below*, and in England at Moccas Court (Herefordshire), *right*. In both houses the changes are rung on the elements within the designs; and in both different wide and narrow panels are combined. At Moccas the room is taller, allowing an upward extension of the design that recalls the panel *left*, and the panels are surrounded by delicate floral borders by Réveillon; the original blue grounds, however, were painted out in a misguided attempt at 'brightening'.

105, 106 A rare Réveillon paper in mint condition, never hung. The panel (*above*, and actual-size detail *right*) appears as no. 600 in the firm's records and can be dated with certainty to 1788. In this exceptional work, the manufacturer used not only traditional block-printing in distemper but painting with diluted inks and the application of gold leaf. Réveillon had realized how important it was to use the best designers, especially those trained at the Gobelins, if he was to catch the eye of buyers. This paper triumphantly vindicates his decision.

The papers at Le Chalumet, however, can be dated to 1794–97, so they are not by Réveillon but by his successors, Pierre Jacquemart and Eugène Balthazar Crescent Bénard de Moulinières. After its looting, Réveillon had reopened his prestigious manufactory in the Faubourg St-Antoine in the autumn of 1789; but in May 1791 he passed the business over to Jacquemart & Bénard, who rented it for a year before becoming the official owners in May 1792.

If Réveillon was the leading manufacturer of decorative panels, there were other firms in Paris, and perhaps in Lyons as well, who produced very fine examples of the genre. Arthur & Grenard employed designers from the Gobelins, and were described in the *Almanach Dauphin* in 1777 as 'without doubt one of the oldest and most notable manufacturers in the capital'. The firm produced arabesque panels, but it attracted attention chiefly for a superb pair of decorative panels centred on grisaille scenes of Pygmalion and Galatea and Euridice bitten by a snake. Rich bands of multicoloured flowers set against a marbled ground frame the scenes and the imitation reliefs above, and ornament the faces of the flanking pilasters. The overall composition is closer to the tradition of English print-room papers than are any of the designs of Réveillon or Jacquemart & Bénard.

No manufacturer has yet been identified for a remarkable Pompeian-style paper at Chinon (Indre), but the richness of the scheme deserves a close examination. The Antique figures, griffins and female herms[5] reveal a talented designer and engraver, as do the various medallions decorated with landscapes and Antique nudes which surround the central composition. An even more sumptuous Pompeian panel survives at Guntersblum in Germany. The paper has been attributed to Réveillon,[6] certainly correctly; records at the house indicate a date of 1790. The composition is remarkable, and all the details are rendered with minute care.

Any discussion of the mural panels of Réveillon and his circle would be incomplete without a look at the way in which their designers adapted to the events of the Revolution. We know that Jacquemart & Bénard were 'put in charge of works concerning the various ministries, the various festivals and public ceremonies, and notably the installation of the Convention in the Palais des Tuileries and the adaptation of the neighbouring houses of the *émigrés* [i.e., opponents of the régime, who had fled] to accommodate the various sections of the Government of the day.'[7] An idea of such decoration is provided by an arabesque paper which refers to the Fête de la Fédération of 14 July 1790 and to the Constitution. Changes between the design (by Réveillon) and the paper (by Jacquemart & Bénard) show that imagery might be modified as the Revolution progressed. Another paper, incorporating tricolour rosettes, belongs to the same category of politicized designs.[8]

These revolutionary papers, with their unequivocal message, were in fact used only in public buildings, such as ministries, the Assemblée Nationale, town halls and law courts. In private, bourgeois and revolutionaries went on living in settings that would not have shocked anyone from the Ancien Régime: faced with disturbances and uncertainties outside, they felt the need to make for themselves a haven of peace and tranquillity. Certainly there were changes in motifs and in colours; but those were due not to the events of the moment but to the emergence of new generations with new tastes and to contemporary developments in the chemistry of dyeing.

opposite
107 'L'Eau et le Feu', a paper by Réveillon composed as a half-drop pattern; block-printed in colours, *c.* 1780. This example, in the château of Cardet (Gard), is hung as a panel surrounded by a border also printed by Réveillon.

108 A panel by Arthur & Grenard of Paris incorporating a scene of Pygmalion and Galatea; block-printed in grisaille and colours, *c.* 1785. This is one of a pair of panels composed of several printed papers, which are remarkable for surviving intact.

below
109 A Pompeian scheme at Chinon (Indre), perhaps manufactured in Paris; block-printed in colours, 1780s(?).

110 Part of a Pompeian scheme in the castle at Guntersblum (Rhineland-Palatinate) by Réveillon; block-printed in colours, 1790.

111 Judge Joseph Lecoq of Arras
with his family: detail of a painting
by Dominique Doncre, 1791. Judge
Lecoq had just assumed a new post
under the Revolutionary government;
the event is recorded in his drawing
room hung with arabesque papers
redolent of the Ancien Régime.

112 A few arabesque papers,
intended for public buildings, were
produced with allusions to the
Revolution. This panel celebrates the
Fête de la Fédération of 14 July 1790
and the Constitution. The original
design by Réveillon (no. 1053),
complete with tricolor ribbons,
survives; but there the legionary
standards at the bottom left and right
are topped by a dolphin and an
eagle, whereas in the existing block-
printed paper those royal emblems
are replaced by caps of Liberty –
suggesting that it was issued by
Jacquemart & Bénard in 1793, after
the death of the king.

The beginnings of *décors*, and large allegorical figures

A major wallpaper genre emerged around 1800 which was destined to have a long life: the *décor* – known in the English-speaking world as pilaster-and-panel decoration or fresco paper. Developed at the same time as scenic papers, it is still current today, though now generally used only on one wall in a room. The earliest documented scheme in France is one dated 1799 which was deposited in the Cabinet des Estampes of the Bibliothèque Nationale by the Parisian manufacturer Legrand. A coloured engraving of the bucolic *décor* gives an overall impression of the design, while samples of the wallpaper components show what its actual structure and character would have been. (Regrettably, the ensemble is now too fragile for photography.)[9]

The 'Galerie mythologique' issued by Joseph Dufour in Paris in 1814 belongs to this category of paper. Designed by Xavier Mader, it consists of six main panels and six groups of accessories. The images are printed in grisaille heightened with ochre, blue and green, in the fashion of the time, and stand out against grey, green, or blue-green grounds. In describing this particular scheme, the contemporary observer Sébastien Le Normand gives a perfect account of how these *décors* were used:

> On either side of the main subject there are groups of accessories, which vary according to the subject.
>
> The widths of this hanging may be put up close together, in sequence, so that the subjects are separated only by the groups of accessories; but this disposition is not as handsome or as rich as that in which, depending on the size of the walls in a room, the panels are treated as isolated pictures, and the groups of accessories are placed to taste in the spaces at the sides. . . .
>
> Each subject should be framed by a border. . . .
>
> These hangings . . . produce the most splendid effect, and replace paintings hung on the walls of reception rooms.
>
> This sort of hanging is perfectly adapted to form panels of any size, because of the way in which the intermediate groups of accessories can be placed next to the subjects or spaced out. . . . In a word, when this hanging is well managed it should give the effect of a painting set against a tapestry.[10]

Dufour had already issued a design of the *décor* type in 1808, a series of personifications of the months designed by Evariste Fragonard, son of the famous Honoré. Five of the wallpaper panels are known,[11] together with the original design for another of the months.

113–115 Detail of the 'Galerie mythologique' by Dufour of Paris, showing one of the panels and two flanking groups of accessories: block-printed on a grey ground in grisaille heightened with ochre, blue and green, 1814.

JUGEMENT DE PARIS.

A survey of the large decorative panels produced in the 18th and early 19th centuries would be incomplete without a look at the allegorical figures that became such a popular wallpaper product after 1800. While not as large as the arabesque-type panels or as the *décors*, they could be life-size, and their role in the decoration of a room was similar to that of the larger panels.

116– 119
A set of four figures of Bacchus and his followers, placed on pedestals and designed to look like patinated bronze, were in all probability printed in Lyons in the years 1800–1810. Evidence that Lyons manufacturers produced allegorical figures comes from a document dated 29 Germinal an VI (March 1799): in this, Deyrieu Frères are informed that the Minister of the Interior will see to the publication of 'their advertisement relative to eight emblematic figures of their devising. Eight life-size figures representing Liberty, Equality, Justice, Reason, Law, the Republic, Virtue and Philosophy.'[12] The document incidentally sheds light on the use of Revolutionary subject-matter and on the commercial dynamism of Lyonnais manufacturers on the eve of the 19th century, armed with a technical mastery that was based securely on long experience of designing for textiles.

A set of personifications of the four seasons, also devised to look like bronze statues, was produced by Zuber in Alsace around 1810. The designs, interestingly, were supplied by Evariste Fragonard, whom we have already met designing for Dufour. A further set of the seasons, this time imitating stone statues, was issued in Paris by Jacquemart around 1830. Four seems almost to have been a magic number for such panels. Four dancing figures produced about 1825 have been attributed to the Parisian firm founded by the designer Xavier Mader after his departure from Dufour. They are so similar to the decoration in the dining room in the château of Malmaison that they may well have been designed by the decorative painter Béranger, or based on designs by him.

121
In France, such figures were fully incorporated into the composition of *décors*. House-owners were able to give their walls individuality by choosing to juxtapose particular figures. The choice was helped, of course, by the wallpaper merchant, and effectively at an earlier stage by the manufacturer, but the idea of choice was so attractive that by the mid-century pilaster-and-panel decorations eclipsed scenic papers in popularity. (On the later *décors*, see pp.74–75.)

Accessory decorations and ceiling papers

As we have seen, wallpaper in the late 18th and early 19th centuries took up and was integrated into the architectural vocabulary of the house. Panels on a smaller scale were produced to decorate overdoors, overmantels, and chimneyboards – a genre known in France as *attiques* and *camées* (see also above, p.72). Effectively paintings evoked by block-printing, *attiques* might be square or rectangular, and could be quite large. Their picture-like quality could be enhanced by the way in which they were mounted on the wall: one *frise à paysage* printed with a landscape in the manner of Hubert Robert (perhaps even a copy of a work by Robert) is surrounded by a beaded giltwood frame in typical Louis XVI style.[13]

122– 126

116–119 Four panels of Bacchus and his followers, probably produced in Lyons: block-printed in colours to resemble patinated bronze, *c.* 1800–1810.

120 Original design by Evariste Fragonard for the month of April. for a set of the months produced by Dufour in 1808. The gouache drawing bears lines made by the engraver's stylus in tracing the pattern through a kind of carbon paper onto the woodblocks (one for each colour). On the final paper printed from the blocks the image would appear in reverse (see Ills. 135, 136).

121 Original design for a *décor*, or pilaster-and-panel set. incorporating figures; gouache, perhaps from the region of Lyons, *c*. 1815–20. Each of the three parts proposes a different solution for the frieze, the pilaster. the panel and the borders. Printed examples of the central lower border exist in several public collections.

124   A pair of panels presented in 1799 by Legrand to the Cabinet des Estampes of the Bibliothèque Nationale in Paris show clearly by their format that they were intended as overdoors. The two Classical scenes – of Diogenes and Alexander[14] and Zeuxis – are rendered as low reliefs set against a dark ground.

126   Different in manner are two early 19th-century overdoors which must have been intended to complete a room hung with a panoramic paper: here grisaille, overprinted with touches of blue and beige, is used to depict landscapes where people disport themselves in an elegant Italianate countryside.[15]

In the 1830s a particular genre of decorative panel emerged in which famous paintings of the day were reproduced in a black-and-white grisaille with particularly strong contrasts between shadows and highlights. A painting by Jean

122   Louis Boilly, *Nous étions deux, nous voilà trois* (We were Two, and Now We are Three), was reproduced in this way – via an engraving – as part of a pair of panels, and so too were two pictures by Baron Gérard: *Homer and his Guide*

123   (probably the picture shown at the Salon of 1813) and *Belisarius* (much admired at the Salon of 1795, where it was purchased by the Dutch ambassador, Mayer, and eventually acquired by the Leuchtenberg Gallery in Munich). No manufacturer has yet been identified for either set.

An explanation for the translation of paintings into black-and-white may lie in the new fashion for lithographs, a medium that was coming into wider use at the time. In the relationship between prints and wallpaper, the latter had the great advantage of size. In colour reproduction, too, wallpaper had the edge: it is no coincidence that the first posters stuck up on walls in towns were printed by the same technique as wallpaper.

Art-lovers in the early 19th century who could not afford original paintings, sculpture or plasterwork could thus buy printed *attiques* or *camées* in which

73,   they could enjoy historical, mythological or religious scenes, vases of flowers and
74   stucco ornaments, either in grisaille or in colour. But while some of the panels were faithful copies of pictures well known at the time (if not always recognizable today), that was not true of all. In other cases, the paintings were transformed, due to the technical constraints or stylistic conventions of the wallpaper medium. The number of colours used might be reduced, to keep the cost down; both modelling and tonal relationships might be altered by the nature of woodblock printing; a painting's format might be adapted to fit the surface to be decorated; or extra features, such as vegetation or a foreground terrace, might be added by the printers for whom such elements formed part of their design vocabulary.

127   The dado was another area of the room for which decorative papers were devised that featured small versions of fashionable paintings, combined with

ornamental panelling. Four pictures incorporated in dado decoration preserved in several public collections include a *Mediterranean Seaport* now attributed to Jean-Gabriel Charvet.[16]

The papers we have been considering so far were hung only on walls; but in the 18th- and early 19th-century house decorative panels could also serve to ornament ceilings. A ceiling paper of the 1780s, contemporary with most of the mural panels described above, is composed in the same general way as the Pompeian papers, with medallions containing figural scenes or ornaments placed against a green ground. In the centre is the goddess Diana in her chariot pulled by deer. The design is completed by sumptuous printed borders cut out to fit the specific shapes, as were the four Antique figures placed in the corners. A ceiling paper of the early 19th century survives in a house in the village of Vaugneray (Rhône). Printed in 1814 by Dufour, it is modelled on a painting; and its designer has sought to give the effect of a room opening up into a dome by his use of a circular shape surrounded by fictive plasterwork. Sébastien Le Normand described how such a ceiling paper worked:

> The central subject and its surrounding border are fixed in their dimensions. . . . Two elements are adjustable to any size of ceiling: the plain ground can be extended or reduced, and the outer border can be wider or narrower, or can even be eliminated altogether, when the cornice of the room serves to finish off both the wall-hanging and the ceiling.[17]

To conclude: many different types of large decorative panel were available in the 18th and early 19th centuries. The earliest feature landscapes or pastoral and amorous scenes. Later came arabesque panels, then *décors* and reproductions of fashionable paintings or sculptures as *attiques* or *camées*, as dado ornaments, and even as ceilings. All are intimately linked to the architecture of the rooms which they so elegantly decorated. It would not be an overstatement to say that they were largely responsible for raising wallpaper in France to the status of the traditionally 'noble' decorative materials – wood panelling, leather, fabric and tapestries.

opposite
128 A ceiling decorated with *en feuille* printed papers made by an unknown Parisian manufacturer; block-printed in sepia and colours, *c.* 1780. At the centre is the goddess Diana in her chariot. The dark and light areas of the background, the borders of flowers and fruit, the medallions, and the figures in the corners were all cut out from individual sheets of paper.

above
129 A ceiling paper in a small corner room in the Grand Maison Valentin at Vaugneray (Rhône), designed by Xavier Mader and manufactured by Dufour; block-printed in colours, 1814. Here the subject is the toilette of Venus. As often happened in the 19th century, this pattern was reprinted a few years later by Desfossé of Paris, proprietor of the original blocks.

6 Wide Horizons: French Scenic Papers

ODILE NOUVEL-KAMMERER

'Scenic' or 'panoramic' papers occupy a unique position in the world of wall-paper. They are the most spectacular expression of the lengths to which manufacturers would go to display the full range of their skills, and their story is that of the challenge which manufacturers set themselves to reconcile art with industry, the élite with the general public, and taste with mass-production, all without making any fundamental changes to the usual methods of production.

What are the main characteristics of scenic papers, and how do they differ from other wallpapers?

Mural decoration is not a straightforward matter, for consideration of the subject is complicated by the variety of roles which walls play in the life of the person living within them. At the most basic level, walls are the framework of a dwelling, the boundaries of a space, the guardians of an individual's privacy. But beyond that delimiting function, language enters in, at however simple a level: walls make a powerful decorative statement – from the pure white surfaces of a Carmelite's cell to a rich silk hanging, from tiny flowers repeated a thousand times over to complex narratives of the life of a famous figure or expansive photo-murals offering views out over exotic beaches. The wall becomes a site of discourse, whether consciously or unconsciously. And in the case of scenic wallpapers, that discourse becomes a message.

At many times and in many countries there have been decorative programmes that integrate the entire vertical surface of a room – frescoes, tapestries or painted wooden panelling in Europe, fragile screen-walls made of paper with painted decoration in Japan – and more often than not, these schemes invite the viewer to look into them and to forget the physical barrier of the walls. Producers of scenic wallpaper were aware of such precedents, but they did not seek to copy them. They set themselves up as inventors, to the extent that they developed novel methods of composition and fabrication, and they responded to the demands of customers in their own age. And it is that combination of printing technology, economic conditions and fashion that largely explains the phenomenal success of the wallpapers.

The essential characteristic of scenic papers is the absence of repeats. As with most wallpapers, the subject-matter is drawn from the world of nature outside the house; but where they might have a flower, a bouquet or some foliage, here there is an entire landscape. The names given to the first papers in this new style are revealing: they were called '*papiers peints–paysages*' (landscape wallpapers) or '*tableaux–tentures*' (paintings as wall-hangings). What the manufacturers had done so ingeniously was to free the pattern from its traditional subordination to the individual strip of paper. Until now, the function of paper had been to unify the walls of a room visually. The only solution that was satisfactory at the same time technically, economically and aesthetically was to use a motif and repeat it in a simple and legible pattern. In the case of scenic

papers, however, the manufacturers turned their backs on that orderly vision and proposed instead a new and bold solution: a single vast pattern on a number of pieces which fitted together to form a landscape. Each piece is treated as an element within a coherent and structured ensemble. One might, therefore, suggest the following definition of scenic wallpaper: it is the depiction of a continuous landscape without any repetition of scenes or of motifs, printed on a series of paper pieces that join up one with another, designed to cover all the walls of a room in a house, at a price that was not prohibitive, with the aim of creating a distinctive atmosphere.

The beginnings of this new, and exclusively French, genre are unclear. Curiously, no information on what was a novel and important kind of mural decoration is to be had either from the manufacturers themselves or from the dictionaries and technical treatises of the time, which are extremely precise in

130 The Drawing Room of the Princesses Sophie and Marie of Bavaria at Nymphenburg outside Munich, c. 1820. The walls are hung with 'La Grande Helvétie', a Zuber design of 1815. It has been given framing pilasters of paper and a rich frieze at the top. The furniture is kept low, to allow the scenic vistas their full effect.

their descriptions of other types of wallpaper. Sébastien Le Normand, writing in 1822, concluded that 'the real reason for this gap in the description of the arts is due to the secretiveness that artists have always maintained on the subject of their procedures, and the difficulty which other people who might have described them found in getting access to the workshops.'[1]

96   Scenic wallpapers seem to have emerged in France as an outgrowth of the development of decorative folding screens at the end of the 18th century. Each leaf of a screen was usually covered with a single width of textile or wallpaper. Some had begun to introduce the notion of variety between the leaves, by using different scenes printed from woodblocks or else copper engravings enhanced with colours. Little by little, the vertical nature of the composition yielded to a 131 horizontal emphasis. In the screen of 'Les Emigrés', for instance, produced in the 1790s, the strongly horizontal composition extends from one panel to the next and is divided into a series of planes: the foreground, marked by naturalistically depicted plants and rocks, leads back to the figures, the street, the houses, the trees, and the mountains outlined against the sky. A scenic paper 132 produced at about the same time, 'Les Métamorphoses d'Ovide', is very similar in its composition: each of the mythological scenes is depicted on one piece, with the title at the bottom, but as in the screen the scenes are linked together and the overall picture is unified by the foreground, with its large plants, and the landscape in the background, which stands out against an expansive sky.

  The importance given to the sky in designs for screens is not accidental. Landscape painting was enjoying a revival with great popular success, and the masters of that genre insisted on the importance of atmosphere in creating the feeling of 'nature' in a work. The development of the technique by which scenic wallpapers were produced is in a sense the culmination of this quest to render effects of air and light in two dimensions. Like other wallpapers, panoramic schemes were printed by means of woodblocks, each block supplying a specific colour. Since no motif was ever repeated, and since a great many colours were used on each strip, the number of individual blocks required to produce a scenic paper was exceptionally high – ranging from several hundred to as many as four thousand for the most complex schemes. Printing could only take place once the ground had been laid in; and that ground, in the case of scenic papers, was the sky. When a scenic wallpaper is hung in a room, the horizon line should be at eye level: the sky therefore occupies about two-thirds of the height of the pieces, while the landscape occupies the lower third. Since the sky is so visible, it had to be perfect in its execution, without the slightest defect to catch the eye and destroy the illusion of depth and open air. It so happened that in 1819 Zuber developed a new method of brushing in the ground, known as *irisé* (see above, p. 61), which made it possible to pass imperceptibly from one colour to another through the most subtle shading. Applied to scenic papers, this technique at last resolved the problem of the horizon and the transparency of the sky. One of the charms of the large panoramic schemes lies precisely in the pure, often cloudless blue skies which flood the room with a diaphanous light.

  If we lack information on the beginnings of scenic wallpapers, we do know that they were shown at the Expositions des Produits de l'Industrie Française in Paris between 1806 and 1849, and then at the international exhibitions; and through the reports of the juries we can trace the phrases that were successively 143 applied to them.[2] In 1806 the jury referred to '*paysages*' (landscapes) and '*ten-* 141 *tures*' (wall-hangings); in 1819, it mentioned '*tableaux en grisaille*' (paintings in grisaille) and '*paysages coloriés*' (coloured landscapes); in 1834, we find 'paintings on paper to depict landscapes, familiar scenes, and historical subjects'; and at the Great Exhibition of 1851 in London, the French commission 149 ranked the 'Grande Chasse' set produced by Délicourt among 'the most remarkable works [*oeuvres*] in the Exhibition'.[3]

131 A screen papered with panels taken from a series known as 'Les Emigrés'; block-printed in colours, 1790s. The buildings and figures can be rearranged to produce endless variations.

132 Part of 'Les Métamorphoses d'Ovide'; block-printed in green and sepia, 1790s. Three scenes are shown here, at varying distances in the landscape. The paper is hung all around the walls of a tiny cabinet room (the door frame is just visible at the left); to preserve continuity, it is pasted across a cupboard. The images are based on illustrations by Charles Monnet to a translation of Ovid by the Abbé Banier published c. 1770.

The changes in terminology reflect a major debate that was going on throughout the 19th century concerning the decorative arts. Of the two words used by the jury in 1806, one, *paysage*, refers to painting, while the other, *tenture*, refers to tapestry: the jury is clearly hesitating whether comparison should be made to a major art (painting) or to a minor art (tapestry). As the century progressed, scenic wallpaper came to be ranked with the major arts, a classification confirmed by the application to it of the word *oeuvre* in 1851. This was part of a general trend to dissolve the distinction between ornamental and high art. What the manufacturers had set out to do was to resolve the apparent contradiction between the two: to produce a mural art fine enough to be regarded as an *oeuvre*, while at the same time selling to a relatively wide clientèle and therefore keeping up-to-date with changes in fashion and taste.

The notion of '*papier panoramique*', with its emphasis on the continuous and enveloping nature of the decorations, did not come in until the 20th century in France. At the same time, American and British writers began to refer to 'scenic' or 'panoramic' papers, and Germans to '*Bildtapeten*'.

Manufacture and marketing

The terms used to refer to scenic wallpaper may have varied, but its technical characteristics and the methods involved in producing it remained very much the same from the late 18th century to the final decline of the genre around 1865.

Scenic papers had to be adaptable to the most diverse wall areas, whose height and total length could not be predicted. The fact that the manufacturers were dealing with a single design which extended beyond the limits of one strip of wallpaper commonly to between 20 and 32 pieces made their task difficult indeed, and led them to compose these vast mural landscapes on a modular basis that was much more complex than in any paper with a repeating pattern.

The compositional principle underlying panoramic papers is fundamentally architectural in character. Each of the pieces that go to make up the landscape is divided horizontally into two zones: the upper part is the area of the sky, which consisted of a brushed-on ground, while the lower part contains the landscape proper, which was block-printed. To ensure that the horizon line came at eye level, the base of the landscape was usually positioned 0.8 or 1 metre (32 or 36 inches) from the ground. (This was also the height of the furniture placed against the wall, which thus functioned as a sort of balustrade.) Since rooms varied in height, the manufacturers produced pieces that were about 4 metres (13 feet) long, roughly divided into 1.5 metres (5 feet) of landscape and 2.5 metres (8 feet) of sky, which could then be trimmed as necessary when the paper was hung. The system was very similar to that used earlier for Chinese wallpapers.

In width, the pieces had to join up perfectly so that the landscape appeared as a continuous image. To keep the viewer amused and intrigued, the '*papiers peints–paysages*' were conceived as large compositions punctuated by a number of distinct scenes or *tableaux*. At regular intervals in the sequence, trees or huge rocks provided what was known at the time as *séparation*.

Almost all scenic papers allow for a perfect join between the last and first pieces – a significant indication of the manufacturers' determination to create a work of art which would make the whole room into a single image with a unified viewpoint. It was certainly not uncommon, however, for the total length of the walls of a room to be shorter than that of the chosen scenic paper. In that case, the owner could opt to use only part of the scheme. Doors and windows nearly always presented major interruptions to a continuous reading of the subject, and their placing in a wall would lead to the choice of particular scenes to fit the space. The harmonious effect of the finished room was crucially dependent on the proper positioning of the individual scenes on the walls.

130,
143
Many panoramic papers were hung with the accompaniment of accessory elements in wallpaper intended to enhance the decorative effect of the ensemble. In such cases, the scenes were treated like gigantic paintings and were framed within elements of variable width which clearly demarcated each wall and isolated the individual episodes. This arrangement was by no means the rule, however, and owners who wanted to emphasize the narrative quality of the design would have the paper hung without accessories – sometimes even cover-

132 ing the doors, to reduce to an absolute minimum any intrusions into the overall unified vision of the landscape.

Each new scenic wallpaper demanded an immense amount of work on the part of a team of professionals, for whom the project represented a major aesthetic, commercial and financial gamble. The sequence of operations was well established, and each required much greater care than in the case of ordinary wallpapers. First came the choice of the subject. It was usually determined by the manufacturer, who would judge the commercial viability of this or that theme by applying his knowledge of current fashions. The production of a decorative scheme involved such high financial investment that profitability had to be a major consideration.

Once the subject had been chosen, the manufacturer commissioned an artist to submit a design for the composition in the form of preliminary sketches. The process by which the manufacturer chose the artist is relatively obscure, and equally little is known about the networks of designers, since – as in the world of textiles – the rule was for them to remain anonymous. The vast majority of scenic wallpapers are unsigned, and not one of the publicity texts issued to promote the papers mentions the person who created the composition.[4]

The designer would usually begin by gathering information on the chosen subject, collecting together any documentary material that he could find, usually
133 in the form of published prints; these had the advantage of providing ready-made *tableaux* which could then be combined together in a precise and coherent way. There was more to the designer's job, however, than merely putting together a collage of these prints. For a *'paysage'* to be successful, the composi-
138 tion needed rhythm, notably through the variety and scale of the individual scenes; and it also needed carefully balanced colours, and a sense of depth. In other words, starting from a mass of documentary material which was almost invariably on a small scale, the designer had to create a work which would have the effect of, as it were, opening up the wall, and allowing the viewer to escape into another world. The real art of the designer of landscape papers lay in his mastery of enlargement, his understanding of the workings of proportion – in a word, his ability to judge the final effect.

The method followed seems to have been the same everywhere. The designer
137 first made a small-scale study which he submitted to the manufacturer. The latter might then insist on modifications of his own. Once the manufacturer had
135 approved the design, the artist made an actual-size drawing which would serve as the model for cutting the blocks. Each colour on the drawing was numbered to indicate the order in which the blocks would be printed.

138 While all this work was going on, some firms undertook to produce a lithograph – based on a small-scale design – which would be used to advertise the new paper. These lithographs also allowed salesmen to show their customers the range of existing scenic wallpapers without having to unroll the papers themselves, an operation that was always complicated and cumbersome. The illustrations were accompanied by a text praising the particular scheme.

The role of the artist in the creation of a new *'paysage'* was by no means simple:
133,
134
he looked to prints for inspiration, but at the same time felt free to modify them. In this collage-like process, the question of authorship becomes blurred, and manufacturers were as secretive about production as they were about design.

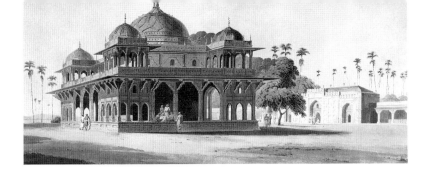

Composition and production

133, 134 Existing images provided models. For 'L'Hindoustan', first block-printed in colours by Zuber in 1807, Pierre Antoine Mongin took Thomas and William Daniell's *Oriental Scenery* and William Hodges' *Select Views in India* and subjected the scenes to collagistic rearrangement. The Daniells' 'Mausoleum of Mucdoom Shah Dowlut, at Moneah' of 1795 (*above right*) becomes a pavilion on a lake (*right*), next to the temple at Tanjore and surrounded by details from other prints in the series.

TÉLÉMAQUE

The first stage in the production of a paper was a small-scale study of the complete design (*top*). Next came actual-size drawings (*far left*), whose design was transferred to the woodblock for cutting by tracing with a stylus whose marks can be seen on the gouache. On the resulting paper (*left*) the design appears in reverse. Finally, the manufacturer might issue a lithograph (*above*) showing the appearance of the complete paper, carefully composed and articulated by features such as trees.

far left and left
135, 136 Actual-size drawing and block-printed piece of 'Renaud et Armide', produced by Dufour in 1831. Using a mixture of Indian and Egyptian styles, the unknown designer shows the tomb of Clorinda and a fallen pagan statue.

top
137 Preliminary study by Joseph Fuchs for 'Le Brésil', first produced by Desfossé in 1862. The artist has indicated in pencil how the composition might be divided into pieces.

above
138 Publicity lithograph for 'Télémaque' by Dufour, *c.* 1818. The story reads left to right, from Telemachus' arrival on the island of Calypso, past her palace, to his departure.

Who is the real author of a scenic paper – the painter responsible for the print used as a model, or the designer who conceived the scheme as a whole? The debate was opened at the Exposition des Produits de l'Industrie in 1819, when certain artists expressed their anxiety at the success of this new genre, which

141 displayed their own ideas, in revised and enlarged form, before a wider public: 'If paper, which is constantly being perfected, eventually becomes as good as painting – as it will any minute – much more cheaply, what will become of those of us who have only our talent to live off?'[5] Despite this attempt on the part of artists to lay claim to a fashionable product, manufacturers almost always continued to maintain the rule of anonymity as far as the designers were concerned. Each panoramic paper was an adventure, a genuine team effort, in which the complementary skills of designer, engraver and printer were brought together under the direction of the head of the works. By refusing to attribute the paternity of a paper, refusing to create 'stars', the manufacturers could

134. retain a monopoly on the work of a particular designer (thus Jean Zuber
140. retained the services of Mongin for several years), and could keep their sources
83 of inspiration secret.

Changing styles

All the earliest 'paysages' show people enjoying a blissful existence in hospitable, paradise-like natural surroundings – a vision which was based on accounts by famous travellers or on prints by or after those few artists who had journeyed abroad. The first two 'paysages' made their official appearance simultaneously

143 at the Exposition des Produits de l'Industrie in 1806: they were 'Les Sauvages
140 du Pacifique' by Joseph Dufour, then at Mâcon, and 'Les Vues de Suisse' by Jean Zuber of Rixheim. Each one depicted a country other than France and presented picturesque and unfamiliar ways of life. Dufour made the reasons for his choice clear in the promotional booklet issued at the same time as the paper:

> We believed that we would earn the appreciation of the public by bringing together, in a clear and accessible way, the multitude of peoples who are separated from us by the vast oceans, so that without leaving his apartment, merely by looking around him, the armchair traveller may experience for himself the journeys that provided the subject-matter and think he sees the figures mentioned there, may compare the text and the painting, and dwell on the peculiarities of appearances, on costumes, etc. . . . .[6]

The scenic wallpapers of this period combined a search for a new type of mural decoration with a manifest desire to impart information: 'the different scenes in this landscape are based on the customs of the country', declared the promotional text for 'La Grande Chasse au Tigre dans l'Inde', issued by Velay in Paris before 1818; 'the costumes are accurate, and they and the buildings have been copied from drawings made on the spot.' A similar desire to instruct

139 and improve lies behind 'Paul et Virginie', a wallpaper issued by Dufour in 1824 illustrating the main episodes of Bernardin de Saint-Pierre's famous romance. With their 'paysages', manufacturers offered a cultural programme for children and adults in the form of what were effectively comic strips on a mural scale. They were stimulating to the imagination, instructive, and in line with bourgeois morality, containing no suggestive scenes (apart from Rinaldo in the arms of Armida, in Dufour's 'Renaud et Armide' of 1831), no unbearable suffering (Virginie's dead body lying on the beach is described in the novel, but absent from the wallpaper: who could bear to see it every day in their drawing room?), and no strenuous labour.

Scenic wallpapers cast the occupant in the role of spectator. The drawing room or dining room walls became the mirror of an idealized daily life. The 19th-century bourgeois enjoyed the reflection of a projected vision of human life

102

in a paradisal setting. This ideal spectacle was convincing in direct proportion to the coherence of the composition, which determined the suggestive power of the paper as a whole through the unity of scale, colours and viewpoints.

141   The only exception to this rule is 'L'Histoire de Psyché', with its exceptional three-dimensional quality. Some of its scenes are not set out-of-doors: instead, they invite the spectator to step at once from his or her own interior into that of an Antique palace (admittedly quite an 'open' interior). Furthermore, the scenes do not join up to form a single sequence: instead, each is self-contained and unrelated to adjacent events, to the extent of having figures that are surprisingly different in scale. The fact is that 'Psyché – which had been partly responsible for the artists' reactions that we noted at the Exposition des Produits de l'Industrie of 1819 – is unique, and seems not to have inspired any imitations.

What happened next was a decisive change in the part played by nature. Hitherto it had served as the setting for scenes of human activity, and had been confined to two important zones in the composition of the panorama. In the foreground (also known as the *terrasse*), picturesque vegetation appeared in close-up, in a style similar to that of botanical illustrations, and presented thousands of tiny details to delight the attentive eye. In the background, on the other hand, tall trees rendered in a deliberately generalized way served to close the horizon. Finally, clumps of trees, distributed fairly regularly in the foreground, served to separate the scenes and to provide a rhythm for the composition as a whole. In the 1840s the emphasis shifted, and human scenes gave way to the depiction of virgin, uninhabited, primeval nature. In this the scenic wallpapers were reflecting a wider public interest in plant varieties that was expressed in other spheres as well (see above, p.64).

145   The first of this new type of paper seems to have been 'Isola Bella', issued by Zuber in 1843. Nature here is invasive and exuberant: an extraordinarily varied flora punctuates a paradisal landscape in which there is not a soul or a trace of human habitation. The method of composition changed too. Prints became less important as models, and the manufacturers turned instead for their landscapes 145–147, 151 to noted *peintres de fleurs*. With their perfect knowledge of botany, these 'flower-painters' formed a highly specialized category of industrial artists; among them were Eugène Ehrmann, Georges Zipélius and Edouard Muller.

If the manufacturers chose exotic types of vegetation in the 1840s, it was because of an ever-growing public appetite for exotic places. After 'Isola Bella', 146 in 1849 Zuber launched 'Eldorado', where the four major areas of the globe – America, Europe, Asia and Africa – were subtly differentiated. The idea of presenting the whole world in a single room was taken further still in gigantic compositions such as Zuber's 'Les Zones Terrestres' of 1855, which included an 147 extraordinary vision of the 'glacial sea', and in Desfossé's 'Eden' of 1861, where 148 the plants have become so large that there is almost no sky. The vastly increased scale of these landscape papers raises the question of reality and illusion: were they actually meant to deceive the eye? What is certain is that they were meant to enchant it. This was the age of conservatories and winter gardens, which were often used for romantic encounters, and the scenic papers of the time project an image of nature that is lush and welcoming.

The move from inhabited landscapes – exotic, based on literature, or occasionally familiar – to atavistic visions of nature expressed a profound change in outlook. The initial aim had been to enhance human life by showing it in harmony with the natural environment. Now, what the decorators sought was to create a new world in the home. The function of the papers was transformed: whereas the inhabitant had formerly been the *spectator* of a play or a novel or effectively of human life, admiring an image of mankind as in a mirror, now he or she became a *performer*, acting out his or her own life within a paradisal setting, a made-to-measure microcosm offering all the variety of the universe.

The desire to instruct and improve, as well as to delight, lies behind many of the first wave of scenic papers.

Subjects might be drawn from novels or travel books; 'L'Histoire de Psyché', uniquely, consists of separate scenes, whose ambitious character looks forward to the prestige papers of the mid-century. Its display at the Exposition des Produits de l'Industrie in 1819 was seen by some painters as a threat.

139 Part of 'Paul et Virginie', a paper first issued by Dufour in 1824, block-printed in ochre and sepia. The images are based on illustrations after J. F. Schall to Bernardin de Saint-Pierre's novel, set in the West Indies. Right, the children meet the slave Domingue; left, later, Virginie sails for Europe and is drowned.

140 Detail of 'Les Vues de Suisse', designed by Pierre Antoine Mongin for Zuber, 1804; block-printed in colours. This was one of the earliest scenic papers, shown at the Exposition des Produits de l'Industrie Française in 1806.

141 'Psyché au bain', from 'L'Histoire de Psyché', issued by Dufour in 1815. This scene was probably designed by Louis Laffitte and perhaps redrawn for the blockcutter by Xavier Mader. Four pieces, block-printed in sepia, are here shown juxtaposed, with their original selvedges and identifications at the bottom.

PSYCHÉ AU BAIN. en 4 lés 8.   PSYCHÉ AU BAIN. en 4 lés 7   PSYCHÉ AU BAIN. en 4 lés 6.   PSYCHÉ AU BAIN. en 4 lés 5.

'. . . bringing together the multitude of peoples who are separated from us by the vast oceans. . .'

142 Boston, from 'Vues d'Amérique du Nord', designed by Jean Julien Deltil for Zuber and first issued in 1834, block-printed in colours. The view is based on a print after J. G. Milbert, combined with a picturesque foreground.

143 Detail from 'Les Sauvages de la Mer Pacifique', designed by Jean Gabriel Charvet for Dufour of Mâcon, 1804, shown at the Exposition des Produits de l'Industrie in 1806; block-printed in colours. This scene shows the inhabitants of the Sandwich Islands, with the death of Captain Cook in the background. It has been hung framed by pilasters, but the paper could also form a continuous panorama.

144 Detail from 'Vues du Brésil', designed by Deltil for Zuber and first issued in 1830; block-printing in colours is combined with *irisé*. The scenes are taken from J. M. Rugendas's *Voyage pittoresque dans le Brésil* (1827). The complete paper, in 30 pieces, cost 60 francs in 1831.

After 1840, exotic plants and unpeopled landscapes came to the fore.

145 Part of 'Isola Bella', seemingly the earliest of the new type of papers, first issued by Zuber in 1843. For the complete scheme, 550 blocks were required to print 85 colours, below an *irisé* sky. This botanically learned design is traditionally attributed to the flower-painters Eugène Ehrmann and Georges Zipélius. All the plants, such as the tall *Magnolia discolor* in the centre and the banana to the right, were carefully identified by the designers.

146 The scene representing Europe in 'Eldorado', designed by Ehrmann, Zipélius and Joseph Fuchs for Zuber and first issued in 1849; block-printed in colours.

147 'La Mer glaciale' – the glacial sea – from 'Les Zones Terrestres', designed by Ehrmann for Zuber and first issued in 1855; block-printed in colours.

148 A piece from 'L'Eden', designed by Joseph Fuchs for Desfossé and first produced in 1861. The main subject here is the Gloire de Dijon rose, which had been introduced in 1853. It is set off against bright green larch and dark cedar which fill the space. The complete paper required 3,642 blocks to print its 23 pieces, and cost 150 francs.

Manufacturers were determined to establish wallpaper as an art, rather than a craft, and to this end they exploited the scale of scenic papers. Two makers stand out: Eugène Délicourt in 1851 and Jules Desfossé in 1855.

bottom and opposite
150–152 Desfossé's stand at the Paris Exhibition of 1855 featured pictorial panels associated with famous artists, in a setting of the firm's floral papers, all block-printed in colours. In the centre was the 'Jardin d'Armide', where James Pradier's statue of *Prudence* was shown in a bower designed by the outstanding flower-painter Edouard Muller. At the left was 'Les Pierrots',

signed by Thomas Couture, who was painting the same subject in oil at the time and supervised the paper's production in the factory. At the right was 'La Bacchante Endormie', with an astonishing nude based on Auguste Clésinger's statue, *Woman Stung by a Serpent*. These two outer pictures were printed on single sheets of paper 1.85 × 2.35 metres (6 × 7½ ft) in size.

above
149 The 'Grande Chasse' series designed by Antoine Dury for Délicourt won first prize for wallpaper at the Great Exhibition of 1851 in London, having proved to the judges that the industry was 'capable of the highest artistic effects'. The 16-piece set required 4,000 blocks, and sold in 1854 at 190 francs. This is one of its five components, the stag hunt.

The pursuit of prestige

One of the chief ambitions of wallpaper manufacturers was to rescue their products from the class of 'minor arts' (where most of what we now call 'decorative arts' were consigned) and raise them to the status of 'major arts' (in the company of architecture, painting and sculpture). In this they were participating in the general development of the decorative arts and seeking to prove an important point: that all art is one, and that what is beautiful can also be useful. They were helped in their crusade by the international exhibitions. At the first of these, the Great Exhibition held in London in 1851, Délicourt showed the 'Grande Chasse' set, designed by Dury and printed on 16 pieces – one of the large-scale depictions of nature of the type we have just been considering – and the critics hailed it by the prestige term *oeuvre*: 'Monsieur Délicourt's *chasse* proved that the wallpaper industry is capable of achieving the highest artistic effects, and that it has definitively won its place among the most splendid productions sanctioned by taste.'[7]

At the 1855 Exhibition held in Paris, Desfossé presented a remarkable and entirely novel display, for which the firm had enlisted the help of leading painters and sculptors. In the middle was the 'Jardin d'Armide', designed by Muller around a copy of James Pradier's sculpted figure of *Prudence*. This was flanked by Thomas Couture's *Pierrots* and by *La Bacchante Endormie*, based on another sculpture, Auguste Clésinger's *Woman Stung by a Serpent*. Facing it was *La Prière*, also by Couture.

Desfossé's aim was plain. For some fifty years manufacturers had been producing their decorative schemes on the fringe of the world of serious art. Desfossé was determined to break with that tradition, and to ennoble wallpaper by bringing it into the world of 'high art'. As we saw, scenic wallpapers had at first been called *tableaux* – paintings – and Desfossé's gambit was to pursue that line of association to its logical conclusion. To start with, he secured the cooperation of extremely well-known artists such as Thomas Couture, who agreed to work with him under completely novel conditions. Couture's *Pierrots* provides a particularly interesting example. Jules Desfossé asked the artist to supervise every stage of the manufacture of the wallpaper in person, from the cutting of the blocks to the final printing, and apparently the paper was in fact completed before the oil painting. It is rare in being signed, and rarer still in the form taken by the signature: printed at the bottom are the words 'Thomas Couture Manufacture J. Desfossé' – publicly linking the name of a factory with that of a famous artist in a daring project.

Desfossé's next innovation was to use as the support not the standard paper but a single sheet, as large as 1.85 × 2.35 metres (about 6 × 7½ feet), which called for immense skill in handling during drying and printing.

Finally, the link between the scenes was no longer provided by formal continuity or even by the unity of tone that one finds in all panoramic papers – even in 'Psyché', where the independence of the individual scenes appears in the present context as strikingly avant-garde. In Desfossé's scheme, each picture stands by itself and obeys its own rules. There is no indication that Couture paid any attention to Muller's 'Armide'. And yet each picture was intended to form part of a moral narrative, and is only fully understood in relation to the other three. In taking up the traditional principle of putting together a sequence of scenes, Desfossé here manifested in its most intense form the ambiguity latent in any scenic paper: each is at the same time an element in a coherent narrative and a unique work, the presentation of which at the Exposition Universelle of 1855 took the form of a picture gallery.

Thinking along the same lines, Zuber produced several pictorial papers, including Swiss landscapes, such as 'Les Vaches' and 'Le Berger', and a romantic image of the sea in 'La Vigie de Koat-Ven' of 1861.

Thus in the end the manufacturers had won their apparently mad initial gamble to give wallpaper a double nature: to make it the most important element in the decoration of a room, uniquely opening up the walls to distant vistas, and at the same time to transmit cultural images to the widest possible audience, with the endorsement of the leading artists of the day. It was a gamble that could succeed only under particular circumstances, and those circumstances could not be expected to last. After about 1865 the production of new **317** panoramic wallpapers ceased until the 1970s, when a few papers in contemporary style were issued.

What all these scenic papers did was to allow 19th-century men and women to dream of dwelling in paradise, while wars and revolutions raged outside. The most surprising illustration of this quest for paradise was the production of the **153** 'Monuments de Paris' paper by Dufour around 1815. Once the decoration is hung in a room and the last pieces are joined up, one seems to be on an island from which one looks across the water – the River Seine – to a mythical city of Paris, rearranged in an imaginary way. The room becomes an isle of refuge, from which the viewer can share the paradisal vision enjoyed by the figures on the bank in the foreground. All the panoramic designs, even those with the most ostensibly violent subjects, were treated in a peaceful mode and project the sort of image of landscape as Eden promoted by Rousseau's writings. In that respect they faithfully reflect the Age of Enlightenment, which fascinated the men and women of the 19th century and still has power to move us today.

153 'Les Monuments de Paris', on the walls of the dining room of Stonor Park (Oxfordshire). This popular pattern was first produced by Dufour c. 1815, and also reprinted by Desfossé & Karth later in the century from the original blocks. The Stonor paper, hung in 1978–79, came from another house whose owners had acquired it in Paris in the 1930s – a time when scenic papers again became very fashionable. Among the 'monuments' visible here, from left to right, are the Palais du Luxembourg, Panthéon, Place Vendôme with its column, Arc de Triomphe du Carrousel, Collège de France and Notre-Dame.

7 An Ocean Apart:
Imports and the Beginning
of American Manufacture

RICHARD C. NYLANDER

Until the beginning of the American Revolution (1776–83), England was almost exclusively the source for wallpaper in the American colonies. Subsequently French imports gained ground, particularly in the upper end of the market. At the same time, domestic American manufacture, with limited origins in the mid-18th century, took heart from Independence and began to expand into a competitive and successful industry.

Papers from England

Newspaper advertisements, manuscripts, and surviving wallpapers reveal that fashionable English patterns quickly found their way into the houses built by wealthy colonists in urban areas. The first reference to wallpaper in America is recorded in the estate inventory of the Boston (Massachusetts) stationer Michael Perry in 1700: listed in his stock are '7 quires of painted [i.e., stained or printed] paper and three reams of painted paper.'[1] Like most early references to wallpaper, it is descriptive of quantity but not of design. No samples of late 17th- or early 18th-century designs have been uncovered in buildings, but partial samples of three different patterns survive as covers for five almanacs printed in Boston dating between 1700 and 1727.[2] A floral design with a diaper background on a pale red ground and a marbled pattern on green cover almanacs for 1700 and 1718 respectively. The three almanacs from the 1720s are covered with late 17th-century wallpaper depicting a stag hunt, samples of which also survive in the collections of Colonial Williamsburg in Virginia and the Whitworth Art Gallery in Manchester, England. It is likely that at least some of these early designs were applied to the walls as individual sheets. Invoices and account books document the purchase of 'painted paper' in quires into the 1730s. Beginning at about the same time, however, 'Stampt Paper in Rolls' and 'Roll Paper for Rooms' become the terms more frequently used in newspaper advertisements.

Before the mid-18th century, wallpaper was purchased from stationers, who carried an entire range of paper products, or from merchants as a special order. Beginning about 1750, newspapers began to carry notices which announced the arrival of upholsterers from England. In the 18th century, paper-hanging was a branch of the upholsterer's trade, and it is likely that these newly arrived immigrants brought some stock with them.

Advertisements for English paper hangings become more numerous in the 1760s and 1770s in newspapers printed in Boston, New York, Philadelphia, and Charleston (South Carolina). This increase no doubt reflects the wider acceptance of wallpaper as a necessary component of the fashionable English interior and

22

therefore one to imitate in the colonies. The advertisements describe the quality of the papers being offered, using such words as 'fine', 'handsome', or 'uncommonly elegant', but rarely describe the pattern types that were available. Among the few descriptions listed between 1742 and 1766 are 'Flowered' (1742), 'Mock India' (1756), 'in the Gothic and Chinese Taste' and 'beautiful Painted Landscapes' (1761), 'Flock, or velvet, and Mock Chinese' (1763), and 'neat flower pieces for chimneys' – i.e., chimney-boards or fireboards, which concealed fireplaces in the summer when they were not in use (1766). Perhaps the most complete list was presented by the upholsterer William Bucktrout in the notice he placed in the *Williamsburg Gazette* for 9 May 1771. It includes 'embossed, Stucco, Chintz, Striped, Mosaick, Damask, and common'.[3] Some of the damasks would have been the large, formal flock papers described above.

154,
155   As ambitious in design and scale were pillar-and-arch patterns, of which more evidence survives in America than in Great Britain. The basis of these designs is an arch springing from a pair of columns, the capitals of which are usually of

154 In a *Family Group* attributed to the Irish artist Philip Hussey, *c.* 1760, the room is hung with a pillar-and-arch wallpaper block-printed on a grey ground. Curiously, a different pattern is used on the chimneybreast. Fragments of the main pattern, bearing Georgian Excise stamps, have been found in two mid-18th century houses in New England seaports.

155 This length of an English pillar-and-arch paper, *c.* 1760, is all that would fit between the mop board and the ceiling in the parlour of Timothy Johnson's house in North Andover (Massachusetts). The pattern is block-printed in black, white and brown on a grey ground.

the Corinthian order. The effect on the walls was of a continuous colonnade, somewhat like the arcades of Classical or Renaissance buildings. A variety of elements could be placed within the arch – a bust, a vase of flowers, a balustrade or a garden ornament. Often an entire building was shown there in perspective, enhancing the illusion that the observer was looking through a colonnade that opened directly onto a street or a town square.

Pillar-and-arch wallpapers were occasionally referred to as 'Architecture' papers. Their architectural nature was further enhanced by the colours in which they were printed, most often black, white and brown on a grey ground. The 42-inch (1.07 m) repeat of most of them required two sets of wood blocks or 'prints' (usually about 21 inches – 53 cm – square) to complete a single design element. The scale made the papers appropriate for use in large spaces, and indeed American newspaper advertisement of the late 18th century suggest that they be placed in entries (stair halls) or halls (large reception rooms). In an effort to be stylish, however, some people used pillar-and-arch papers in low studded rooms where scarcely two repeats would fit between floor and ceiling.

The dramatic impact of the large damask and pillar-and-arch patterns was counterbalanced by a wide range of more moderate-scale patterns that were readily adaptable to the parlours and chambers of less ambitious homes. Their repeats fitted easily within the standard printing block; some were small enough to require only a half block.

Textiles provided an almost endless source of designs that could be translated into wallpaper. Changing fashions in woven and printed fabrics, such as silk brocades, worsteds, block-printed chintzes and plate-printed cottons, were echoed in papers that ranged from elaborate multi-coloured compositions to simple sprig patterns printed in one or two colours.

Flock wallpapers were also available in smaller patterns. A common type depicts vines which sprout large leaves and flowers as they trail up to the ceiling.

155

below
156 Two widths of an English paper, block-printed in eight colours, which was one of two 'mock Chinese' designs purchased by Jeremiah Lee in about 1769. The colonial merchant also chose block-printed mock-flock papers in blues and green, and custom-made hand-painted hangings (see Ill. 160) for his mansion in Marblehead (Massachusetts).

opposite
157 Dr Philemon Tracy feels a patient's pulse while seated in a floral-papered room, *c.* 1790. The paper is hung both above and below the chair rail.

158 A sprig paper, block-printed in England *c.* 1760–80. This classic design might be difficult to date were it not for the Georgian Excise stamp on the reverse. The original light pink ground colour is visible on the left-hand margin.

159 An elaborate English floral paper, block-printed *c.* 1720–40. The vivid colours that appealed to the 18th century consumer are apparent on the left side.

Often the background was overprinted with an intricate diaper pattern, termed
32 'mosaic' or 'mosaick' in the 18th century (see above, p. 30). But even this wall-paper style, which simulated a more expensive fabric, was itself available in a less costly imitation. In mock flocks, so called, the areas that would have been covered with chopped wool are instead strewn with powdered colour in a dark shade.

A wide variety of silk brocades were also rendered in wallpaper. An elaborate
159 floral design at Williamsburg is further enhanced by a stripe imitating an intri-cate lace. Less complicated floral trail brocades provided the inspiration for a multitude of simpler papers. Often the vine meanders up a striped background. Both floral trail designs and plain stripes are seen in popular English 18th-century genre prints depicting middle-class interiors, such as those published by Robert Sayer and Carrington Bowles.

158 Sprigs were the simplest of all the floral designs derived from textiles. They were printed in regular repeating fashion in one or two colours. This simple pattern type has never lost its appeal: some Georgian designs could just as easi-ly have been made in France or the United States in the 1820s or purchased from Laura Ashley in the 1980s. Sprig papers may have belonged to the cate-gory that most paper-stainers called 'common', a group which included an end-less variety of small geometric designs. These were hung in the secondary rooms of a house and may also have been used as ceiling papers.

41. The most exotic 18th-century wallpaper patterns were based on block-
156 printed chintzes or inspired by fanciful interpretations of Chinese designs, known today as 'Chinoiserie'. Either could have been termed 'India figures'. 'Chintz figures' were perhaps the most colourful of all mid-18th-century wall-papers; occasionally stencils were used as well as blocks to apply the colours.

Our knowledge of English imports is augmented by invoices for wallpapers among the accounts for numerous houses built in the colonies in the mid-18th

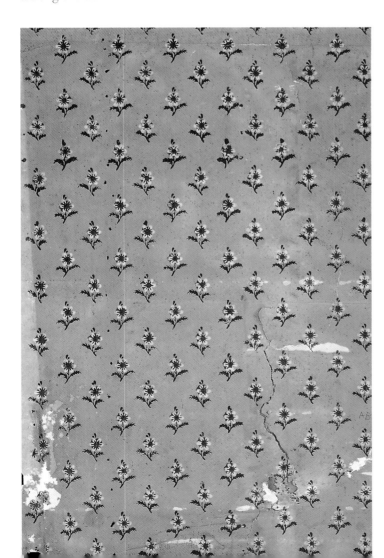

century. Most often these record only the number of rolls or a brief description of the pattern. They seldom answer questions about the hierarchy of patterns chosen for particular rooms of a single house or how the wallpapers were intended to complement other decorative elements.

The drawings found among the records for refurbishing the Proprietary House in Perth Amboy (New Jersey) for the Royal Governor William Franklin and his wife between 1773 and 1775 provide some insight into the choice of wallpaper and suggest details about 18th-century conventions of colour coordination within a room.[4] Notations on the crude floor plan list the room name and the type and colour of the wallpaper that the managers in charge of the refurbishing thought appropriate. For the Drawing Room 'a handsome *Yellow* Paper – suitable for Yellow Silk Damask Curtains, Chairs, &c' was required. The Dining Parlour was 'To be papered with a neat *red & white* Paper – The Curtains to be red & white Check of the best kind.' The 'Breakfasting Parlour' was 'To be papered with a neat *Green & white* Paper – Curtains to be Green Check.' For the Governor's Study or Office 'A common *Green* Paper will do, as great Part of the Wall will be covered with Books, Maps, &c.' The Housekeeper's Room was the only one on the ground floor that 'Needn't be papered'.

The chambers upstairs followed the same pattern. 'A *Yellow* Paper, to suit Yellow Damask Furniture' and a '*Green & white* Paper to suit Green Check Furniture' were needed for the secondary bedchambers. The 'Best Bed Chamber' was 'To be papered with a handsome *Crimson* colour'd Paper – to suit a Crimson Damask Bed & Furniture'. Apparently the only room where the governor and his wife had any choice was their own bedchamber: the plan notes that 'The Paper to be *blue & white*, striped, of a particular Pattern' had already been 'sent for to England'.

For the entrance hall, in addition to the floor plan, more detailed elevations with measurements and locations of doors and windows were included because it was 'to be papered with Paper made on Purpose to suit the Pannels, Chimney &c and if it won't add much to the Expence (which it is thought it will not) to have the Falls of the Passaick & Cohoes represented in black & white in Imitation of Copper Plate on a Buff coloured Ground from the Prints of those Falls sold by Jeffereys: The same kind for the Staircase on which the Falls of Niagara to be painted or stained.'

The exact nature of the popular English wallpaper styles that were used in the American colonies is best established by the examples that have remained on the walls of 18th-century houses or the fragments that have been uncovered during the course of repairs or restoration. The most elaborate extant examples are the hand-painted hangings that were installed about 1769 in three rooms of the Jeremiah Lee Mansion in Marblehead (Massachusetts) and those originally hung in the Stephen Van Renssellaer House in Albany (New York) in 1768.[5] Like the papers planned for the entrance hall of the Proprietary House, these examples were custom-made to fit the spaces they were to decorate. They were designed to imitate walls hung with large oil paintings in elaborate Rococo frames. The views selected for Jeremiah Lee were Classical and Romantic scenes copied from engravings of paintings by Giovanni Paolo Pannini and Joseph Vernet. More frequent survivals are rooms of flock wallpaper. There are five, each with a different design, in New England alone, and additional fragments uncovered in numerous houses attest to the popularity of flocks or 'velvet' papers in the colonies.

Equally stylish were rooms hung with solid or 'plain' coloured wallpapers edged with printed or papier maché borders. This style is illustrated in 18th-century pictures of the period in both England and America. Johann Zoffany's 1769 painting of Sir Lawrence Dundas with his grandson and John Singleton Copley's 1772 portrait of Ebenezer Tyng depict rooms papered with the two

160

160 Hand-painted panels in grisaille taken by an English paper-stainer from engravings by Pierre Antoine de Machy (1723–1807) fill the large wall areas in the drawing room of the Jeremiah Lee Mansion at Marblehead (Massachusetts).

most popular colours of the period, blue and green respectively. In each room the wallpaper has been embellished with a pierced gilded border, probably made of papier maché. George Washington and Benjamin Franklin each ordered plain coloured wallpapers from England in the 1760s.[6] Plain papers also became available from France beginning in the 1780s. In 1782 John Welsh, a Boston merchant who later changed his occupation to that of paper-stainer, wrote to his brother in France to order '*plain* clear sky blue, *plain* crimson, & *plain* green papers mostly of the first mentioned & so on in proportion ye other colours with n^t [neat] borders of papier marchii, white and gilt according to your fancy – wch are fash^o in Europe'.[7]

Plain papers remained fashionable into the 1790s. Green and blue continued to be the most popular colours, but as one New York paper-stainer stated, any colour could be supplied to his customers 'agreeable to their fancy' or 'to suit their Furniture'.[8] In 1795 Ebenezer Clough of Boston listed an entire range of colours including 'PLAIN Blues, Greens, Buffs, Red, Yellow, Stone, Pinks, Purple, – Purls, and any other plain coloured Grounds, which the Public may want'.[9] All were available not only ready coloured but in rolls, thereby saving the labour of pasting individual sheets of uncoloured paper to the walls and then painting them with the desired shade.

A small watercolour, traditionally said to show the parlour of Count Rumford's house in Concord (New Hampshire), shows the room hung with a plain green paper with a festoon border at the cornice level. The picture almost perfectly illustrates the description of a room in Boston in 1792.

161

The dining and drawing rooms, which opened from the hall on either side, had cornices of stucco: and the walls were hung with a plain green paper, relieved by a broad, highly coloured border, representing flowers and shells. The furniture of both apartments was of mahogany, carved and inlaid . . . With the exception of the entrance hall, the carpets on both the lower stories were Brussels and Axminster. Graceful wreaths of flowers, on a white ground, formed the pattern in the drawing room.[10]

161 *A Harpsichord Recital at Count Rumford's, Concord, New Hampshire*, by Benjamin Thompson, *c.* 1800.

The use of borders was not restricted to rooms hung with plain papers. Their importance in 18th-century decoration is underscored in a letter from a Rhode Island firm to its English supplier in 1784: 'The paper hangings, came without border, and are now laying useless.'[11] A few years earlier John Welsh in Boston had complained to his agent in France: 'do let the borders match better – the grounds ought to be alike.'[12] His comments imply that a certain compatibility existed in the 18th century between wallpapers and their borders. Many examples found *in situ*, however, indicate that pattern and colour were not coordinated to the degree that they are today.

Papers from France

Beginning in the 1780s, imports from England received stiff competition from French wallpapers. John Welsh noted in 1782 that 'altho the paper hang^{gs} come high from France, they are quick sale.'[13] The removal of export duties in 1787 made French products more affordable to the American consumer. They were imported by dealers in paper hangings and by upholsterers, many of whom had emigrated from France. Francis De L'Orme was one such upholsterer 'lately arrived from Paris' who settled in Charleston (South Carolina) in 1790. His stock included 'an assortment of handsome Paper-Hangings from Paris, in the latest Taste, some emblematic of the late Revolution'.[14] By 1795, he was selling '3,000 pieces of paperhanging with rich borders' as well as 'very fine landscapes for chimney pieces'.[15] These last articles were probably panels designed as overdoors, which found ready use in America to decorate fireboards.

Vast quantities of French wallpapers were also shipped to Philadelphia in the 1790s. In addition to the patterns he produced himself, William Poyntell carried a large assortment of imported papers. In 1792, he advertised that he had 'purchased an invoice of Three Thousand Pieces, Just arrived from France, New Patterns, and brilliant colours'.[16] Only six years earlier he had purchased an equal number of papers from London. Poyntell was so pleased with his new French collection, he announces, that he created a sample book, complete with borders, to make it easier for patrons to make a selection. He increased his stock every year, reaching a total of 12,000 rolls in 1797. They ranged 'from the lowest priced kind to the most superb patterns'.[17] Surely the latter were the luxurious products in the style made famous by Jean-Baptiste Réveillon's factory that have been discussed in earlier chapters.

William Strickland, an English visitor to the United States in 1794, commented on the popularity of French wallpapers in his description of Clermont, a house near Hudson (New York). 'The principal rooms which are of good dimensions are hung with french papers, which are chiefly used in this country, the patterns being much more beautiful and elegant, and lively, than what are manufactured in and exported from England and much cheaper in proportion to their merit.'[18] The artistic quality and the astonishing range of colours, so different from the more sombre and monochromatic palette of the English wallpapers they were used to, clearly had captured the attention of the American public, and French wallpaper styles dominated the American market for most of the next century.

The beginnings of American production

The documentary and physical evidence points to the predominance of English wallpaper in the American colonies before the American Revolution, with French papers becoming popular after the war. When, then, did domestic production begin? The newspapers give us some tantalizing clues as early as the 1750s and 1760s. In 1756, John Hickey, a silk-dyer in New York 'lately from Dublin', advertised that he 'stamps or prints paper in the English manner and hangs it so as to harbour no worms'.[19] Nine years later, almost to the day, the

Boston News-Letter reported that 'John Rugar produced several Patterns of Paper Hangings made in this Province' at a 'Meeting of the Society for promoting the Arts, etc.' in New York.[20] Also in New York, in 1767, John Scully advertised that he 'Manufactures all kind of Paper Hangings, of the newest Patterns'.[21] In 1775, Edward Ryves, another Irish immigrant, and a partner named Fletcher advertised 'A new American Manufactory' for paper hangings in Philadelphia, and claimed they were 'the first who have attempted that manufacture on this continent'. Their long notice emphasized their effort 'to excel in neatness of patterns and elegance of colour' as well as commenting on 'the heavy expense attendant on so extensive an undertaking'.[22] Nothing else is known of these early endeavours, and to date no wallpapers documented to any of these individuals are known.

Our knowledge of American paper-stainers and their products increases dramatically after the Revolution. The mood after the Treaty of Paris was one of great optimism for the future of the new Republic. In the six years between 1784 and 1790 almost a dozen paper-stainers established new businesses in Boston and Philadelphia. In newspaper advertisements they were overwhelmingly confident of their ability and the quality of their product. The tone of a lengthy notice placed in the *New-York Journal, & Patriotic Register* for 20 July 1790 by the Boston partnership of Prentiss & May is typical of many advertisements that promoted American wallpapers as equal to imported papers but less expensive.

> The progress of manufactures, in our youthful country, affords a flattering presage of expeditious maturity— nothing is wanting but the encouragement of well wishers to their country, in promoting them; and it is in general conceded, that they are at least as cheap, and equal in goodness to the foreign. The manufacture of Paper Hangings is brought to so great perfection, that should the manufactures meet with encouragement, they will soon be enabled

162 This French paper of the 1780s with its fanciful genre scene was hung in a bedchamber of the Tobias Lear House in Portsmouth (New Hampshire). It was block-printed on recycled paper: the opaque ground colour covers the text of an unbound book. The left-hand edge has been misjoined to another piece of the same paper.

163 An arabesque paper and border, probably made in Boston *c.* 1790–1810. Neither the colouring nor the block-printing compares with the French wallpaper from which it was no doubt copied. Fragments of this design have been found in several New England houses, attesting to its popularity.

to supply the United States entirely, and thus detain many thousands of pounds per annum within these boundries which would otherwise be sent to Europe.[23]

Joseph Dickinson of Philadelphia also praised domestically produced wallpapers. In 1785, he announced that he was 'determined to undersell all importation' and that he would 'warrent both paper and colours to stand equal, if not preferable, to any imported', claiming that both were 'calculated to suit the nature of this climate'.[24] In one advertisement he added a note that he hoped would have even more appeal to the practical-minded consumer: 'Flies and smoke opperate to soil paper in common rooms if the grounds are too delicate; to prevent which I have pin grounds that fly marks will not be perceptable upon. Also dark grounds, which the smoke will not considerable effect, in the course of twenty years.'[25]

The raw materials needed to produce wallpaper were readily available. The Revolution had given a boost to the production of paper itself. Over twenty paper mills had been established in the colonies between 1690 and 1776, but their production had to be supplemented by imports from England, France and the Netherlands. Once independence was declared, imported papers were harder to come by. Several states encouraged the setting up of paper mills to meet the demand, and by the end of the war an estimated eighty to ninety paper mills were in operation. By 1810, this number had increased to two hundred. Annual production was 425,000 reams of paper valued at $1,690,000.[26] In that same year, mills in Massachusetts produced 22,500 pasted-sheet rolls for paper hangings and three paper-staining manufactories in Philadelphia alone produced 115,000 'Pieces stamped'.[27]

The production of American wallpaper did not differ substantially from the practice in England. The 1798 billhead of Ebenezer Clough of Boston provides the best contemporary illustration. On the far left, the paper-stainer and his apprentice are taking individual sheets of handmade paper and joining them together to form rolls. A press ensures that the sheets are securely glued together. The completed 12-yard (11 m) rolls are stored on shelves until they are needed. On the far right, the paper-stainer, again with the help of his apprentice, is grinding dry colours and mixing them in barrels. Immediately to the left, he is applying the background colour to the rolls with large brushes. In the final vignette, the paper-stainer has just applied the printing block to the paper and is about to strike it with a mallet to insure a good impression. The block is only half as wide as the paper, indicating that he is probably printing a small-figured pattern. Comparison with similar vignettes at the top of a broadside for the Blue-Paper Warehouse in London issued c. 1720 shows essentially the same method.

Only one wallpaper pattern can be attributed to Ebenezer Clough. It celebrates America's first president, George Washington, who had attained the

PATRIOTISM

164 Detail of the billhead of Ebenezer Clough of Boston, 1798, showing the paper-stainer and his apprentice at work.

opposite
165 Wallpaper celebrating the Independence of the United States, by an unidentified manufacturer in Boston or Philadelphia. c. 1785–90. The figures are placed within a pillar-and-arch framework.

166 'Washington's Monument', produced by Ebenezer Clough of Boston in 1800. A sample of the same design, bearing the stamp of the Hartford (Connecticut) paper-stainer Zechariah Mills, has recently come to light.

status of a heroic figure by the time of his death in 1799: within a pillar-and-arch frame, Liberty and Justice weep over an urn inscribed 'Sacred to Washington'. Clough was justifiably proud of his paper and advertised it in Boston's *Columbian Centinel* in 1800 as 'WASHINGTON'S MONUMENT'. After a lengthy description of the design, he reiterated the call to support American manufactures: 'As the above attempt to perpetuate the memory of the Best of Men, is the production of an American, both in draft and workmanship, it is hoped that all true-born Americans will so encourage the Manufactories of their Country, that Manufactories of all kinds may flourish, and importation stop.'[28]

165 Another popular wallpaper with a patriotic subject, this time an allegorical depiction of the American Revolution, was made by an anonymous paper-stainer in either Boston or Philadelphia. The new nation is shown as an Indian princess crowned by a feathered headdress and carrying a bow and quiver. The figure of a man with a tricorn hat in the centre represents America's ally France; his foot is trampling 'BRITISH LAWS' and he is handing a copy of the Declaration of Independence to a mourning Britannia.

Only a handful of similar commemorative designs can be cited as uniquely American wallpapers. In an effort to satisfy their customers's desires to be fashionable, most paper-stainers continued to copy imported designs. Although Appleton Prentiss was proud of the wallpapers he made in his Boston shop, he did not fail to let his customers know in 1790 that 'the figures are chosen from

167 the newest European patterns'.[29] Prentiss's unique billhead, dated 1791, gives us some idea of the wallpapers that he actually produced. They include simple

EUROPEAN FASHION

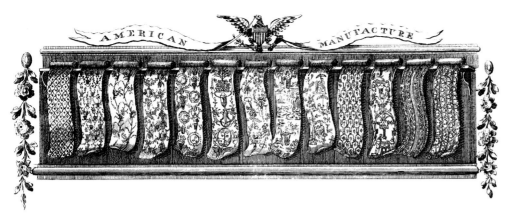

167

167 geometrics, floral trails, arabesques, a Chinoiserie design, a pillar-and-arch pattern and several borders. At least three are copied directly from known French wallpapers; others are decidedly English in appearance. The elaborate nature of some of them is hinted at in one of Prentiss's advertisements which mentions patterns printed in sixteen colours. It is impossible to tell which, if any, of the designs in the billhead are Prentiss's own creation.

Many of the small-scale simple repeating designs made by American paper-stainers in the 1790s and the first decade of the 19th century might be considered to be the rather unsophisticated products of naive craftsmen. In fact they reflect a popular trend in English wallpapers during the same time: similar patterns have been found in fashionable London town houses and in commodious mansions in the United States. Those of the highest quality were printed on polished or 'satin' grounds and often fine pin dots outline the principal motifs. The wallpapers chosen for the large rooms of the Boston house built for Harrison Gray Otis and his wife in 1796 all have repeats measuring between $2\frac{1}{2}$ and 10 inches (9–25 cm). They include stripes, block patterns, and for the best room a floral pattern printed on a satin ground intended to imitate a silk damask. All were embellished with narrow borders.

Wallpapers in the same taste were chosen by Lady Jean Skipwith to decorate the rooms of her new house, Prestwould Plantation, in Clarksville (Virginia). In 1795 she wrote of her plan to her agent in London:

> We wish to have our House papered; but as we are not well acquainted with the prices of the different sorts of papers we defer ordering it till some future opportunity. In the mean time will thank you to send us patterns of different qualitied papers, with the prices of them. We do not mean to go to the length of India [i.e., Chinese] Paper, only plain English and Irish. I am very partial to papers of only one colour, or two at the most – velvet [i.e., flock] paper I think looks too warm for this country.

In all, eleven different patterns with matching borders were purchased for her from the London paper-stainer James Duppa. The invoice dated 1799 includes such intriguing pattern names as 'Angle Leaf Greens', 'Angle Worm purples', 'Cloud & Mitre', 'India plaid on Olymp^{n}', 'Sattin Grass' and 'Bengall Stripe on Buff'.[30]

169

Other well-documented wallpapers in the same style were ordered in 1807 by James Rundlet of Portsmouth (New Hampshire). Just three months after the frame of his house was raised, 112 rolls of wallpaper and borders for seven rooms were shipped from England. The most expensive paper was reserved for the best parlour, where it remains on the walls today. The shipping invoice identifies the pattern as 'Peach Damask', and the end of one roll is stamped 'James Bate, Manufacturer. 45. Cheapside, London'. The border that was hung with it was more expensive than Bate's paper and was probably imported from France. It bears a strong resemblance to products of Jacquemart & Bénard and is called 'Paris Flock Border' on the invoice.[31]

171

167 Detail of the billhead of Appleton Prentiss of Boston, 1791. The patterns represent fashionable papers produced in the late 18th century by Boston paper-stainers in their attempt to 'suit any taste'. Most correspond to pattern names noted in 1789 in Prentiss's invoice book. They include, from left to right, a small geometric figure (possibly 'star & ribon'), 'flower pots', a floral trail paper (probably 'Vines'), four imitations of elaborate French designs (including 'bird in Ring', 'Basket' and 'parrotquiets'), a pattern depicting garden statuary and birds ('Swans'), a Chinoiserie design ('China fig.'), a bow knot design ('Nott'), a pillar-and-arch paper ('Arches'), and two rolls of uncut borders ('Narrow Borders' and 'festoon').

168 A vine and stripe paper and border block-printed by Zechariah Mills of Hartford (Connecticut) between 1802 and 1807, from the Daniel Hough House at Lebanon (New Hampshire). The wheat and leaves were printed in a glossy varnish green that stood out against the original light blue ground. Because the ground has faded the intricate pea weed pattern in white is now barely perceptible behind the trailing vines.

169 'Sattin Grass' and 'Laurel Border' by James Duppa of London: block-printed in colours, c. 1799. Lady Jean Skipwith ordered this pattern with a highly polished satin ground for the drawing room of her house, Prestwould Plantation, in Clarksville (Virginia).

170 *North Parlor of Dr Whitridge's, Tiverton, Rhode Island, 1814*, by Joseph Shoemaker Russell, c. 1850. This watercolour illustrates a room hung with a floral stripe or vine pattern. A contrasting border was used only at the ceiling level.

By the beginning of the 19th century French wallpaper styles had almost eclipsed English ones in popularity, and there is ample evidence that many of the French imports were copied directly by American manufacturers. Comparison of the two at the turn of the century, however, does not substantiate most American paper-stainers' claims that their products were of equal quality.

163   An American-made pattern of Cupid standing on top of an urn may well have been copied from a French example imported into Boston, but it could never deceive anyone who had seen a real French paper: the execution of the details is not nearly as fine; perhaps in an effort to cut down on expense, the number of colours has been reduced to four, and the orange and blue combination typical of so many French designs has lost all of its subtlety.

Competition must have spurred those who wanted to succeed at the craft to improve their wallpapers. In 1813, Moses Grant, Jr, a Boston paper-stainer, referred to 'the rapid improvement of this branch of manufactures'.[32] Indeed, it becomes difficult to determine the origin of many wallpapers merely on grounds of quality. Several distinct French pattern types enjoyed enormous popularity in the United States. Two of the most fashionable between about 1810 and 1825 were drapery patterns and 'landscape figures'. The magnificent and realistic renderings of drapery panels like those produced by Dufour found their way into a limited number of American homes. More readily affordable and perhaps more suitable for the scale of most American houses were the less elaborate and often

172   more stylized versions. Henry Virchaux & Co. produced a number of these at their Philadelphia factory around 1814. In an attempt to make sure that no other firm copied his wallpapers, Virchaux submitted several of his original designs for copyright and a number of them survive in the Library of Congress in Washington, D. C.

In the so-called 'landscape figure' papers, the design consists of large and small motifs alternating between stripes and placed on a background that is

171 'Peach Damask' and 'Paris Flock Border', ordered by James Rundlet of Portsmouth (New Hampshire) in 1807. The dark background colour was block-printed over the pink satin ground which appears as the flowers and leaves of the pattern. This unused sample is stamped with the maker's name, James Bate of London, as well as a 'First Account Taken' Excise stamp.

172 Drapery wallpaper by Henry Virchaux of Philadelphia, c. 1814. The following text accompanied the sample when Virchaux submitted it to the Library of Congress for copyright: 'Ground imitating drapery, ornamented with festoons, garlands of roses in Arabesque upon one side two ribands entwined forming a column. Messrs. Virchaux & Co. intend to execute this design of their own invention on every different ground with correspondent colours, at their manufactory of paper Hangings.'

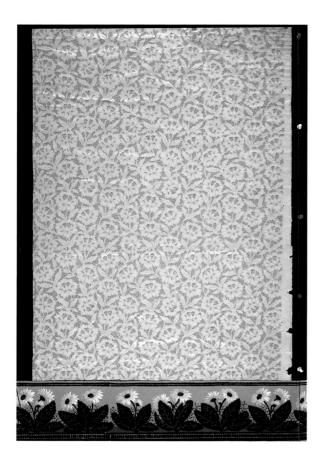

often enriched with a small over-all pattern. An almost endless variety of motifs could be placed between the stripes. Pastoral scenes are the most common, followed by Classical figures and scenes from some exotic part of the world. In New England, many landscape figures were made between 1811 and 1817 by the Boston firm of Moses Grant Jr & Co. Grant was the son of a successful paper-stainer and the grandson of an upholsterer, so he knew his business well. Although he must have used French wallpapers for inspiration, the 1813 advertisement mentioned above, for 'Fancy Landscape Paper hangings', clearly boasts that 'the *Design, Paper, Colours* and *Labor are American*'.[33]

Little is known about who drafted the designs for the wallpapers that were produced in America in the late 18th and early 19th centuries. In 1797 William Poyntell needed craftsmen to carve printing blocks and placed the following notice in the *Pennsylvania Packet*: 'Print Cutters Wanted. Neat workman at drafting and cutting, may have employ for the winter.'[34] In 1810, Moses Grant & Son advertised that 'in order to afford their customers the greatest choice . . . several artists are constantly employed in cutting new patterns.' A year later, the successor firm, Moses Grant Jr & Co., stated that the paper-staining was 'under the superintendence of one of the first American artists.'[35] Unfortunately, no names were given. Some artists, however, must have received their training as apprentices in paper-staining manufactories. William Doyle, for example, was a paper-stainer in Boston between 1795 and 1803 and went on to pursue a successful career as a painter of portrait miniatures, while Thomas Cole had drawn patterns for his father's paper-staining business in Steubenville (Ohio) in the early 1820s before going on to become a distinguished landscape painter.

The Grant firm was one of over two dozen that produced wallpaper in the first twenty years of the 19th century. Toward the end of this period, competition with French imports became stiff, and when the 1820 census was taken many paper-stainers complained bitterly. Samuel James of Providence (Rhode Island)

173 'Landscape Figure', paper, block-printed in the popular shades of grey of the period, by Moses Grant Jr & Co. of Boston, between 1811 and 1817. Grant used the pastoral scene of the man catching a fish in newspaper advertisements and on his billhead.

reported that he had 'formerly employed 6 Hands, now only 1 about half the time owing to the market being glutted with French papers'. Thomas Redman of Boston relayed the following comments about his business to the census taker: 'During that time France was involved in War [i.e., until 1815], quite good, but now ruined by excessive importations from thence. We want a duty on them.'[36]

Although duties were increased on most imports in 1821, it was not until 1824 that a higher duty of 40 per cent was applied to wallpaper. Even so, it did not totally discourage French imports. Between 1829 and 1834, the French firm of Zuber dealt directly with almost a hundred small dealers and importers from Portland (Maine) to New Orleans (Louisiana). The higher duties would have had less impact on sales of a product directed at the top end of the market, consisting primarily of scenic views and more expensive patterns with *irisé* or 'rainbow' grounds.

The higher duties on imported wallpapers did, however, give the impetus needed to get the smaller American shops back on their feet, and several newcomers established themselves in order to meet the growing demand. One of these was Janes & Bolles, who produced wallpapers in Hartford (Connecticut) between 1821 and 1828. Some of their papers are preserved today in a rare sample book, the only known survival in the United States earlier than the 1890s. The book contains one landscape figure and several geometric patterns; the majority, however, are designs printed in one or two colours in which small motifs are arranged to create striped effects. Janes & Bolles did not attempt to copy the more elaborate French styles, such as the popular *irisé* papers. Other firms did, but with only moderate success.

The productivity, labour force and raw materials of a small firm probably comparable to Janes and Bolles, in the western Massachusetts town of Lee, are documented in a report compiled by Secretary of the Treasury Louis B. McLane in 1833. The Paper Hanging Manufactory of W. & W. & C. Laflin, which had been in operation only three years when the report was published, employed sixteen men and six women. The women were paid slightly less than half of what the men earned. The firm produced 132,000 rolls of wallpaper worth $19,800 annually. Raw materials for the same year costing $14,745 included 4,000 reams of paper, 60,000 lbs (27,000 kg) of sizing, 2,000 lbs (900 kg) of pot ashes, the same quantity of pearl, 1,200 lbs (540 kg) of alum, 4,000 lbs (1,800 kg) of paints, 3,000 lbs (1,350 kg) of Paris White, 10,000 lbs (4,500 kg) of clay, 200 gallons (758 l) of oil, 1,000 lbs (450 kg) of rope, and 150 cords of wood and 12,000 lbs (5,400 kg) of imported dye woods. The report also states that the Laflins' wallpapers were sold mainly in New York.[37]

The number of warehouses where the consumer could purchase both imported and domestically produced wallpapers also increased in the 1830s. Although they were located primarily in cities, they supplied countless booksellers and general stores in rural areas with stylish papers. A label inside a band box made by John C. and Charles Cook provides a clue to taste outside the towns: it reads, 'Paper Hangings (of bright colours) of a style generally in demand by COUNTRY MERCHANTS for their trade, will always be kept in great variety.'[38]

Newspaper advertisements during this period often include prices. In 1823 Clarendon Harris of Worcester (Massachusetts) offered both French and American wallpapers ranging in price from 25 cents to $1.00 per roll. Thirteen years later, John R. Nickels, also of Worcester, was selling 'super SATIN PAPERS at from 25 cents to $1.25 per Roll, – Common do 12 1/2 cts. to 37 1/2 – which are equal to the French.' Nickels's papers were made locally by Joseph Barrey, who claimed that they were 'equal to the Paris or Rexheim Papers'.[39] Another of Barrey's advertisements gives us a very complete idea of both production and cost on the eve of mechanization. In 1837 he placed the following notice in the *Massachusetts Spy*:

J. M. BARREY is constantly manufacturing PAPERS suitable for PARLORS, ENTRIES, and Chambers, &c, which he will sell wholesale or retail lower than his usually low prices; viz. 5,000 rolls at 12 1/2 cents; 8,000 rolls at 14 cts. (good article); 3,000 rolls at 17 cents; 6,000 rolls at 25 cents; 12,000 rolls Satins, elegant gloss, at 37 1/2 cents; and a large lot of higher priced Satins. Also, FIRE BOARD PATTERNS, from 37 1/2 cents to $3.50. Also, a large lot of splendid VELVET and Common BOARDERS from 2 cents to 33. Also, a large assortment of BAND and HAT BOXES, by the gross, dozen, or single. Also, Green, Blue, Black, Yellow, Buff, and Grey, Plain Satin and Common Papers.[40]

Surely with this quantity available at such a range in price, even an individual at the low end of the middle class could afford wallpaper. It would only take one day's wages at the average rate of a dollar a day to purchase enough of Barrey's 'good article' at 14 cents a roll to paper one room of a house.

Mechanization

Mechanization was the next obvious step in order to respond to the increasing demand for stylish wallpapers. As we will see in the following chapter, European experiments to speed up production began in the early 19th century. England in particular pressed ahead, capitalizing on her invention of steam-powered multi-colour printing by roller in 1839. American attempts lagged a little behind, and the first mechanically printed wallpapers are generally said to have been produced in 1844 by Howell & Brothers in Philadelphia, on an English steam-powered machine. Two sources published in the 1890s, however, cite an instance of mechanization almost a decade earlier. An article in a trade journal

174 Wallpaper sample book of Janes & Bolles of Hartford (Connecticut), between 1821 and 1828. Twenty-nine samples are included, many of which are the same pattern printed in different colours on a variety of grounds. Although some of the blue grounds are brushed on, the pattern marked with the firm's name and the number '802' is printed on a paper stock made from unbleached rags.

B.F.Nutting del.

Pendletons Lithog.

WAREHOUSE OF J. BUMSTEAD & SON,
No. 113 WASHINGTON ST. BOSTON.

of 1890 reported that in 1835 'Josiah Bumstead & Son are credited with invent-ing a [hand-cranked] machine to print wallpaper in one colour, which, though crude, was a vast improvement on the hand process for rapid work.[41]

Josiah Freeman Bumstead kept a daily journal of his business from 1840, five years before he took over the company in Boston from his father Josiah, until his death in 1868. The ten volumes record the experiments that led to success-ful full-scale machine printing by the mid-1850s. Bumstead presents a fairly complete picture of this process as it gradually developed in the United States, because he comments not only on his own production but also on that of many other factories in New York, New Jersey, Baltimore and Philadelphia who were confronting the same problems and solving them in slightly different ways.[42]

The decade of the 1840s appears to be the period of greatest experimentation in the mechanization of all aspects of wallpaper production. Grounding machines spread an even coat of colour by means of cylindrical brushes. Also perfected now were satining machines, which produced satin or polished grounds by running dampened paper under brushes that revolved at a high speed. The earliest machines for both processes used horse power. In 1841, Bumstead noted that the satining machine used by the above-mentioned Joseph Barrey could do forty rolls 'with small whipping up of the horse'. The ground-ing machine that Bumstead purchased for his own use in 1845 was capable of producing 100 rolls per hour. By the end of the decade, both types were driven

175 The warehouse of J. Bumstead & Son, Boston, c. 1825–36. 'Chimney Board Prints' and the newest styles of wallpaper patterns hang in the well-lit balcony area of the retail shop. It is interesting to note that Bumstead stored his stock in bins, a method depicted in the trade cards of the English manufacturers James Wheeley and Richard Masefield one hundred years earlier.

by steam power. The problems of hanging and drying the greatly increased quantities of paper were solved as well.

There were also experiments to print wallpapers with a roller rather than a woodblock. Looking back on the work of an employee, Bumstead records that Charles Baxter had produced 34,978 rolls of wallpaper on a one-colour machine in 1839, and comments on similar practices in other firms. By the end of 1842, he had a two-colour machine in operation. Most of these were operated by hand, and as late as 1846 Bumstead commented that 'Barrey's printing machine goes much harder than mine. It takes a stout man to turn it.'

Additional machines were invented to meet the demand to print in more than one colour. By the mid-1850s, when Bumstead printed an elaborate pictorial billhead, the Waldron Company of New Brunswick (New Jersey), established in 1848, had succeeded in making a machine that could compete with English ones – generally considered to be superior, but very expensive. The billhead illustrates most aspects of Bumstead's operation. The new four-storey factory building was efficiently powered by steam. The traditional hand processes of block-cutting and block-printing or table work are seen on either side of the view of the retail store where the wallpapers were sold. Below the block-printer, two men are operating a satining machine. Mechanized printing is pictured directly opposite. The woman in the lower left is rolling the finished paper. (Rolling wallpaper was just one of the jobs undertaken by women in Bumstead's factory. They were also employed to do flocking and apply gilding; a few did printing.) The final vignette shows two paper-hangers with the tools of their trade leaving for a job.

Bumstead's was representative of several small firms at mid-century which combined the traditional methods of 'paper-staining' with the newer technology. Hand-block-printing continued to produce the best quality papers. Because of their limitations, machines were initially used only for ranges that were sold as 'common' or 'cheap'. It was not until the late 19th century that mechanized production would take over the industry almost completely and America would establish a place of its own in the international wallpaper market.

176

177

176 The billhead of J. F. Bumstead & Co. of Boston, 1856, depicts both the firm's retail shop and the factory, where traditional block-printing and recent advances in mechanized printing were carried on simultaneously.

177 A Rococo Revival wallpaper by J. F. Bumstead & Co., c. 1845–60. The design is block-printed in ten colours on a matt white ground. The pattern number '80' is stamped on the reverse.

8 The English Response: Mechanization and Design Reform

JOANNA BANHAM

The influence of the industrial Revolution

The history of wallpaper in the mid-19th century is dominated by two issues – the growth of new middle-class markets and the massive expansion of the industry arising from the introduction of steam-powered machines. Since the 1780s international trade had been dominated by France, whose manufacturers excelled in the production of expensive luxury goods. With the rise and expansion of the middle class, however, a type of consumer emerged whose desire to affirm the economic status and social respectability of their class was expressed partly in their enthusiasm for decorations and furnishings with which to adorn their homes. The first half of the 19th century witnessed an unprecedented increase in the demand for cheaper and more varied wallpapers. This demand not only generated a need for faster and more efficient methods of production that were capable of supplying the mass market: it also led to a gradual shift in the balance of world trade. From the 1850s, the commercial supremacy previously enjoyed by France was increasingly challenged by the manufacturing prowess of those nations employing machinery.

By 1860, machines were in use in many of the larger centres of manufacture in Europe and the United States; but interest largely depended upon the degree to which each country was industrialized. Thus progress was comparatively slow in Holland, Germany and France, while in England, where many other industries had already been mechanized, machine-printing was most actively and enthusiastically pursued. It was also in England that critical reactions to mass-production were most mixed. The introduction of machinery coincided with a crisis of confidence in native design that resulted in vehement attempts, on the part of certain critics and designers, to check what they perceived as the degenerate nature of contemporary work and to establish 'correct' principles of design. This chapter therefore concentrates upon developments within the English scene. It focuses initially upon the origins and subsequent effects of machine-printing, and then upon the arguments and efforts of those associated with the Movement for Design Reform. In addition, it aims to provide a survey of the main ideas and styles pertaining to the manufacture of wallpaper in the mid-century.

Mechanization

The first experiments in improving the efficiency of wallpaper production concerned the laying down of grounds, and in 1814 the English paper-stainer Timothy Harris patented a method of mechanically colouring the paper.[1] This was followed by attempts to speed up the block-printing process: in 1823, Harris's compatriot William Palmer produced a hand-operated device which mechanically raised and lowered the blocks on and off the colour tray (a rectangular container for the paint) and the paper.[2] Next came interest in rotary techniques: in 1826 Jean Zuber of Rixheim patented a design for a horse-

Timeline

132

powered machine in which the pattern was printed from engraved metal cylinders.[3] Like later wallpaper-printing machines, this invention adapted methods previously used in the production of textiles, but the difficulties inherent in the endeavour were twofold. Firstly, the thick distemper paints favoured in wallpapers did not lie evenly within the intaglio lines; and secondly, the grounded paper did not accept the pattern as readily as did the more absorbent textiles. In an attempt to overcome these problems Zuber's machine used thin-bodied varnish colours rather than distemper paints. Nevertheless, the results were still quite patchy and, despite the fact that the firm continued printing from engraved cylinders well into the 1830s, the technique was not widely exploited.

Similar experiments with cylinder-printing were also taking place in the United States. There was clearly no shortage of interest amongst manufacturers

178 A typical early 19th-century wallpaper, with a large, brightly coloured floral pattern – slightly old-fashioned for the date, 1838 – is shown by Mary Ellen Best in her painting room in York.

179 Twenty years later, the London parlour in Augustus Egg's *Past and Present, No. 1* features a subdued and formal red flock wallpaper whose Gothic fleur-de-lis pattern owes much to the intervening influence of Pugin and the Design Reform Movement.

on both sides of the Atlantic in speeding up production, and thus lowering costs, during this period. Yet it was not until 1839 that designs for the first truly successful steam-powered machine appeared. The credit for its invention went to an English firm.

The introduction of machine-printing in England might well have occurred prior to this date, but its development was held up by the high cost of Excise duties levied on wallpaper and by the restrictions governing the supply of continuous paper. By 1830, the tax on wallpaper represented a double duty of 3*d.* payable on each pound of paper used and a further 1¾*d.* charged on every yard of paper stained.[4] Manufacturers opposed these levies bitterly and campaigned fiercely for their removal on the grounds that they were both economically punitive and undemocratic. Giving evidence before a Government Inquiry in 1835, several claimed that the duty payable on an ordinary roll of wallpaper (1*s.* 3*d.*) amounted to as much as half of the price for which it was eventually sold.[5] Others pointed out that as the tax was the same on cheap as on more expensive goods, it penalized less wealthy consumers and favoured the luxury end of the market.[6] Furthermore, the Excise authorities themselves were increasingly conscious of the difficulties of enforcing the tax. Their officers were required to visit each workshop at least twice a day, to stamp every yard of wallpaper personally, and to submit copious returns every fortnight. The 1835 Inquiry therefore concluded that collection of the tax was expensive and that, by keeping the price of wallpaper high, it was detrimental to the expansion of the industry and placed English manufacturers at a disadvantage with their rivals abroad. Accordingly, in 1836 the duty on paper was halved and that on paper-staining was abolished. In 1861, the remaining tax on paper was removed.

The lightening of duties on native products was paralleled by the gradual decline of import tariffs charged on foreign goods. These had stood at 1*s.* a yard since 1825 but in 1846 they were reduced to 1¾*d.* and, following the signing of the 1860 trade agreement with France, they lapsed completely. The original protectionist intention behind this tax was, by the 1850s, giving way to the increasing influence of commercial and political interests lobbying for Free Trade. The overall growth of the industry during this period also meant that – to manufacturers at least – the threat of foreign competition no longer seemed as daunting as it had previously appeared. In the short term imports doubled, but in 1851 Jean Zuber declared: 'this heavy competition impelled the English manufacturers to such exertions that now, with a duty one sixth of that of 1825, we find a difficulty of introducing merchandise to the same amount as then.'[7] A decade later, in 1861, figures relating to the sale of wallpaper generally revealed that the value of work exported from the United Kingdom far exceeded that of imports and stood at £105,984 and £15,395 respectively.[8]

An even more serious handicap to the development of wallpaper-printing machines than Excise duties was the lack of paper produced in continuous rolls. The existing procedure of joining small sheets together manually prior to printing was inconvenient, costly and slow. Moreover, the hand-made rolls tore under the enormous pressure generated in machines, while the joins came unstuck when the paper was dampened during printing. The existence of continuous paper was therefore an essential prerequisite for mass-production. As early as 1798, the Frenchman Louis Robert had devised a means of manufacturing long lengths with precisely this end in mind; but the economic conditions in France proved unfavourable for the commercial exploitation of his design. In 1800 it was sent to London, where patents were taken out in 1801 and, with financial backing from the stationers Henry and Sealy Fourdrinier, Robert's original machine was modified and improved. By 1805, it was possible to produce paper in rolls 27 feet long by 4 feet wide (8.23 x 1.22 m) and it was only the restrictions imposed by the Excise authorities that prevented the immediate use of

180 An eight-colour English surface-printing machine in action in 1867. The paper, in a long continuous strip, runs around the central cylinder past the rollers, each of which is fed from a trough of colour (replenished from the tubs in the foreground). The scene is in Paris, at Gillou & Thorailler, described as the most technologically advanced of French firms at the time – one of many foreign manufacturers who took advantage of English expertise in this field.

181 Surface-printing roller used by the F. E. James Company in the United States in the mid-19th century.

continuous lengths within large sections of the English wallpaper industry.
These were lifted about 1830. By then machine-made paper was also widely
available in America and France, and from this time on, efforts to perfect mechanized methods of wallpaper production were intensified.

The first successful machine, patented in 1839, was developed by Potters &
Ross, a calico-printing firm based in Darwen (Lancashire) – later the manufacturing giants C. & J. G. Potter & Co. Like earlier attempts, it adapted rotary
techniques whereby the paper was drawn over the surface of a large central
drum and received an impression of the pattern from a number of engraved
metal cylinders (one for each colour) that were arranged around its base. Each
cylinder was supported above a trough of colour and was fed with pigment by
a continous cloth belt which also helped to regulate the supply of paint. Initially,
the cylinders were made of copper and the designs were cut into the metal, with
the pigment being carried in the intaglio lines.

It proved impossible, however, to produce solid areas of colour by printing
with engraved rollers, and about 1840 Potters introduced rollers made of wood.
The pattern was raised on the surface (as it was in block-printing) and formed
out of thin strips of brass that were tapped into the wooden core. On their own,
these metal strips printed outlines and fine details, and when combined with
areas of tightly packed felt they provided a surface that was capable of printing
small masses of solid colour. This modification represented a great improvement
on previous techniques. With the exception of one or two refinements made to
the colour feed, and the addition of steam-heated chambers where the paper was
drawn to dry after printing, Potters' machine needed few additional alterations
and became the standard model for subsequent 'surface-printing machines' for
the next fifty years. Further evidence for its success is provided by the demand
for such technology abroad. As early as 1844, Howell & Brothers in Philadelphia
reputedly imported a single-colour machine,[9] and in 1850 Jean Zuber & Cie in
France ordered a six-colour version from James Houston & Co. of Manchester.[10]
Other American and European companies followed suit, and for much of the
1850s English manufacturing techniques were generally thought to be the most
efficient in the world.

The first machine-printed patterns went on sale in 1841 but, despite the
excitement that they generated within some sections of the industry, machine-

printing was not without its teething problems, or its limitations, in the early years. Registering the design accurately was difficult and, initially, the number of colours that could be printed was rarely more than one or two. Prior to the introduction of faster-drying, chemically-adapted paints, the impression often became blurred and the colours 'ran' when the paper passed beneath the rollers at speed. The patterns themselves also differed from block-printed work in several respects. Firstly, the size of the repeat was relatively short and the motifs were comparatively small in scale. Secondly, the emergence of cheap synthetic pigments, such as the vivid artificial 'French' ultramarine, chrome yellow, and two piercing shades of Scheele's and Schwienfort green, resulted in hues that were generally brighter in tone.[11] And thirdly, machine-printed patterns were on the whole less elaborate than their block-printed counterparts. Scenic papers, pilaster-and-panel decorations, and the multi-coloured naturalistic effects favoured particularly in French work were beyond the capabilities of the new technique, which was best suited to the production of simpler designs. Striped patterns proved especially successful, and as machine-production became more widespread, papers including alternating bands of trailing foliage, scrollwork and interlacing strapwork proliferated. Diaper and trellis designs were likewise extremely common, as were finely detailed all-over florals and pictorial effects. Many of these patterns were printed with rollers primarily made up of metal pins and bars and contained comparatively small areas of solid colour which were carefully arranged so as not to overlap. Their appearance was distinctively linear: to many contemporaries they lacked the depth and richness characteristic of block-printing. But, cheap and fast to reproduce, they catered to the tastes of the lower sections of the market who had not been able to afford hand-work.

Given these limitations, it is not surprising that responses to machine-printing were so ambivalent. On the one hand, national pride was much bolstered by the technical advances that had been made, and at least one authority was prompted to declare: 'in all the material essentials of the manufacture we are fully on a par with the French'.[12] Similarly, the idea that machine-printed wall-paper could reach a larger audience and might represent a useful diffuser of taste also received widespread support.[13] At the same time, however, many observers were disappointed with the technical quality of its results. As dis-satisfaction with English design grew, mechanization was increasingly blamed for the apparent deterioration in artistic standards.[14] This view was particular-ly prevalent amongst Design Reformers, who perceived a growing conflict between mass-production and good taste. (Their ideas are discussed more fully in the next section.) Nevertheless, not even its fiercest opponents could deny the speed or economy with which wallpaper could now be produced, and by 1850 machines capable of printing perfectly registered patterns in up to eight differ-ent colours were being used by several of the most prominent manufacturers including Lightbown, Aspinall & Co. of Pendleton (Lancashire) and Allan Cockshut & Co. of London. The effect upon the industry was profound. Production rose from 1,222,753 rolls in 1834 to 5,500,000 rolls in 1851, and by 1874, when twenty-colour machines were not uncommon, it had grown to a staggering 32,000,000 rolls.[15] Prices, meanwhile, had reputedly dropped to as little as ¼d. a yard.[16] Within the space of just one generation, wallpaper had become a commodity available to all but the very poor.

The effects of mechanization upon the internal organization and conditions of work within the industry are more difficult to gauge. Contemporaries claimed that the introduction of machinery helped to break the monopoly previously enjoyed by 'a few great houses' and paved the way for the efforts of new entrepreneurs.[17] Certainly, the numbers of firms involved in the manufacture of wallpaper rose quite markedly during this period. The London Post Office Directory lists 87 paper-stainers in operation in 1840; by 1860 this figure had

below
182 Ivy trellis pattern by Potters of Darwen (Lancashire); surface-printed, 1840s. The small scale, few colours, and somewhat unadventurous nature of this design illustrate the limitations of machine-printing in its early years.

opposite
183 Sample of a surface-printed paper by W. B. Simpson of London, included in the reformist *Journal of Design* in 1849 with the comment: 'if the French beat us in art, we now have the palm for cheapness, which the public so much applaud.' The pattern is inspired by contemporary chintzes. Colour is restricted to small areas. The dot-like effect in the background, often used to enliven simple designs, was produced by blunting the ends of metal pins driven into the printing roller.

184 Detail of a sample of a 'bedroom paper-hanging' by John Woollams & Co., included in the *Journal of Design* in 1851. This shows how in early surface-printed papers the colours could blur and run.

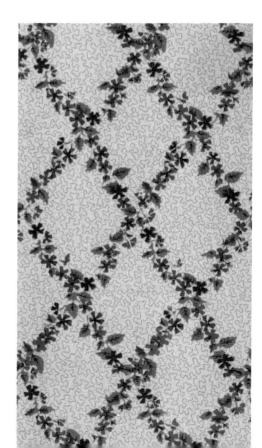

grown to 169. Yet it would be wrong to assume that machine-printing replaced more traditional methods of production overnight or, indeed, that the two techniques were kept entirely separate. The cost of purchasing and installing machines was extremely high. Also, for as long as surface-printing was regarded as qualitatively inferior to block-printing, demand for hand-produced work remained strong and many firms continued to specialize in this work. Often both techniques co-existed within the same factory or workshop. Old-established and successful hand-printing companies, such as Jeffrey & Co. and John Woollams & Co. in London, added machines, while newer concerns like Heywood, Higginbottom & Smith and Potters set up block-printing tables to supplement their machine work.

Conditions within both areas of manufacture were mixed. Block-printing was physically quite strenuous and many printers complained of poor eyesight caused by years of attending closely to the accurate register of the patterns.[18] Also, repeated exposure to the dust produced in the flocking process and to the lead and arsenic contained in certain pigments entailed other risks, and a report of 1832 declared that few hand-workers could carry on past the age of fifty.[19] The introduction of machinery relieved some of these hardships. The constant lifting and carrying of the heavy wooden blocks, for instance, was no longer required, and the use of arsenical paints was prohibited in 1862. Nevertheless, the heat in the drying rooms was intense and factory operatives worked longer shifts than their hand-printing counterparts, often going without a break for up to fifteen hours a day.[20] The loss of specialist skills and the reduction in the numbers of workers needed to man the machines were also causes for concern. When Clarke's of High Holborn, London, installed a machine the workforce went on strike and Government troops had to be called in to protect the establishment.[21] Clearly, the advent of mechanization was not welcomed by those who were actually involved in operating the process.

Design Reform

As in other countries, the middle decades of the 19th century were marked by an unprecedented eclecticism in design. Writing in 1840, the London decorators H. W. & A. Arrowsmith exclaimed: 'the present age is distinguished from all others in having no style which can properly be called its own.'[22] The dominant trend was towards historical styles, and the most popular patterns, especially for the more expensive kinds of block-printed work, derived from 18th-century Rococo prototypes. They were characterized by intricate detail and bulbous curves and featured ornate floral sprays set within asymmetrical foliate scrollwork. Equally popular, as far as consumers were concerned, were wallpapers containing highly naturalistic cabbage roses and other floral motifs. Both pattern types had originated in France and spread internationally, satisfying a passion for richly elaborated ornament that was evident in almost every area of mid-century design. They appealed particularly to a prosperous, self-confident bourgeoisie and their dense patterning and strong colours harmonized well with the other furnishings and ornaments within the middle-class home.

Gothic and Renaissance styles were also much in demand amongst this group. Public interest in the Middle Ages had been greatly stimulated by writers such as Walter Scott, and many of the 'Gothic' papers of the period, in which pointed arches frame scenes of ancient ruins or picturesque landscapes, clearly reflected a Romantic, as opposed to antiquarian, view of the past. Renaissance patterns, by contrast, were more authentic and utilized motifs derived from 16th-century strapwork or arabesque designs. The former were favoured within traditionally masculine settings such as libraries and dining-rooms while the latter – which included complex pilaster-and-panel decorations – were reserved for more formal areas like drawing-rooms.

Somewhat further down the social scale came the market for imitation marbles, woodgrains and pictorial effects. *Trompe-l'oeil* marble and stonework patterns served as cheap substitutes for more expensive materials within passageways and halls – as they had earlier, but now for a lower social class. The function of pictorial papers, which commemorated important historical events or illustrated popular pastimes, is less clear. Contemporaries pointed to their educational value, particularly within working-class homes,[23] but their appeal was probably stimulated more by novelty than self-improvement, and it is difficult to imagine exactly where, apart from nurseries and schoolrooms, such designs might have been used.

above
185 Page from a sample book of Jeffrey & Co. of London, an old-established firm that specialized in expensive hand-prints. *c.* 1837–44. The papers shown required two, thirteen, and ten 'prints' or blocks respectively.

opposite
186 Floral pattern by William Woollams & Co.: block-printed in colours, 1849.

187 Floral pattern with Rococo scrollwork by John Woollams & Co.; block-printed in colours, *c.* 1860.

188 Two block-printed wallpaper borders of the mid-19th century. With their *trompe-l'oeil* mouldings and scrollwork in Renaissance style, these were previously thought to be French, but they are probably by William Woollams. The uncertainty highlights the strength of French influence in this period.

189 Pilaster-and-panel decoration by Townsend, Parker & Co. (from Matthew Digby Wyatt's *Industrial Arts of the 19th Century*). The only English wallpaper to be awarded a medal at the Great Exhibition of 1851, it is also strongly French in type. It was much admired by the Jury, but critics including Richard Redgrave deplored the elaboration and artificiality of such work.

190 A design based on English print-room papers (cf. Ill. 51): block-printed in colours, 1840s.

While consumers delighted in the breadth of choice available, critics viewed the unregulated use of period styles less positively, and the decades from the 1830s to the 1860s witnessed the emergence of a growing crisis of confidence in the quality of English design. This crisis affected many areas of manufacture, but it was especially keenly felt within the sphere of wallpaper because this was one area where native firms had formerly excelled. Commentators like the decorator John Gregory Crace looked back longingly to the 18th century as a time when English wallpapers had been widely regarded as the finest in the world.[24] Crace also drew attention to the superiority of French firms. Rivalry between the two nations was exacerbated during the 1840s by the severe economic conditions of the decade and by the fiercely competitive nature of international trade. Commercial considerations were compounded by issues of national pride: 'To be obliged to cry "peccavi,"' as one writer put the case in 1849, 'and at once acknowledge an inferiority to our continental neighbour is almost too much for flesh and blood to endure.'[25]

Much of the blame for deteriorating standards was attributed to the inferior education of English designers and deficiencies in public taste, and several attempts were made to remedy these shortcomings throughout the 1830s and 1840s. In 1837, for example, the Government established state-subsidized Schools of Design with the specific intention of training artists for industry. During the 1840s, it also sponsored a series of exhibitions aimed at instructing the populace in the principles of good taste. Neither, however, proved very successful. A Select Committee Report of 1849 revealed that almost all the companies investigated continued to copy or purchase their best designs from France,[26] while the spread of mechanization had apparently only served to accelerate the drop in standards within more popular spheres. Indeed, according to many critics, manufacturers bent on policies of vigorous commercialism spared no pains to satisfy 'a public who prefer the vulgar, the gaudy, the ugly even, to the beautiful and perfect'.[27] The industry as a whole appeared to be in the throes of a rapid and demoralizing decline.

Matters reached a climax at the Great Exhibition, held in London in 1851, which was intended as an international showcase for the best of English manufacturing and design. Over fifty wallpaper firms participated, displaying work from many parts of Europe and the United States. The British goods were remarkable principally for their evidence of technical skills. Heywood, Higginbottom & Smith, for instance, exhibited a fourteen-colour machine-print, while William Woollams & Co. showed a pilaster-and-panel decoration which required more than sixty blocks to print. Another pilaster decoration produced by Townsend, Parker & Co. received a prize medal. Yet, despite virtuoso demonstrations of this kind, the Exhibition failed as an attempt to reaffirm the supremacy of English wallpapers within the eyes of the world. The highest honours were awarded to the Parisian firm of Eugène Délicourt, and the vast majority of native work on show simply served to underline the widespread acceptance of French styles.

Commercial and nationalistic considerations aside, many of the criticisms of the Exhibition focused upon the excessive realism and elaboration of contemporary work. They owed much to ideas first formulated by the architect and polemicist A. W. N. Pugin (1812–52). Pugin's solution to the eclecticism of his age lay in his championship of Gothic art, which he viewed as the only permissible style on moral as well as aesthetic grounds. He was especially critical of *trompe l'oeil*, sham medieval work: within the sphere of wallpaper, he castigated 'what are termed Gothic pattern papers . . . where a wretched caricature of a pointed building is repeated from the skirting to the cornice in glorious confusion – door over pinnacle, and pinnacle over door' as both 'defective in principle' and visually absurd.[28] Pugin's objections to these patterns

189

149

191

141

were twofold. Firstly, he disliked their inappropriate use of Gothic imagery; and secondly, he strongly disapproved of their illegitimate use of shading, perspective and pictorial forms. 'A wall', he argued. 'may be enriched at pleasure but it must always be treated consistently.'[29]

In place of three-dimensional effects which produced a disturbing and dishonest illusion of depth, Pugin advocated flat treatments and conventionalized motifs that would enhance, not contradict, the two-dimensional nature of the wall. His passionate admiration of Gothic art led him to recommend the use of heraldic emblems and the stylized fruit and foliage forms to be found in medieval manuscripts and textiles. Many of his wallpapers were also flocked so as to recall the appearance and texture of 'ancient hangings'. Others utilized the bright colours and geometric arrangements derived from medieval tiles and stencilled work. Both types featured in his designs for the decoration of the Houses of Parliament, or New Palace of Westminster, in London. This project occupied him more or less constantly from 1844 until his death and included over a hundred wallpapers which ranged from large severely medieval patterns to simple stylized floral designs.

192–195

Although the appeal of Pugin's work was somewhat limited – even sympathetic observers described it as 'too ecclesiastical and traditional in character'[30] for general use – his insistence upon historical authenticity was much admired, and his axiom that 'all ornament should consist of the enrichment of the essential construction of the building'[31] rapidly became accepted within critical circles as the correct principle upon which wallpaper design should be based. This idea was taken up by the civil servant Henry Cole (1808–82), the painter Richard Redgrave (1804–88) and the designer Owen Jones (1809–74), who spearheaded the mid-century campaign for Design Reform. During the 1850s this group worked together at London's South Kensington Schools where they launched a tireless crusade against what they perceived as the excesses of modern work. Unlike Pugin, however, their efforts were motivated as much by commercial as aesthetic concerns: their principal objectives were to raise standards within industry and to improve the standing of English wallpapers abroad. Cole, in particular, was a determined advocate of education within both the public and

191 'Pattern of Modern Gothic Paper'. from A. W. N. Pugin's *True Principles of Christian or Pointed Architecture* (1841). Such papers. with their toy-like architecture and perspective vistas, were descended from 18th-century pillar-and-arch patterns (see Ill. 53); by Pugin's time they were 'a great favourite with hotel and tavern-keepers'.

192 The Prime Minister's Room in the Palace of Westminster. The wallpaper, designed by Pugin *c.* 1848, was inspired by 15th-century hangings and incorporates heraldic leopards, Tudor roses and conventionalized pineapple motifs.

Pugin wallpapers for the Palace of Westminster.

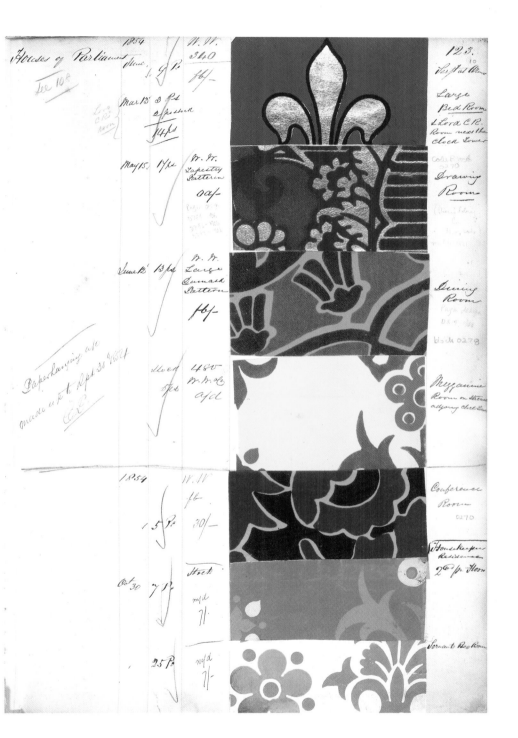

193 *left* Page from a sample book compiled by the decorators Crace & Co., showing a range of block-printed and flocked papers by Pugin, *c.* 1851–54, highlighting the variety of styles. There is a striking contrast between the rich papers for the drawing room and bedroom of the Sergeant-at-Arms (a senior official in the House of Commons) and the simple patterns for the servants' bedrooms.

194 *above* Fragment with a design copied from a 15th-century Flemish carpet, attributed to William Woollams & Co.; block-printed and flocked, *c.* 1850.

195 *below* A small-scale geometric pattern, *c.* 1851, incorporating the national emblems of England, Scotland and Ireland in a manner that recalls the appearance of medieval tiles.

the private domain. He was one of the fiercest critics of the largely ineffectual Government Schools of Design and in 1853 he was appointed Secretary to the new Department of Practical Art in London which was set up to reform the training provided by provincial colleges and schools. He had also sponsored the wider dissemination of 'correct' principles via the reformist *Journal of Design and Manufactures* (1849–52) and in a series of public exhibitions that had illustrated examples of good and bad taste. Thoroughly Utilitarian in outlook, he believed that designs for wallpaper should contain nothing that could not be justified by recourse to logic or fact. Thus animals, landscapes and other pictorial motifs were outlawed. In a thinly disguised caricature of his ideas, a Government Inspector in Charles Dickens's novel *Hard Times* (1854) regaled a class of schoolchildren with the following treatise on taste:

> Let me ask you girls and boys, would you paper a room with representations of horses? . . . Of course not. . . . Do you ever see horses walking up and down the sides of rooms in reality – in fact? . . . Of course not. Why, then, you are not to have, in any object of use or ornament what would be a contradiction in fact . . . . You must use . . . for all purposes, combinations and modifications (in primary colours) of mathematical figures which are susceptible of proof and demonstration. This is the new discovery. This is fact. This is taste.[32]

185,
187   Redgrave's anger was provoked by the more elaborate examples of the Rococo Revival style, which he decried as 'the florid and gaudy compositions, consisting of architectural ornament in relief, with imitative flowers and foliage . . . rendered with the full force of their natural colours'.[33] In place of naturalistic treatments, he preached a doctrine of conventionalization: his students were
200   instructed to employ flattened plant shapes that conformed to geometric principles.
201   The systematization of nature reached its apogee in the wallpapers of Owen Jones, who worked extensively for such upmarket firms as Townsend, Parker & Co., John Trumble & Sons of Leeds, and Jeffrey & Co. Jones believed that modern work should be founded upon the achievements of the past and, to this

196 Detail of a railway station pattern by Potters of Darwen; block-printed in colours, *c.* 1853. This pictorial wallpaper was selected by Henry Cole to demonstrate 'False Principles of Decoration' at the Museum of Ornamental Art, Marlborough House, London. It was accompanied by the text: 'Perspective representations of a railway station, frequently repeated and falsifying the perspective'.

end, he made an extensive study of historical styles which culminated in the publication of the encyclopaedic *Grammar of Ornament* in 1856. In the preface to this book he defined certain incontrovertible laws that governed the nature and appearance of design. One was that 'All ornament should be based upon a geometrical construction.'[34] Another was that flowers and other living objects should be replaced by 'conventional representations . . . sufficiently suggestive to convey the intended image to the mind, without destroying the unity of the object they are employed to decorate.'[35] Nature, in Jones's own work, is conventionalized to an almost mathematical degree – far more so than in the formal representations recommended by Redgrave and Cole – and motifs are arranged in mechanically plotted rows. Many of his patterns also reveal his liking for the stylized curves to be found in Islamic art, which his writings and designs did much to popularize. Yet perhaps the most influential of his wallpapers were those employing simple abstract motifs such as triangles and stars printed in primary shades of red and blue. These derived again from Arab and Egyptian decoration and inspired a host of imitations.

So, how successful was the Design Reform Movement in realizing its aims? The teachings of Redgrave and the design orthodoxy preached by the South Kensington Schools encouraged the more progressive sections of the industry to accept simpler, stencilled effects, and from the mid-1850s stylized floral and diaper patterns proliferated within the more expensive kinds of machine- and hand-printed work. Similarly, the influence of Pugin and Jones did much to inspire a fashion – albeit shortlived – for authentic Gothic and Moorish designs. Also, the close scrutiny of contemporary work helped focus attention upon the importance of 'correct' principles and went some way towards weakening the stranglehold of foreign styles. Indeed, by 1860, many critics felt that substantial improvements had been made. At the International Exhibition held in London in 1862 the majority of prizes were awarded to English firms and there was widespread condemnation of elaborate, illusionistic French designs.[36]

In the long term, however, the achievements of the Design Reform Movement were more theoretical than practical. The call for simple, flat effects clearly fell on deaf ears as far as the majority of consumers were concerned: naturalistic styles continued to dominate the commercial sections of the industry well into the 20th century. Moreover, even within avant-garde circles the appeal of 'correct' principles soon began to pall and the doctrines of the design establishment appeared increasingly restrictive. The next generation of artist- and architect-designers favoured a return to freer and more organic styles: the painter Edward Poynter, who succeeded Redgrave as Principal of the South Kensington Schools, claimed 'this determined insistence upon the necessity of a purely flat kind of decoration has produced a kind of work, quite as unfortunate, if not more so, than the vulgar rococo ornament which it has superseded.'[37]

The failure of mid-century efforts to revolutionize the appearance of English wallpaper was partly due to the fact that although mechanization took much of the blame for poor design, the Design Reformers' response was mainly in the medium of block-prints. With the exception of Christopher Dresser (1834–1904) and Lewis F. Day (1845–1910), both of whom worked closely with machine-printing firms, a similar problem faced the designers associated with the subsequent Arts and Crafts Movement – none more so than William Morris (1834–96). Morris's reputation towers over the second half of the 19th century and, understandably, many historians have over-estimated the impact of his wallpapers, particularly upon the popular end of the market. For, despite his avowed intention to produce 'an art made by the people, for the people',[38] the patterns of his firm were printed by Jeffrey & Co., almost all of them by hand, and retailed at prices that the working classes could not possibly afford (between 3s. and 16s. a roll).[39] They were bought instead by those aesthetically

197

198, 199

Reformed design

197 Geometrical pattern by Owen Jones reflecting Islamic influence, manufactured by Jeffrey & Co.; block-printed in colours, late 1850s.

198 One of many Neo-Gothic patterns inspired by the teachings of Pugin and the Design Reform Movement: a paper attributed to F. A. Slocombe and produced by Corbiere Son & Brindle; block-printed in colours, c. 1868.

199 A particularly rich and elaborate example of the Moorish style popularized by Owen Jones: diaper pattern by John Woollams and Co.; block-printed in colours, flocked and embossed, 1867.

200 Sample of a block-printed ivy pattern designed by Richard Redgrave and manufactured by W. B. Simpson, included in the *Journal of Design* in 1849. In accordance with his view that wallpaper should be 'a background to the furniture, the objects of art, and the occupants' of a room, Redgrave recommended subdued colours and quiet, unobtrusive patterns that were retiring in effect. This design was produced specifically as a background for pictures.

201 Stylized floral pattern by Owen Jones, manufactured by Jeffrey & Co. for the Viceroy's Palace in Cairo; block-printed in colours, *c.* 1865.

minded sections of society who inhabited fashionable new areas of Oxford and London. They were equally popular with artistic markets abroad. From the 1870s Morris & Co. wallpapers could be purchased in the United States from outlets in Boston, Philadelphia and New York, and in the following decade they were available on the Continent from agents in Paris, Frankfurt and Berlin.[40] They were also imported into Australia via Melbourne.

In this respect Morris benefited greatly not only from the rise in wages and living standards described in the next chapter, but also from a new awareness of the need for 'Art' within the home. This idea was actively promoted in contemporary manuals such as Charles Eastlake's *Hints on Household Taste* (1868) and Macmillan's Art at Home series (1876ff.) and was closely linked to the growing influence of Aestheticism, a creed or movement that became increasingly important in many parts of Europe and the United States. Aesthetic styles of decoration favoured the tripartite division of the wall and encouraged the use of matching or complementary patterns in the dado, filling and frieze. Motifs and colours were also often indebted to an appreciation of Japanese design, employing geometric and stylized natural forms and hues that were for the most part soft, subtle and sombre. The key designers associated with this style – Christopher Dresser, B. J. Talbert and Walter Crane – were much admired abroad. Together with that of Morris, their work came to be identified with a distinctive English school of decoration whose members had an increasingly significant influence upon international design.

Morris's work represents something of a compromise between the extreme realism of pre-Reform floral patterns and more formalized designs. His earliest wallpapers were strongly affected by Gothic art, employing stylized motifs arranged symmetrically in accordance with the doctrines laid down by the South Kensington circle. By the 1870s, however, he was increasingly interested in interpreting the curves of living plants in lines that responded to the evidence of his eyes rather than the dictates of a compass. From the late 1870s his admiration for Renaissance ornament and the stylizations associated with traditional techniques such as weaving moved his patterns away from the intertwining, curvilinear lines characteristic of his earlier work towards more formal elements.

While debates concerning the conflict between manufacturing and design continued in the last quarter of the century (Arts and Crafts designers, for example, were just as anxious about mass-production, although the motivation behind their attacks was often political), by the late 1860s faith in British manufacturing had been much restored and English firms were world leaders in terms of the sheer quantity of wallpapers produced and sold.[41] They had also scored important victories in terms of design. At the 1867 Paris Exposition Universelle many of the prizes were awarded to British firms, and the critic for *The Builder* was proud to declare:

> The improvement in the character of the design for both common and expensive wallpapers is one of the most pleasing features of the Exhibition, and none the less so because our own manufacturers occupy a prominent place in this advancement. At the time of the first International Exhibition (1851) there was no branch of furniture in which so utterly bad taste prevailed as in paperhangings . . . In the present exhibition we miss the atrocious natural imitations of fruit, flowers, and landscapes once so popular among all classes, and in place of them, sober, conventional treatments of foliage, exhibiting considerable skill in design and arrangement . . . are well adapted for backgrounds in rooms of every description. The English makers are fairly entitled to stand at the head of exhibitors in this class, for though the French distinguish themselves as much as ever in the high qualities of their manufacture, there is less sound taste observable in their productions. . . .[42]

202

203

202 'Daisy' by William Morris, manufactured by Jeffrey & Co.; block-printed in colours, 1864. The pattern was based on an embroidered hanging that appears in a 15th-century manuscript of the chronicler Froissart.

203 'Jasmine' by William Morris, manufactured by Jeffrey & Co.; block-printed in colours, 1872. One of the most organic of Morris's wallpapers, containing flowers and foliage that branch out in all directions to create an impression of tangled and luxuriant growth. Such patterns were to be immensely influential in the later 19th century both in Britain and abroad.

9 Proliferation:
Late 19th-Century Papers,
Markets and Manufacturers

CHRISTINE WOODS · JOANNE KOSUDA WARNER · BERNARD JACQUÉ

In 1883 the *Journal of Decorative Art* stated that the manufacture of paper hangings in Britain had developed to 'an extraordinary extent' since mid-century. There was considerable activity in all industries associated with domestic furnishing during this period. Owing to demographic and social changes, demand had grown substantially and mechanization played a considerable part in its satisfaction. In wallpaper manufacture some flat patterns and flocks were still being printed by hand with wooden blocks; a number had outlines printed in this way and colours brushed on by hand through a stencil (a technique commonly used in the 17th and 18th centuries, which enjoyed a resurgence of popularity from the 1890s well into the new century); others had surfaces embossed by hand or by machine and were coloured by hand. But, by 1883, the vast majority were machine-printed, either in distemper by wooden rollers with a relief pattern on the surface or in oil colour by copper rollers engraved with an intaglio design. Papers could be made to look and feel more substantial by being embossed with metal rollers or could be given a satin-like sheen or sparkling ground. Some wallcoverings were made from a combination of substances, for example cork and rubber, and imitated decorative effects such as stamped leather and moulded plaster. By the turn of the century, the consumer could choose from an enormous range of products, the variety of which was considerably greater than can be found today.

This chapter focuses on the growth of demand for wallcoverings, discusses how the demand was satisfied by designers, manufacturers and merchants, and describes some of these remarkable products, samples of which, no doubt, still lurk beneath our present woodchip and textured vinyl.

Consumers and fashions

Between 1851 and 1911 the population of England and Wales doubled, and by the turn of the century almost 77 per cent lived in urban areas.[1] Income, too, almost doubled over the same period, and the number of white-collar employees increased dramatically. While in the 1880s most people could still be categorized as poor, with agricultural workers, for instance, generally earning less than £50 a year, by then a considerable number could expect £160 per annum – the threshold for income tax – or very much more. Doctors, solicitors and architects fell into this category, joined at the end of the century by bank clerks, curates and commercial travellers.

This larger, urbanized, and relatively more affluent population required housing, and in the mid- to late 1870s there was a boom in speculative building. Until the turn of the century nine out of ten homes were rented from private landlords. Middle-class tenants commonly undertook the cost of redecoration; the poor accepted the landlord's scheme of decoration.[2] As incomes rose and the variety of consumer goods increased, so did consumption of household

Britain
CHRISTINE WOODS

furnishings and decoration, the acquisition of which, amongst other activities, demonstrated social status. Within houses, there was even greater differentiation between the decoration of specific areas, such as halls, staircases, drawing rooms, bedrooms and ladies' boudoirs: wallpaper was eventually thought suitable for bathrooms and kitchens too.

QUOTE

The proliferation of publications providing guidance on furnishing is indicative of the importance accorded to the making of correct choices. Matters of taste were widely discussed but, as it was largely middle-class women who were responsible for the establishment and maintenance of what came to be known as 'the home beautiful', it was they who ploughed through the barrage of (often conflicting) advice in *The Ladies' Realm*, *The Lady's World*, and other magazines that sprang up to cater to 'that large borderland between the very rich,

204 Surface-printed and embossed wallpaper issued by Cotterell Bros, merchants, of Bristol in the early 1890s. This trailing floral pattern, which incorporates motifs derived from 18th-century textiles, has been made to resemble an embroidered silk damask by the embossing of an additional pattern.

who can hand over their houses to one or other of the high-class decorators, . . . and the very poor, who have neither money nor ambition'.[3]

According to one decorator, wealthy clients often quibbled over a few pence per piece when choosing wallpaper. Efforts at economy could not have been made easy by the widespread adoption in the 1870s and 1880s of the style of interior decoration mentioned in the previous chapter which split the wall surface into three sections: the dado, which might culminate in a rail and/or a printed paper border; the filling, usually an all-over repeating pattern; and the frieze, which was often separated from the filling by yet another paper border and extended up to the cornice or ceiling (which might also be papered). This arrangement, advocated particularly for areas most likely to be seen by visitors, compelled the consumer to purchase several different wallpaper products, the cost of which varied tremendously. By the 1890s fashion had begun to move away from tripartite decorations in favour of a plain or textured filling used in conjunction with a patterned frieze. While this simpler arrangement was no doubt cheaper, the most fashionable wallpaper friezes were usually hand-printed and were themselves comparatively expensive.

It is difficult to estimate to what extent the consumer lower down the social scale was concerned with fashion. The proliferation of machine-printed dados and friezes suggests that there was a substantial market for cheap versions of 'artistic' ideas (see above, p.148), but it seems likely that these found their way into the homes of the lower middle classes rather than houses decorated by builders or landlords for the working classes. For this end of the market, the *Journal of Decorative Art* in 1887 deemed it unnecessary 'in these days of cheap paperhangings' to specify any particular kind, other than the washable variety which, it thought, would contribute to the making of an artisan's dwelling 'sweet, clean and beautiful'.[4]

The British wallpaper industry catered for almost all levels of income. Even upmarket firms such as Jeffrey & Co., of Islington, London, which in 1892 was manufacturing embossed leather wallcoverings at 24*s.* per yard as well as paper imitations at 10*s.*, included printed papers at 6*d.* a roll in its ranges.[5] Nevertheless, it was at decorators catering for the newly affluent middle-class market, with incomes from £200 to more than £1,000 per annum, that most advertising was directed.

Manufacture and distribution

The 1877 edition of *Kelly's Post Office Directory of Merchants and Manufacturers* contains 84 entries under the heading 'Paperhanging Manufacturers', more than 50 of whom were located in London or its suburbs or had London offices or agents. Half of those situated elsewhere in Britain were located in Lancashire and just under a third of the remainder were in Scotland. Several southern firms had agents in Scotland and a number had, by the late 1870s, established export markets in Europe and elsewhere. For example, the products of the Manchester firm of Heywood, Higginbottom & Smith were, according to the *Journal of Decorative Art* in 1883, 'despatched to all parts of the globe'; and another Lancashire firm, C. & J. G. Potter, had agents in Paris and Hamburg. Numerous others made it their business to be included in the listings of publications such as the *British Mercantile Guide*, which was circulated throughout Europe and the Colonies. Many British names became almost as well known in Australia and America as at home, and by the 1890s Jeffrey & Co.'s more expensive papers were being sold in Scandinavia.[6]

Some of the companies listed in the directories, like Arthur Sanderson & Sons in London, imported and distributed papers as well as manufacturing them and by 1900 a quarter of the provincial firms listed were also engaged in distribution of some kind – some almost wholly so. Essex & Co., also of London, which

205 'The Alcestis', 'La Margarete' and 'Lily and Dove' tripartite decoration, designed by Walter Crane and block-printed by Jeffrey & Co. of London specially for display at the Philadelphia Centennial Exposition, 1876. It won much critical acclaim and an award for the firm, although it is not clear how well it sold.

[handwritten margin note: Downfall in status]

225 later became known for its production of designs by C. F. A. Voysey, had begun in 1887 as a merchanting operation.

Some firms became known for special products, such as the 'stamped golds' issued by Wylie & Lochhead of Glasgow and the imitation wood and marble effects produced by the London firm of Southall & Snow. Others concentrated on particular genres: J. Stather & Sons of Hull, for example, focused on 'washables'. Most manufacturers, however, dealt in a wide range of products made by machine while keeping a small section of the factory aside for hand-block-printing of more expensive qualities. In 1900 the established London firm of William Woollams & Co. included in its range 'artistic' wallpapers, machine- and block-printed, 'sanitary' and washable papers and raised flocks (where repeated flocking leaves a deep relief), and also sold a wide variety of wallcoverings produced by other manufacturers.[7] Some had extensive establishments – the

206 numerous separate departments of Lightbown, Aspinall & Co.'s mill at Pendleton (Lancashire) covered almost four acres by the turn of the century – while others

207 had several operations going on simultaneously in the same small workshop.

Mechanization and growth in demand enabled well-organized firms such as these to carry a stock of 8,000 or so huge rolls of paper (each one 1,200–1,500 yards (1,100–1,370 m) long) and to be confident that the 950,000 rolls of printed wallpaper made from it would sell. In 1883 Heywood, Higginbottom & Smith boasted that it was producing nearly 6,000,000 rolls annually.[8] The vast increase in production was remarkable in itself, but the period 1870–1900 also saw the development of an unprecedented variety of products, many of which were the result of the marriage of new technology with entrepreneurial spirit.

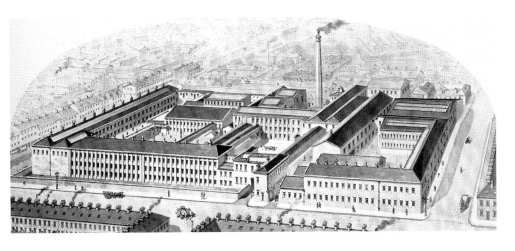

206 Bird's-eye view of Hayfield Mills, Pendleton (Lancashire). The founder of the Lightbown Aspinall firm, who had trained at Potters of Darwen, established his business on the outskirts of Manchester in 1846. As it expanded new buildings were added until the factory, shown here c. 1905, covered almost 4 acres (1.6 ha).

207 Interior of the Charles Knowles & Co. factory, London, c. 1904. This firm, established in 1852, produced block-printed papers by many well-known designers. In the early 1890s, it introduced machinery and became known for chintz, damask and striped designs. In this part of the workshop 'The Rowans', a Voysey-type design, is being block-printed whilst, in the foreground, a frieze in Art Nouveau style is being hand-stencilled with an enormous round brush.

153

New products

It was now common for twenty-colour surface-printing machines to be in operation. A writer in the *Journal of Decorative Art* commented in 1883: 'To see a
piece of paper go in at one end of a machine plain, and come out on the other
side printed in twenty colours, all complete, is a very wonderful sight.' But the
papers produced in this way were, like the hand-prints, printed in distemper,
which was not washable – something of a disadvantage in an age when
atmospheric pollution created in the home by oil lamps, gasoliers and coal fires
was considerable, and was compounded by the dirt and grime which seeped into
the house from the industrialized world outside.

Manufacturers had been trying to produce a washable wallpaper since at least
mid-century. At the 1851 Exhibition W. B. Simpson displayed examples printed
in distemper which had been hardened in some way afterwards, but it wasn't
until 1853, when John Stather's oil-printed patterns appeared, that washable
wallpapers were recognized as a commercially viable proposition. Even so, the
process took some time to develop: in 1873 it was still worth while for *The
Practical Magazine* to publish a laborious 'improved' recipe for the water-
proofing of traditionally printed wallpaper. But also in the early 1870s
Heywood, Higginbottom & Smith produced a monochrome washable paper
printed in oil colour from copper rollers, and English 'sanitary' wallpapers were
launched. Further experimentation culminated in the issue by several firms, notably Lightbown Aspinall, of polychrome 'sanitaries' in 1884 – appropriately,
the year of the International Health Exhibition. According to the founder of
Walker & Carver (also of Pendleton), a pioneer of their development, the new
papers 'at once hit the public taste.'[9]

The main advantage of the oil-printed papers was the resistance of the colours
to water, which was enhanced greatly if they were coated with size and varnished. The majority were also strikingly different in appearance. Until now,
shaded effects and blended colours could only be obtained by hand techniques,
usually stencilling. The 'sanitary' production process enabled, for the first time,
the machine-printing of shaded effects in the same tone from a single roller.
Thus a smaller number of engraved rollers could produce at low cost multi-
colour patterns featuring soft, subtly blended effects and fine lines eminently
suitable for realistic designs and pictorial patterns. Not only had the industry
produced, at long last, a washable wallpaper, but its patterns could be produced
so cheaply that almost anyone could afford to buy them.

The success of 'sanitaries' encouraged the production of a great variety of
designs. By 1896 the 'set' produced by Potters alone included more than 650
borders and friezes,[10] and as some cost only a little more than the cheapest
surface-printed papers, it was suggested that they be used in the homes of the
working classes. The better qualities were also advocated for hallways, kitchens,
etc., in middle-class dwellings, and many have survived to this day in the bath-

below
208 'Sanitary' machine-printed
wallpaper issued by David Walker of
Middleton (Lancashire) in the late
1880s. Many of the earliest
'sanitaries' were highly successful
imitations of woodgrain effects.
Their popularity continued into the
20th century; and numerous
variations on the theme were also
produced, such as this one, which
incorporates floral motifs and
strapwork.

opposite
209 'Marble' effect issued by the
merchants S. M. Bryde & Co.
c. 1895. Surface-printed papers like
this dado were common in the last
quarter of the century, as were less
elaborate imitations of marble
produced by hand.

210 Varnished 'tile' pattern, surface-
printed by Lightbown Aspinall
c. 1892. Clearly influenced by the
fashion for Japanese design, this is
typical of many papers produced for
kitchens, sculleries, passages and
bathrooms.

211 Wallpaper pattern book showing
a 'sanitary' dado, filling and frieze
manufactured by Lightbown
Aspinall. *c.* 1892. This elaborate
tripartite decoration (available in
three different colourways) cost
2*s.* 6*d.*–3*s.* 3*d.* per roll for the dado
and 1*s.* 6*d.*–2*s.* for the filling. The
dado comprises a dense patchwork of
unrelated motifs (like most machine-
printed dados of the period), and is
combined with a much lighter filling
of trailing poppies and leaves. The
fine lines and shaded tones made
possible by the 'sanitary' process give
these decorations a radically
different appearance from that of
their hand- or machine-produced
distemper-printed counterparts.

rooms of late Victorian and Edwardian houses. By the 1890s many of the major manufacturers had followed the lead of the Lancashire firms, and the genre remained a major part of the industry's output until well into the 20th century.

'Sanitary' wallpapers were rarely admired by commentators on design matters. Nevertheless, as the *Journal of Decorative Art* asserted in 1884, 'in these days of International Health Exhibitions' no popular support would be given to an invention which could not claim to be 'sanitary'. Thus, despite its association with products considered by some to be downmarket and lacking in artistic merit, the word was rapidly taken up as a term of commendation by manufacturers of other new wallcoverings which bore little or no relation, visually or in composition, to the myriad washable wallpapers which proudly bore this appellation on their selvedges. Among these were Lincrusta and Anaglypta, two of the most famous late Victorian wallcoverings, which are still available, virtually unchanged, more than a century later; indeed, many examples sold in the 1880s and 1890s are still giving good service in Europe and elsewhere.

Lincrusta-Walton, developed in 1877, was the brainchild of Frederick Walton, inventor of linoleum, and its composition was similar, comprising largely a mixture of oxidized linseed oil, gum, resins, and wood-pulp spread onto a canvas backing. But visually it was very different, having a relief pattern machine-embossed on the surface by engraved iron or steel rollers. It was immediately successful, not least because although not a 'sanitary' paper, it was considered unrivalled in terms of its hygienic properties. Lincrusta was completely waterproof; someone established that it could even be cleaned with

below
212 Frederick Walton's new showroom in central London, 1900. Increasing demand for Lincrusta, together with Walton's development of another popular relief decoration, Cameoid, led to his expansion into adjacent premises – a move which enabled a more extensive display of his products, in particular ceiling decorations and high-relief friezes. From the *Journal of Decorative Art*.

opposite
213 Anaglypta decoration, featuring a peacock in the Art Nouveau style, designed by Charles Haité. From the *Journal of Decorative Art*, 1900.

214 'Arabian', an Anaglypta filling designed by Christopher Dresser, still featured years later in the 1909 catalogue of *Anaglypta and Salamander Decorations*.

weak dilutions of acid, and it was therefore particularly recommended for use in public buildings. In addition, it could stand up to the kind of wear and tear that would have ruined paper wallcoverings.

215 Artistically, Lincrusta was deemed almost perfect when compared with the much-criticized 'sanitary' wallpaper. It lent itself to the most intricate designs, and it could either be left untreated or it could be painted, stained or gilded. Its solid backing and flexibility facilitated ease of handling and hanging so it could be fixed without problem to wood or plaster. Between 1879 and 1884 sales trebled.[11] This was not surprising when its surface perfectly reproduced materi-

247– als such as wood, plaster and tooled leather for as little as 2s. per yard. Even
249 other imitations, such as the superb embossed wallpapers introduced by the French manufacturer Paul Balin in the 1860s and imported by Sanderson, cost two or three times this amount, while the price of the real thing was prohibitive. Lincrusta was considered suitable for the walls and ceilings of halls, stairways, dining and other rooms and was even recommended as a covering for doors. Outside the home it was suggested for the decoration of motor cars, railway carriages and ships. In 1887 it was much improved when the manufacturer replaced the canvas backing with waterproof paper. By the 1890s special ceiling, dado and frieze patterns were available, and Lincrusta was being produced in a wide range of colours. In 1891 it was proudly revealed that in one month the firm had sold 23,000 yards (21,000 m) of one design.[12]

250 Lincrusta provided a substitute for traditional relief decorations, but it was also open to avant-garde use, as in Hector Guimard's extreme Art Nouveau patterns for the Castel Béranger in Paris (1896). The aesthetic reformer Christopher Dresser is known to have supplied some of the first designs for the company, at least one of them in the Anglo-Japanese style.

Although less expensive than traditional relief decorations, Lincrusta was still out of reach of the mass market. Anaglypta, however, introduced in 1886, was made of cotton fibre pulp and produced by a much simpler and cheaper process of hollow moulding similar to paper-making. Its inventor, Thomas J. Palmer, was the manager of Frederick Walton's London showroom, and it is hard to understand Walton's reluctance to develop the product. Palmer had no option but to set up in business to produce it himself, in association with Storey Bros of Lancaster. Walton must have regretted his decision, because the new product, launched in 1887 at the Manchester Jubilee Exhibition, was received with enthusiasm and by 1893 it was considered to be one of the most important wallcoverings on the market.

213 In many respects Anaglypta (the name was taken from a Latin term meaning carved in relief or embossed) came a good second to Lincrusta. Also manufactured in both high and low relief, it too had a multiplicity of uses in domestic and public buildings, and its hollow back made it so lightweight that for ceilings it was considered superior. Once sized and painted it was as hygienic. Although production of Anaglypta was taken over in 1894 by Potters and relocated to Darwen, Palmer remained the driving force behind the issue of an enormous number of patterns both of the traditional imitative kind and of a modern variety, which enabled Anaglypta to be used in what were considered to be fashionable homes. By 1897, the firm was accustomed to receiving hundreds of orders each day, including one for 700 rolls of one dado pattern for a single building; in that year as much as 77 miles (125 km) of one design was

214 sold.[13] Christopher Dresser was one of the well-known names providing designs for the company right from the start. His patterns, mostly abstract or Oriental in inspiration, continued in use until after the turn of the century.

The fashion for Lincrusta and Anaglypta led to the development of a host of other wallcoverings which were produced by a number of different processes from a wide range of materials, including mixtures of cork and rubber

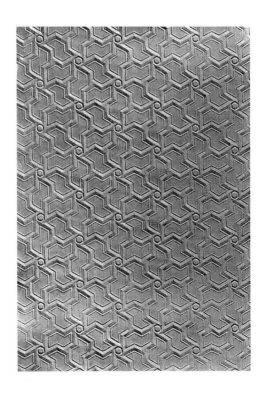

(Subercorium and Calcorian) and asbestos (Salamander). The majority were made from rag or wood pulp in some form (Lignomur, Cameoid, Cordelova).

Also hygienic, but much more sumptuous and fashionable, were papers imitating the gilt leather wallcoverings produced in Spain and Holland in the 16th and 17th centuries. Heavily embossed and lacquered paper wall decorations which resembled tooled leather at a fraction of the cost were made in Japan for export to Europe in the early 1870s, but at that time their patterns were considered to be too distinctively Japanese for most English interiors.[14] In the 1870s and 1880s Jeffrey's produced several 'imitation leather papers', but by the mid-1880s the Japanese product, its designs much modified to suit European taste, had largely overwhelmed the British market, despite competition from French manufacturers such as Paul Balin.

The British firm mainly responsible for the influx of Japanese leather papers was Rottmann, Strome & Co., whose founder, Alexander Rottmann, in the early 1880s established a factory near Yokohama for their production. He was soon sending them to Britain 'in shiploads'[15] and exporting to North America and Australia. Their luxurious appearance was achieved at considerable expense; in the mid-1890s they cost between 20s. and 80s. (£1–£4) per roll of 12 square yards (10 m²). Tinfoil was beaten into the hand- or machine-embossed pattern and several coats of lacquer were then applied, which made the metal look like gold.[16] Colours were subsequently applied by hand through stencils, and the result could be indistinguishable from the original decorated leathers from which the designs had been copied. Some of Rottmann's patterns employed adapted Oriental motifs which, together with their provenance, capitalized on the fashion in the 1880s and 1890s for Japanese art and design. Even papers made in Britain gained by association.

In common with some other embossed decorations, imitation leathers were produced in a wide range of high- and low-relief patterns and were considered very suitable for the decoration of entrance halls, stairways, dining and drawing rooms, libraries and studies in fashionable middle-class homes, where, sanctioned by advice from authorities on interior decoration, they could be combined in schemes with flat printed wallpapers or relief decorations such as Lincrusta.

Not all embossed wallcoverings had raised patterns. The passing of a printed wallpaper through an embossing machine could improve the 'finish' by providing a slight texture and add interest in the form of additional pattern, both at extremely low cost. Imitations of textiles such as damasks benefited particularly from developments in embossing techniques.

Although wallpaper has been printed in imitation of textiles, leather, wood, stone, etc., throughout its history, the production of imitations of a wide variety of materials was a particular feature of the last quarter of the 19th century. Stather's early 'washable' paper had been printed to resemble oak planks, and by the 1890s a number of firms, including Lightbown Aspinall, were issuing sample books crammed with varnished 'tiles' (both 'sanitaries' and surface-prints) for use in kitchens, sculleries and bathrooms. The range of varnished and unvarnished 'marbles', produced by hand and by machine, would astonish the prospective wallpaper buyer today. These new products were manufactured in their thousands alongside the myriad surface-prints and hand-printed papers and flocks issued each season to a market hungry for novelty.

Designers[17]

In order for manufacturers to be able to satisfy the ever-growing demand they needed a steady supply of designs. It seems that, prior to the mid-1870s, France was one significant source; many paper-stainers, on the other hand, depended largely on the cutters of their printing blocks for the provision of patterns, the drawings being 'thrown in as a kind of bait' by the craftsmen to secure the block-

215 Fragment of a Lincrusta-Walton filling installed in the John D. Rockefeller House in New York in the 1880s. Lincrusta was produced in a wide variety of designs. This asymmetrical pattern of formalized flowers and leaves is a perfect expression of the extremely fashionable Aesthetic style.

216, 217 Two examples of Rottmann, Strome & Co.'s Japanese leather papers. By the time these decorations were universally popular in the 1880s their patterns owed more to the West than the East. In the drawing room illustrated in the *Journal of Decorative Art* in 1884 (*below*) the dado, thought to be 'thoroughly Japanesque', incorporates dragons 'sailing at each other in a fierce, free fashion', but the filling above it is based on Spanish gilt leather and the frieze is also European in style. Something of the texture of these lacquered, stencilled and painted papers is suggested by the detail of 'The Alicante' (*above right*) – indicatively, a Spanish name – registered in 1897.

248

216,
217

208–
210

MADE IN JAPAN   THE ALICANTE REGD No

cutting business.[18] The main advantage of the arrangement was that the patterns were designed in such a way that they could be produced easily and cheaply. This appears to have been a major consideration until late in the century, when trade directories still provided lists of 'pattern-drawers'.

Some manufacturers, however, including Potters, had begun to establish their own studios in the 1860s, a sensible move when we consider that this company spent in the region of £7,000 per annum on designing, drawing, cutting and printing sample patterns.[19] The trend gained momentum in the 1880s and 1890s, when some firms (e.g., the Darwen Paperstaining Co.) were issuing several hundred different designs each season. Little is known about the organization of these company studios. It seems likely that, in common with their counterparts in the textile industry, most in-house designers did not attend the national Schools of Design but were trained on the premises and were not required to produce original work: instead, schemes were taken from pattern books and historic samples or were re-workings of previously successful styles. In addition, they were expected to adapt the work of freelance designers.

From the late 1870s, freelances such as A. F. Brophy had established successful businesses supplying designs to wallpaper – and other – firms, and in the last twenty years of the century improvements in the teaching of commercial art enabled ever more individuals to earn a living freelancing for industry. It was in this climate that Arthur Silver set up his studio in London in 1880 and quickly began to sell to wallpaper manufacturers (John Line was an early client). By the mid-1890s the Silver Studio was employing designers whose work was associated with particular styles, and by the turn of the century it was exporting more than 50 per cent of its output to Continental Europe and America.[20]

Many patterns were purchased from designers working on their own behalf from home. In November 1899 alone, Sanderson supplemented the output of its own studio with more than a dozen items bought from Paris as well as England, paying between £2 2s. and £6 each. A prolific designer around that time could earn an average of £400 per annum.

While most employees in commercial and company studios were destined to remain anonymous, a few freelances became well known outside the trade. Indeed, in the 1880s and 1890s the association of a known name with a particular manufacturer appeared to add considerable value to a firm's products. Many of those whose names were perceived to have most cachet had trained not as commercial designers but as artists or, more commonly, architects.[21] One of the first wallpaper manufacturers to employ such people was Metford Warner of Jeffrey & Co. Before the late 1860s, Jeffrey's had printed some designs privately, notably for Morris & Co., and executed a few special commissions, including a series of papers designed by Owen Jones for the Viceroy's Palace in Cairo; but otherwise the firm had obtained almost all their designs from commercial pattern-drawers or French studios. Now, in response to criticism in the first edition of Charles Eastlake's *Hints on Household Taste* (1868), Warner commissioned a range of patterns from a group of architects (including Eastlake himself, who had trained as an architect though he never practised), none of whom had ever designed wallpapers before. Despite a mixed reception for his project from the trade press, he went on to commission designs from the artist Walter Crane. By the mid-1880s, the reputation of Jeffrey's had been enhanced considerably by its employment of such figures as the architect E. W. Godwin and the furniture designer B. J. Talbert, and numerous other firms had followed its example.

The importance of this departure from established procedures should not be underestimated. The employment of leading members of the English artistic élite had a noticeable effect on both manufacturers and designers – not least because the new, so-called 'artistic', patterns incorporated ideas associated with

218 Design for a wallpaper by Harry Napper, 1897. Napper joined the Silver Studio *c.* 1890 and managed the firm for two years after Arthur Silver's death in 1896. Under his direction it produced a continuous stream of Art Nouveau designs such as this filling, which features the stylized flowers and jagged leaves characteristic of his work.

219 Design for a door and wall decoration by Arthur Silver, *c.* 1885. Despite the unusually deep border at the top of the dado, this scheme – clearly influenced by Japanese art and design – is simpler than many tripartite arrangements, pointing towards future banishment of highly decorated dados in favour of prominent friezes.

220 Surface-printed wallpaper issued by Firth, Ray & Prosser, whose merchanting business was confined largely to the North of England. This asymmetrical Anglo-Japanese design is one of many included in the firm's book for 1886 and shows the influence of Aesthetic styles on production for the middle market. By the 1890s, hundreds of similar designs were being produced for more humble homes.

fashionable English art movements of the period. Taking ideas from Design Reform, Aestheticism, Japan, and the Arts and Crafts Movement, with its commitment to the honest use of materials, wallpaper (like textiles) developed a vocabulary of two-dimensional motifs, often extreme stylizations of plants or even animals and birds, which, with their strongly marked outlines, produced a rhythmic decorative effect. Such designs, which contributed to the development of Art Nouveau, were very different in appearance from the largely French-inspired patterns hitherto produced by most manufacturers. The association of the word 'art' with wallpapers became widespread, and the new styles were widely copied by both studio and freelance designers.

214,
223

However, the relationship between manufacturers and their artistic associates was not always an easy one. While Christopher Dresser and Lewis F. Day were willing to 'meet industrial conditions', most artists and architects had little or no knowledge of industrial processes, and a good deal of re-working must have been necessary to render some of their patterns suitable for machine production. Metford Warner considered early designs for wallpapers by Godwin and the Gothic Revival architect William Burges 'rather mad'; but Walter Crane was perhaps the most extreme in his refusal to compromise with 'the demands of commerce'. He admitted that the artwork he submitted to Jeffrey's was 'comparatively rough and sketchy', but was not inclined to finish it further because he didn't like to see his original idea 'lose vigour and character'; he also refused to design 'in any given style', and so Warner, who gave his designers a free hand, was often presented by Crane with something entirely different from what had been anticipated. Given these difficulties, it was a great advantage to manufacturers aspiring to produce artistically progressive papers to be able to call on the sophisticated professionalism of the Silver Studio – or to be able to rely on their own personal talent.

222

Few manufacturers had themselves been trained in the decorative arts, although retrospective accounts suggest that, like Harold Sanderson and Metford Warner, they often supervised both the choice and the colouring of designs issued by their firms. One notable exception was William Shand Kydd, who attended one of the Schools of Design and worked for several firms before establishing his own business in London in 1891, later becoming known particularly for his block-printed and stencilled friezes. His use in stencilling of sponges or crumpled chamois skins, as well as a variety of brushes, to obtain graduated washes and areas where several colours blended, created subtle, rich effects impossible to produce with block- or surface-printing, and the 'sanitary' process could not give the same quality of colour. It is clear that Shand Kydd's training and experience were of paramount importance in the subsequent success of his firm, which is remembered largely for the innovative designs and rich colouring of its products.[22] Most of his friezes of the 1890s featured the swirling, organic motifs associated with the Art Nouveau style, their shapes emphasized by hand-block-printed outlines.

opposite
221 'Tulip Garden', designed by Arthur Silver *c.* 1894 and hand-stencilled onto grasspaper. The original from which this reproduction was made resulted from Silver's experiments with Japanese woven grasscloth, which was usually backed with paper. Stencilled fillings were not as common as friezes because it was difficult to conceal joins in the pattern if they cut through shaded areas. 'Tulip Garden' was designed to avoid this happening.

222 Block-printed and stencilled frieze by William Shand Kydd, *c.* 1895, typical of his Art Nouveau style. More than 3 feet (1 m) deep, it would have been part of a fairly expensive scheme, providing the main decorative focus above a panelled wainscot or plain wallpaper.

223 An opening from *Selected Handprinted Wallpapers*, issued by Jeffrey & Co. for the season 1894–95. This pattern is by Lewis F. Day. Other designers represented include Walter Crane, C. F. A. Voysey and Lindsay Butterfield. This book was sent to Sweden, to Erik Folcker's avant-garde shop Sub Rosa in Stockholm.

224 'Compton', a block-printed
wallpaper designed by J. H. Dearle
and produced for Morris & Co. by
Jeffrey & Co. in 1896 – the year of
Morris's death. Dearle subsequently
became Art Director. The firm had a
distinctive house style, and such was
the prestige of the founder that many
of Dearle's patterns, including this
one, have been mistakenly attributed
to Morris.

225 Design for a wallpaper by
C. F. A. Voysey, 1895. Although he
later condemned the Art Nouveau
style, its sinuous aesthetic can be
seen clearly in many of Voysey's
early patterns such as this six-colour
design, priced at £8. 8s.

226 'Artichoke' by Walter Crane,
hand-block-printed by Jeffrey & Co.,
1895. This is one of several papers
produced after Crane had been asked
to reduce the number of colours and
scale of his designs in order to cut
production costs. Some of his
pictorial, elaborate patterns had
taken two widths and more than one
block depth to achieve a single
repeat. Here he has taken the idea of
superimposed layers from Morris,
whom he greatly admired, while
retaining an idiosyncratic vitality
of line.

In the competitive mood of the late 19th century considerable effort went into the establishment of reputations which put particular firms at the forefront of 'art' manufacture; but it was also important that a balance be maintained between this type of production, which was more often than not hand-printed and expensive, and the less innovative, largely machine-produced patterns required by less well-off consumers, some of whom, although more conservative, nevertheless wanted their decorations to reflect the current fashions. One of the difficulties faced by manufacturers was that, while they went to considerable lengths to produce a wide range of products to suit all sections of the market, they did not have direct contact with consumers.

Distribution

Trade in wallpapers was conducted via merchants and decorators, largely through the medium of pattern books. Middle- and upper-class customers might see displays of wallpaper at their decorator's premises, a trade showroom, or in one of the department stores, but the majority of consumers chose from the books supplied by a decorator.

Manufacturers, and merchants selecting from manufacturers' and importers' ranges with an eye to regional demand, usually produced at least two books a season, each containing 150–500 or so samples, and some produced many more.[23] In 1888, the Manchester merchants J. Davenport & Co. issued three books – one of hand-printed papers and the other two of 'cheaper and more general class of goods'. That same year a firm of Bristol merchants, Cotterell Bros, broke all records by producing a book containing more than 800 samples. The title page of a Cotterells book published in the early 1890s indicates that this firm made available a wide variety of products, all selected from the ranges of various manufacturers specifically to suit customers in the Bristol area;[24] there were hand-prints at 11s. a roll, surface-prints from 3s. to 7s. 6d., and 'sanitaries' at 1s. By the turn of the century the capital investment in pattern books was huge, and large manufacturers whose books were widely distributed were spending more than £10,000 on their production regularly.

It was from merchants that decorators obtained pattern books and samples to show to their customers. The selection that the latter eventually saw depended on the decorator's opinion of the client's requirements, in terms of taste as well as expense (and according to some critics, on the amount of trade discount given by merchants on certain products). It is clear from his memoirs that the London decorator Mawer Cowtan never recommended machine-printed papers to his aristocratic clients.[25] Lower down the social ladder, the inhabitants of small houses made their choice from one or two pattern books selected and supplied by the local 'builder, plumber and decorator' from whom they had obtained an estimate for the work, while those in the cheapest rented accommodation had to choose from a pattern book sent round by the landlord.

Since decorators at all levels – including some who, like Rhoda and Agnes Garrett, with their *Suggestions for Home Decoration* (1877), published advice directed at the middle classes – were instrumental in guiding consumer choice, both manufacturers and merchants found it necessary to publicize their new ranges regularly in the trade press.

Publicity

By the last decades of the 19th century the level of competition was such that it had become essential for many firms to advertise.[26] This was particularly true for those engaged in the manufacture of items of fashion – which depended on the public's awareness of new lines – if only because it enabled them to retain their share of a market saturated with goods.

clockwise from upper left
227 Illustration from a sample book produced by Cotterell Bros of Bristol to display their 'Clifton' wallpapers, early 1890s: a surface-printed tapestry paper and frieze. Tapestry papers usually comprised traditional floral patterns or 'medieval' scenes glimpsed through masses of foliage, over which fine lines were printed to simulate woven effects.

228 Another illustration from Cotterell's 'Clifton' sample book, showing a 'sanitary' machine-printed dado, border, filling and frieze. Images of this kind were essential if merchants were to convey the full impact of large-scale design repeats. A further feature which could be brought to the attention of the decorator immediately was the way in which pictorial dado papers were designed to be cut to fit the incline of the stairs and other features.

229 Surface-printed filling by the Darwen Paperstaining Co., 1892. One of many small florals in a pattern book of cheap products which also contains tile, woodgrain, tapestry and marble imitations printed in no more than three colours on a thinly grounded woodpulp paper.

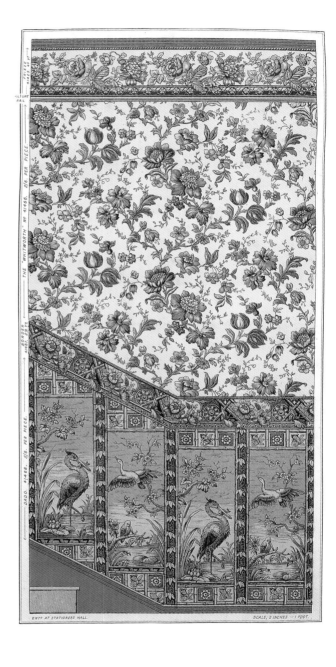

While merchants and decorators were suspicious of attempts by manufacturers to appeal directly to the public, participation in international exhibitions gave wallpaper firms an opportunity for the promotion of products to a wide audience at home and abroad. In addition, the inclusion of wallpapers in the London Annual Exhibition of Fine Arts for the first time in 1873 raised both their status in artistic circles and the general awareness of them as products having decorative potential.

By the 1880s the award of numerous medals for excellence, at international events as well as at home, ensured mention in newspapers keen to report British achievement and in contemporary magazines which featured articles on home decoration. The financial outlay involved was, however, considerable, particularly as the displays at major international exhibitions tended to feature specially designed wallpapers which, by associating a manufacturer's name with a well-known artist or architect, enhanced the firm's reputation generally rather than ensuring sales of the papers themselves. Indeed, although many of Walter Crane's designs won important awards for Jeffrey's, the artist himself remarked that nearly all the producers of his work complained they could not sell it,[27] and sales of many of the most acclaimed designs may not even have covered their manufacturing costs.[28] Nevertheless, as competition increased, manufacturers had little alternative but to maintain their reputation for artistic excellence despite the expense, particularly if they hoped to see their products favourably reviewed in magazines directed at the middle-class market.

For artistic circles, wallpapers were reviewed and illustrated in *The Art Journal*, *The Magazine of Art* and *The Studio*. The opinions of those writing on interior decoration in women's magazines had a far wider audience, and were of importance to manufacturers not least because, in addition to offering general advice about colour schemes, etc., they frequently mentioned papers by name and illustrated those considered to be of special merit. Not all the comments were favourable: in 1898, despite critical acclaim from the artistic press, a number of Jeffrey's papers were damned by a writer in *The Ladies' Realm*, who thought that although the designs by Walter Crane, Lewis F. Day and Heywood Sumner were 'very fine in themselves', they could never be made to look well in a room.

Writers on decorative art generally devoted their attention to the concerns of the more well-to-do, and it was upmarket manufacturers who were enabled by journalism of this kind to circumvent merchants and decorators and bring their products directly to the notice of potential customers. Firms catering for the 'general' trade had to rely on reviews in trade magazines. The *Journal of Decorative Art*, founded in 1881 and directed at 'the Decorator, Architect, Builder and all Art Workers', reported on a wide variety of events where wallpapers were displayed, such as the Manchester Jubilee Exhibition (1887), displays organized by the Arts and Crafts Exhibition Society (from 1888), and trade fairs in London and the provinces. Like other journals, it also featured occasional articles on individual wallpaper firms, enabling them to bring new products, and special promotions or services, to the notice of their customers. In addition, new wallpaper collections were reviewed each season. At this level of the market, if a pattern warranted special mention it usually had to be referred to by a production number rather than a name. The modest papers were also rarely illustrated: they were not expected to set new trends.

By the 1890s, in addition to receiving editorial coverage of this kind, wallpaper manufacturers and merchants were advertising regularly in journals and magazines directed at the decorating trade. Some advertisements featured illustrations of their showrooms and/or their latest patterns, and almost all included lists and descriptions of a wide range of products, the whole often enclosed in a decorative border.

205

230 This chaste Sanderson advertisement of 1898 features a decorative frieze similar to that found in many of the firm's papers of this period, all of which, it asserts, are 12 yards (11 m) long. This is a reference to short measures, which were a constant cause of complaints from decorators.

It has been suggested that the spread of advertising in the 1880s and 1890s offended middle-class sensibilities,[29] and that may explain why some firms catering for this section of the market advertised relatively little. Indeed, the Sanderson brothers refused to display their awards, preferring to rely on their already substantial reputation for high-quality wallpapers. In the 1890s the word 'artistic' all but disappeared from upmarket promotions, no doubt because it had been swiftly appropriated by merchants, who used it relentlessly to describe cheap products. Several manufacturers deleted all reference to their product ranges and issued more restrained advertisements, which merely associated their name with a current fashionable style – usually by means of a simple outline drawing – or with a well-known artist or designer.

The majority of firms, however, catered for what was regarded as a less discriminating clientele, and they bombarded their customers (the decorators) with information in a manner which reflected the intensity of activity and level of competition at that end of the market. For them the most important consideration was to make it known that they had the largest stock and the best selection at the lowest prices.

Changes in industrial organization

By the turn of the century the market was saturated with cheap wallpapers and there was talk of undercutting of prices. Competition between manufacturers was keen, and in 1899 'The Wall Paper Manufacturers Ltd' (generally known as the WPM) was incorporated as a joint stock company, merging the interests of thirty-one firms which between them controlled almost 98 per cent of the British wallpaper industry.[30] It is clear from the agreements drawn up between the constituent companies (which included such well-known names as Potters and Lightbown Aspinall) that initially the WPM's main concern was for large-scale machine production. Several firms known for their high quality hand-prints retained a degree of independence by maintaining separate control of their showrooms and distribution.

Although the WPM promoted the idea of variety (each branch had its own design studio where individuality was to be 'specially encouraged'), some mills were closed, the workforces were cut, administration was centralized and prices were rigidly controlled. Merchants, who had been used to playing off one manufacturer against another in order to obtain the discounts on which their profit margin depended, suddenly found that if they did not restrict their dealing to the WPM's products, discounts would not apply. Jeffrey's and other firms whose owners had preferred to remain independent were persuaded to enter into 'working agreements' with the WPM and thus, at a stroke, almost all competition, however insignificant in comparison, had been virtually eliminated.

Conclusion

At the time of the Great Exhibition of 1851, despite the existence in Britain of successful machine-printing, the possibility that wallpaper would become commonplace seems not to have been considered seriously by the majority of manufacturers. However, most industries associated with the decorative arts were to experience a period of increasing activity during the last three decades of the century and firms producing patterned wallpapers were no exception. By 1900 the industry had come to rely on large-scale concentration of production for a mass market and was radically different from that of the 1850s.

Widespread adoption of surface-printing in the 1840s had provided the initial impetus for changes in manufacturing processes, the success of which (coupled with increased demand) had, by the 1890s, encouraged large, well-organized firms to erect new mills, adopt the most up-to-date labour-saving machinery and appliances, invest in research and development, and improve production costs. At home, the availability of a huge variety of wallpaper products (of which only a few have been described here) allowed both rich and middle-income groups to purchase from a wider range than before. In addition, although some decorators considered anything costing below 2s. per roll beneath their notice, the production of wallpapers priced at as little as 1d. provided an increasing number of consumers at the lower end of the social scale with an opportunity to exercise some control over their domestic circumstances.

In 1888 the *Journal of Decorative Art* remarked on the benefits to be reaped by the general public from a market rich in an increasing range of choices. However, the democratization of wallpaper caused considerable unease, both within some sections of the industry and outside. Throughout the late 19th century manufacturers and merchants whose products had traditionally been restricted to the middle and upper classes were having to come to terms with the dramatic demographic and social changes which had taken place since mid-century. To do so they were having to employ new strategies in order to defend themselves against competitors who regarded themselves as industrialists and distributors increasingly dependent on the more modest middle and lower classes, who wanted a fashionable article at a lower price. It can, surely, be no coincidence that the efforts of major figures in the trade to raise the status of wallpaper occurred in the 1870s when output had reached 32,000,000 rolls per annum, most of it machine-produced.

It is undeniable that the collaboration between manufacturers and leading exponents of the Aesthetic and Arts and Crafts movements was instrumental in the development of a new, and what was perceived as a quintessentially English, style of surface pattern design, the success of which in international markets increased confidence in British design at home. The prestige of association with members of the artistic élite also allowed some manufacturers to supply machine-printed wallpapers to the lower end of the market whilst publicly distancing themselves from such production. R. W. Essex, for example, 'abhorred' 'sanitary papers' because he thought they lacked 'artistic character', but he sold them in large quantities.[31]

Unlike British textiles which, in part, owed their success abroad to innovative production, the majority of 'art wallpapers' were hand-printed. Those that were printed by machine were produced in such a way as to imitate their hand-blocked counterparts. Thus, the success of British wallpapers, which were renowned for their 'modern' design both at home and abroad, remained linked to traditional methods of production – methods which were themselves associated with manufacture for a wealthy élite.

By the turn of the century, however, only a dozen or so firms were still manufacturing hand-printed papers (many of which were simple one- or two-colour designs which would compete in price with machine goods) and it was estimated that more than 90 per cent of the industry's output was machine-produced[32] – much of it by the 'sanitary' printing process, which resulted in a product which was uncompromisingly different in appearance from that printed by hand. According to the prospectus of the WPM in 1900, British firms occupied the leading position in world wallpaper manufacture and had little to fear from foreign competition in the home and colonial market. There was an established trade with the Continent in cheap machine-printed papers; and there was also a substantial demand, from both the Continent and the United States, for more expensive products.

The surge of confidence which swept through the British wallpaper industry during the last three decades of the century had removed its dependence for new designs on French studios, had facilitated both the stimulation and satisfaction of demand for technological ingenuity and visual novelty, and had enabled many manufacturers to experience a golden age of expansion.

231 'Sanitary' machine-printed wallpaper, *c.* 1899–1902. The development of this process provided manufacturers with a marvellous opportunity to produce cheap commemorative and other pictorial papers for the popular market. This one features heroic scenes from the Boer War, probably based on sketches published in the *Illustrated London News*.

By the late 19th century the American wallpaper industry was well established. Due to advances in machine-printing, prices were lower than they had ever been. Charles Eastlake's *Hints on Household Taste*, which had its first American publication in 1872 and was reprinted some eight times by 1886, brought the ideas of the English Design Reformers to an eager public, providing illustrations and practical advice. Two-dimensional stylization was now the model for American paper-hangings, ending the long reign of realistic French-inspired florals and textile imitations. Native designers were producing 'artistic' patterns based on the examples of Owen Jones, William Morris and Christopher Dresser.

It is interesting to note that by 1876 American manufacturers were confident that the papers they produced would find a ready market in England. A report in the London *Furniture Gazette* on 'American Paper-Hangings in the English Market'[1] observed that Americans could not lead the fashion but that they 'strive by their superior mechanical skill to make papers in those designs a little cheaper than their rivals.' The correspondent continued: 'There are good designers now in the United States, and it is undoubtedly true that a large number of the richest and most popular patterns in favour among discriminating people in America are of native invention.'

Americans bought a lot of wallpaper during the 1870s and 1880s. One of the largest manufacturers, Howell & Brothers of Philadelphia, was producing 6,000,000 rolls per year in 1874.[2] The *Furniture Gazette* in 1879 reported that 'The people of the United States spend $8,000,000 per annum for wallpaper, their requirements being about 57,142,860 rolls, or 457,142,400 yards [418,011,000 m] – which would be sufficient to girdle the earth at the equator and leave several hundred yards to spare.'[3]

During this period, approximately twenty-five firms supplied the demand, the largest of them producing hand-block-prints as well as machine-printed papers. Factories were clustered on the East Coast and found in Philadelphia, New York, several places in New Jersey, and Boston. Three of the biggest were Howell & Brothers (1835–after 1900) of Philadelphia; Christy, Constant & Co. (1844–85) of New York (later Christy, Shepherd & Garrett); and Janeway & Carpenter (*c.* 1850–after 1900) of New Brunswick (New Jersey). Christy, Constant & Co. in 1868 owned ten surface-printing machines, four of which were capable of printing twelve colours at a time. Machines were also used there for grounding and satining. Twenty-five to thirty hand-presses served to block-print the higher grades, including gilded and flock papers.[4] Machines capable of printing six, eight and twelve colours, based on English models, had been available by the mid- or late 1850s from the Waldron Company of New Brunswick (New Jersey), and in 1876 Waldron was commissioned by Howell & Brothers to make one of their large surface-printing machines for Howell's display at the Philadelphia Centennial Exhibition: visitors to Machinery Hall could watch wallpaper being printed on a machine 10 feet high and 10 feet long (3×3 m).

One of the most innovative firms, Frederick Beck & Co., was founded in New York in 1860. During the 1880s the company produced imitations of Dutch stamped leather, in which the design was embossed by machine and then hand-painted. Beck's mica papers were remarked upon in the press, and praised as 'exquisite' and 'immensely fetching'.[5] (Japanese mica was used as a ground and then a pattern was printed over this shimmering surface.) Beck opened a factory in Stanford (Connecticut) in 1883 to produce Lincrusta-Walton, the relief moulded wallcovering, and also manufactured another English invention – 'sanitary' papers, with a washable surface printed in oil colours by means of engraved rollers (see above, p.154).[6]

Most companies, Beck included, produced modest papers for modest budgets. The *Furniture Gazette* reported that American paper-hangings were cheaper than they had ever been: 'Wallpapers which were sold wholesale five years ago

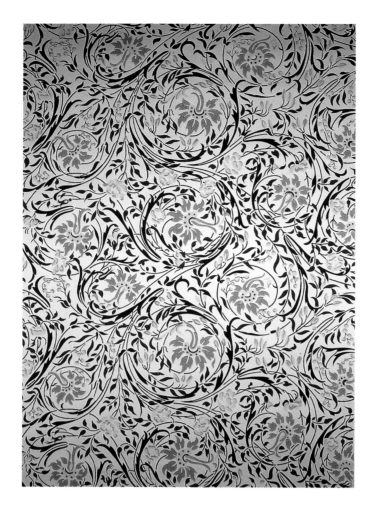

232 'The Perdita', a paper in William Morris style by Thomas Strahan & Co. of Chelsea (Massachusetts); surface-printed in colours, 1880s.

233 Dining room of the Mark Twain House, Hartford (Connecticut). A paper with a deep red ground covered with golden embossed lilies was chosen by the firm Associated Artists for their redecoration of the writer's home in 1881.

opposite
234 Patent for a Lincrusta-Walton frieze, issued to Augustin Le Prince on 12 August 1884 for Frederick Beck & Co. of New York. Beck was the only company to produce Lincrusta in the United States during this period. The designer described this piece as 'in the Persian style, having a border in the style of Louis XVI'.

AUGUSTIN LE PRINCE, OF NEW YORK, N. Y.

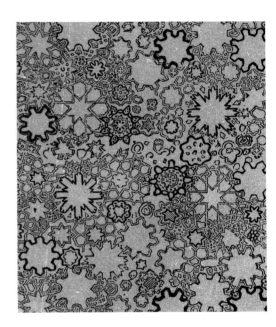

at from 12½ to 13 cents a roll are selling at from 6 to 6½ cents a roll. Those which sold five years ago at 45 to 50 cents have now come down to 24 and 25 cents; and a corresponding decline has taken place in all other grades.'[7] The preferred tripartite wall decoration of dado, filling and frieze, introduced in the 1870s, was available in all price ranges.

The Philadelphia Centennial Exhibition of 1876 not only gave visitors a glimpse of how wallpaper was made; it also gave many people a taste of the English art manufacturers' products. The display of the prizewinning London firm Jeffrey & Co. included papers designed by William Morris and Walter Crane, which met with wide approval. The Morris patterns had been imported and sold in the United States since 1870 by J. M. Bumstead of Boston.[8] The taste for papers modelled after Morris designs was commented upon in 1884 in the magazine *Carpentry and Building*:

> It is quite remarkable how quickly the supply for cheap and truly artistic papers has responded to the demand. The paper manufacturers have employed the best artists and have given prizes for good designs. They have taken hints from Morris and his followers . . . . There was a time when if one wanted a good paper for his wall he must pay the enormous prices asked by William Morris and Co. of London. Now he can find quite as good designs as Morris ever made by looking over the stock of any first-class American papers at not more than one-third the price of the no better papers from England.[9]

Another important English designer whose work was emulated by Americans was Christopher Dresser. He was an exponent of ornament derived from nature and, as we have seen, he also used motifs found in Indian, Moorish, Chinese, and especially Japanese art in his wallpapers. In 1877 he designed papers for the Philadelphia firm of Wilson & Fenimores. Patterns based on Japanese and Indian motifs, as well as flattened natural forms, were also supplied by the American decorating team Associated Artists (1879–83); Louis Comfort Tiffany, Candace Wheeler, and Samuel Colman designed wallpaper for Warren, Fuller & Co. of New York (1880–1901). Indeed, 'the idea that only flat, abstracted patterns were permissible was so pervasive that it could be the butt of a joke.'[10]

The 1890s saw a major change in wallpaper styles. Gone was the tripartite treatment, to be replaced by the wide frieze and sidewall or filling paper.

top and above
235 Surface-printed Anglo-Japanesque wallpaper, 1880s. The asymmetrical framework of fans, circles and arches combined with the two-dimensional treatment of flowers and animals is typical of the Anglo-Japanesque mixture of English design tenets and traditional Japanese design principles.

236 Detail of a ceiling decoration designed by Louis Comfort Tiffany, from *What Shall We Do With Our Walls*, published in 1880 by Warren, Fuller & Co. with an essay by Clarence Cook. Warren, Fuller & Co. has been compared with the English firm Jeffrey & Co. for their use of well-known artists as designers.

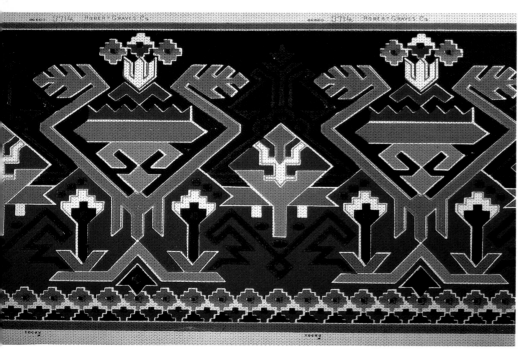

American wallpapers of the 1890s

237, 238 Two friezes, machine-printed by the Robert Graves Co., of New York. Manufacturers used a wide variety of techniques and styles to distinguish their product. Graves's upper frieze includes shading and gold glitter; the lower one interprets American Indian motifs.

239 A showroom, from a poster printed in Cleveland (Ohio) c. 1895–1900. American manu-facturers supplied the consumer – by this period, significantly, a woman – with a new selection of papers every year; patterns were also imported from Europe. The two suites of designs at the top consist, reading from left to right, of a rich pattern for the main wall area, a frieze, and a simpler ceiling paper. Dados were no longer fashionable. Styles shown are Adamesque, Rococo Revival, realistic floral, and Art Nouveau.

The public may have grown tired of the correct 'rules' promulgated in the past decade. Architects and interior designers who catered to a wealthy clientèle were recommending luxurious wooden panelling or textile applications for walls. But for the average American, paper was still the preferred way to decorate a home economically. A roll of American wallpaper was 8 yards long by 20 inches wide (7.3 × 0.5 m). In 1898 the *New York Times* reported that the average grades sold for between 4½ cents and $2, and that thirty-four manufacturers were producing 200,000,000 rolls each year.[11] Production had been steadily increasing since mid-century: in 1850 it was 15,000,000 rolls, in 1870 45,000,000, and in 1890 100,000,000.[12]

237–239 Realistically portrayed flowers, Rococo Revival scrolls, Adamesque motifs, stripes, damasks and American Indian style patterns were also available. Colour shading, gold glitter, metallic pigments and overprinting with fine lines appeared on many of the average-price designs produced during this period.[13] Machine-printing had reached its technical high point, and papers were overburdened with these special effects.

The Decorator and Furnisher in 1890 commented on the quality and large volume of wallpaper then being produced in America, and touched on its great appeal:

> There are exaggerated and capricious patterns with lurid contrasts of color originated by the manufacturer to create in his customer a desire for something that is all the rage, and fashion instead of the love of good decoration is appealed to. But ignoring the offensively cheap papers, there are grades of wallpaper having designs that produce a refined physical and mental enjoyment. Unlike other costly forms of art which exist for only a few, wallpaper exists for all, and the man of moderate means may surround himself with all that is artistic in design and color.[14]

240 A New York City barber shop, 1903. By the end of the century wallpaper was widely used, even in commercial establishments. The frieze and sidewall or filling combination had replaced the popular tripartite wall decoration of previous decades.

'The French are so quick that they have no need of steam, and so skilful that they never get tired.' The journalist Auguste Luchet's conclusion following the 1862 Exhibition in London may raise a smile today, but it points to a truth about French practice: while mechanization increased, France, more than almost any other country, maintained a large traditional sector based on manual skill. The wallpaper industry was no exception.

Printing from an engraved copper cylinder had been perfected in 1826 by Jean Zuber & Cie in Rixheim; the surface-printing technique made its appearance in France in 1843 with a hand-powered machine at the Parisian firm of Bissonet. It was not until 1850 that a steam-powered six-colour printing machine was introduced, imported from England by Jean Zuber & Cie; but the number had grown to 50 by 1867, to 150 in 1878, and to 200 in 1900, with French machines joining in. Zuber subsequently acquired a sixteen-colour German machine. In 1887 it was possible for O. E. Lami, a proponent of mechanization, to write: 'thanks to their low cost, machine-printed wallpapers are now a common item of consumption – so much so that the number of manufacturers of luxury papers has gone down significantly and the latter have had to reorganize their plant and incorporate machines.' The advantages of machine-printing were all too obvious: in the course of a survey carried out in the 1880s, the firm of Zuber calculated that a twenty-colour machine could print in one day what would take a hand-block-printer four years! This was reflected in the prices. Wallpaper had cost several gold francs a roll, but now it could be bought for as little as 15 centimes, and it came to decorate the most modest interiors, like that of the laundress Gervaise in Emile Zola's novel *L'Assommoir* (1877), or those of the manual workers and lower middle-class inhabitants of the rooms shown in Eugène Atget's late 19th-century photographs. All observers agreed in seeing the process as one that made luxury and comfort available to all classes.

180

241

France

BERNARD JACQUÉ

241 Interior of a worker's flat in rue de Romainville, Paris, photographed by Eugène Atget in 1910. On the walls is a modest paper with a simple Art Nouveau motif. The chimneyboard in front of the fireplace, sealing off the draughts, is covered with pieces of floral-patterned paper – a last gasp of the tradition of papering such a feature.

177

Machine-printing did not at first have a significant aesthetic impact, even when one considers the rapid improvement in quality achieved during the 1850s by the use of more colours and increased accuracy of engraving and registration. Zuber's ledgers, for instance, show that designs made for block-printing were transferred to machine-printing without any account being taken of the thinness of the colour or the lack of definition in the resulting paper.[1] Gradually the influence of Owen Jones's *Grammar of Ornament* (1856) began to be felt, in flat patterns with colouring that was strident in the 1860s and gradually softer as the century wore on. Flowers remained very popular, now of a type which a critic in 1889 dubbed *ornemanière* (meaning stylized rather than naturalistic), based on a wide variety of styles. Many rich damask patterns were produced in dark 'heraldic' colours and designs that were strongly Renaissance in character (the style known as 'Henri II', which lasted into the 1930s); but the same patterns occur in block-printed versions as well. By the 1880s the availability of sixteen- and twenty-four-colour machines (with a maximum of twenty-six colours at the firm of Isidore Leroy) made it possible to imitate hand work even more successfully. These gigantic machines were also used by their owners to produce showpieces for display at the great international exhibitions – even *décors* similar to those manufactured by hand, technically dazzling in the mechanics of their production, but sadly deficient in artistic quality.

Far from dying out, block-printing remained in use for luxury wallpapers, and was also more cost-effective for short runs of papers requiring few colours. In Paris there were still eight hundred printing tables in 1866; they were common enough in 1881 for the decorative arts historian Charles Blanc to be

242 A pattern made up of popular books, including *Don Quixote* and works by Jules Verne and Sir Walter Scott, surface-printed by Isidore Leroy, 1889. Books are treated here in a very different way from the rows of sham spines available as wallpaper earlier in the century. This example comes from one of the albums compiled by the designers Claude Frères, recording outstanding designs year by year.

opposite
243 A paper with a pattern of flowers in the stylized manner described as *ornemanière*; block-printed, *c.* 1880.

244 A paper for a child's room featuring Pierrots, 1900. With its ten colours on a plain ground, this is a characteristic example of machine-printing at the end of the century.

178

able to describe the process meticulously,[2] and large firms continued to use them right up to 1914. Hand work was also required for the manufacture of embossed papers, which could command retail prices high enough to justify the sophisticated processes used in their production.

Block-printing retained its own specialisms, such as the three-dimensional flower patterns which had come in in the 1840s and continued to be produced until the early 1880s without any notable evolution, except for the introduction of new coordinated textiles in the form of glazed cotton. Ornament patterns, too, saw no significant change, beyond a multiplication of three-dimensional motifs: eclecticism remained the norm, with Rococo and Louis XVI particularly popular in the 1850s and 1860s, followed by Renaissance in the last decades of the century. All required a lavish number of colours.

What little impetus for change there might have been was discouraged by the continued international popularity of these quintessentially French products – chiefly in the United States but also in Britain, which became the leading customer for French wallpapers after the Free Trade agreement of 1860.[3] (In 1863 exports to Britain amounted to one-eighth of total production.) Traffic in the other direction was negligible, as France continued to import little from abroad. It was thus only gradually that Arts and Crafts influences from Britain were reflected in the colouring, which became less brilliant but also less intense and paler, and in the patterns, which became more stylized and two-dimensional, either completely flat or in very shallow relief. Simultaneously, in the 1880s, French exports experienced a marked fall in the face of strong foreign competition.

Block-printing continued to reign triumphant in the realm of the *décor*. In the 1860s, all the leading companies produced Louis XVI schemes. Design became quieter and the colouring more discreet: usually they had white satin grounds heightened with gold, brightened by panel compositions of rustic scenes in pastel tones. Antiquity reappeared, particularly at the Paris Exposition of 1867, but the form it took now was very different from the Neoclassicism of the beginning of the century: the designs were linear and deliberately flat, the colouring sharp and refined, reflecting contemporary discoveries about the polychromy of Greek and Roman buildings. Having said all this, however, one has to admit that whatever its stylistic sources one *décor* looks much like another, especially when it comes to those that were mass-produced in this period of intensified urbanization. Both their basic schemes and their proportions were tied to the standardization of wallpaper manufacture and of building technology. Louis XVI sets remained in production until the end of the century, but after 1870 the only new *décors* introduced were very expensive schemes, especially in the Renaissance style, where effects of graining were used to imitate wood panelling; then the genre disappeared altogether. Its fate was sealed by the decline in hand-block-printing, since *décors* could not be mass-produced by machine.

245   Another area where block-printing maintained its dominance after the introduction of machinery was in the production of wallpapers imitating tapestries with added embossing and intaglio printing of a grid of fine lines to give them a 'woven' appearance. The earliest example seems to be the 'Décor Gobelins' issued by Zuber in 1866, which is modelled on 18th-century tapestries with elaborate borders, notably the celebrated 'Loves of the Gods'. Taste then looked further back to the 16th century, with verdure patterns and evocations of Flemish tapestries rendered in sombre tones. These papers were produced either as repeating patterns which would have been completed by borders, or as more elaborate compositions to be fitted together like scenic papers. Gradually they displaced both *décors* and scenic papers from the display stands at international exhibitions. The Paris Exposition of 1900 saw the appearance of tapestry panels in Art Nouveau style.

Finally, however, this kind of work disappeared in the face of economic pressures. The production of *décors* slowed down and then ceased, and printing tables were dismantled. It is significant that when Zuber took advantage of the lull caused by the First World War to draw up an inventory of its blocks, the firm chose to destroy many of them.

Craft production had lingered on in one other area, that of relief papers. The embossing process had first appeared in the 1840s and then took off in the 1860s, in France and Belgium (in Louvain, Brussels and Liège) and in Germany (at the firm of Herting).[4] Britain was slow to join in until the development of Lincrusta in 1877. Most were machine-made, but the finest of all embossed wallpapers were those produced by hand methods in Paris by Paul Balin, who had begun as a manufacturer of luxury papers before taking out a patent in 1866 which he later modified several times.[5] His aim was frankly imitative. He collected historic textiles and embossed leathers, and tirelessly scoured the public and private collections of decorative art that were beginning to be put together throughout Europe: an advertisement records, for instance, that he attempted to copy with the utmost fidelity 'a 17th-century silk velvet in the Industrial Museum of Lyons'. As a son of his own eclectic time, however, he was quite prepared to reproduce an embroidery pattern as embossed leather. He continued to produce such papers until his death in 1898, never showing the slightest hint of influence from the Design Reform movement.

The technique itself was not innovative: the effect was produced by squeezing the paper in a press between two plates, one bearing the design in relief and one having it recessed. But the great attention that Balin paid to the strength of the press, the quality of the support (more like card than paper), the perfection of the register and the impeccable execution of the finishes were what gave his products the 'realistic modelling' of which he boasted. His wallpapers are uncannily convincing: illusionism was taken to an unprecedented pitch of perfection – so perfect, indeed, that in the end the perfection kills the illusion. That is today's view, however, and not that of the late 19th century, when people took delight at the thought of living in a setting that was both historic and brand new.

Papers like Balin's cost a fortune: while earlier wallpapers had cost several gold francs for a whole roll, these were ten gold francs or more for one metre! The explanation lay in the number of processes involved and in the need for a large and highly skilled workforce. Embossed wallpapers were esteemed by connoisseurs, and after Balin had been awarded a prize at the Vienna Exhibition in 1873 samples were acquired by all the major decorative arts collections. They were bought privately, too, not only in France but in Britain (where they were imported by Sanderson) and in the United States.

The conservative character of the French wallpaper industry – which may be attributable as much to aesthetic factors as to economic, social or technical ones – prevailed until 1914, and was responsible for losses in some foreign markets such as the United States, where, after the Centennial Exhibition in Philadelphia in 1876, English 'reformist' patterns rapidly gained ground.[6] It is an important phenomenon, however, and one which has long been ignored in histories of decorative art, focused as they have been on the avant-garde. The fact is that the French industry remained extremely vigorous and also very active in the export market, showing that this more traditional manner was not merely very popular but was actually quantitatively dominant. A collection of thirty albums put together by the designers Claude Frères between 1870 and 1900[7] is instructive: each volume contains a selection made, with manufacturers in mind, of the outstanding products of the international wallpaper industry in a particular year – and what emerges is that traditional designs greatly outnumber innovative patterns, even at the height of the vogue for Art Nouveau. Perhaps the most surprising thing is that the patterns of this period are still copied and produced today.

245 Wallpaper simulating tapestry, *c.* 1890. This composition was found on the wall of a bourgeois house in Lyons. It imitates a verdure tapestry hanging, with three block-printed widths in the centre surrounded by two different borders and a special pattern at the base. The texture of cloth is suggested not only by a fine grid of lines overprinted in intaglio but by slight embossing.

The papers of Paul Balin

Some of the most magnificent papers of the 19th century are those produced by Paul Balin. In his hands wallpaper became a magical material, capable – at a very high price – of confusing the eye between reality and imitation. Trained with Desfossé, in 1863 he took over the Parisian firm of Genoux, and from 1866 he perfected the embossing technique. He won awards at the international exhibitions at Paris in 1867 (featured on his letterhead) and Vienna in 1873, and his papers were exported abroad and collected by museums. He identified his sources with care.

10 Unsteady Progress:
From the Turn of the Century
to the Second World War

SABINE THÜMMLER · MARK TURNER

The Continent of Europe

SABINE THÜMMLER

For most of the first thirty years of the 20th century the production of wallpapers in Europe grew steadily. German output rose from 60,000,000 rolls in 1900 to 100,000,000 in 1932. This owed less to the adoption of additional machinery than to improvements in efficiency – a pattern that can also be seen in the expansion of many small family firms into middle-size concerns of between 10 and 250 employees. But increasing production brought price-cutting and charges of unfair competition. In an attempt to regulate and stabilize the industry a number of trade organizations were formed: the WPM in Britain in 1899 (see above, p.169); in Germany the Verein Deutscher Tapetenfabrikanten in 1889, the Verband Tapetenindustrie in 1907, the Tapeten-Industrie AG-TIAG in 1908, the Kartell Deutscher Tapetenindustrieller in 1909 and the Verband Deutscher Tapetenfabriken in 1911. The measures they introduced were successful until the world-wide economic crisis of the late 1920s and early 1930s, when a number of companies went bankrupt. Those that remained, however, operated very efficiently and competitively.

The majority of output in these years was machine-produced for the mass market. France, with its tradition of high-quality luxury wallpapers, maintained a certain amount of hand-printing, especially during the Art Deco period, but in Germany, for the most part, both avant-garde and less design-conscious patterns were machine-printed.

Art Nouveau and Jugendstil

The ideas and practitioners of the British Aesthetic and Arts and Crafts movements had had a significant impact on Europe at the end of the 19th century, as we have seen, but by the start of the new century their influence was in decline. For the next fifty years the Continent was far more active in pursuing 'modern' design. Its first manifestation was in Art Nouveau, which appeared at its artistic zenith in the Paris Exposition Universelle of 1900. Within Art Nouveau – in Germany, Jugendstil – two basic tendencies can be distinguished: one was a formal language with an emphasis on the botanic and organic, which presented plant motifs as flat linear patterns; the other showed a tendency towards linear abstraction, transforming models from nature into geometric structural forms.

In interior decoration, the dark, subdued brownish colours of the last quarter of the 19th century were replaced by pale, pastel tones. At its most extreme, the artistic ideal was the integrating *Gesamtkunstwerk* (total work of art), wherein architecture, furnishings, even everyday objects were all equally imbued with art, employing a unified formal language. Houses complete with interior decoration, including wallpapers, came from the pen of a single designer. In Hector Guimard's papers for the Castel Béranger in Paris (1894–98), motifs ultimately derived from natural forms appear as energetic sweeping curves and lines of force. The Belgian Henry van de Velde, who also belonged to the abstract linear

250

tendency in Art Nouveau, designed a wallpaper in 1895 to match the style of his furniture: consisting of the movement and counter-movement of sweeping curves, it played with positive and negative forms.[1]

In Germany the first Jugendstil wallpapers to appear were in the floral manner; there are examples by Walter Leistikow and Hans Christiansen and by Otto Eckmann, whose stylized swans became almost the emblem of Jugendstil. Eckmann at first produced patterns with burgeoning, intertwining forms, but as he developed he tended to move increasingly towards abstract designs, such as the 'Pheasant' wallpaper of 1901/2: this consists only of delicately curved, symmetrically arranged lines, while the bird motif is carried in the frieze.

Patterns derived from long-stemmed flowers such as lilies or poppies, and from water-lilies, reeds, waves and swans appeared very often in wallpaper, and

251

250 Detail of a ceiling panel in Lincrusta-Walton, designed by Hector Guimard for the Castel Béranger, Paris, c. 1896.

251 Detail of the frieze and filling papers of 'Fasan' ('Pheasant'), designed by Otto Eckmann and surface-printed in colours by H. Engelhard of Mannheim, 1901/2.

185

favourite colours were pastels, especially lilac, lemon yellow, turquoise and white. Walls were either articulated with wallpapers into three parts (dado, filling and frieze) or treated in the manner which was by now 'smarter' in England, with a single division at door-height. In that arrangement the lower part was often hung with wood panelling or mock panelling in paper, while the upper part was hung with patterned paper extending up to the ceiling.

Jugendstil was a widespread phenomenon, and all companies catering to a middle-class market included designs of this type in their higher-priced output. But it soon had its critics. A writer in *Die Tapete* declared in 1908: 'The modern wallpapers which appeared around 1900 . . . astound us with the boldness of their form and colours, but they will never succeed, because the public soon grows weary of the confused tangle of lines on the wall.' The author went on to praise the new artist-designed wallpapers, including those of Josef Hoffmann, whose chief characteristic, compared with papers of the beginning of the century, lay in their 'modest renunciation of draughtsmanship'.[2] Influenced by the Scottish architect Charles Rennie Mackintosh, Hoffmann devised a clear, geometric variant of Art Nouveau, distinguished by purity of line and a restriction of the palette to contrasting tones such as black and white. A number of his papers appeared in the collections issued by Erismann & Cie of Breisach in connection with the Deutscher Werkbund after 1908.

But although Jugendstil dominated (and has continued to dominate) discussion of design, in the end in interior decoration it was just one phenomenon among many. It was able to make its presence felt alongside the historical styles, but could not displace them, as had been its original aim. The wallpapers available in the first years of the 20th century spanned the range from Art Nouveau, through floral designs influenced by Art Nouveau to a greater or lesser extent, to wallpapers in historicist styles and accurate historical imitations, such as the embossed wallpaper by UPL (Usines Peters-Lacroix), Brussels, in the style of Baroque gilded leather hangings. Engelhard was known for its high-quality flocks and embossed papers. Flammersheim & Steinmann in Cologne was a particularly traditional firm specializing in historic patterns. Many middle-sized companies, such as Norddeutsche Tapetenfabrik Hölscher & Breimer, produced a broad range of products for a wide market.

By the second decade of the century naturalistic flower wallpapers had returned to fashion. They either had a loose arrangement of bouquets or else made use of blossoms set so closely together that the background was completely concealed. At first more restrained colours were preferred, but in the course of the decade colours became ever stronger and more intense. Tapestry textures created by means of fine parallel hatching over the pattern, first seen in the late 19th century and popular since then in Britain, regained popularity in Continental Europe.

Deutscher Werkbund and Wiener Werkstätte

In contrast to England and France, where papers for the top end of the market continued to be block-printed, efforts were made in Germany to create good design appropriate for machine production. On the one hand the products had to be affordable to a broad range of social classes, and on the other they had to be tasteful, beautiful and practical.

In 1907 the Deutscher Werkbund was formed in Munich in Jugendstil artistic circles. The Werkbund, which was to have a great influence on the development of design far beyond the borders of Germany,[3] was an association of artists, artist-craftsmen and industrial companies which aimed to modernize the aesthetic appearance of industrial products while at the same time considering suitability of materials and fitness to function. Manufacture by machine and the product's practical and tasteful design became the most important aesthetic

252

253

227,
245

252 A wallpaper by Josef Hoffmann, surface-printed in colours by Erismann & Cie of Breisach, *c.* 1910, shown in a room designed by Koloman Moser.

253 A French floral paper, surface-printed in colours before 1914.

premises. Peter Behrens, Otto Eckmann, Josef Hoffmann, Joseph Maria Olbrich and Richard Riemerschmid were among the participating architects and artist-craftsmen who produced wallpaper designs for machine production. Two wallpaper firms became members: Erismann in 1908 and Coswig in 1912. The former issued a series of patterns designed between 1907 and 1914 by Riemerschmid, which exemplified Werkbund ideals: typically the surface is articulated with small shapes, usually leaf motifs, set closely together so that the repeats are almost invisible, and given rhythm by means of undulating stems or irregularly arranged fruit motifs.

254 A new formal language appeared in wallpaper collections around 1915. It was characterized by repeating patterns resembling woodcuts, with clearly defined shapes and strongly contrasting colours, in which cup-shaped blossom motifs were a particular favourite. The centre of this development was Vienna, where the Secession style was expressed in the work of the Wiener Werkstätte.

The Wiener Werkstätte were founded in 1903 as a workshop under the artistic direction of Josef Hoffmann and Koloman Moser, with the aim of bringing art to all areas of life. At the beginning Wiener Werkstätte products reflected the geometric style of Hoffmann and Moser, which was close to the Deutscher Werkbund in its striving for *Sachlichkeit* (objectivity, matter-of-fact-ness) and its emphasis on structural principles in design. The arrival of Eduard Josef Wimmer in 1908 and Dagobert Peche seven years later led to a shift from functionalist design towards imaginative, fantastic decorative forms. The work of Peche, with its linear rhythm, flamboyant harmonies and strange ornamental forms, determined the second phase of the Wiener Werkstätte, and here the predominance of the decorative principle had parallels with French Art Deco.

255 Peche created a bizarrely stylized plant world entirely independent of traditional styles: his 'magic flowers', distant abstractions of their prototypes in nature, are always depicted two-dimensionally, with characteristic elongated,

254 Wallpaper designed by H. D. Ulrich; block-printed in colours in Vienna, 1915.

255 'Cythere', designed by Dagobert Peche and produced by Flammersheim & Steinmann of Cologne; surface-printed in colours, 1921.

lancet-shaped leaves and slender blossoms. His wallpapers are printed in dusty colours and their background is often striped in a sequence of tones of a single colour. The wallpapers were initially printed by the Viennese firm of Max Schmidt; later, in 1921–23, Schmidt was succeeded by Flammersheim & Steinmann of Cologne.

Art Deco

The tendency towards extremely refined ornamental forms for luxury objects tailored to an upper-middle-class clientèle, which is visible in Peche's work, reached its high point in Art Deco, which grew out of floral Art Nouveau in France between 1905 and 1908. At first it defined itself in contrast to plain functional design and the strivings of Modernism, and it was typically expressed in exclusive interiors using precious materials.

Among the influences which gave rise to Art Deco were a return to Rococo stylistic features and enthusiasm for the productions of Diaghilev's Ballets Russes, which triumphed in Paris from 1909 onwards, with stage designs created by Léon Bakst in Oriental style and strident colours. There was a vogue for unconventional combinations such as red with orange, or blue with green. Egyptian elements and features borrowed from Cubism and African art also made a contribution. Besides stepped forms, the preferred ornamental motifs were flowers such as roses, daisies and dahlias, whose round heads were stylized in two-dimensional forms with strongly emphasized outlines. The couturier Paul Poiret was one of the first to transplant the look of the Ballets Russes, in his designs for clothes, and in 1911 he opened the Atelier Martine to provide equally exquisite interior decoration. The Atelier's wallpapers, designed in a spontaneous, sometimes deliberately naive style, were distinguished by their large-scale patterns and glowing colours. Henri Stéphany produced wallpapers with patterns in strong colours that show Constructivist and even Cubist elements of form. Other leading designers of the period were Maurice Dufrène, Paul Dumas and above all Emile Jacques Ruhlmann. The climax of this first phase of Art Deco was the Exposition Internationale des Art Décoratifs et Industriels Modernes held in Paris in 1925, which gave the style its name. To be seen there was a room created by Ruhlmann exemplifying the luxury of a totally designed interior: silk fabric harmonized with exclusive furniture in a transposition of the Louis XVI style.[4] A slight variant of the pattern was also issued as a wallpaper.

After its invention in France, Art Deco was very soon taken up in other countries. In Germany a related formal language was developed in what were known as Expressionist wallpapers. *'Formwille der Zeit'* (the will-to-form of the age)

256 A room hung with 'Les Gazelles', designed by the Atelier Martine of Paris, c. 1923.

257 'Roses', designed by Emile Jacques Ruhlmann; block-printed in colours, 1925.

was an often-used slogan, indicating that, as with Art Nouveau, no historical models were to be imitated: instead, there was to be a modern language of forms appropriate to the times. Under the influence of stylistic features from Expressionism and Cubism, a sharp-edged type of ornament with contrasting brilliant colours was devised. Glowing, intense colours were seen as the expression of the age.

In this spirit Oskar Treichel, Josef Margold and Wenzel Hablik designed their fantastic ornamental motifs abstracted from nature. Hablik created wallpapers with purely graphic patterns, such as meandering lines or serrated strips or plant ornament. A wallpaper of 1928 has an upward-spouting golden tree trunk made up of individual cloud-like segments, with an irregular covering of green leaves and dark red cup-shaped blossoms.

From the mid-1920s a new type of wallpaper pattern began to develop. It was strictly two-dimensional, and was influenced by a style of decoration first seen on ceramics of this period, where motifs were spattered on in shaded tones through stencils. Abstract geometric shapes derived from the principles of Constructivist painting provided the formal elements of design: circles, triangles or rectangles appeared with one side clearly defined, while the other merged with the background colour.[5] Some of the papers which followed this trend were printed with individual scattered flowers, probably to make them acceptable to a wider range of customers. Another new aspect of this decoration was the possibility of introducing a horizontal pattern and thereby emphasizing space.

258 'Grand Damas', by Emile Jacques Ruhlmann, block-printed in colours, 1925.

259 Wallpaper designed by Wenzel Hablik and produced by Werner & Sievers of Oldesloe: surface-printed in colours, 1928.

Reaction to pattern

From these wallpapers it was only a small step to the simplest, plainest linear patterns, such as Franz Jaeger's squares of fine lines, designed in 1927 for Hölscher & Breimer in Langenhagen, or the stripes of Paul László formed from longitudinal hatching which widens and narrows, designed about 1929 for Flammersheim & Steinmann. Here the decisive value was placed on colour, but from 1925 onwards pastel shades in finely graded modulations began to predominate; harmony rather than contrast was desirable, and patterns used a single colour with delicately balanced undertones and secondary tones.

In spite of this reticence, a hostility towards wallpapers developed among architects and artists. With the Neue Sachlichkeit movement came a reaction against the ornamental and decorative, and coloured paint was increasingly regarded as the surface treatment that was truest to materials. Le Corbusier was enthusiastic about using whitewash to paint walls (though this did not prevent him from developing a range of papers of his own for the Salubra company at Grenzach-Wyhlen in 1932). Wallpaper was accused of always wanting to represent something other than what it was, and was regarded as a surrogate because it imitated fabrics and used representational means to create spatial illusion. In the eyes of critics, designers had run through all the stylistic periods and were now merely cultivating the weirdest paper blossoms.

Paint or wallpaper? The question which had been discussed since the beginning of the 20th century now flared up with new violence. The years before the world economic crisis that began with the Crash in 1929 were the great age for building housing estates, and the design of the small flats was governed by the notions of neutrality and functionalism. It is true that on the market there were wallpapers intended for housing estates, but most had large-scale ornament in strong, dark colours, distorted by cheap printing. Consequently most architects opted for the colour possibilities of paint. To counter this, some manufacturers invited architects to collaborate in the creation of patterns specially for housing estates, such as the 'Siedlungskarte' designed by Hans Leistikow for the May-Siedlung (by the architect Ernst May) in Frankfurt, produced in 1925 by Marburger Tapetenfabrik. The best-known collection was the 'bauhaus-tapeten', or Bauhaus wallpapers, which were first issued in 1930 as a result of cooperation between the manufacturer Gebrüder Rasch of Bramsche and the Bauhaus, and which have continued (with interruptions) to the present day.

The Bauhaus, founded in 1919 at Weimar by Walter Gropius as a school with workshops for design crafts, architecture and figurative arts, had a decisive influence internationally on architecture, the shaping of living space and the design of objects of practical use. One of its fundamental principles was that objects should be practical, durable, cheap and elegant. Hannes Meyer, who succeeded Gropius in 1928, went a step further towards a socially orientated design. Meyer's aim was to make a few standard products which would be suitable for everybody, and which through industrial production could be sold at a reasonable price to reach the widest social strata. In this field the greatest commercial success was the 'bauhaus-tapeten'. Their design was entrusted to the wallpainting workshop under Hinnerk Scheper. Scheper had been using coloured paint as a means of accentuating architecture, and for this he preferred delicately nuanced, very pale colours: walls were covered with broken pastel-colour mixtures on highly polished, matt, roughened or textured surfaces. The fourteen patterns in the first wallpaper collection achieved similar effects, utilizing shimmering cross-hatchings, vertical and horizontal lines, or delicate lattices and grids crossed by thicker lines, and wavy combed lines. In each pattern three closely related pastel tones merge optically to create an effect of vibrating colour on the wall surface.

190

260 Pattern 'b5' from the 'bauhaus-tapeten' collection produced by Gebrüder Rasch of Bramsche; surface-printed in colours, 1930.

261 An example of the mass-market *Effekttapeten* or special-effects wallpapers inspired by Bauhaus designs, produced by Norddeutsche Tapetenfabrik of Langenhagen; surface-printed in colours, *c*. 1935.

261 The Bauhaus papers had an effect on the mass market, contributing to the development in the course of the 1930s of what were known as *Effekttapeten*, *Rauhfasertapeten* and *Strukturtapeten*. The *Effekttapeten* (special-effect wallpapers) had minimal patterns: they were usually completely covered in blurred patches of graduated colour, creating a dim, streaky surface. Sometimes the surface was enlivened with gold dust, and the papers were often partly embossed or lightly textured to imitate textiles. *Rauhfasertapeten* (woodchip wallpapers) came in a single colour or were enlivened with some colour decoration, but either way they were always coloured and not, as they are nowadays, regarded as a raw material for one to paint oneself. This led in the mid-1930s to the development of the *Strukturtapeten* (textured wallpapers), with strong three-dimensional machine-embossed patterns based on leather grain, fibrous paper, veining or plaster, and no other ornament; like the special-effect papers they were simply intended to enliven the wall surface.

Reinterpreting the past, heralding the future

A concurrent but very different taste was for classic wallpaper motifs such as floral designs or adaptations of historical styles. Quick, realistic sketches of wild flowers, branches with leaves and blossoms, landscape motifs often in Chinese style, were printed on a mottled or a woodchip ground. Because the paper had a special-effect or a woodchip texture, the pattern did not stand out clearly and often merged to a greater or lesser extent with the background. Here again little gold highlights against the brownish, 'tea-stained' matt colours were popular. Historical models were either copied accurately, though treated in a completely flat manner with softened outlines, or were given modern modifications. This 262 sort of pattern can be seen in Rasch's 1937 'Weimar' collection. The designs by Paul Schulze-Naumburg translate historical flat ornaments, usually textile patterns with heraldic motifs or floral scrolls, into a modern wallpaper language and give the effect of stencil printing.

263 In 1938 the Amt der Schönheit der Arbeit (Office for the Beauty of Work) in Berlin issued a special collection which, in the spirit of political conformity, the whole German wallpaper industry was to print. It was designed by the architect Richard Lisker.[6] (Lisker had been Professor and then Director of the Städelsche Kunstschule in Frankfurt since 1924; in 1939 he was to be summarily dismissed.) Amazingly, the wallpaper patterns are not in the *altdeutsch* style

262 Detail of a wallpaper designed by Paul Schultze-Naumburg from the 'Weimar' collection, produced by Rasch; surface-printed in colours, 1937.

263 Detail of a wallpaper designed by Richard Lisker from the 'Schönheit der Arbeit' collection; surface-printed in colours, 1939.

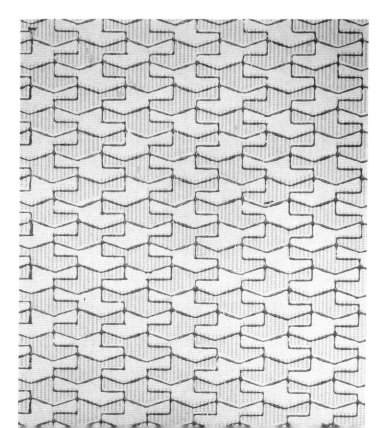

propagated by Schulze-Naumburg, which we might have expected from the National Socialists: instead we find twenty-five designs with echoes of the Bauhaus, in woodchip textures and linear patterns. The motifs, such as sparsely arranged arrows, mazes and grids, printed in bright, fresh colours on a white ground, were not successful at the time. (Similar effects did, however, become popular in the 1960s.) The collection can be seen as a development of the architects' designs by László and Jaeger mentioned above.

The outbreak of World War II in 1939 and the ensuing period of shortages meant that not much new in the way of wallpaper could be developed on the Continent, and some of the tendencies clearly apparent in the late 1930s had to wait more than a decade before they were developed. In 1939 a collection appeared from Rasch under the title 'Wiener Künstler Tapeten' (Viennese Artist Wallpapers). It was produced under the direction of the old master Josef Hoffmann, and described as 'lively, fashionable woodchip wallpaper'.[7] The designs showed slender, flat stylized leaf and flower motifs strewn loosely over the ground. Quick chalk-outline sketches with flat, stencil-like colouring and bright, fresh tones pointed to a style which was to become widespread in the 1950s.

It was the wallpaper industries in Scandinavia, which had been less affected by the war, that took the lead in design in the 1940s. There were two strands. One was functionalist: small restful patterns, printed in monochrome or embossed, were devised to provide a restrained background for furniture and pictures. The other was representational: these patterns were often characterized by delicately linear floral forms in light springtime colours on a pale ground. The Swedish company Norrköpings tapetfabrik had been collaborating in both modes with architects and designers since the 1930s; characteristic representational papers include Elias Svedberg's 'Callas', produced as a machine-print in 1946. Scandinavian work had been admired by the European design establishment before the war and it was to prove very influential, as we shall see in the following chapter, in the immediate post-war period.

Looking back, one can see that the textured and special-effect wallpapers, which produced restful walls without ornament, were the most characteristic innovation of the first half of the 20th century. In the long run, however, they led to the decline of wallpaper in favour of smooth walls painted white or in a plain colour.

264 Swedish wallpaper, surface-printed in colours before 1950.

At the turn of the century the use of wallpaper was almost universal on both sides of the Atlantic. However, critics and architects were beginning a strengthening campaign to encourage the public to abandon pattern in favour of paint, panelling and other less demonstrative forms of wall treatment. A critical loathing of wallpaper developed which was to last for thirty years or more. It is paradoxical that it was the Arts and Crafts Movement, which fostered such wonderful achievements in wallpaper, that ultimately gave rise to its decline.

Both Britain and America had a rapidly expanding middle class which took a great interest in all matters appertaining to the home and its furnishings. This class of society was particularly attracted to the Arts and Crafts ideal of a domestic architecture and decoration that valued honesty and simplicity and was based on the vernacular tradition. To many people in the early 1900s the idea of living in a house that appeared to have endured over the centuries and that was in harmony with its surroundings was an extremely attractive one. Arts and Crafts architects in Britain drew their inspiration from domestic architecture of the Tudor, Stuart and Georgian periods, delighting in the way these houses reflected local building materials and climatic conditions. In the United States, many also felt their cultural roots to be British, and so had no difficulty in claiming British vernacular architecture as their rightful tradition, too. Yet others looked to American colonial styles as being most appropriate. Spanish Colonial, for instance, was felt to be particularly suitable for California and Florida. The vernacular revival quickly filtered down to the popular housing market over the first two decades of the 20th century. Arts and Crafts ideals found their most successful popular expression in the American bungalow. Although originally associated with California, these homely and versatile dwellings quickly became popular throughout the United States. Whilst many were built in the Craftsman style, they were easily adapted to other types which suited the locality, climate and personal taste of the owner. Generous porches helped integrate the bungalow into its surrounding landscape, and its free-flowing adaptable interior spaces provided a welcome contrast to the formality of the old 19th-century parlour and dining room arrangement. The British mass housing market did not fare so well. Speculative builders paid lip service to the vernacular revival by using such selling attractions as lattice windows and stained glass, bogus half-timbering, tile-hanging and pebble-dashing. However they determinedly clung to the old town house plan of small rooms leading off narrow corridors.

Naturally, this all led to a growing interest in appropriate interior decoration. Architects and critics recommended using genuine antiques or furniture inspired by simple British (or colonial) styles. They were given much support by the journals on home decoration. Particularly important were *Country Life* in Britain and *House & Garden* in the United States, which both reached a wealthy and influential, albeit small, section of society. Thanks to developments made in the 1890s in the technique of halftone printing, these magazines were able to provide good quality black-and-white photographic illustrations, the importance of which it is hard to overestimate. For the first time readers were able to see what the interior of an unspoilt Cotswold manor house or a millionaire's lodge in the Adirondacks really looked like. It did not go unnoticed that whilst genuine Tudor farmhouses had oak panelling, whitewashed walls and brick inglenooks, they did not have patterned walls. Thus began a fashionable prejudice against wallpaper which was to last until the 1930s.

The vast majority of people, however, still wanted to use wallpaper, the popularity of which is borne out by the impressive rise in production during the first half of the 20th century. In Britain output increased from 50,000,000 rolls per annum in 1900 to nearly 100,000,000 in 1939. In the United States it grew to over 400,000,000 in 1947.[1] The situation was summed up in 1945 by the English architect and critic H. S. Goodhart-Rendel:

194

An architectural historian, working through such records of the early years of the twentieth century as the annual *Recent Domestic Architecture, The Studio Year Book* and the 'Lesser Country Homes of the Day' published serially in *Country Life*, would be justified in inferring that by the outbreak of the last war the paper-hanging trade in England had almost ceased to exist.

The historian would be wrong. Wallpaper was still made and used in great quantities, but not in houses likely to be illustrated in art publications . . . . It was the patronage of people who had never heard of Shaw or of Lutyens or of Voysey that kept wallpaper alive, of people with a natural healthy taste for the ornamental which no highbrow forms could quell.[2]

The Arts and Crafts inheritance

Before the First World War, while wallpaper continued to receive general approbation, there was a vast range of choice, depending largely on income and personal taste. In both Britain and America the use of the decorative dado paper was on the decline. Its removal was not just part of the general simplification of decoration: it was also seen to be an out-of-date fashion, reminiscent of the cluttered 'artistic' parlours of the 1880s and 1890s. Dados were still used in halls and dining rooms, where the walls were subjected to considerable wear and tear, but their frequent adoption in tenement stairways and hospital corridors hastened their demise in domestic settings.

Instead, up to about 1915, there was a craze for friezes. They had been widely used for thirty years or more, but now became much deeper and were offered in a far greater range of subjects. The British wallpaper historians A. V. Sugden and J. L. Edmondson wrote in 1926: 'Conventional, allegorical, topical, scenic, naturalistic, broad in effect or full of detail as fancy dictated, the frieze has given every possible scope for ingenuity in method of production. It came fully into its own about the beginning of 1900 and continued in favour until a few years ago.'[3]

265   Arts and Crafts followers favoured a wide demonstrative stylized landscape used in conjunction with plain or panelled walls. Another option, even closer to the Arts and Crafts spirit, was a hand-stencilled pattern of conventionalized flowers and leaves. Most of the better manufacturers, including Essex & Co., Sanderson and Jeffrey & Co., had their own stencilling departments, sometimes using this technique in conjunction with block-printing. The firm that specialized in this type of production, however, was Shand Kydd, which was particularly famous both in Britain and the United States for the quality of its work and its

222   striking use of colour. Shand Kydd's friezes used very lush, organic Art Nouveau designs, based on acanthus scrolls, lilies and poppies. They were so successful that one American manufacturer proudly claimed: 'Our new friezes that have been attracting so much attention are done in the "Shand-Kydd" effects.'[4]

But the fashion was by no means confined to Arts and Crafts houses. By 1905 virtually every manufacturer carried a range of friezes, and they were very popular as machine-prints for the mass market. Home decorating journals recommended certain subjects for specific rooms: woodland scenes in rich and evocative colours for dining rooms; hunting scenes for smoking and billiard rooms; and seascapes for bathrooms. The simple stylized motifs of Art Nouveau were also used, but their popularity declined rapidly and by 1910 they were really only used for the cheaper patterns.

266   A longer-lasting form of this fashion, continuing into the 1930s, was the nursery frieze. This had developed from the late 19th-century papers which were derived, directly or indirectly, from the work of well-known childrens' book illustrators such as Walter Crane and Kate Greenaway. By 1910 many British and American manufacturers carried a range and high quality British examples were imported into the United States by companies such as W. H. S. Lloyd in New York.

Revivals

By far the best-selling friezes (and filling or sidewall papers) in the first decade or so of the 20th century were those loosely inspired by late 18th-century French decoration. In *The Decoration of Houses*, published in New York in 1897, the architect Ogden Codman, Jr, and the society hostess and novelist Edith Wharton described interiors with 'plenty of white paint, a pale wallpaper with bow knots and fragile chairs dipped in liquid gilding and covered with a flowered silk and cotton material.'[5] To accompany papers imitating silk moiré and damask there were appropriate friezes, mostly on the theme of rose and ribbon swags, with or without architectural scrollwork. A further development was the 'crown hanging' where the frieze and filling were combined in one continuous 4-yard (3.66 m) length. Roses, wisteria and ivy were thus able to tumble down the wall or climb up to form an arbour below the cornice.

The undemanding prettiness of such papers and of the simpler, pastel coloured, Classical Revival patterns enabled them to blend comfortably with a wide range of furnishings. Whilst not suitable for plain and substantial Arts and Crafts or Mission furniture, they went happily with antiques and reproductions. Above all they formed a pleasant background to the everyday Victorian pieces that most people were obliged to live with. Machine-printed for the impecunious or block-printed for the rich, their popularity was universal.

Similarly, late 18th- or early 19th-century chintzes enjoyed a comeback. Most of the old-established British block-printing firms kept chintz pattern books, presumably for rich clients who had always used such papers regardless of changing tastes. In the early 1900s a number of firms, including Lightbown Aspinall and Potters, produced some very pretty machine-printed versions. These immediately became best-sellers and encouraged the *London Journal of Commerce* to remark: 'The pendulum swings, and old-world chintzes, despised by the "greenery-yallery" school of the seventies, now appear again on the walls of the best houses.'[6] In the United States interest in such papers was fuelled by Kate Sanborn's *Old Time Wallpapers* (1905). Chintz patterns for both textiles and wallpapers were further encouraged by the society decorator Elsie de Wolfe's book, *The House in Good Taste* (1913). Although the author's attitude to wallpapers in general was extremely ambiguous, she actually used them frequently, both in her own and in other people's homes. In the period leading up to the First World War, one American firm in particular, M. H. Birge & Sons of Buffalo (New York), seems to have specialized in reproductions of old chintz patterns.

It was inevitable that the social and economic upheavals of the War should have repercussions on the wallpaper industry. Production virtually ceased in Britain and shortages of materials and labour on both sides of the Atlantic were reflected in higher prices. In Britain the reluctance on the part of the rich to use wallpaper resulted in the disappearance of manufacturers that had hitherto achieved an international reputation for excellence. Many, including Essex, Jeffrey's and Charles Knowles were absorbed by Sanderson. The loss of these small and innovative firms meant that scope for new and experimental design was much diminished. Two new monthly magazines were started, *Homes and Gardens* (1919) and *Ideal Home* (1922). Both carried regular articles on wallpaper, but readers must have been puzzled by the fact that none of the houses featured ever had papered rooms. Inevitably, the conclusion must have been drawn that patterned walls were not an ingredient of the house in good taste.

In the United States the situation was somewhat different. Whilst Elsie de Wolfe and other notable lady decorators of the 1920s and 1930s encouraged their rich clients to adopt a sophisticated version of the English country house interior, with an emphasis on expensive block-printed chintzes and silk damask, they were prepared to tolerate the use of wallpaper in their design schemes.

clockwise from far left
265 Part of a wallpaper frieze, probably manufactured by Potters of Darwen (Lancashire); surface-printed in colours, *c*. 1905. A typical rustic scene, equally popular in Craftsman bungalows in the United States and suburban 'semis' in Great Britain.

266 Design for a frieze by Harry Silver, 1904. This stylish Silver Studio pattern in Arts and Crafts style was probably intended for Jeffrey & Co. of London.

267 A 'crown hanging' from *Wallpaper Ideas*, a catalogue produced by the Robert Graves Co. of New York, 1908.

Wealthy East Coast Americans in the early 19th century had been fond of using French scenic papers, so it was possible to argue that they were part of traditional decoration. Following on from Kate Sanborn's *Old Time Wallpapers*, numerous articles on scenic and historic papers appeared in American home decorating journals. Heavy increases in taxation after the war led to the dispersal of the contents of some of Europe's grandest houses, enabling Americans to buy fine pieces of furniture, and they naturally requested their decorators to provide appropriate settings. French manufacturers such as Zuber received a welcome boost to trade in meeting the demand for reprinted scenic papers. Interest was further stimulated by the publication of Phyllis Ackerman's *Wallpaper, its History, Design and Use* (1923) and Nancy McClelland's *Historic Wallpapers* (1924). Phyllis Ackerman wrote: 'Certainly no early American house, especially in the New England style, whether it be old or modern copy, is perfect without some of the old-fashioned wallpapers.'[7]

By the late 1920s the American wallpaper industry was able to provide plausible reproductions of scenic papers for those who were unable to afford French imports. Henry Bosch, of Chicago and New York, also offered a range of copies of 18th-century Chinoiserie papers. Even the mail-order companies such as Sears, Roebuck & Co. and Montgomery Ward & Co. offered cheap but very cheerful pastiches. In Britain scenic papers, whether imported from France by Cole & Son or contemporary versions by Sanderson and John Line, were never as popular.

Post-war: papers for the mass market

In both America and (slightly later) Britain there was a post-war suburban housing boom which provided modest homes for people on relatively low incomes. It was at this end of the market that most wallpaper activity was concentrated. The big American manufacturers, distributors and mail-order firms directed their most strenuous efforts at this sector. Sophisticated sales techniques by mail-order companies ensured that the owners of houses bought in this way were conscious of the architectural style of their property – be it Cape Cod, Dutch Colonial or English Cottage. The wallpaper catalogues also sent out by these companies played upon pride of ownership by suggesting papers which would be stylistically appropriate. In Britain new homes were mainly bought by young couples anxious to escape the drab and dirty older inner suburbs. These people would not normally be readers of such publications as *House & Garden*, and their approach to decoration owed far more to mid-Victorian popular taste than to the Arts and Crafts Movement. Anaglypta or Lincrusta (if it could be afforded) was widely used in rooms which received a lot of wear and was still painted dark brown or oak-grained to hide the dirt. The British working class had grown used to having brightly patterned wallpapers and considered a room unfinished without it. It was subject to changes of fashion, of course, but the comparative cheapness allowed frequent replacement.

Throughout the 1920s cheap British and American wallpapers were similar in design. The major difference lay in the use of colour. Mass-market American papers were predominantly pale in hue, with beige, grey, light green or blue grounds, whereas in Britain there was a period of brilliant colours, and lacquer red, black and dark blue grounds. In both countries pale and pretty chintz papers were the usual form of decoration for bedrooms; in America they were also widely used in other parts of the house, and subtle differences were stressed with regard to their suitability for a particular architectural style: a coarse-textured background, for instance, was suggested for a Mediterranean revival home ('imitates Spanish palm finished plaster'[8]). Imitation tapestry papers were considered suitable for Tudor cottages on both sides of the Atlantic. By the late 1920s softened Cubist shapes were becoming increasingly common, often in the

270

269

271

upper row
268 A 'tapestry' wallpaper issued by the British conglomerate WPM; surface-printed in colours, *c.* 1925. Such patterns enjoyed great popularity on both sides of the Atlantic in the 1920s and 1930s.

269 'The Cathay', an English cut-out border by John Line & Sons Ltd; block-printed in colours, 1928.

lower row
270 A page of scenic wallpaper panels from the catalogue of Montgomery Ward & Co. of Chicago, 1932. Similar decorations were available in Britain, but they were never so widely used as in the United States.

271 Cover page of a Sears, Roebuck & Co. wallpaper catalogue, 1930. This is a typical American 'Miami Moderne' paper, surface-printed in fashionable pastel colours.

cenic Beauty For Your Walls
Ward's Great 60th Anniversary Brings You
Landscape Papers at Popular Prices

Olympia Fields—for Classic Loveliness

OLYMPIA FIELDS is our most beautiful scenic wall paper. It creates the effect of frescoed walls with the same delicacy of details and perfect coloring. See the illusion of distance—you seem to look *into* the picture to the hills beyond. Reproduced from original oil paintings by a special lithographing process on fine quality heavy paper that re-creates the original colors with authentic loveliness. Shown here with lower part of wall, or dado, papered with PERSIAN BLEND, Page 17, with band border and ceiling to match. Also effective for a panel treatment.

Comes in sets of 3 sections (shown complete above). Each section is 5½ feet high and 4 feet wide, giving a repeat of 12 feet. Sold only in sets of 3 sections. *We Pay Postage.*
576 R 64—Per set (12 feet).........................**$9.95**

Modern Homes Use Scenic Wall Papers

In your large formal rooms—reception hall, spacious dining or living room—we recommend the rare beauty of these new scenic papers. Both are reproduced from beautiful oil paintings and give the effect of frescoes on the wall. *Southern Beauty* and *November Woods* are most effectively used as a frieze at the ceiling line with a harmonizing paper of simple design such as our Blend shown on Page 17. Southern Beauty may also be used in same treatment as Olympia Fields above.

Southern Beauty Frieze
New Beauty Wherever You Use It

uriant tropical scene, with handsome palms and bright blossoms—nally rich in coloring. A gorgeous decoration for formal rooms. feet long, 40 inches wide. Picture shows one-third complete frieze. cries makes a panorama of interest and charm. Use it in large and rooms. For harmonizing sidewall pattern we suggest our 576 R 820. 576 R 794, Page 23; 576 R 776, Page 35; 576 R 800, Page 24. ee sections, 5 feet long, each different but forming continuous scene. y in sets of three sections. *We Pay Postage.*
.........................**$3.35**

November Woods Frieze
Rich Colors for Library or Living Room

November woods after the frost has wrought its color magic in trees and shrubbery. This colorful frieze brings the charm of outdoors into the room in which you use it. Nature lovers will delight in its realistic color treatment. Ten feet long, 28 inches wide. Picture shows one section of frieze.

In two sections, 5 feet long, each different but forming continuous scene. Sold only in sets of two sections. For sidewall pattern to combine with November Woods we suggest our 576 R 794, Page 23; 576 R 810, Page 17; 576 R 816, Page 15; 576 R 790, Page 26. Ship. weight 3 lbs.
576 R 60—Per set (10 feet).........................**$1.70**
6 1—Per set (15 feet).........................

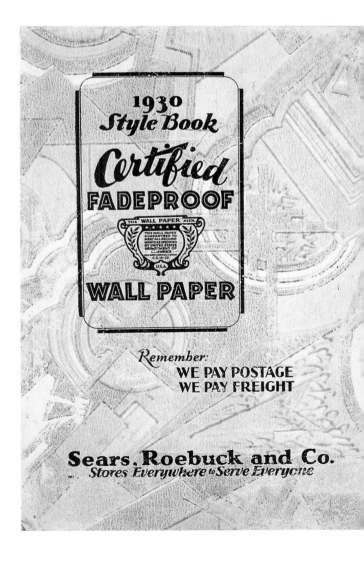

1930 Style Book
Certified FADEPROOF

THE WALL PAPER ASS'N
THIS WALL PAPER GUARANTEED TO MEET ALL REQUIREMENTS OF THE SPECIFICATIONS BY UNITED STATES DEPARTMENT OF COMMERCE C.S.16-29 U.S.A.

WALL PAPER

Remember:
WE PAY POSTAGE
WE PAY FREIGHT

Sears, Roebuck and Co.
Stores Everywhere to Serve Everyone

form of overlapping squares or oblongs, juxtaposed with sprays of flowers. Cut-out borders in geometric or floral patterns were an essential embellishment, usually hung immediately below the picture rail or cornice. Plainer, geometric borders could also be used to frame panels of imitation tapestry or scenic paper.

A notable characteristic of British wallpaper during the 1920s was the large number of novelty designs available, with richly coloured and exotic patterns for parlours, halls and staircases. Oriental subjects were particularly favoured; Arabian themes were inspired by the popularity of films such as *The Sheik* (1924); and the discovery of the tomb of Tutankhamen in 1922 resulted in a brief craze for ancient Egyptian motifs.

Papers by artists

Because of wallpaper's comparatively humble status in the 1920s few artist-designers could be bothered with it, and manufacturers, for their part, were reluctant to experiment. An artist who did venture into commercial wallpaper design at this time seem to have regretted it. The American painter Charles Burchfield worked for M. H. Birge from 1921 to 1929, largely providing scenic and landscape papers. But, although Birge was one of the best American firms and credited him on the selvedge, Burchfield wrote that the work he did there was 'directly opposed to my ideals in art'.[9]

In Britain, one artist who made an outstanding contribution to wallpaper was Edward Bawden.[10] He trained as an illustrator and calligrapher at the Royal College of Art in the early 1920s and was inspired to take up wallpapers by

272 'Robins and Crocuses', designed by Charles Burchfield for M. H. Birge & Sons of Buffalo (New York); surface-printed in colours, 1923.

273 'Conservatory', by Edward
Bawden, lithographically printed at
the Curwen Press, Plaistow (Essex),
1929.

274 Cover of a catalogue issued by
Montgomery, Ward & Co. of
Chicago, 1939. Examples are shown
of '18th Century', 'Early American'
and 'Modern' designs.

202   seeing William Morris's 'Daisy' pattern in one of the period rooms at the 1924 Empire Exhibition at Wembley. His tutor, Paul Nash, recalled that by 1925 Bawden was 'obscurely printing a series of very original wallpaper designs cut on linoleum and rather painfully printed, if I remember rightly, by foot pressure.'[11] They were subsequently lithographed by the Curwen Press, a printing company based in Plaistow (Essex). One result of this process was that they had to be produced in small sheets, like early wallpapers. Bawden's first papers were

273   highly pictorial and some, like 'Conservatory' and 'Riviera', reveal his prescient 'fondness for the Victorian scene and especially for the Victorianism of the English watering place.'[12] In his later papers this pictorial quality diminished, though they continued to draw strongly on mid-19th-century motifs. The Curwen Press commissioned four more designs from him in 1932 which were sold as the 'Plaistow Wallpapers'.

Documentaries, Victoriana, and modern

Prejudice against the use of wallpapers in the 1930s was fuelled out of motives very different from those of the earlier purists – by advocates of the Modern Movement, which was hostile to ornament in principle. Surface decoration was provided by texture rather than pattern. Nevertheless, as the decade progressed and the Depression abated, the future of wallpaper began to look brighter. In the United States a number of important and well-publicized restorations, most notably at Colonial Williamsburg (Virginia), encouraged an interest in historic wallpapers. They also featured in exhibitions at the Buffalo Fine Art Academy in 1937 and at the Cooper-Hewitt Museum, New York, in 1938. This all served to stimulate a demand for accurate copies of old papers. Nancy McClelland formed her own company, Nancy McClelland Inc., in 1939, to make reproductions from her private collection, and Katzenbach & Warren began to produce approved designs from Colonial Williamsburg. Birge issued a range based on samples in the Cooper-Hewitt. Much ingenuity was shown by manufacturers in unearthing scraps which had been used to line hat-boxes and trunks, as the possession of an interesting provenance added greatly to a wallpaper's status. All this activity can be seen as an extension of the growing interest in Victorian decoration which had its esoteric beginnings in the early 1920s and was by the mid-1930s popular with interior decorators on both sides of the Atlantic. The style was a refreshing antidote to the Modern Movement. Block-printed striped or diaper wallpapers could still be obtained from the better manufacturers and were regarded as an essential ingredient in creating a truly 19th-century effect. Importantly, sophisticated people became used to having wallpaper again.

By the late 1930s there was also a growing demand in the United States for well-designed contemporary patterns. Shows such as the Contemporary American Industrial Art Exhibition at the Metropolitan Museum, New York, in 1932 and the proliferation of home decoration journals like *Better Homes & Gardens* and *House Beautiful* promoted a general awareness of modern design. Refugees from Germany and Austria, some of whom were employed by the wallpaper industry, imported European design developments. Tommi Parzinger, whose large-scale, simple patterns based on leaf forms were very successful, worked for Katzenbach & Warren, which also employed Ilonka Karasz. Her highly figurative designs are very closely related to those of Edward Bawden, portraying stylized neo-romantic landscapes and patterns based on domestic architectural detail such as gables and porches. She had previously worked in the studio of the interior designer Donald Deskey, who was responsible for the innovative aluminium wallpaper depicting scenes from the tobacco trade for the smoking room of the Radio City Music Hall in New York. The American public was first shown the potential of large-scale abstract-patterned wallpapers at the New York World's Fair in 1939. This highly important and influential exhibi-

275 View of the exhibition of 'Bardfield' wallpapers by John Aldridge and Edward Bawden at Muriel Rose's Little Gallery, London, 1939. The papers were printed from lino blocks. Most of the patterns visible here are by Aldridge, notably 'Royal Oak' (left foreground and end wall, left), 'Moss' (end wall, right), 'Cornucopia' (right wall) and 'Lace' (far right).

tion was overshadowed by the outbreak of the Second World War, but not least of the innovations it made was to show architects and designers how wallpaper could be used in public buildings and how a demonstrative pattern could define space in domestic interiors when used in conjunction with a plain or quietly patterned paper. (This was to become a very popular decorating device in open-plan interiors in the United States and Britain in the 1950s.)

British attempts in the 1930s to market modern design for wallpapers met with limited success. The architect F. R. S. Yorke in 1932 reflected current Modern Movement thinking in rejecting wallpaper in favour of more novel treatments such as silver foil or plywood.[13] Only Sanderson and John Line made any significant progress in encouraging contemporary styling. Sanderson manufactured an elegant geometric design by the Australian-born architect Raymond McGrath, called 'Finella', which was used in the studios McGrath designed for the BBC at Broadcasting House, London, in 1932. Sanderson and John Line also produced silver and gilt abstract patterns and papers that cleverly imitated the fashionable woods of the decade such as maple or birch. Both firms prepared beautifully illustrated catalogues of their Modernist papers which were obviously aimed at architects and interior decorators.

As in the United States, there were indications by the late 1930s that wallpaper was once more becoming fashionable. John Line reissued an album of delightful early 19th-century chintz patterns and Cole & Son, previously famous for importing French wallpapers, acquired the rights to designs by Marion Dorn, though she and her husband E. McKnight Kauffer left in 1940 for the United States, where her papers were subsequently produced by Katzenbach & Warren. Coles also bought the lino blocks for what became known as the 'Bardfield' papers, produced by Edward Bawden and his friend and neighbour John Aldridge at Great Bardfield (Essex). The Second World War halted their production, but they became justifiably famous in the early 1950s when they were used at the Festival of Britain.

275, 276

276 Edward Bawden in his studio at Great Bardfield (Essex), 1939, surrounded by material related to his wallpapers. He is leaning on a partly cut lino block.

Popular papers of the 1930s fell into two categories: they were either racy Cubist patterns with their mathematical severity softened by sprays of leaves and flowers, or they were textured papers – 'porridge', as they came to be known, because of their colour and lumpy appearance – which were used in conjunction with borders. Borders during this period scaled astonishing heights of inventiveness, including corners and skirting-board friezes as well as those designed for below the cornice. They ranged from glamorous Miami Beach Moderne to semi-naturalistic trees and herbaceous borders.

Wallpaper production was halted in Great Britain and much disrupted in the United States by the Second World War. However, in Britain the movement for progressive design reform which had begun in 1915 with the formation of the Design and Industries Association finally saw its influence extended to affect national policy with the establishment of the Council of Industrial Design in 1944. This official Government body and its allies found their most effective tool in what were often brilliantly staged exhibitions. One of the earliest and most influential was the Exhibition of Historical and British Wallpapers held in London in 1945. Like its American counterparts, it set out to show the public not only the distinguished history of wallpaper but its potential in the modern house. It was imaginatively organized by T. A. Fennemore, chairman of the Central Institute of Art and Design, with the support of the wallpaper industry. Fennemore ensured the success of the exhibition by persuading the connoisseur and traveller Sacheverell Sitwell to write the introduction to the catalogue and by showing room sets by the country's leading decorators, including Cecil Beaton and Grace Lovat Fraser. Some of the best-known artists and designers of the day, among them Enid Marx, Graham Sutherland, Laurence Scarfe and Clifford and Rosemary Ellis, were asked to submit designs for wallpapers. The public, after years of 'porridge' and wartime deprivation, was enchanted with the exhibits. When the aristocracy, in the form of Mr and Mrs Reresby Sitwell, were photographed in 1947 for *House and Garden* standing in an archway of ivy leaf trellis paper, the industry knew that, once again, wallpaper had achieved its rightful position in the decorative arts hierarchy.

For the rest of the 1940s wallpaper was kept very much in the public eye through exhibitions on both sides of the Atlantic. The 'Bardfield' papers were shown at the 'Britain Can Make It' exhibition in London in 1946. In America, as we shall see in the next chapter, it was possible to translate interest into activity, but in Britain chronic shortages of materials continued until the 1950s. Despite this, the Board of Trade put great pressure on British wallpaper manufacturers to expand their American export market and thereby earn the country some hard currency. This led to the production of the 'Lancastria' set by the Lightbown Aspinall branch of the WPM:[14] the result of a close collaboration between American and British designers, these papers were to British eyes of an astonishing inventiveness. Their scale was twice that of the ordinary home-produced papers and they featured subjects such as flamboyant tropical flowers and leaves or large single roses in cartouches – designs which were to become clichés in the 1950s, but which in the 1940s were wonderfully exciting and new. Many were sold with a plainer companion paper of a simple stripe or polka-dot pattern.

Ultimately it was successful developments in screen-printing techniques during the 1940s that enabled wallpaper to embark on one of the most important periods in its history. Whilst block-printing was still carried out by a number of firms in Britain during the 1950s, it was almost extinct by the late 1940s in the United States. Instead, the comparatively low cost and flexibility of screen-printing meant that American and British manufacturers need no longer be slaves to the demands of the mass market, but could risk experimental work by young designers.

left column
277 Poster for the Exhibition of Historical and British Wallpapers held in London in 1945. The patterns shown are representative of papers by the poster's designers, Clifford and Rosemary Ellis.

278 Design for a paper by Laurence Scarfe, 1945, intended for the Exhibition of Historical and British Wallpapers. The pattern combines Surrealist and Victorian motifs.

right
279 Wallpaper from one of the 'Lancastria' collections produced by the WPM, *c.* 1950. This design is typical of the large-scale figurative papers devised for export to the United States but widely admired in Britain.

11 Post-War Promise:
Pattern and Technology up to 1970

JOANNE KOSUDA WARNER · LESLEY HOSKINS

The lifting of what the *New York Times* called the 'design freeze' in the American wallpaper industry came in November 1945. Wallpaper had been deemed a non-essential commodity by the War Production Board, and there had been a 20 per cent reduction in the number of wallpaper styles; 25 per cent reduction in the number of new patterns; 20 per cent reduction of all sheets in sample books; 50 per cent reduction in the use of critical materials; complete elimination of bronze and aluminium powder; and reduction in the weight of raw paper stock.[1] The industry had limped along during the war years, selling off most of the holdings in their warehouses. With restrictions lifted, manufacturers went into full gear to meet pent-up consumer demand.

As we saw in the previous chapter, American consumers had become accustomed to using wallpaper in their homes. It was available from a variety of sources. Retail outlets sold from sample books composed of the products of one or more manufacturers. Merchants could choose designs which would appeal to customers in their part of the country. A shop located in New England, for example, could expect to sell more 'period'-style patterns than one in California. Wallpaper was sold through decorating materials outlets, through department stores and through hardware, book and drug stores, but by far the most popular way of buying was directly from a paper-hanger. While the selection may have been limited, the convenience of choosing in your own home made it worthwhile.

The post-war spending boom, consumer attitudes, and low stocks combined to give the industry a tremendous boost. In the 1946–47 season over 400,000,000 rolls were sold, a figure equal to the entire rollage of the 1920s.[2] Manufacturers were sailing on a cloud and in 1946 instituted an industry-wide award in honour of Justin P. Allman, the first president of the Wallpaper Wholesalers Association. The historian Nancy McClelland was chosen to receive the initial Allman Award because she had 'done more than any other person to bring wallpaper to the high place which it occupies in the consumer's mind today.'[3]

The initial boomlet flagged, however, and the 1951–52 figures reported that sales had dropped to 182,000,000 rolls. Manufacturers had expected good results in the new decade based on the public's previous buying habits, but purchases throughout the 1950s never kept pace with the enormous increases in the number of new homes built, in population, or in national income. America's favourite decorating product was seen as old-fashioned, and by 1966 machine-printed output had dropped to 69,000,000 rolls. In spite of the introduction of new products and updated designs wallpaper never regained its former market share.

The industry during the 1950s was composed of some thirty-nine machine-printing companies, a handful using lithography or some special process, and some seventy independent companies hand-screen-printing, either issuing their

The United States
JOANNE KOSUDA WARNER

206

own designs or acting as contract printers for others. The market was dominated by the two largest machine-printers, United Wallpaper and Imperial Paper and Color Corporation. United was made up of factories located in Pennsylvania, New Jersey, New York and Illinois, while Imperial comprised several small producers located in New York State. Imperial's mill in Plattsburg (New York) did everything from handling the logs for the paper to printing and packaging the final product. The manufacturers produced a new line every two years (until 1960, then every year) and the consumer had a large selection of designs from which to choose. Imperial's new range for 1950 alone was composed of approximately eight hundred different patterns and colourways.[4]

For the mass market, medium- and higher-priced papers were produced by the largest manufacturers, who possessed modern machinery and could make

280 Advertisement for United Wallpaper showing surface-printed designs available to the post-war consumer in America, from *House & Garden*, April 1949.

United

Has the widest selection of beautiful patterns and colorings of any wallpaper in the world...

and...

You will find United Wallpaper in more of America's fine homes than any other brand.

Look for the seal on the back of every genuine United Wallpaper. Newest styles now available at better dealers everywhere.

UNITED WALLPAPER

INC.

GUARANTEED—Washable, Fadeproof, Wall-tested, Style-tested—as marked on the back of each quality roll.

any type. The small machine-printers, with their limited equipment, usually dealt in the low- and medium-priced papers. Machine-prints priced at $2–$6 accounted for over 90 per cent of the rollage sold in the United States.[5]

Do-it-yourself features

It was the largest companies that could afford the cost of research and development. The two technical innovations of the 1950s, vinyl and pre-pasted wallcoverings, were initiated by the giants, United and Imperial.

Vinyl wallcovering, which came of age in the 1960s, was introduced by United in 1947. Their product, 'Varlar', was composed of a printed layer of polyvinyl chloride bonded to a paper backing. (Polyvinyl chloride, or PVC, was the first plastic compound to be widely used after the war.) United sponsored demonstrations where 'Varlar' was smeared with grease, lipstick and ink and then scrubbed clean with soap and water. In 1934 Imperial had brought out a washable paper in which the starch binder or size was replaced by a protein size and the surface was given a chemical treatment after printing, but that early innovation was no match for the truly scrubbable surface of vinyl.[6]

A shortage of paper-hangers (who had moved on to other industries) and increased labour costs after the war made hanging a more expensive and difficult project than it had been. The industry responded with pre-pasted wallpaper, the other major innovation of this period. United had brought out a pre-pasted product known as 'Trimz' around 1940, but it had languished with the cut-backs. Now papers that you could hang yourself, without a mess, were again introduced. Pre-trimming the selvedges at the factory was another time-saving device, and in 1953 Imperial began to treat its entire line in this way. In 1954, its pre-trimmed, pre-pasted papers were advertised with the slogan 'Just wet and hang.'

However, there was competition from the paint industry, which cut into the wallpaper market by introducing pre-mixed colours and latex paint. Wood panelling was also seen as a desirable alternative by consumers. Do-it-yourself papers were one solution; but the consumer was even more interested in a fresh, modern look and the manufacturers weren't supplying one. In 1948 *Interiors* magazine commented: 'the manufacturers who are most satisfied with their financial condition are the same ones who have consistently pursued a daring policy with respect to design.'

Screen-printing

While the technical improvements of the 1940s–60s belong to the machine-printer, the design innovations were most frequently found in the area of handscreen-printing, which came into its own after the war. Start-up costs were low and printing inks had been improved, leaving designers free to experiment without the restrictions of the print roller and long runs. Usually compared to stencilling, screen-printing requires one screen for each colour to be printed. A frame is stretched with a synthetic fabric mesh and the negative elements of the design (which are not to print) are blocked out. The positive areas remain open mesh and ink is pushed through the holes with a rubber squeegee. The screen is moved down the length of the roll laid out on the print table, printing one colour at a time. Screens and colours are added until the design is complete. Small runs can be produced this way as well as custom colours. The labour costs of hand-screen-printing made these papers the most expensive type: in 1950 the price range was $6–$12 per roll.

Beginning in the late 1940s, a number of small specialist companies produced distinctive designs for this medium. James Seeman started his New York company in 1946 with mural designs and hand-painted and hand-screened scenics. The two-man studio of Jack Denst and Donald Soderlund started

281 'When in Rome', designed by Clarence Hawking for Denst & Soderlund; screen-printed on paper-backed silk, 1950–55.

282 Detail of 'Byzantine Curtains' by Ilonka Karasz, from the Katzenbach & Warren samplebook *Mezzotone Papers*; printed on light-sensitive paper from a full-size drawing, 1948.

302

screen-printing in Chicago in 1947. One of their first efforts was 'Totem', images of carved masks in a large repeat. In 1948 Katzenbach & Warren of New York offered screen-printed murals designed by Henri Matisse, Joan Miró, Roberto Matta and Alexander Calder. A year later, Calder designed a wallpaper and fabric for Laverne Originals of New York with a mobile-like pattern of stars, planets and the moon. In 1950 Piazza Prints of New York issued Saul Steinberg's witty 'Wedding' and 'Trains' as well as a paper depicting Raphael's decorations for the Logge of the Vatican. About the same time, Ben Rose in Chicago and Gene McDonald in New York were producing modern abstractions with titles like 'Tic Tac', 'Index' and 'Facade'.

While some companies were specifically commissioning established artists to design wallpaper, the fine arts and architecture were also a tremendous influence on young designers. Laverne Originals' Estelle and Erwine Laverne 'considered their work as fine art applied to hand crafts, and that as such it is not only a solution to the economic problem but it is a contribution to the culture of the country as well.'[7] 'Wallpaper design is more than making a living', Jack Denst asserted: 'I am concerned with the beauty of art and its effect on our civilization.'[8]

Modern effects

The *New York Times*, reviewing new wallpaper for 1949, optimistically reported that the design of the machine-prints was fast catching up with the hand-screened variety. Florals were drawn with a fresh technique and freely spaced to avoid monotonous repeats, metallic highlights were numerous and daring, and dark-coloured backgrounds (such as elephant grey, cocoa brown or teal blue) were used. The *Times* also noted: 'many of the new papers were never intended to cover all four walls of the room but rather to be used on one wall or as a single decorative panel, as hand-made papers have been for some time.'[9] To take advantage of the interest in screen-printed 'designer' papers, United produced a line in 1953 which included screen-prints and indicated the designer's name on the back of each sample.

A truly innovative firm was Katzenbach & Warren of New York. In 1948 they organized and sponsored a travelling exhibition called 'Modern Wallpaper', in which furnished room corners illustrated new effects: two different papers were used in the same room or large panels with bold designs gave drama to the spaces. Two years later William Katzenbach won the Allman Award, and in 1951 he and his wife Lois wrote *The Practical Book of American Wallpaper*, with an introduction by Nancy McClelland. The chapter entitled 'New Dimensions' discards the concept of papering a room in the same way as you would cover a box and features instead a combination of plain and papered walls.

In 1954, with their 'American Futures' collection, Katzenbach & Warren were one of the first companies to offer papers produced by the photogravure process. The design is photochemically etched onto a copper cylinder or a wrap-around plate, yielding a great variety of tone when printed. Soft watercolour effects are possible as well as fine detail. Etched rollers had been much used in the 19th century, but photo-etching was a new development. Katzenbach was hailed by *Interiors* magazine as 'Consistently avant garde in both design and technical innovations', and praised for giving his designers – who included Ilonka Karasz, William Justema and Marion Dorn – scope to exercise their talents via such technical means as photography, photo-engraving and intaglio printing.'[10]

The patterns offered to American consumers were often described in the press as unconventional, abstract or compact. What comes across most clearly is that everyone was interested in 'modern' designs. What was meant by the term was open to interpretation. According to the *New York Times* in 1948, 'A modern

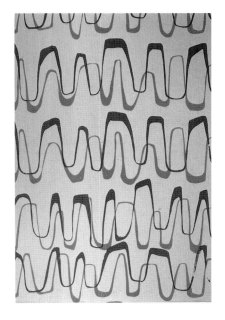

283 Screen-printed wallpaper with a 'modern' pattern of green and blue wavy lines, 1948.

284 'How to familyproof your funtime room': an advertisement for Imperial's scrubbable 'Glendura' wallcovering, from *American Home*, 1957. In this open-plan interior, kitchen and living room are distinguished by different patterned wallpapers.

design . . . might be a straw mat or a spider web, an abstract symbol of rain, or again a single flower, larger, more brilliant than any that grows in a garden. One thing it definitely is not: the old familiar line-up of morning glories or plumes marching up and down and around the walls in endless repeat.'[11] Three broad categories seem to emerge. A 'modern' design could be a traditional pattern that had been re-styled or coloured, such as damask patterns applied to grasscloth or printed in pink on a coffee ground. Patterns based on precedents in the fine arts were also very important. Finally, some papers described as 'modern' were meant to meet the requirements of modern architecture. The one-storey, open-plan house dubbed 'ranch' in 1948 was considered the 'modern' house. Built by the thousands all over the United States, these small, inexpensive homes had 'living areas' instead of separate rooms. A papered wall vied for space with the very popular 'picture windows', compelling designers to come up with novel forms (e.g., sound waves or amoeba shapes) as well as panel decorations to meet the needs of contemporary rooms.

These three forms of response by the wallpaper industry were firmly established by 1950. The designer George Nelson noted that in 1941 it had been almost impossible to find modern fabric or wallpaper but by 1949 everything had changed.[12] Education, consumer attitudes and the 'Good Design' programme, aimed at raising the general awareness of design for the home, had all affected the look of the products that were available to the post-war customer.

The New York Museum of Modern Art's 'Good Design' exhibitions produced in tandem with the Chicago Merchandise Mart, the country's largest home furnishing retail centre, raised the public's awareness of design. They were held at MOMA and at the Merchandise Mart and ran for five years starting in 1950. Edgar Kaufmann, Jr of the Museum headed a three-man jury whose other members were a designer, craftsman or teacher and an involved businessman; together they chose what they considered the most 'courageous and progressive' work emerging from the home furnishing industry. The winning entries were eligible to bear the 'Good Design' label, found on objects sold all across the country.

Problems regarding the organization's choice were reported in the October 1952 issue of the *Wallpaper Magazine*, the industry publication (later *Wallpaper and Wallcoverings*). The editors were curious as to why 'the good design selections have been restricted to the exclusive hand-screened papers in price brackets well beyond the reach of the mass of buyers'. Kaufmann replied that the jury, which relied on submissions from manufacturers, had seen too few in this area. The editors chided the industry and urged more entries: 'while other manufacturers grab at the opportunity to compete for the Good Design label, wallpaper producers have been sitting on their hands.' The next year, Kaufmann, the designer Russel Wright and the president of the Herman Miller Furniture Company of Michigan made the selections, which included United's machine-prints 'Blossom Tree' and 'Dunbarton', utilizing tree motifs drawn in a folk-art style, and M. H. Birge & Co.'s 'Thicket', a machine-print designed by Francis Mair. Also selected were Jack Denst's screen-print 'Broken Ladder' – horizontal lines interrupted by square-headed posts – and 'Facets', 'Pepitas' and 'Lines', created by the architect and industrial designer Alexander Girard for the Herman Miller Company, which came in his striking colour combinations of orange on white or magenta on light grey.

While segments of the population were exposed to a museum definition of 'good design', an even larger group were influenced by what they saw on television and in magazines. Television told people what was stylish and new, much in the same way as the movies had done for previous generations. The number of magazines devoted to the home increased and readers were treated to more colour photographs and advertising.

upper row
285 'New England', from the James Seeman Studios samplebook *James Seeman Scenics*; screen-printed by James Seeman Studios, 1951. This five-panel paper sold for $75.

286 'Angela', designed by Gene McDonald; screen-printed by Gene McDonald Inc., 1953.

lower row
287 'Marbalia', designed by Erwine Laverne for Laverne Originals; hand-marbled, 1957. The 'Marbalia' mural, first produced in 1948, had been a 1952 Good Design selection by the Museum of Modern Art, New York.

288 A surface-printed 'modern' pattern by United Wallpaper. *c.* 1955.

In 1954, *House Beautiful* gave its readers a tour through the current wallpaper scene by devoting the March issue to 'The Wonderful Ways of Wallpaper'. The editorial pages started with this copy:

Tired of the flat, grayed monotony of much of today's decoration? Enrich it with the bright, textured world of wallpaper! Lonesome for the past in your starkly modern house? Summon it back with a traditional beauty. Want to bring your period pieces up to date? Then paper your walls in a modern manner. Are your rooms too small? The new 'scenics' will give you a sense of space.

Elizabeth Gordon, the editor, was awarded the Allman Award for 1955 for her work on this issue.

House Beautiful's judgment, 'this is the decade for textures', is borne out by the many papers of the 1950s imitating textiles, woven woods, and stone, which provided a non-assertive background for pictures and furniture. In 1946, United had commissioned from the textile designer Dorothy Liebes a line of wallpaper based on her hand-loomed fabrics. The 'woven' papers were lightly embossed and printed with metallic pigments to resemble the lurex and novelty yarns that she used. At a cost of 90 cents to $1.50 per roll, they met with an enthusiastic response. In the 1950s grasscloth, tapa cloth, hemp and woodchips were used, as well as geometric designs or small evenly spaced motifs that gave the appearance of a textured surface. They blended well with other papers: a simulated tweed combined with a leafy pattern, for example, worked well in a ranch house and lent a modern feel to an older home.

Scenic or mural papers saw a resurgence as a way to give the illusion of space to shrinking rooms. They were available to cover one wall, one panel, or – by 1948 – the entire room, like traditional panoramic papers. James Seeman of New York and Albert Van Luit of Los Angeles produced a wide range whose themes ranged from Oriental subjects to Desert Highway 66. In 1948 photo-murals were introduced for the moderate budget, on wallpaper rather than on photographic stock, with scenes of the Vermont countryside and the New York skyline.

Bringing nature indoors was a preoccupation with designers, or so it seemed: leaves, trees and plants were arranged in straight lines or allowed their natural form. Vera Neumann, best known for her printed textiles, designed wallpaper for Schumacher of New York in the late 1940s. In 'Leaf Quilt', she added texture to the leaf shapes by overlaying them with lines, dots, diamonds and checks.

The Scandinavian influence, with its emphasis on nature and folk motifs, was felt in wallpaper designs in the years around 1950. The robust plant life drawn by Bent Karlby, a Danish architect, found a ready audience in America: 'Hogweed', 'Wild Strawberries' and 'Marine Fauna' were the titles of some of his imported screen-prints of the early 1950s. Because of their popularity, Schumacher presented a group of American-made Karlby designs.

The papers considered most modern by the magazines were those covered with doodles, squiggles, loops, sound waves, prisms, vertical graphs, Miró-like forms, amoeba shapes, and even flying saucers. Representing the current fascination with science, technology and modern art, these patterns were the acceptable style for a modern interior. A group of artists, architects and design-ers including Ray Eames, Salvador Dalí and George Nelson were commissioned by Schiffer of New York to design a collection of printed fabrics in 1949. In 1950 the 'Stimulus' collection was expanded to include wallpaper with designs made to relate to their fabric counterparts, not copy them. The hour-glass form in George Nelson's fabric 'Diavolo', for instance, was more widely spaced in its paper counterpart.[13]

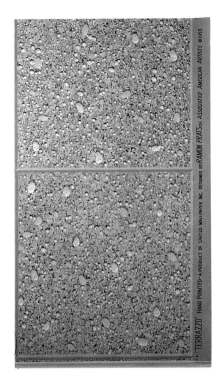

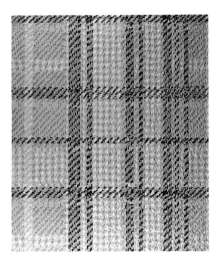

289 'Terrazzo', designed by Raymond Prats for United Wallpaper: screen-printed, 1953.

290 'Tailored Twill' from the United Wallpaper samplebook *Weaves, from Exclusive Hand-Loom Originals by Dorothy Liebes*: surface-printed in colours, 1947.

The modern screen-prints just mentioned captured only a small part of the market. Elsewhere, traditional wallpaper styles remained popular – but they were given a new twist. Damasks, Chinoiserie and country-style patterns were re-coloured or re-scaled to fit the current trends. Louis Bowen, Inc. of New York stencilled Renaissance-style floral arrangements in brown, grey or pink over white grasscloth for a fresh look. Neoclassical patterns were printed in black and white, and period designs were 'streamlined' in the quest for modernity.

Historic patterns

One type of wallpaper that did not change with the times but grew in importance was the 'documentaries', based on historic papers, which had begun to be issued before the war (see above, p. 202). Nancy McClelland, herself one of the producers, explained the thinking and process in the August 1949 issue of *Interior Design and Decoration*:

> A paper should be reproduced first in its original drawing and color as a basis for a new pattern, and all of our different papers start with the original colors. After that, we reproduce them in combinations, which, though not the original, are yet colors of the period of the paper. In that way, the papers retain the feel of a document. . . . Today, documents are more popular than ever because they are understood more in relation to their original historic background. But primarily they are bought because they are livable in all sorts and sizes of rooms, in all parts of the country.

A few companies specialized in these papers: William J. Galligan, Wilton Owen, Thomas Strahan and Hobe Erwin Editions. Others – Thibaut, Greeff, Birge and Schumacher – included document-inspired designs in their general lines. Machine- and screen-printing were used for these papers.

While a small part of the wallpaper industry was sparked by the wide range of creative designers working during this period, throughout the 1950s paper lost ground to paint and wood panelling which were heavily promoted to the consumer. The pre-trimmed and pre-pasted lines were not manufactured and promoted as widely as they could have been. But by far the biggest problem remained the public's perception of the product as old-fashioned, and sales in 1956 fell to 160,000,000 rolls. One of Imperial's designers wrote in 1958:

> We have begun to recognize that wallpaper is a style product; indeed we have been made all too painfully aware that without style it just doesn't sell. At Imperial, we have made great strides during the past two years, and one of our greatest discoveries, I feel, was that the American public has been steadily outpacing the wallpaper industry since World War II.[14]

For those concerned with the success of wallpaper, the 1960s began with the realization that change would have to come. As a start, the use of a past best-seller as an indicator of what would sell in the future was discouraged. Manufacturers and distributors increased advertising budgets and addressed the consumer directly in home magazines. And to promote its overall visibility, wallpaper was placed in advertisements for other products.

New materials and manufacturers

330

A major technical innovation of the 1960s was strippable paper, aimed at the do-it-yourself market. Several materials could supply the base: non-woven rayon fibres, or a mixture of woodpulp and synthetic fibres bonded with resin. A light vinyl film is laminated to these substrates and printed. 'Tyvek', a spun-bonded olefin, was a non-laminated printing base used by Schumacher and other companies. By 1967 mass-produced wallpaper was pre-pasted, pre-trimmed and easily stripped, and by 1969 pre-trimmed screen-prints were also available.

213

Vinyl wallcoverings had by far the biggest impact on the industry during the 1960s. A huge market opened for them in hospitals, offices and hotels. By 1965 dealers reported that they accounted for 50 per cent of sales.[15] The public was enticed by the promotion of the product and by its washability and durability. Even the Katzenbach & Warren 'Colonial Williamsburg' line was produced with a vinyl finish. The enormous growth of the vinyl market attracted large companies to the wallcoverings business. Outsiders either bought an existing company or opened a new division of their own. General Tire offered its 'Genon' collection which contained vinyl imitations of tweed, linen, silk, woodgrains and stone. B. F. Goodrich Tire offered 'Koroseal' fabric-backed vinyl in 1960. The Borden Company, later to become a giant multinational wallcoverings concern, entered the field by acquiring Columbus Coated Fabrics – originally a producer of oilcloth, later of vinyl-coated fabric – in 1961.

The technological developments of the 1960s changed the look of wallcoverings. For flock papers, the traditional wool was replaced by acrylic fibres. They were deposited on the adhesive by means of an electrostatic charge which caused the flock to stand up, resulting in a thick texture. They also made the surface washable, an important selling point in the vinyl-dominated market.

A silvery mirror-like surface for walls was supplied by 'Mylar', Dupont's polyester film, as well as by metallic foil grounds printed by rotogravure or screen-printing. They were sometimes combined with cork or flock for surface interest.

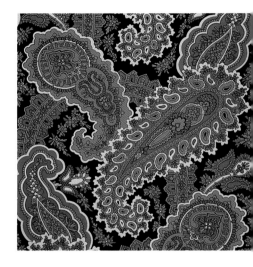

Screen-printing also underwent changes in the 1960s. Semi-automation speeded up the process by mechanically moving the screen along the print table. Rotary screen-printing is fully automatic: the screen takes the form of a wire mesh cylinder, and colour is applied through the centre of the cylinder. Such a machine can print colour at great speed, resulting in high volume and reduced cost. Flexographic printing, which was used in England during this period (see pp. 221–22), was not adopted by American manufacturers until the mid-1970s.

The hand-print look, involving flat expanses of colour, was considered fashionable and tied to the 'youth' market. The younger generation was seen as more willing than their parents to experiment with colour and pattern. *Interiors* reported in 1967 that

291

> repeat patterns are getting bolder. Colorways will be more vivid. New color palettes are emerging which include earth-tone hues, more rusts and the ever-popular no-color, black and white. Textures will be apparent in almost all collections and will range from the Mod 'wet' look to flocks on flocks, flocks on embossed grounds, or flocks on raised pigment paints. Grass cloths and weaves will still be numerous, having the added advantage of grass fibers dyed with fade resistant dyes and weaves locked in with vinyl coatings.[16]

291 'Kicky', from the United Wallpaper samplebook *Bravo – Young Ideas for the New Generation*; surface-printed and flocked, 1967–68. Most patterns in this book are large-scale, brightly coloured florals and geometrics printed on strippable, pre-pasted vinyl.

292 'Malabar', produced by Woodson Wallpapers, Inc.; screen-printed, 1968–69.

293 'Razzmatazz', designed by William Justema for the Stamford Wallpaper Co.; flocked, 1967.

During the 1960s, designers were still seeking inspiration in the fine arts, but that world had evolved into Pop and Op Art. Pop artist Andy Warhol silk-screened his own wallpaper, 'Cow', in 1966. Generally inspiration was found in the worlds of fashion, film, music and popular culture. United produced papers with the cartoon image of Batman, graffiti, American flags, and boldly coloured

293 simplified flowers. William Justema's Op Art-like 'Razzmatazz' was printed in black flocking on a white ground in 1967. Jack Denst won an Allman Award for 'Environment 15', which he characterized as a combination of high-rise and mobile murals as ready to go as the young executive generation itself.[17]

By the end of the decade, the machine-printers, screen-printers, vinyl, foil and flock manufacturers had joined forces to promote wallcoverings to the consumer. After struggling through the decreasing sales of the 1950s and the vinyl revolution of the 1960s, the industry realized that there was a future for the papered wall in American homes.

214

European wallpaper flourished in the two decades from 1950 to 1970.[1] A genuinely popular excitement about modern design in the 1950s was followed in the 1960s by the introduction of new technology which was to revolutionize the industry and its products.

The rehabilitation of wallpaper

Sales and output grew steadily during the period.[2] The interruptions of the war and the subsequent shortages of fuel and paper had created a backlog of demand which lasted into the 1950s and which was intensified by the major building and repair schemes that were undertaken throughout Europe. Housing was a particularly high priority and the baby boom of the early 1950s reflected a rush into domesticity. America was very influential, setting standards of efficient industrial production and glorifying consumption – something more attainable as the standard of living rose from the mid-1950s onwards.

All these factors contributed to a voracious market which was further encouraged by exhibitions promoting well-designed goods, such as the Festival of Britain in 1951 in London and 'H55', organized by Svensk Form in Stockholm in 1955.[3] The wallpaper industry enthusiastically participated in this method of promoting its wares and began organizing its own public displays. The French manufacturers put on 'Les Papiers peints et les décorateurs du XVIIIème siècle à nos jours' (Wallpapers and Decorators from the 18th Century to the Present) in Paris in 1953. The Deutsches Tapetenmuseum in Kassel, with the support of the German industry, maintained permanent displays and organized special exhibitions such as the 1951 'Alte und Neue Bildtapeten' (Scenic Wallpapers, Old and New). Forty-four European companies and one from the USA showed their recent work at 'ITA 60' (Internationalen Tapeten-Ausstellung, or International Wallpaper Exhibition) in Munich in 1960.[4] Individual firms also put on public exhibitions, for instance Sanderson's 'Three Arts', held in 1954 at its London showroom.

The positive response to such shows revealed a critical rehabilitation. Modernist disapproval, so damning in the two decades before the war, melted away and architects, increasingly involved in housing developments, found paper to be a useful and relatively cheap decorative finish. Patterned walls regained respectability; a wide variety of types and styles came on to the market to satisfy different tastes, classes and pockets.

294   Probably the best-selling designs throughout the 1950s were porridge and pudding patterns, almost indistinguishable from those of the 1930s. Surface-printing was the cheapest way of producing these indistinct, mottled effects, but the sturdier results of embossing (both simple and the more expensive duplex) continued to have very good sales, especially in Britain.[5] Plastic-printing was also ideal for producing all-over 'worm-cast' patterns and was especially popular in Germany, in spite of Norta Hannover's reputation for embossed papers. Introduced in the late 1930s, the basic process was similar to traditional surface-printing (see p.135) except that liquid plaster or clay was substituted for distemper to give a relief effect. Only one or two rollers were used and the machines turned slowly because of the lengthy drying of the medium. Later variations included colouring the plaster, using engraved rollers, impressing or printing into areas of still damp clay, and over-printing onto a dry surface.

At the same time traditional styles could be found everywhere. In France, firms such as essef and Follot continued to issue the tartans and realistic florals that appealed to the taste for bold patterns. Germany was less florally inclined, although the firm H. Strauven had considerable success with its pastel sketchy versions. The Netherlands had its Dutch tiles and windmills. Regency stripes and small classical motifs were fashionable in Britain in the early 1950s, especially at the upper end of the market.

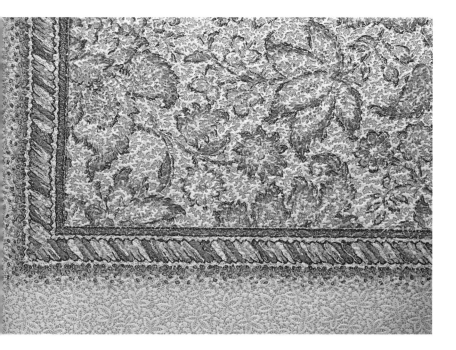

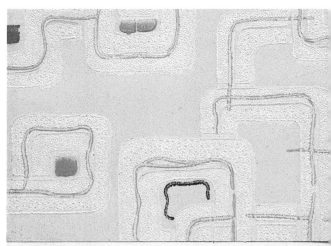

"*Polyessef*" lessivable. Réf. 6.456-P2, le rouleau 720

Despite the small size of this bedroom or bed-sitting room the decoration—in restrained contemporary style—provides plenty of interest, and encourages a feeling of cosy comfort. A neat wallpaper of modern design is combined with light-grey wall paint, and the small pictures are well placed to add to the interest of the scheme. Well-bound books in a modern bookcase complete the "picture". The ceiling could be in ivory distemper.

LE REVÊTEMENT. MURAL PLASTIQUE

lessivable

- Se pose comme le pap
  sans précaution spécia
- Se lessive comme une
  à l'huile
- Gamme complète de
  et dessins variés
- Se place dans cuisines,
  bains et endroits les plu

POLYESSE

LE REVÊTEMENT MURAL PLASTIQU

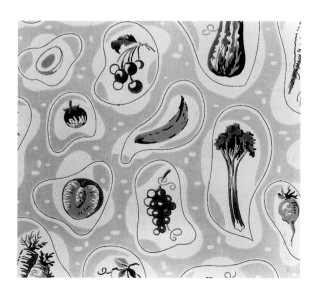

'Contemporary'

^{295–297} But the style most characteristic of the 1950s, throughout Europe, was the 'contemporary'. Now instantly recognizable as of its period, it was essentially modern, even futuristic, and its spiky, wiry attenuations could be found in fine art, architecture and all the decorative arts. In wallpaper, it usually employed a cursive, calligraphic line and small abstract or geometric motifs. Common colours were grey, yellow, red, mauve and black and the ground was often darker than the printed motifs. The slight blurring and relief of surface-printing suited these patterns well but plastic-printing was also used, especially on the Continent.

²⁹⁶ Although the 'contemporary' style emerged at the beginning of the 1950s, it took some time to gain wide currency in the wallpaper mass market. In 1952 such patterns formed only 4 per cent of British output; by 1956 the figure was 20 per cent; by the end of the decade they made up a large proportion of sales. Their popularity was given a great boost by domestic and women's magazines, themselves a growing industry. With ever more space to fill, and with an enormous readership, much of it among the younger part of the female population, the journals focused on interior decorating, both stylistically and practically. This fed the sales of wallpaper of all kinds but it gave special emphasis to the modern patterns which reproduced very well in the new high-quality colour spreads. The resulting public demand was actually a problem at first because merchants and decorators, notoriously conservative, were slow to recognize the potential of the 'contemporary', preferring to deal in known sellers. It was largely consumer demand, fuelled by the press, that led to the wider availability of the new patterns in subsequent years.

²⁹⁵ The most up-to-date way of using these often obtrusive patterns was to confine them to a 'feature' wall, with a quieter paper elsewhere. The fashion ²⁸⁴ derived from America, where it suited the large, open-plan layouts of many of the newer houses: strong designs could give decorative focus, and changes of pattern differentiated areas. The European taste for American style picked up on this scheme, which adapted well to the new housing types. Post-war exigencies imposed size restrictions but the interiors were carefully planned and often employed through-rooming or space-saving combinations of functions. Living/dining and kitchen/dining rooms, once the dubious privilege of the working classes, became usual and even fashionable.

Integrating the kitchen more closely with the living areas directed decorative attention at what had previously been seen as a utilitarian service area. The kitchen had been a focus for modernity and efficiency since the 1920s, but it was also central to the domesticity that was so important in the 1950s. Whether willingly or not, a woman's role was widely seen as that of skilled housewife and mother. In France there was legislation aimed at producing larger families. But after their wider responsibilities of the war years, it would hardly have been appetizing for women to return to drudgery in some hidden nether region. Instead, the kitchen became an integral part of the house. Cheerful kitchen ²⁹⁷ papers came onto the market, often featuring fruits, vegetables, utensils or recipes, both in the 'contemporary' vein and more realistically depicted. The inclusion of exotic species was a sign of expanding consumer horizons. There ³⁰⁰ was also a spate of travel-based patterns – wine bottles and Continental street scenes were especially popular – reflecting the availability of cheaper and easier travel and a more international outlook.

Artist and freelance designs

Mass-produced patterns were usually anonymous: that is, they were either designed in-house or were bought in from the big commercial studios, like Willy Hermann's in Berlin. But the 'Good Design' movement of the 1950s which, like the mid-19th-century Design Reform movement, aimed at improving both the standard of manufactured items and public taste, encouraged certain companies to become involved in commissioning work from artists and freelance designers. This process had started rather earlier in Sweden than in the rest of Europe, and the designs commissioned in the 1930s, most notably by Norrköpings tapetfabrik, provided a source of both motifs and style for Continental Europe when it took to pattern again after the war. The Swedish magazine *Form*[6] continued to promote the idea of cooperation between artists and manufacturers and in 1953 organized a competition for wallpaper designs. Over eight hundred entries were received. The winning design, 'Slån', by Gerd Göran, was put into production by Norrköpings tapetfabrik. But, influential as its effects had been, this kind of cooperation declined during the 1950s and by 1962 the Swedish Handicraft Union felt itself able to judge only 10 per cent of the more than six thousand current wallpaper patterns to be of good quality.

Some German manufacturers established links with art schools in the 1950s. (A similar association had occurred in the early part of the century.) For example, the Werkakademie Kassel was employed by Marburg, the Werkkunstschule in Krefeld by Rheinische Tapetenfabrik, and the Folkwangschule in Essen by Pickhardt & Siebert. Rasch recommenced its 'Bauhaus' collections in 1949. The first set was made on pre-war rollers, but from 1950 onwards new designs were added, many of them the responsibility of Hinnerk Scheper. Like the earlier ranges, they offered low-toned textural patterns.

The 'Bauhaus' collections called upon a generic design pedigree but in 1950 the head of the firm, Dr Emil Rasch, who had a strong and lasting belief in modern art as the source of good design, instituted another group of wallpapers, 'Künstler Tapeten' (Artists' Wallpapers), featuring patterns commissioned from artists and designers of international standing. The central theme of the 'Künstler Tapeten' was more the reputation of the contributors than a stylistic coherence – although all of the designs were modern and many of them could be categorized as 'contemporary'.

The more successful 'Künstler' patterns were often produced not by 'fine' artists but by freelance designers, a number of whom were mainly active in the textile industry, where there was a longer tradition of commissioning outsiders. 'Studie', for example, first issued in 1950 and re-issued time and again, was the work of Margret Hildebrand, the best-known designer in post-war Germany. Lucienne Day, who had a similar reputation in Britain, contributed six designs, displaying her characteristic control of line and space. Finely outlined cityscapes or groups of figures (motifs which also often appeared in anonymous patterns) formed a significant part of the earlier series. Designers working in this idiom included the Germans Tea Ernst and Cuno Fischer, the Frenchman Raymond Peynet and the Japanese-American Shinkichi Tajiri.

Heightened public awareness of 'design' in the 1950s meant that the promotional value of these collections (and of others like them throughout Europe) outweighed straightforward sales considerations. Salvador Dalí's 'Don Quixote' (*c.* 1960), for example, though eye-catching, was not a bestseller.[7] The company's press department worked hard at keeping the designers in the public eye, putting on 'Künstlerisches Schaffen – Industrielles Gestalten' (Artistic Creation – Design in Industry) in 1956. This was a significant exhibition which showed the papers alongside paintings, sculptures and other design work by the contributing artists. Although only a relatively small part of Rasch's total output, the 'Künstler Tapeten' enhanced the reputation of the company as a whole.

Similarly, Marburg employed Elsbeth Kupferoth, another very successful and high-profile young German designer, to style and contribute to the influential 'Neue Form' (New Form) collections of the early to mid-1950s. Her designs, with their scratchy verticals, were extremely popular and led to many imitations.

below
298 'Studie', designed by Margret Hildebrand for the 'Künstler Tapeten' range produced by Gebrüder Rasch of Bramsche; surface-printed, 1953/54. This version is in black and white.

opposite, left and right columns
299 'Slån', designed by Gerd Göran and produced in Sweden by Norrköpings tapetfabrik; surface-printed on embossed paper, 1953.

300 'Paris', designed by the sculptor Shinkichi Tajiri for the 'Künstler Tapeten' range by Rasch; surface-printed in colours, 1953/54. Cosmopolitan motifs presented in delicate line were a marked feature of 1950s patterns.

301 'Colophon', designed by Elizabeth Griffiths for the second 'Palladio' collection, produced by the Lightbown Aspinall Branch of the WPM; hand-screen-printed, 1957. A large-scale architectural paper whose lines suggest the effects of traditional woodcuts.

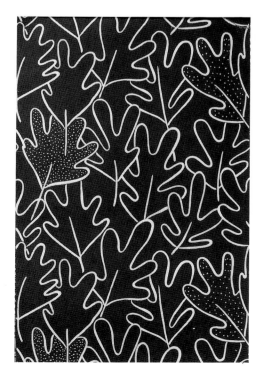

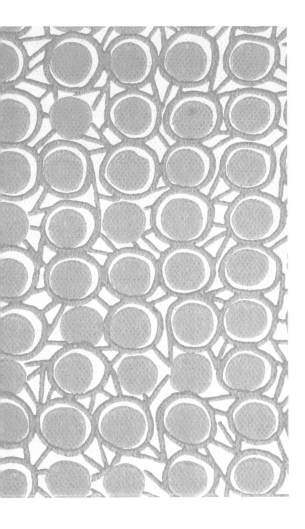

Later, 'Neue Form' was edited by Professor Kurt Kranz of the Hochschule für bildende Künste in Hamburg.

Some 'designer' papers were more impersonal and modernist. The Swiss company Salubra in 1959 issued a second set of Le Corbusier papers (the first had been put out in the early 1930s) which employed abstract geometric shapes that built up into interchangeable patterns. In the Netherlands, between 1951 and 1959, Rath & Doodeheefver brought out the 'Goed Wonen' (Better Homes) collections. Goed Wonen was an organization that had been set up in 1946 to improve standards of everyday design and over the years its members contributed to the pattern books which took its name.[8] Without repeats and using only low colour contrasts, the designs, like their 'Bauhaus'-type predecessors, were predominantly abstract. They were therefore very practical – easy to hang and slow to mark – but also fitted into an 'architectural' approach to interiors that valued unity of space and the essential structure over surface decoration.[9]

Although they were usually more expensive than the run-of-the-mill studio patterns, in Continental Europe the designer papers were almost always machine-produced. This required a substantial investment in tooling up and it argues for a belief both in the principle of industrial art and in the commercial power of good design.

In Britain, however, the more special patterns tended to be hand-printed, sometimes by woodblock but increasingly by the silk-screen process that was introduced into the wallpaper industry in the late 1940s. Silk-screening was slow but had low origination costs and used cheap (female, semi-skilled) labour. It was therefore ideally suited to producing short runs which could be sold at the upper end of the market. The influential 'Limited Editions' collection issued by John Line in 1951 used this method alongside block-printing. It included patterns by artists and freelance designers such as John Minton, Jacqueline Groag and Lucienne Day and was also innovative in providing quieter companion papers to be used in a decorative scheme alongside the more demonstrative patterns. John Line was a keen participant in modern design and was the wallpaper manufacturer chosen to participate in the Festival of Britain scheme to use motifs drawn from crystal-structure diagrams.[10]

British artist and designer work in wallpaper was often more 'personal' than its Continental counterpart and the silk-screen process was ideal for keeping the effect of the artist's own marks, thus giving the impression of handicraft as much as of factory production. The early 'Palladio' collections, much admired as examples of the best in modern design,[11] made full use of this effect. 'Palladio' was issued every two years, from 1956 until the late 1960s, initially by the Lightbown Aspinall branch of the WPM, later by Sanderson. Conceived by Lightbown's director, Richard Busby, and styled until 1963 by the freelance designer Roger Nicholson, they were sets of large-scale designs, intended for use by architects in public buildings. Colours were usually strong and elegant: in the 1950s greys, whites, maroons and dark greens were typical. Most of the patterns were commissioned from freelance designers and there was considerable variation in style, with textural versions of the 'contemporary' ranged alongside representational illustrative patterns. In the latter category were a number of designs celebrating the English countryside and traditional popular art, a celebration which was one of the main themes of the Festival of Britain and which, through the work of artists like Edward Bawden, Enid Marx and Barbara Jones, had become an important part of British pattern-making in the early 1950s.[12]

New products and processes

Wallpaper sales in the 1950s were also boosted by the growth of do-it-yourself and by moves towards an American style of help-yourself retailing which put more emphasis on display than on specialist services. Manufacturers introduced

302

301

302 Silk-screen-printing at Sanderson's factory at Perivale (Middlesex), *c.* 1960. For a description of the process, see p. 210.

a number of new products intended to make things easier for the amateur paper-hanger. Many of them came from the USA, but in Europe they were usually pioneered in the UK where DIY arrived earlier than on the Continent.[13] Easy-mix wallpaper pastes were available from about 1953. Trimming the selvedges off papers was never an easy job, even for professional paper-hangers, and decorators' shops would often do this for their customers; in the mid-1950s the manufacturers themselves stepped in, offering semi-trimmed papers. These were perforated along the selvedge which, when struck smartly against the side of a table, was supposed to come away cleanly. But they were never completely satisfactory and fully trimmed papers were introduced in about 1960. The display requirements of retailing made it preferable to produce rolls of wallpaper wrapped in clear film for protection, with the pattern visible on the outside. (Traditionally, they were rolled pattern in.) The decorating trade grumbled that papers treated in this way kept rolling up on the pasting table, but it eventually became standard practice. In 1961 the WPM introduced the first British ready-pasted papers and in the late 1960s several manufacturers were bringing in easy-strip, laminated papers which allowed the top, patterned layer to be peeled off when re-decorating. The remaining layer could be left on the wall or easily removed by damping and scraping in the normal manner.

One particularly important matter was 'washability', which in North America was already standard. Different levels of washability were required for different markets. At one end, a wipable surface that allowed the fingerprints and paste marks of the amateur paperhanger to be removed was all that was needed. One way of achieving spongeability was to give ordinary surface-printed papers a waterproof coating. This had previously been done with varnish (as in the case of the old 'sanitaries'), but new vinyl resins or latex derivatives had the advantage of not yellowing with exposure to light. Such coated papers were available from the early 1950s. Rasch's 'Lotura' range, imported from Sweden, was one example. By the later 1960s almost 30 per cent of British wallpapers were reckoned to be washable.

Newer, and more of a challenge in the contracts field, where there was a call for really tough, scrubbable finishes, were various kinds of vinyl wallcoverings. These had particular success in Switzerland, Britain and the Netherlands, which developed products like 'Suwide' and 'Balacuir'. Many of them were fabric-backed and were produced by companies who were diversifying out of floor-coverings or leathercloths into wallcoverings. The early versions were tough and thick, often self-coloured, usually embossed but sometimes printed. Their disadvantage was that they were heavy, stiff and expensive. This prompted ICI (which had had some success in the UK with its fabric-backed product, 'Mural Vynide') to adapt the technology to make something more like wallpaper. By 1961 the company was producing 'Vymura', a paper coated with PVC and then printed with specially developed inks. It was originally aimed only at the contract market but soon expanded very successfully into the domestic arena. It had no direct competition for several years and its early designs show a freedom from commercial restraint which later disappeared.

Such vinyl papers were never popular on the Continent but the printing technique they employed – photogravure – was one of the two new methods introduced in the 1960s which soon almost entirely ousted traditional technology.

Photogravure printing uses metal rollers, photochemically engraved with tiny cells of a regular size, the depth of the cells controlling the intensity of colour produced. Each roller is furnished with colour by an ink roll or spray, and a doctor blade scrapes its surface clean, leaving ink only in the engraved cells. It then turns against a rubber cylinder which presses the paper, passing between the two, into the engraved cells to take up the colour. The second new process, flexographic printing, was introduced at much the same time. Similar in princi-

New processes:

Photogravure

& Flexographic

ple to traditional relief or surface-printing, flexo employs rubber rollers and oil-based colours. The economic superiority of the new processes ensured their success. They saved on the cost of materials by depositing only a very thin layer of colour which could be dried quickly, thus enabling the machines to run very fast. At a time when sales were still rising, production costs and performance in a large and competitive market were very important.

1960s styling

The new methods gave a smooth, cool, even finish, very different from the blurry impasto of surface-printing. It now became possible to lay areas of transparent colour over each other; the engraved dots of gravure could produce shading and an infinite range of mixed colours from a limited number of printing inks. The resulting rather flat, impersonal effects were in tune with general developments in popular taste. Widespread interest in 'good design' had very much declined by the middle of the 1960s and wallpaper manufacturers were again getting most of their patterns from their own studios. Although Rasch was still producing its 'Künstler Tapeten', by 1964/65 it was no longer naming the designers. 'Palladio' continued to give names, but the personal artists' marks which had been so much a feature of the earlier patterns largely disappeared in favour of large, less textural, areas of bright colour. The papers in 'Palladio Mondo', an offshoot machine-printed collection introduced in 1962, were anonymous.

The 'contemporary' had all but gone by the end of the 1950s and no predominant style took its place. The post-war modernist ideal of 'functional' and enduring design was challenged by consumerism and built-in obsolescence. 'Why can't the public have what it wants?' asked the design critic Reyner Banham.[14] What the public got, in wallpaper, was a mixture. The WPM's best-selling design was a sketchily realistic blue rose. Sanderson's new 'Triad' collections, issued biennially from 1962 onwards, offered patterns ranging from crayonny abstracts through spiky teazles to 'Victorian' sprigs and floral trails. The importance of 'Triad' lay not so much in its designs as in its introduction of 'coordination' (a package of feature wallpaper, companion pattern and associated printed fabric) to the middle market (see below, p.231). Even Rasch, so dedicated to modern design in the 1950s that old samples and commercial examples were not allowed in the design studio, complemented its modern ranges with 'Country', a coordinated collection including traditional stripes and 19th-century rosebuds. Perhaps the most characteristic feature of 1960s patterning was the well-spaced arrangement of motifs, often with a vertical emphasis, on a bright white ground.

The 'architectural' market was now making more use of a wide range of textiles and natural materials – canvas, hessian, corks, woods, woven grasses and so on – laminated onto a paper backing. Like the earlier large-scale patterned papers, they were often confined to one feature or wall in a room. At the same time, gravure printing combined with photographic techniques of designing and engraving could produce extraordinarily realistic imitations of these effects at a fraction of the cost. Imitating other materials has always been a function of wallpaper, but the new processes gave it renewed popularity. Textile, wood and stone patterns were used everywhere in the house; tiles, mosaics and marbles were more often confined to kitchens and bathrooms.

Youth was potent in the culture of the 1960s and wallpaper manufacturers were anxious to capture the elusive young customers, tempting them with collections like 'Rave' from John Line, 'Carnaby' from Rasch and 'Scene' from the WPM. Many of the new designs reflected the art and activities of the young. There were patterns with the colours and forms of Pop Art and Op Art. The Beatles and the Flintstones made an appearance. Art Nouveau was rampant in graphics and fashion and the whiplash curves of the 1890s appeared with

303 Page from a WPM log book showing surface-printed papers with a washable coating, early 1960s. Several of the patterns are obviously intended for kitchen or bathroom use. The blue rose design in the column on the right (A28738), issued by the Allan Cockshut branch, was one of the best-sellers of the period.

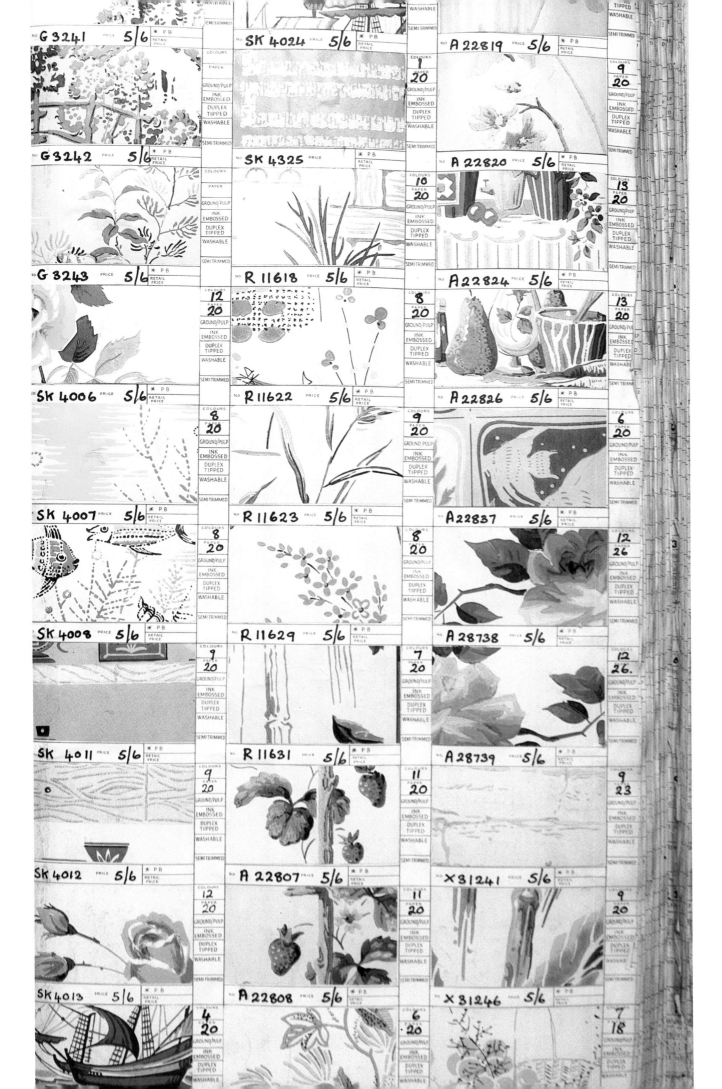

considerably less delicacy of line on textiles, bags, wrappings and, of course, wallpaper.

Youth culture was especially strong in Britain and had less effect elsewhere. For the most part, Continental wallpaper design in the early part of the decade showed no strong theme and little colour. Two collections of the late 1960s marked a clear change: Salubra's 'Style-Folklore' and Marburg's 'Arte'. The most popular design in the latter had huge sunburst circles arranged regularly on a rectangular grid, in strong, tone-on-tone colours. Giant circles and waving vertical bands soon gained a very wide currency. It was partly the influence, once again, of Scandinavian design, which was now impressing the rest of Europe with the big, bright, geometric patterns of its textiles and Rya rugs. A mixture of ethnic or traditional craft styling with obviously industrial products was a characteristic feature of more fashion-conscious interior decoration: these wallpapers were often shown with white plastic furniture and stark white paint. Although the first 'Arte' set was surface-printed, the subsequent widespread adoption of new printing technology contributed to the promotion of such designs: one of the things that flexo and gravure did best was to print large, flat areas of overlapping colour at low cost.

In contrast to the sheer mass and variety of the production of the major manufacturers, a number of small companies seized the chance to offer papers of a clearly identifiable individuality. In France, Mauny had been block-printing fine wallpapers (many of them for export to America) since the 1930s. Patterns introduced in the 1960s used modern imagery and names – 'Chelsea' and 'Cosmos', for example. Nobilis had been set up in 1928 (from 1942 in association with Suzanne Fontan) and continued producing its soft, fresh, traditionally-based patterns. Manuel Canovas and Jean Vigne both started issuing papers in 1967 in Paris and, in London, Osborne & Little's first collection came out in 1968. These three new companies all used the silk-screen method to produce short runs of unusual patterns for a sector of the market which, in the 1950s, had been served by the major manufacturers themselves.

But now the big companies were concentrating more on technical innovations than design. Later, as we will see in the next chapter, the very excellence of the new technology contributed to the overproduction that was to bedevil the industry. They were also facing the beginning of changes in the organization and structure of their industry. Everywhere, retailers and wholesalers were growing larger and more powerful. The situation was especially acute in Britain where the Monopolies Commission ruled that the giant WPM should discontinue the restrictive trading arrangements and retail price maintenance that had enabled it to dominate the industry since the turn of the century. Shortly afterwards, in 1965 the WPM was taken over by the Reed Group and subjected, unwillingly, to a programme of rationalization and centralization. Nonetheless, it was the newcomer Coloroll and new methods of marketing that were to dominate the 1970s.

305

308

opposite, left column
304 The illustrations in pattern books ('lithos', in the trade) became increasingly 'inspirational' during the 1960s. This British example shows an Art Nouveau pattern in youthful and fashionable colours, issued *c.* 1970 by Shand Kydd, which was now operating as part of the WPM under the ownership of Reed International.

305 Litho showing 'Messina' from Marburg's 'Arte' collection, designed by Brigitte Doeg and coloured by Hilde Eitel; surface-printed, 1968/69. Fabrics to coordinate with the papers were available through textile specialists.

opposite, right column
306 Machine-printed wallpaper issued by Crown (WPM) in 1969/70. The bright colours on a brilliant white ground, the stylization and the spacing were an appeal to the young market.

307 Imitation textile paper by Marburg; photogravure-printed on an embossed ground, *c.* 1965.

308 'Chelsea', by Mauny of France; block-printed in aquamarine on white, 1962.

225

12 Off the Shelf:
Design and Consumer Trends since 1970

MARY SCHOESER

In search of high-volume sales – or 'bread-and-butter' lines – the wallpaper industry entered the 1970s with great optimism.[1] With their flat, sleek styling, the bright, large-scale patterns of the early 1970s seem far removed from the 'country' and 'document' florals or low-key textures and 'unis' that characterize the popular designs of more recent years. Yet developments of the early 1970s set the stage for subsequent changes, which in many respects can be seen as reactions both to the scale of the more outlandish early 1970s designs and the 'gung-ho' mood of the industry in the same period.

309. 310

The first few years of the 1970s were bright in every respect, with growth in sales coupled with creativity in both design and production techniques. These trends could be found in large and small manufacturers alike; although Vymura's once dominant share of the market for paper-backed vinyls (see above, p.221) had already dropped to 35–40 per cent, in their studio Robin Gregson-Brown and his team of some dozen designers and colourists had two years in which to produce each new pattern book of 120–150 designs, a luxury that was not to last out the decade. In 1972 in Germany, Marburg issued a range of wallpapers designed by the artists Otmar Alt, Werner Berger, Allen Jones, Peter Phillips, Niki de Saint-Phalle, Jean Tinguely and Paul Wunderlich, and at the same time was perfecting a method of laying vinyl on paper that was to rival Vymura's. Catering to a much smaller market, Osborne & Little in England solidified their reputation for hand-screenprinted innovative designs and by about 1976 had generated sufficient demand to warrant the transfer of all but their border production on to flexographic machines. Jack Denst Inc. in Chicago was well known for Denst's bold, graphic murals and wallpapers and was custom hand screen-printing from a selection of 1,000 colours. (With the cost of, for example, red ink rising from about $10 then to $70 now, this has been reduced to 175 colours, matched to the Formica range.)

311

The early 1970s' brightness was expressed literally in the enthusiasm for metallic surfaces, which had begun late in the previous decade. Vinyl-coated foil, paper-backed foil and Mylar (developed as a protective covering by NASA) were printed with a variety of mainly dark-toned geometric patterns, although Winfield Design Associates, a San Francisco-based firm which in 1972 applied for an American patent for its foil-paper lamination process, also produced more elaborately patterned Klimt-like 'incandescent' designs by Ted Ramsay, as well as foils textured with what they called an 'arcane mineral powder', producing the effect of a metal patina. Largely American-led, this fashion also incorporated witty collections such as 'Love Stories' of 1977, in which Jack Denst included a Mylar printed with dollar bills called 'Alimony'.

312

313

Mylar, foils and metallic pigments found a niche in the European decorators' repertoire, especially via Paris, where the Boutique Américaine had represented American manufacturers since 1967. There were also numerous ranges that included designs printed on plain paper grounds with metallic pigments, as well as solid-colour metallic-printed papers or unadorned foils. All were relatively expensive and were therefore typically found in hotels, restaurants, nightclubs and retail outlets. But they also married well with the taste for richly toned interiors, whether sparsely furnished with glass, chrome and leather in the late International Style or crammed with the more exotic, Bohemian accessories as epitomized by the new Biba shop, opened in London in late 1973 and described at the time by *Vogue* as 'a Nickelodeon land of Art Deco with potted palms and mirrored halls'.

The Art Deco revival had begun in the mid-1960s, when it was part of the tongue-in-cheek Pop idiom. By the early 1970s the momentum of Pop was still apparent in wallpapers, whether in designs incorporating photo-realism, the bold outlines and enlarged dots of Roy Lichtenstein's 'comics', or simply the

309, 310 Vymura's 'Peony' of *c.* 1970 (shown in a roomset and in detail) is typical of many of the bold bright paper-backed vinyls which dominated the British market at the time. It was designed in the Vymura studio, headed by Robin Gregson-Brown.

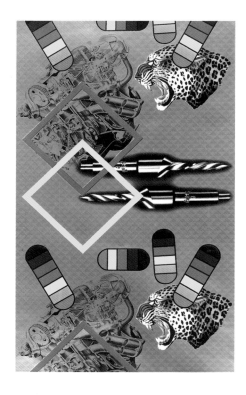

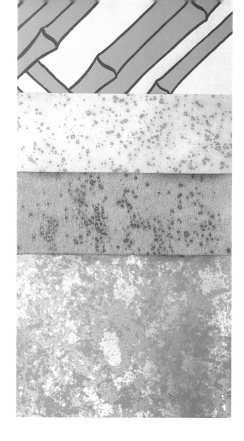

311 'Kenya' by Peter Phillips, one of the 'xartwall' series of artist-designed wallpapers produced by Marburg of Germany in 1972. Its six colours are gravure-printed on a base of aluminium steamed polyester foil, laminated onto paper.

312 This selection of wallcoverings of the 1970s by Winfield Design Associates of San Francisco includes foil/polyethylene/paper laminates intended to simulate aged metals. At the top is 'Bamboo Pavilion' (1972), at the bottom 'Lunado' (1976). Most of the firm's designs of this period were created by David Winfield Wilson.

313 'Alimony', designed by Jack Denst of Chicago in 1977, depicts enlarged dollar bills hand-screen-printed on bronze Mylar. It is shown in Denst's own house.

opposite
314 The 1970s trend towards 'personality' advertising is summed up by this example from Sanderson of Britain, whose successful 'VIP' campaign ran from 1973 to 1977. In 1975 the actress Susan Hampshire was associated with 'Kenzan', a screen-printed vinyl.

315 massive scale that created an all-encompassing effect. Even traditionally styled papers were subject to these trends, with the Chinoiserie patterns so favoured by decorators often sporting birds 18–24 inches (45–60 cm) high. However, by the mid-1970s the big bold style was being transformed by the wave of romanticism that favoured tiny florals.

The narrowing of the gulf between fashion and interiors was a lasting legacy of Pop Art, which also blurred the line between commercial and fine art. At the same time, fashion and interiors were merging in a more literal sense, as a result of the entry of a number of fashion designers into licensing agreements with bedding manufacturers. Economic pressures towards diversification also encouraged wallpaper firms to expand into furnishing fabrics and fabric firms to do the opposite. And finally, the changed expectations brought about by the introduction of all-colour magazines and colour television underpinned the gradual move from striking contrasts – easily read in black-and-white – to colours either paler or more closely related in intensity. All these factors began to have a real impact on design in the early 1970s and shaped the history of wallpapers and wallcoverings over the next two decades.

Textures and florals

The course of design since 1970 is not a straight line. If the fashion for retrospective styling can be traced to the second half of the 1970s, so too can the liking for texture and a 'natural' look. Associated with the 'executive' interiors of the 1960s, in the next decade newly styled and coloured textile wallcoverings and laid papers, suedes and imported Korean grass cloths (for which Nobilis in France became well known) were important – even if statistically small – options. Their textural and tonal qualities were imitated by many manufacturers of mass-market wallcoverings, even well into the 1980s.

Many makers of textile wallcoverings and laid papers (in which a loose-weave cloth such as hessian, or parallel yarns in the case of laid papers, are laminated to a backing) were weaving companies, a number of whom were North 316 European, such as AB Kinnasand Wallcovering in Sweden or Bekaert Textiles in Belgium (both of which still operate today). Small suppliers of these and other specialist wallcoverings found success in the 'architectural' markets – notably

Very Susan Hampshire, very Sanderson.

top and above
315 A Pop floral pattern created by the British designer John Wright for Jojo Paper Co. Ltd of Japan in the early 1970s. The illustration in the firm's pattern book reflects the connection with London fashion designers such as Barbara Hulanicki of Biba and Mary Quant.

316 A 1990s version of Novalin, a craft-based paper base laid with 100 per cent linen yarns. By Kinnasand of Sweden, it is now treated with a flameproof coating, but has otherwise remained unchanged since 1979, when it began to be distributed by Turner Wallcoverings Ltd, London.

317 The mural 'Envol' ('Taking Flight') was first hand-screen-printed by Zuber of France in 1974. Background-only panels could be added to extend it on either side.

Italy, Scandinavia, Germany and Japan. These are countries in which little distinction is made between the domestic and contract markets, perhaps because the same countries promote an interior and architectural design style that demonstrates a great interest in walls as solid elements in interior structures and, in addition, maintain a lively debate about modern design. One such international distributor based in Britain was Helen Sheane, whose woollen-yarn laid papers were made in Yorkshire on machines invented by the French architect Jean Pierre Teroy. She recalls that her firm, established in 1971, had their best year with laid papers in 1976, just as very thick yarns were becoming thick-and-thin. (The yarns became finer as the fashion faded in the later 1980s.)

In their pursuit of substance or surface qualities, such 'architectural' papers were sustained by the same impetus that had favoured the metallics; they therefore offered an alternative to a coexisting strand of design which concentrated on pattern. Both tended to integrate wallcoverings into the interior in a way which gradually began to erode the idea of the 'statement' wall. Even murals became extremely muted, as can be seen in the a-historical designs such as those produced by Nobilis, Zuber and Jack Denst and made for modern 'architectural' interiors throughout the 1970s and beyond. The key to the latter development rested in the changes occurring in floral designs.

There had, of course, always been floral-patterned wallpapers, but those of the second half of the 1970s often had several distinguishing characteristics: they were simple, stylized patterns arranged close together in an easily read repeat, often in a limited number of colours. As the decade progressed the patterns became smaller, and the colours, whether pale or dark, became increasingly chalky (with the American versions always a bit brighter, as epitomized by Schumacher's 'Waverley' range of 'calico' patterns on a clear ground).

Co-ordination and retrospective styling

Initially these florals were not viewed as 'period' designs, but were part of a general trend which also favoured more demure geometric patterns based on, and often consisting solely of, trellis or scale networks. Such small geometric or floral patterns were the basis of collections issued across Europe and North America, although latterly the floral variety have become closely identified with Laura Ashley in England, who began to issue wallpapers in about 1973 as an adjunct to an established range of printed fabrics. In this Laura Ashley was not

230

unique, but the firm capitalized on a practice previously the province of the international 'decorator' market, where designs were generally derived from fabrics. Under the old system, the consumer relied on a decorator or specialist-shop owner for knowledge of companion fabrics, paid well for the match, and often waited weeks for delivery. This was the system under which Sanderson's 'Triad' coordinates (launched in the previous decade) managed to establish the middle-market appetite for matching wallpaper and fabric. Even when, in England, Designers' Guild (founded in 1970) introduced wallpapers in 1975 and Osborne & Little added fabrics a year later, the higher price and relatively limited number of purchase points (and the more adventurous designs) meant they had little impact on the mass market.

320

That was to arrive in the form of 'Dolly Mixtures', the landmark small-floral collection designed by Linda Beard and issued by Coloroll from 1978. John Wilman joined the firm in the following year and consciously took the range to the mass market through the large do-it-yourself warehouses or 'sheds' such as Texas (a business concept new to Britain and itself derived from the American mass-merchants such as K-Mart and Target). By the early 1980s Coloroll had the most popular of the British mass market wallpaper + fabric ranges (the fabric came in the form of ready-mades), and was developing a strong presence in America and, through Cofac, in France. When introduced, the papers sold for just over £1 per roll, which can be compared to the average price in 1976 of £14 for an imported Winfield foil.

321

Exactly matching fabric and wallpaper also became a dominant feature of interiors in France, the Netherlands and North America. The largest manufacturer in the United States, Imperial Wallcoverings, was taken over by Collins & Aikman Corporation in 1971, and the latter's large fabric group led naturally to the issue of coordinated papers and fabrics in about 1975. This coincided with the period when, at least at Imperial, wallcoverings ceased to be a commodity (closely related to paint) and began to be viewed as a fashion product. The marriage of fabrics and papers enhanced this process. It also placed papers – often – in a secondary position, with their design dependent upon the initial selection of fabric ranges. In 1982 the chief executive of Sanderson (still at the forefront in the supply of coordinated ranges for the middle market) explained: 'We are changing the emphasis of the company from being a wallpaper company which used a coordinated fabric to being a fabric company which uses a wall-covering co-ordinate.'[2] And so it is for many coordinates today.

318–323

The all-encompassing use of a single pattern for fabric and wallpaper reached its peak in the late 1970s, and laid the ground for more complex forms of coordination, in which elements of a collection were related through colour, theme and the designers' handwriting, rather than by exact match. Sanderson abandoned the straightforward coordination of 'Triad' for the more diverse 'Options' collections from 1980 onwards; like many other companies, Imperial found success with its three- and four-part collections in which the main pattern was accompanied by a plainer coordinate, a very small 'toss' pattern of related florals, a border, and one or more fabrics to match or blend with the group.

Once fabrics had become part of the picture, the stage was set for the development of 'bed-led' design. This trend was helped by the more widespread introduction of central heating, which made bedrooms habitable by day (although it also made redecorating less frequent in the family rooms formerly heated by coal- or wood-burning fires). Coordinated collections for children's and teenagers' rooms became commonplace as the study of niche markets became more sophisticated, and as the 1980s progressed, licensed designs of cartoon and comic book figures jostled for attention with designs originating from manufacturers' own studios. Bed-led design for adults turned from the traditional feminine florals vs 'For Men Only' (one of the Linda Beard/Coloroll collections that

323

318 The decorator look was made easy in Katzenbach & Warren's 'Welcome Home' collection of 1985–89, which included 'Eastborne' (with a matching fabric) and 'Bamboo' in the entryway.

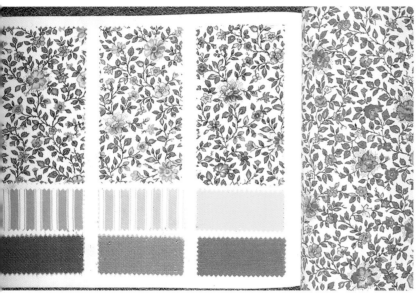

sold well in the early 1980s) to unisex designs in stripes, abstracts or classical patterns. It also required a greater emphasis on point-of-sale displays. This development enhanced the ability of manufacturers and retailers to sell their more complex collections, which might include lamps, tablecovers and painted furniture as well as curtains, bed and duvet covers, wallpaper and borders.

Borders, produced throughout the 1970s, became a more prominent decorative feature in the 1980s. They sported a wide range of patterns, but were particularly promoted as a feature of 'document' patterns that came to the fore in the 1980s, whether hand-block-printed by the long-established firms of Cole & Son and Sanderson in England and Mauny and Zuber & Cie in France, hand-screen-printed in America by Schumacher and Bradbury & Bradbury (founded in 1979 in California especially to provide period papers), or made available through the many decorators and wholesale furnishings firms who embraced this style. After about 1985, bold *trompe-l'oeil* drapery designs distinguished the exclusive ranges from the mass-market 'document' patterns, and were closely identified with Zuber, who, through hand-screen-prints, increased their provision of old patterns.

Interest in wallpapers of the past is clearly demonstrated by the amount of hand-screen-printing which has been reintroduced into the industry by both old and new companies. This interest has been reflected in, and fostered by, an increasing number of books and of articles in magazines for general circulation, and it received further encouragement by the establishment of groups such as Britain's Wallpaper History Society in 1986 and the Association des Amis du Papier Peint in France in 1990. Museum collections and their curators, particularly those in Germany, France, the United States and Great Britain, have been active in promoting a serious reassessment of the importance of wallpaper – not only in period rooms but as an element in the history of manufacture and consumption generally.

Plains and reliefs

With so much seductive pattern on walls today, it is easy to forget that painted plain or textured walls were fashionable throughout the period. For wallpaper manufacturers this meant an increase in woodchip paper sales until the late 1980s (and a continued rise to this day in some markets, such as Germany, where Erfurt is Europe's largest woodchip paper producer). A parallel boom occurred for the manufacturers of embossed and textured 'whites', intended to be painted; these, for example, accounted for about one-third of Crown Wallcoverings' 1977–88 sales. Vinyls and papers with stippled, dragged and marbled effects – many introduced in the early to mid-1980s as companions to design-laden papers and borders – retained their popularity into the 1990s.

The provision of textured papers relied on the survival of the old embossing technique and on new developments in the vinyl wallcoverings industry. Vinyl-coated papers are embossed to give a 'sandblasted' finish that keys the printed design into the vinyl, but throughout the 1970s this was an all-over process that produced a flat effect. In 1971 Vymura also introduced 'Novamura', a vinyl film that is embossed prior to printing and has no backing. This was never popular in certain markets, such as Germany, where a different method of applying vinyl was developed between 1972 and 1975. There, Marburg used the rotary screen-printing process to deposit a vinyl ink containing a catalyst, similar to yeast, that expands when heated. In these 'SUPROFIL' or blown vinyls, plaster-effects were created first, with Anaglypta sales suffering as a result. By about 1980 the use of the technique was widespread and the vinyl-coated wallpaper industry in Britain responded with in-register vinyls, first introduced by Crown in 1982; these have an additional texture engraved over and exactly matching the pattern, which by necessity has subtle colours, so that the engraving is not lost.

left column

319 High-quality wallcoverings such as 'Jardin', printed by Rasch of Germany in 1978–79, continued to employ large-scale patterns. Its bittersweet colours were popular from the mid-1970s until the first years of the 1980s.

320 Sanderson of Britain produced its 'Triad' range throughout the 1970s; shown here is 'Dimity', from the 1976 collection. The tiny floral design was available as a surface-printed wallpaper and had three companion fabrics – matching, striped or plain.

321 The best-selling single range of British wallpapers in the early 1980s was Coloroll's 'Dolly Mixtures', first designed by Linda Beard in 1978. As its name implies, purchasers were offered a degree of off-the-shelf choice with wallpapers and ready-made accessories grouped around colour themes.

right column

322 'Passion Flowers', issued as both wallpaper and fabric by G. P. & J. Baker of London in 1979, epitomizes the peak period for exactly matching coordinates. Wholesale fabric houses supplying the decorator trade had a long tradition of offering papers to match their fabrics.

323 The development during the 1980s of 'bed-led' design and complex coordination can be seen in Crown of Britain's 'Green Planet' collection, part of their 'Kids Kapers' range of 1993–94. The washable papers are printed by both flexographic and gravure methods.

Subsequent developments in screen-printed vinyls allowed for variations in height (low-blows) and the introduction of colour.

The more subtle coordinated look of the 1980s arrived in tandem with the wider availability of sophisticated vinyls, in which the 'architectural' qualities of textural, 'splash and dash' patterns and low-key colour began to be incorporated into related fabrics, producing, overall, a more painterly effect. Walls began to take on their own character – rather than aping other materials, whether plaster or fabric – and to sport overtly modern designs. Even the use of borders in picture-rail and dado-rail positions further stressed the functions of walls. Ironically, mural wallcoverings also typified this trend, as the fashion for *trompe-l'oeil* supported the re-issue of scenic designs and full panoramas of the type associated with Desfossé and Zuber papers of the previous century. Retrospective they may be, but their use confirms that, by the end of the 1980s, walls had regained a separate and distinct role in the decorated interior.

Changes in the industry

In retrospect, the early 1970s represented a high point in many company histories. The effects of the oil crisis of 1973 – higher fuel and petrochemical costs and the elimination of many jobs – led, generally, to fewer new houses being built in the subsequent decade, and West Germany was not unusual in finding that its estimated national per capita consumption of wallpaper (including imports) was the highest in 1973 at 2.5 rolls and the lowest in 1982 at 1.3 rolls, stabilizing at about 1.5 rolls after 1985. (Housing starts are still an important factor in sales: for Imperial Wallcoverings in America, for example, the higher per capita consumption in the Northeast – which is lower than that in Europe – is balanced by the livelier building trade in the Southwest, with the result that these two markets roughly equal each other in total sales.)

In the years around 1980 there was a significant reduction in the size of the industry, in part due to a fall in sales which occurred at the same time as the almost complete change to flexographic and photogravure printing – high-speed processes that demanded larger markets in order to be profitable and were therefore more sensitive to any drop in sales. In addition, the industry was not helped by continued improvements in vinyls and coated papers, which produced a more lasting product, nor by greater use of clean domestic fuels such as electricity. Up until 1978, for example, there were twenty mass-manufacturers in France, the most important of which was Leroy, accounting for about 800 of the 3,500 people employed in the wallpaper industry. Today there are seven: Champenoise, Décofrance, Decorene, Ugepa, Venilia (a subsidiary of Solvay Belge), the newly formed group Inaltéra-Grantil and the Société Française des Papiers Peints (essef). Only the latter three employ more than 100 people.

A similar picture emerged in former West Germany, where bankruptcies eliminated about half of the manufacturers: Norta Hannover, makers of exclusive papers, failed in 1979; Ditzel Bammenthal, first in West Germany to produce pre-pasted strippable blown vinyls (in 1976), and with a branch in France, went bankrupt in 1985. Tapetenfabrik G. L. Peine of Hildesheim, West Germany's largest manufacturer between 1956 and 1976, survived only into the first year of the 1980s. Among the dozen or so remaining companies are Rasch, AS Création and P & S International, which represents the amalgamation of two previously independent companies, Pickaërt and Sieburg. This trend also brought Rath & Doodeheefver and Goudsmit-Hoff together in the Netherlands; in America Katzenbach & Warren was taken over by Imperial.

British manufacture too slimmed down radically, particularly as firms changed hands. Under Reed's ownership, Crown Wallcoverings (part of the WPM) was much streamlined during the 1970s. In 1985 it was taken over by Borden, and it now operates within the context of that American parent

top row
324 The timeless appeal of many historic designs is apparent in 'Bambou et Chèvrefeuille' ('Bamboo and Honeysuckle'), a mid-19th-century French pattern hand-block-printed by Mauny of France.

325 The German company Marburg's blown vinyls are today laden with colour, as seen in the 1992 prize-winning 'SUPROFIL Original' collection.

centre row
326 Bestsellers of 1993, shown as a draughts board. The blue squares are from Crown of Britain's 'Calypso' range of flexographically printed washable papers for kitchens and bathrooms, aimed at the mass market. The other squares show more expensive retail papers by Osborne & Little of Britain: 'Nuage' textures, 'Siena' marbles, 'Coronata' stars, and the 'Sundance' moon and star pattern. The board stands on a favourite of American interior decorators: 'Lotus Damask', a reproduction by F. Schumacher & Co. for Williamsburg Restoration Inc.

327 The North American market is offered a broad choice of price and pattern, even when the desired effect is painterly, as shown in a selection from the 1990–91 production of companies in the Collins & Aikman/Imperial Wallcovering Group (numbered from the left). They were by Louis W. Bowen Fine Wallcoverings (3); Mario Buatta (1); Gear, to a design by Raymond Waites (8); Imperial (5, 7, 9); Katzenbach & Warren (2, 6); and Sterling Prints (4, 10).

bottom row
328 Rasch is one of the few German wallcoverings companies to advertise. This image comes from a series which showed papers from the innovative 'Zeitwände' collection, planned in the late 1980s. The name literally means 'time-walls', but it is a pun on *Zeitwende* – changing times – and the papers were photographed chiefly in East Berlin settings. This is 'Luna' of 1992, a rotary-screen-printed flat vinyl designed by Alessandro Mendini.

329 'In the Dresser Tradition II', a hand-screen-printed historical ensemble by the specialist firm Bradbury & Bradbury of San Francisco. The collection, issued in 1989, was inspired by the late 19th-century British designer Christopher Dresser.

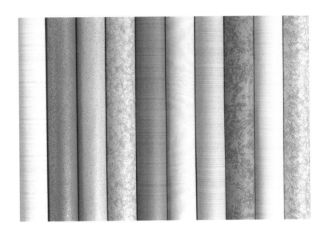

company (one of the 'big three' with Imperial and JenCorp), which also owns Storey's in Britain (and thus commands 31 per cent of the British market). Coloroll, after its rapid expansion of the 1980s, shed many of its subsidiary companies in 1990 and closed the American manufacturer it had purchased, Wall Mates of Long Island; today it has about 15 per cent of the British market.

The USA/UK connections reflect the interdependence of these two countries, with the USA being the most important market for British exports. Coloroll, for example, distributes through Blonder Wallcoverings (a division of Collins & Aikman). John Wilman's own-name brand is handled by Kinney, and fabrics enter the range via Dan River. The lack of in-register vinyl production in America was vital for the survival of this British industry (and Germany's lead in blown vinyl production has gained its entry into the American market). American wallcoverings also come to Britain: JenCorp, America's largest manufacturer of wallcoverings for the contract market, is distributed by Helen Sheane.

However, while the direct trading links between North America and Britain remain dominant, ownership patterns have begun to change. Most indicative of this is Sanderson, taken over from Reed by the American giant WestPoint Pepperell in 1985, and sold to the Dutch firm Gamma Holdings in 1989. Similarly, two British vinyl producers, Kingfisher and Mayfair, were purchased by one of the two major Swiss wallpaper firms, Forbo-Galban, and now have the Forbo name prefixed to theirs. Distribution links have also shown greater diversity recently: Jack Denst Inc. has opened an outlet in Germany at Staunberg, and America itself now has numerous showrooms featuring European papers, particularly in the elaborate period or decorator style, such as those offered by Boussac and Zuber.

The demise of surface-printing in favour of flexography and gravure was regretted by many in the industry, not only because it led to an over-production crisis, but because it brought a different aesthetic into play: a smooth and more transparent colour replaced the opaque impasto-like richness produced by the surface method, and the new faster machines promoted conservative styling intended to appeal to the required large market. The number of different designs produced also decreased as a result. At Crown, for example, the peak for the period was in 1970, when 57,436 patterns and colourways were produced; today the average for the company is about 2,000, the same as that for Marburg and Imperial. Others argue that the older method had not suited the mass market, because price ceilings dictated no more than a handful of colours.

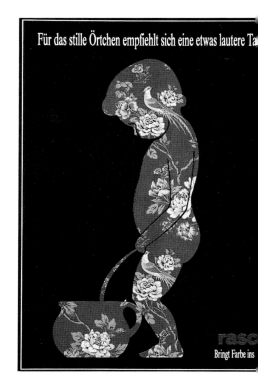

Marketing takes the lead

But for the consumer many of these changes were masked by the dramatic increase in off-the-shelf mass-merchant retailing, an international trend by about 1975 and one which was the growth area for wallpaper sales throughout the 1980s. Catering to the do-it-yourself market, these firms offer a wide choice, long lengths on display or on an accessible roll, reasonable price and everything else to hand. Some, such as Wallpapers to Go in the USA, have literally thousands of patterns in stock. Their buyers exercise enormous power by their choice of designs: six British superstores – Fads, B&Q, Texas, Homebase, Do It All and Great Mills – control 60 per cent of the country's wallcoverings trade.

Manufacturers' response to this development ranges from despair to delight. Many set up their own distribution networks in order to reach their retail buyers directly. The first to do so in America, in 1985, was Imperial. There, faith in the fashion sense of the mass market is marked and the aim is to provide the decorator look without the $80 per roll price tag: in the democratization of exclusive style, there is no doubt that wallpaper companies lead the way. Confidence in the sophistication of the American market was sufficient in the late 1980s to prompt the advertisement of the product under the banner *papiers peints* by

Pierre Deux, an American antiques company founded in 1967; from about 1983 the firm imported French Souleiado papers and some five years later began to commission their own hand-screen-printed document wallpapers. Meanwhile, the French company Boussac promoted its 1989 range of hand-block-printed borders to the American market as 'haute couture for the home'. If further indication of the continued influence of fashion on interiors is needed, there are the Ralph Lauren wallpapers, hand-printed by Motif Design, who also print for Pierre Deux.

Some of this confidence masks the difficulties faced by specialist manufacturers, whether traditional or modern in style. David & Dash, for example, produced avant-garde hand-screen-printed wallpapers throughout the 1980s, but their Miami-based firm closed in 1993. The suppliers of hand-block-printed papers, whose best markets are America, Great Britain and France, face the difficulty of training and keeping paper-hangers skilled at trimming, pasting and complex cutting. In many respects it seems that the small but defiant industry dealing in hand-prints (whether block- or screen-) is maintained not only by the beauty of their papers but also by the consumers' appreciation of the knowledge and skill still preserved by manufacturers and paper-hangers combined. Elsewhere, for instance in Germany, there is less confidence generally in the benefits of a retail-led system, and less wallpaper of any type features in consumer magazines either in the editorial matter or as advertising.

Nevertheless, in both Europe and America the continued success of the mass-merchants has been linked to the white-collar recession of recent years; for in its wake came the value-conscious consumer – identified by the now influential marketing departments of major wallcoverings manufacturers as most likely to be a woman. Consumer pressures have also shown that time is as valuable as money, whether judged in terms of the minutes needed to select and purchase wallpapers from large stocks, or the days elapsed before an ordered wallpaper is delivered. The speed with which manufacturers and distributors deliver ordered papers – always excepting the commissioned hand-prints – has been pushed down from three weeks to two or three days, and the books from which papers are ordered have also become more sophisticated in their arrangement by colour, theme or room-type, in order to make selection quicker.

Consumer testing also shows environmental issues as a major concern, and Marburg, still first in technological advances, have recently introduced SuproNova, a new texture-only wallcovering on a recycled paper base that meets stringent environmental standards. SuproNova brochures stress that it contains no PVC, chlorine, softeners, solvents, heavy metals, formaldehyde or CFCs, and subtitle the product, 'For a beautiful home and safe environment'. Ironically, the most 'friendly' wallcovering is the humble woodchip paper, which has always been made from recycled paper and wood fragments, entirely without colourants – a fact which may yet turn the industry on its head once again before the 20th century is over.

332

opposite
330 Crown's pattern book for
c. 1971 stressed the convenience of ready-pasted and strippable vinyl wallcoverings, still a favourite today. A housewife is shown as the decorator.

331 A 1990 advertisement by Rasch aimed to encourage the spread of wallpaper in the home. It illustrates a traditional pattern with a vivid red ground and, playing on a German euphemism for the bathroom, asks: 'For the quiet little place, may we suggest a somewhat louder wallpaper?'

below
332 SuproNova wallcovering of 1993, the most recent technical innovation in textured 'whites' from Marburg of Germany.

13 Limited Editions: 1995 to Today

MARY SCHOESER

Any account of wallpapers and wallcoverings in recent years can be condensed into one phrase: change, change, and more change. Western mass-produced wallpaper floundered just as the taste for wallcoverings grew, tempted by the customized looks provided by new print technology and product innovations. While the introduction of environmentally friendly, felt-like wallcoverings and backings ('non-wovens') restored some lost ground for 'old guard' corporations, their crumbling state left ample opportunities for smaller concerns to blossom. The latter included both established firms and newcomers, exploiting everything from hand printing to state-of-the-art methods and materials. What these firms share, whether avant-garde or devoted to faithful reproductions, is their passion for their product and the relative ease with which they can respond to changing trends and provide 'haute couture' for walls.

Retrenchment and reorganization

In the UK alone, the financial returns to corporate manufacturers fell to roughly half their former – and already declining – level. This was the result both of lower prices and of a reduction in consumption by 30 per cent, a rate of decline also experienced in North America. In both regions complex acquisitions, joint ventures and mergers occurred, all intended to achieve economies of scale. In 1998 two of the 'big three' – Imperial Wallcoverings and Borden Decorative Products – joined to become Imperial Home Decor Group (IHDG). In 1999 the third – GenCorp – sold its domestic wallpaper and wallcovering operations to Blue Mountain Wallcoverings, a privately owned major contract printer in Ontario, Canada, and its remaining production of wallcoverings for the commercial sector to a new entity, Omnova Solutions.[1] Then in 2000 IHDG (USA) filed for protective bankruptcy; trimmed down, its North American assets were sold to Blue Mountain early in 2004. Only months earlier, the troubled IHDG (UK)/Crown stable had become part of the English CWV Group, which already owned and produced the Coloroll, John Wilman and Vymura ranges.[2]

This state of affairs was roughly replicated in other smaller strongholds of production: France, the Benelux countries, Canada and Italy. While also declining, in 1995 Germany took and retained the UK's place as the foremost country in production terms, in part through acquisitions. For example, by 2003 the Hindrichs-Auffermann AG group[3] included Forbo in the UK (renamed H-A Interiors), Vénilia in France, Novo in Holland and Coswig, operating near Dresden since 1905. Nevertheless, as the large organizations became vulnerable to competition, both from smaller privately owned Western companies and the growing number of manufacturers elsewhere, Hindrichs-

333 Ornamenta, founded by Jane Gordon Clark in London in 1987, became known for designs that disguised their repeating pattern. Then, attracted by the possibility of large single images, it introduced digitally printed site-specific custom wallpapers in 2000. This example of 2001, 'Orange Lily', is a thermal digital print on waxed paper, which absorbs the ink, giving intense colour. Rubbing and polishing add texture and nuanced shading.

Auffermann were among those to suffer, as were the French firms essef and Decofrance.

However, all was not lost, in part because elsewhere an increase in mass-production and consumption was prompted by altered political and economic agendas. Most notably, Russia emerged from its 1997–98 crisis to become the world's largest consumer of wallcoverings, and ahead of the UK in production. The list of exporting countries now represents every continent. From locations such as Estonia, Kazakhstan, Turkey, Saudi Arabia, South Africa, Argentina

334

334 *far left* The largest wallcoverings producer in Turkey is Öncü Grup A.S. Based in Istanbul, it was established in 1965 as a print-cylinder manufacturer, and some twenty years later added its own production, branded Dekor. This design from their studio's 1999–2000 range of rotogravure-printed vinyls reflects the now near-global popularity of informally striped and textured papers accompanied by an accent border.

335 *left* 'Looking East' is a 2002 collection of gravure-printed paper-backed solid vinyls, styled and coloured by David Abbotts, and with a name and pattern-book cover highlighting the Pacific Rim location of its manufacturer, Pacific Wallcoverings Ltd. The company was formed in New Zealand in 1995 by two firms formerly based in Auckland and Ashley Wallpaper (a forty-year-old manufacturer in Pretoria, its present base) and exports to Asia, North America and Australia, as well as to the UK, where this collection was launched in 2003.

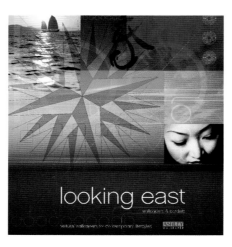

and Mexico come products to serve both regional and Western markets, with the greatest growth occurring throughout the former Soviet states and the Asia-Pacific area, most notably in New Zealand, the Koreas, Taiwan and China. Some expansion was the result of outward investment: Rasch of Germany, now one of the 'top five' firms, initiated production in the Ukraine. Zambaiti of Italy – who produce Murella and other brands and only began making wallpapers in 1974 and vinyls in 1979 – did the same in China in 1994. This followed only ten years after the formation of Yulan (Guangdon Yulan Decorative Materials Company Ltd), the largest manufacturer of Western-style wallcoverings in China; by 1994 Yulan had imported four production lines from the UK and within two years doubled its sales. Delight (Jiangmen Yuhua Wallpaper Factory Company), China's largest manufacturer using Japanese production lines,[4] has also been established for only some twenty years.

New methods and materials

Despite so much upheaval, manufacturers continued to improve and expand their range of products. Innovations included Instant Stencils, launched by IHDG in 2001. These dry rub-off transfers apply a lithographed but seemingly hand-painted motif to non-porous surfaces. Offering a new take on the old

337 The 'Black and White Floral' collection was one of the sets of 'Walls My Way', introduced by IHDG (USA) in 2001: each contained four related images intended to be used singly, in a row, or grouped into a square. These peel-and-stick alternatives to posters were among the early variants of affordable wall art that have since proliferated.

opposite
336 In 2003 the Italian Diego Grandi designed the 'Le Module' concept, which was launched by Sterling Prints through IHDG (USA) and is now offered by the Canadian manufacturer Blue Mountain. It is a non-woven wallcovering available in squares and rectangles to allow for spaced positioning – as here – and in standard rolls for conventional hanging. Its paste-the-wall application made such variety of placement easy.

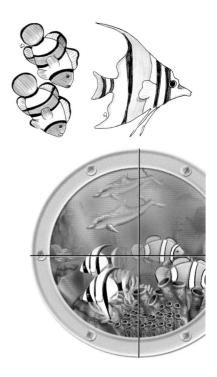

338 *above* For murals and accents such as the offset-printed 'Tropical Pairs', designed by Karoline Daly in 2000, IdeaStix of California introduced a rubber resin patented by Sang Song. In 2004 they extended the concept to personal creativity with PrintStix, home inkjet-printer-size sheets; when ironed, these stick-ons become impervious to showers, dishwashers and microwaves, making it possible to decorate with one's own photographs or artwork.

339 *left* With the Cosmopolitan Collection of 2004, Rasch of Germany combined the idea of individualized wall decoration in paper panels and traditionally manufactured 'plains' that mimic natural materials. All were designed by Bernhard Holzapfel. Shown here is 'Love & Peace', his up-to-date homage to the days of 'flower power', with surrealistically scaled single poppies, digitally printed on a sackcloth-effect ground.

337 methods of decoupage and cut-outs for wallpapers, such transfers can adorn stained or painted wood and walls, glass, ceramics, plastics and metal, as well as
340, 341 paper products – not only wallpaper, but increasingly fashionable interior accessories such as hatboxes, files, storage boxes and folding screens. More robust are vinyl-coated paper motifs, die-cut and ready-pasted. Among the established firms who introduced cut-outs to match borders were Schumacher, in their mass-market Village brand. Others new to the field boosted the selection. McCalls Pattern Company, for example, drew on their long experience with die-cutting of paper for their range of Wallies, the now generic name (from 'wall') by which ready-pasted vinyl-coated appliques are known in North

America. Stronger still are the appliques evolved from self-adhesive vinyl borders such as H-A's Readyroll, but printed on a transparent substrate. These became particularly popular as tile stickers and switch-plate covers, but also come in sets that can be assembled to create murals.

Any doubt as to how to use such appliques was dispelled by television programmes such as America's 'Trading Spaces', which in 2003 launched its own range of Wallies. In the following year viewers of 'Weekend Warriors' on HGTV (a cable service broadcast throughout North America, where it is based, and in Australia, Japan, Thailand, the Philippines, Hungary and the Czech and Slovak Republics) were introduced to the new alternative to 'faux-finish' paint effects: ready-pasted paper to tear, dip and hang in overlapping patches. Indeed, most of these developments aimed to duplicate paint effects, which by the mid-1990s interior designers and sophisticated DIY-ers had taken to heart. The limitations of stick-ons soon became clear, however – generally either the residue

340, 341 'Long Flower', a Rachel Kelly Interactive Wallpaper, was developed while she was a student on the 'Textile Futures' MA course at Central Saint Martins College of Art & Design, London, and launched upon her graduation in 2001. Kelly's 'bespoke' hand-screen-printed papers are designed as panels and accompanied by six paper, vinyl, transfer or foil stickers with which to personalize the composition. This idea was extended to machine-printed papers in 2004.

243

left behind on removal, or susceptibility to damage from high moisture or
338 temperature. These were overcome by IdeaStix, Inc., headquartered in
California and manufacturing in Korea since 2001: suitable for virtually all
non-porous surfaces, IdeaStix motifs are self-adhesive, removable, re-usable,
and water-, heat- and steam-resistant.

The new generation of self-adhesive wall treatments relied equally on
improvements in adhesives and in the product's material. Such partnerships

342 The papers in the Allegory
Collection of 1999 were the first
100 per cent non-wovens offered by
Innovations in Wallcoverings Inc.,
New York, which had manufactured
vinyl interior products since 1975.
'Allegory Vine', by Design Director
Fumiaki Odaka, illustrates the soft
texture and indistinct pattern outline
characteristic of vlies (note the
reverse with its fleece-like qualities).

were also essential in 'paintable' and 'paste-the-wall' developments, which emerged from the wallpaper sector in Germany in 1997.[5] These interrelated innovations were initiated when Erfurt introduced the first embossed paper with a smooth back, and Henkel KGaA its Metylan instant adhesive especially for 'paintables' – woodchip and blown vinyls that were to be painted. This focus on the substrate and adhesive led to flat-backed screen-printed blown vinyls and non-wovens, which were first used to back vinyls and then as wallcoverings in their own right. A non-woven 'paper' combines polyester fibres with cellulose pulp; compared with traditional papers, it is stronger and more opaque, and has greater dimensional stability. These qualities, and the right adhesive, allow non-wovens to be to be hung by putting the paste on the wall rather than the wallcovering (hence the term 'paste-the-wall'), and stripped off dry when change is in order.

Germany (followed by France) has been the most receptive to non-wovens, known as *vlies* – literally, 'fleece'. This in part reflects the German position on environmental issues. Until the early 1990s many German authorities had anti-PVC resolutions, and some still do. Free from vinyl and glass fibres, vlies do not give off gases from volatile organic compounds or shed fibres when removed. Further, unlike vinyl a non-woven 'breathes', so mould and mildew are discouraged. These attributes aided the global rise in the use of vlies, apparent

343 In 2003 the American Maya Romanoff Corporation began patenting a new process to produce a flexible glass-beaded surfacing material, christened 'Beadazzled'. An award-winning innovator, Romanoff orchestrates his corporation's own range of metallic-leafed papers and earth-friendly products such as a micro-thin wood veneer and sand-flocked vlies.

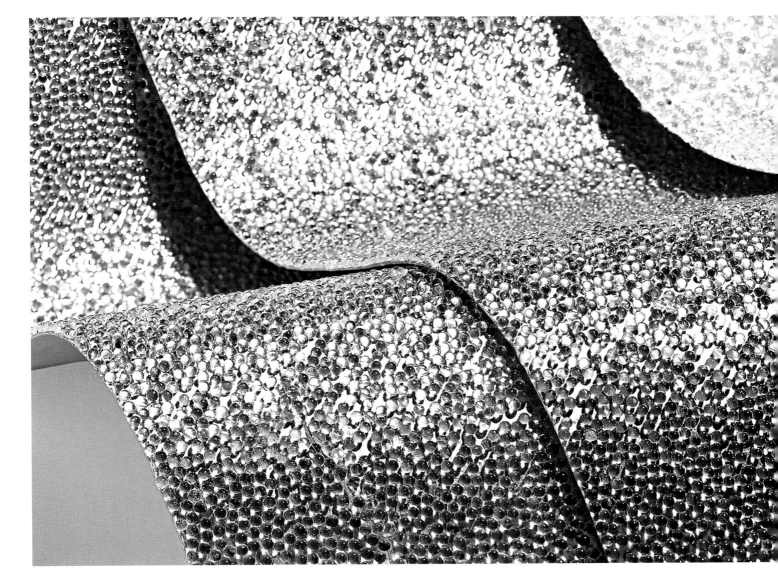

344 The 'On the Beach' Collection of the German wallcoverings manufacturer Marburg is composed from 100 per cent vlies and water-based inks. Designed in 2004 by Art Director Annette Zimmermann, it includes the flower/texture chequerboard and faux water patterns shown here, all with an added relief effect of transparent droplets which appear matte or shiny depending on the light. Production requires a combination of rotary-screen-printing, gravure printing and in-register embossing.

opposite
345 The revival of sumptuous touches in decor is characterized by this detail of 'Desire', a Graham & Brown gravure-screen-printed vinyl of 2001, incorporating metallic ink over pigments. Its designer, Lawrence Llewellyn-Bowen, starred in the last two years of the BBC's 'Changing Rooms', a series on decoration broadcast in twenty countries from 1996 to 2004. During the same period Graham & Brown grew by some 400 per cent, largely through increased sales outside the UK.

346 For golf-lovers, this pre-pasted, strippable, washable vinyl-coated paper comes from the 2003 'Remember When' collection by the Brewster Wallcovering Company of Massachusetts. One of North America's major distributors, Brewster has since 1999 also owned manufacturing units in Canada and the UK in order to ensure its continued provision of a breadth of printing styles. This example is rotogravure-printed.

after 1999 as 'paste-the-wall' products and backings for vinyl-based 'paintables' for domestic interiors. Vlies also contributed to the growing range of acoustical, medical and electromagnetic-shielding 'techno wallcoverings' and, as backings, rendered many vinyl commercial wallcoverings breathable and made possible large expanses of dry-erase surfaces (which, blackboard-like, can be drawn or written on and easily wiped clean).[6] As the technological advantages and earth-friendly characteristics of non-wovens became more widely recognized, concerns about vinyls grew – countered by professionals who detailed for consumers the many good features of vinyl.[7]

344   Worldwide, other winners in the environmental stakes utilize water-based inks and dry processes such as transfer printing. The former are free of cadmium, lead and chromium – traditional constituents in yellow, red and orange pigments, respectively – and so address the 'sick building syndrome'. The latter produce little waste. Both are among the methods used in digitally printed wallcoverings. Although digital imaging technology was already in existence, it was not until 1997–98 that companies such as Metro Wallcoverings (a division of ICI Canada, Inc.) introduced it especially for wallcoverings and, in Massachusetts, Rexam Image Products developed purpose-made substrates, one for direct printing and the other for dry transfer printing.[8] Because digital

printing was slow, its application became most evident in smaller batch-production, typically of borders, appliques and murals, where its photographic realism was put to good use. By 2000 faster digital presses made by Barco, DPS and others allowed the increase in 'on demand' wallpaper printing, as did the development of systems that did not need a special paper. The result was a boom in the creation of unique murals that could be created by printing services using an individual's chosen imagery, as well as by designers responding to specific interiors or developing a limited-edition range. Costs also fell, making digitals about half as expensive as custom block- or screen-printed papers. Rough estimates suggest that today some 10 per cent of wallcoverings are digitally printed.

Tastes and trends

Retro, high-tech, luxurious, humorous, artistic or naturalistic, trends for walls went from mid-1990s subtle paint effects and minimalism to a millennium-induced urge for more complex decor. More adventurous large-scale treatments emerged, filling the void in stark Modernist-inspired interiors and adding an element of risk to complement those furnished in an upbeat retro style. Dependent on rich tones and either exaggerated textures or photographic

344 realism, murals, patterned 'feature-walls', or the all-encompassing use of real or faux natural materials became key. This taste soon inspired a resurgence of wallcoverings catering to devotees of a particular lifestyle, whether represented by fashion brands as disparate as Gucci (in 2003) and Benetton (via CWV, in
345 2004), or created by televised decorators such as Britain's Laurence Llewelyn-Bowen. Together these trends encouraged more licensing of special-interest designs, predominantly borders and appliqués. One can, for example, match
346 dinnerware, while a plethora of designs reflect children's and adults' hobbies and entertainment; in the USA, Blue Mountain's products include designs licensed from Disney as well as from the popular and collectable artist Thomas Kinkade.

The restored interest in 'naturals' rested in part on ecological concerns, which promoted the use of biodegradable wallcoverings constructed with leather, natural fibres and grasses, bamboo, wood veneer, cork or rice paper. New was their broader spectrum of colours, water-based. Speciality products included wall-tiles hand-woven from bamboo, designed in 2002 by Omexco of Belgium in collaboration with Tomita of Japan. 'Naturals' also dovetailed with the fashion for burnished metal and polished stone surfaces, which revitalized
345 the use of metallic inks, metal leaf and Mylar, as well as prompting the
343 introduction of custom-marbled, sand-dusted or crystal-embedded wall-coverings, the latter recently introduced by Fiona, part of Flügger in Denmark. Deeply textured surfaces such as crushed silk, suede, velvet, paintable Jacquard wallcoverings (from Belgium's Bekaert Wall Textiles) and textile-like vlies and vinyls gained from such trends. Faux wood, metal and stone effects became more sophisticated both visually and technically.

Much visual richness relies on computerized advances. Large scanners and
349 digital presses can easily replicate retro Modernist, postwar Contemporary and 1970s Op-influenced designs, and earlier patterns too (without their characteristic pigment-laden surfaces). For those with retro tastes who
350 appreciate the real thing, there are many patterns in the ranges of custom block- and screen-printers and a few manufacturers who, with an eye to consumers' demands for diversity, have retained the near-extinct surface-printing machine side-by-side with high-speed rotary machines and the slower digital and hand-screen presses. Among these are Blue Mountain and York Wallcoverings,
348 founded in 1895 in Pennsylvania and today the oldest and largest manufacturer' in the USA. Design software, greatly improved since 1995, has been a boon to limited-edition makers and the mass-producing industry, while shopping services and texture-mapping systems (to visualize a pattern in an interior) proliferated on the internet after about 2000. Computers now also control lasers to cut out shaped borders and appliqués, a technique first applied in Europe by Domus Parati, founded in 1923 and the oldest surviving wallpaper manufacturer in Italy.

For consumers, the internet has opened up the world of designers and manufacturers. Many company sites acknowledge this by including background information to personalize their services.[9] AS Création of Germany, founded in 1974 with four staff, chronicles its exceptional expansion, including televised promotions and soccer sponsorship. Noticeably, firms remaining in family hands declare this fact with pride, and have fared well. Among these are Zambaiti in Italy, Bekaert (part of Gamma Holdings but with a Bekaert at the
345 helm) in Belgium, Nobilis in France, and Graham & Brown in the UK. Those
348 prospering in the USA include York, the century-old Eisenhart, the major distributors Blonder Home Accents (founded c. 1919) and Brewster
346 Wallcoverings, and the designer-editeur influential since the 1960s, Maya
343 Romanoff. (Editeurs have most if not all of their wallcoverings made exclusively

347 Making a bold statement with domestic imagery. London-based Deborah Bowness combines computer-manipulated photographs, digital printing, hand-screen-printing and real hardware to provide a new twist to photorealism for interior walls. In 'Hooks and Frocks', 1999, a set of real hooks is included with the paper panels so that the faux and the functional collide.

opposite
348 A noticeable trend since the mid-1990s has been the production of murals in faux window and door designs. This American example, 'Tropical Door', was designed for pre-pasted paper by Don Maki of York Wallcoverings' studio and launched in 2002. It is offset-printed, a lithographic technique particularly suited to graduated colours and large images, both seen here in a panel that is 74 ³/₈ inches (189 cm) high and 51 inches (130 cm) wide.

left and below
349 Harking back to mid-20th-century Contemporary styles, 'Rollette' was designed in 2004 by Simon Aldous, Creative Director of the Australian manufacturers colourEverything. Digitally mastered and produced by Flash Photobition, it can be custom-coloured and can have fabric made to match. At 47 inches (120 cm) wide, the paper itself is latex-saturated and reinforced with nylon to make it tear resistant.

350 'Frog Treillage' by Charles Tausch was designed in 1970 for Brunschwig & Fils, New York, and remained in their range until 1984. Thereafter it became the company's most popular custom order until it was re-introduced into their standard range in 2004 with new colourings. Hand-screen-printed on vinyl, it represents the boldly graphic and witty designs of the late 1960s and 1970s that have been revived alongside 'Op' and 'Pop' patterns of the same period.

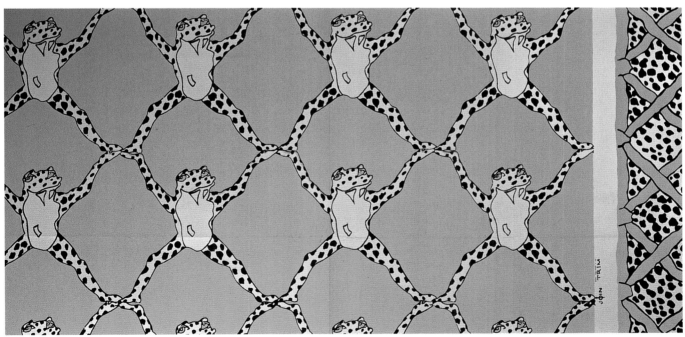

351 Tracy Kendall, who began producing large-print wallpapers in London in 1996, also creates custom hand-stitched wallcoverings such as 'In the White Room', first produced in 2001. Made of hand-cut wallpaper, it aims to capture the rusticated effect of exterior brickwork, and is one of a group of papers exploring the artist's response to the potential of paper itself.

for them by other manufacturers.) The UK, no longer first in commodity production, can claim to have nurtured many such designer-owned enterprises, whether Ornamenta, David Oliver and Jocelyn Warner (since 1997, 1998 and 1999 respectively), or post-2000 entrants such as Rachel Kelly, Hsueh-Pei Wang and Maria Yascuk, the latter two exploring thermochromic and electron-conductive inks, which respectively change colour in response to body heat and allow the incorporation of light-emitting diodes.

When the magazine *Wallpaper** was born in the UK in 1993 it intended its title ironically, as a sneer. Now it is one of the champions of wallpaper's rebirth as the background for a bold 21st-century lifestyle. Meanwhile, wallpaper's former domesticity – and occasional banality – has since the early 1990s inspired installation artists on several continents, among them Deborah Bowness, Robert Gober and Sadie Coles in England and Sydney Albertini, Abigail Lane and Virgil Marti in the US. Wallpaper as a legitimate site for art then arrived, resulting in works ranging from the four wallpapers commissioned by Glasgow's Centre for Contemporary Arts in 1996 to international examples by thirty-three artists gathered together early in 2003 by the curator of Contemporary Arts at America's RISD (Rhode Island School of Design) Museum for the exhibition 'On the Wall: Wallpaper and Tableau'. Whether confronting the boundaries between art and design or the limitations of mass-manufacturing techniques', the 'art paper' often incorporates a subversive commentary conveyed by the use of wallpaper clichés such as topical references, the mimicry of past styles or, as typified by the variously-sized eyeballs in Takashi Murakami's 2002 wallpaper for Studio Printworks, the way a small repeating pattern renders even unexpected imagery innocuous from a distance.[10] A parallel development has been the recognition of paper as a medium in its own right, whether resulting in the wallpapers distributed in Japan by Painthouse (and elsewhere by Bigstone Media Marketing) and designed by Japan's Kyoko Ibe, who is known for her innovative installation art constructed from *washi* paper, or the three-dimensional stitched papers of London-based Tracy Kendall. 'No More White Walls' declared the American Wallpaper Council in 2003, and – for afficionados if not for mass-producers – its optimism seemed to be justified.[11]

333
340, 341

347

352, 353

352, 353 'Wallpaper Gnawed by a Rat' was produced by the pet rats belonging to Front, a Swedish product design group formed in 2003 by four recent MA graduates of Konstfack: Sofia Lagerkvist, Katja Sävström, Anna Lindgren and Charlotte von der Lancken. Seeking to avoid established methods and conventions, they 'manufacture' wallpaper designs by giving a roll of plain paper to a rat, whose chewing produces repeated holes unique to each piece and only revealed by hanging the gnawed paper over a patterned paper.

Postscript: The Rescue and Care of Wallpapers

SARAH MANSELL

The conservation of wallpapers requires specialist knowledge, and it is always best to get informed advice if work needs to be done on a paper. However, an interest in historic papers is not confined to museums and many people make exciting discoveries in their own homes, or have period papers on their walls or in their care. Recording discoveries, general care, and storage are areas of interest to us all. A great deal of damage to wallpapers *in situ* can be avoided with good housekeeping. Burst water pipes, soot falls, furniture scuffs, dirty finger marks and poor storage are all too often the cause of harm.

354 The wardrobe has been pulled away from the wall to show how this once beautiful late 18th-century Chinese paper has been irreversibly damaged by a foolhardy attempt to 'brighten up' the background using ordinary white emulsion paint. Carelessly applied and impossible to remove, this has ruined a once fine paper.

355 This English flock wallpaper of *c.* 1730 has various different kinds of damage. It is dusty, stained and rubbed. There is uneven fading where larger pictures have been hung in the past. Nails have left iron marks and holes. An old, unsympathetic repair can be seen protruding from under the left-hand side of the painting: this has created a tension in the hessian backing, which in turn has split the wallpaper.

356 Historic papers on the wall need to be checked regularly. Here a small area of the painted top layer of an early 19th-century Chinese paper is delaminating from its paper backing. The delicate piece is being stuck down using a pure starch paste and a fine brush. If this had not been done it would have broken off, leaving a missing area.

357 A five-layer 'sandwich' of wallpaper was salvaged from a fine Georgian house in Highgate, London. The papers discovered on separation give a great deal of information about the use and decoration of the room over the last 150 years, of interest to the owners and to historians. From the latest (top left) to the earliest (bottom right), their approximate dates are 1960, 1920, 1890, 1870, and 1840. The English Heritage Study Collection, at Kenwood House in London, has many similar examples of separated wallpaper layers.

358 After the fire at Uppark (Sussex), wallpaper conservator Orde Solomons rescued surviving pieces. These were either reinstated or used as references for reprinting prior to rehanging. Here he is removing areas of an 18th-century flock wallpaper with an electronic vapour machine.

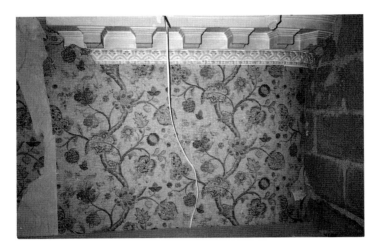

Left Discovery

359 This fragment of *c.* 1800 was discovered during building work, beneath plaster in a Norfolk farmhouse. It is a two-colour block-printed paper typical of the period.

360 This machine-printed paper of *c.* 1930 was found above a false ceiling – a typical area where one might find old wallpaper – in a house in Richmond (Surrey). It is already a useful historic record of how the house was decorated at the time.

Below Display and storage

361 The Cooper-Hewitt Museum in New York uses a moulded perspex frame for the temporary display of rolls of wallpaper. A length can be unrolled to expose a repeat while the weight of the roll is supported in the bottom of the frame. After an exhibition the paper can be removed, rolled and put back into store.

362 A wallpaper study collection may contain many samples of rescued pieces, all in various states of decay. Transparent melinex envelopes will protect them from dust and allow easy handling and study (though they are not suitable for pieces with flaking pigments). Fragile pieces may need a support sheet beneath them.

363 Long drops of wallpaper prepared for storage. They have been wrapped with the design outermost around large cardboard tubes (themselves covered with layers of melinex and acid-free paper), with acid-free tissue interleaved in the rolling process. A dust cover wraps the whole roll, and the tube is suspended on a pole to avoid pressure on the paper.

Until comparatively recently wallpaper conservation has been a 'do-it-yourself' affair. From stately homes to terraced houses the same remedies were applied. Housekeeping manuals of the 19th and 20th centuries abound with enthusiastic advice on how best to carry out minor repairs to wallpaper – most guaranteed, we now know, to mark and destroy the material they were supposed to restore. *The Housewife's Handy Book*, published in London in the late 1920s, is typical: 'bran is a splendid reviver but it will not take out finger-marks that are specially dirty. They can be obliterated . . . in extreme cases with ink eraser. Another plan for removing grease . . . is benzene, which, of course, is highly inflammable. Ink marks usually yield to an application of oxalic acid.' Many cleaning methods were used regularly by conscientious housekeepers until very recently, breadcrumbs being a favourite. Patching, although a practical solution if sensitively done, usually stood out when using leftover lengths or pieces which had not suffered the same light degradation. Heavy-handed use of glue or paste resulted in new staining around repairs, and impetuous attempts to brighten a fading background with paint or chemicals invariably caused irreversible damage.

104.
354

Fortunately continuing developments in the field of paper conservation have addressed the specific problems of wallpaper, and it is becoming a well researched and scientifically supported area of study, with museums and private conservators around the world giving the subject proper attention.

What follows is a brief description of a few alternatives for the care of historic papers: it is *not* a 'How-To' guide. If advice or treatment for wallpapers is needed it is always best to get informed help. (Some suggestions are given at the end of this article.) It is very important to remember that any work done on historic papers must be reversible: nothing should interfere with the authenticity of the original. Moderation is always wise, since in the future better methods of treatment may be devised.

359.
360

Discoveries of old papers, whether large areas or tiny fragments, are usually made when building alterations or redecoration are in progress. They may be found behind door frames, picture rails, panelling, fitted bookcases and window shutters, skirting boards, architraves, fire surrounds, and even under floorboards. Rooms evolve and, as most of us know from our own decorating efforts, layer upon layer may be revealed on the walls themselves.

357

Historic papers have also been found used as linings for chests and deed boxes, on band boxes in the United States, as book covers, and on the walls of doll's houses.

Throughout Europe the earliest wallpapers were tacked directly onto the plaster. By the 17th century most were tacked to stretchers, and by 1700 they were usually stuck to canvas on stretchers. By about 1750 that method had largely been abandoned and papers were stuck directly to the wall, sometimes with a lining paper going up first. Occasionally a coat of varnish was applied over the surface. This was particularly common with the 'sanitaries' or intaglio-printed papers of the late 19th century used for halls, stairways, kitchens and bathrooms. Pastes were traditionally flour-based, sometimes with an addition of gelatine or animal glue, unadulterated animal glue being used for the heavier flocks and embossed wallpapers. Papers with an all-rag content have usually retained their strength well. In the second half of the 19th century, however, paper-making methods began to use wood pulp, containing lignin, which produces sulphurous acids that accelerate the degrading process of the cellulose fibres in conjunction with the ultra-violet in daylight, causing the paper itself to become brittle and disintegrate. Colours from earth pigments are comparatively stable, vegetable dyes proving much more susceptible to fading.

Recording

On discovery, *in situ* photographs should be taken, and a record made of the size, pattern (size of repeat, colour), type of paper (for example, is it in handmade sheets? is it machine-made? is it good quality rag, or weak wood-pulp?), location, and condition of the piece, together with any identification marks. Where feasible tracings can be made, but great care must be taken not to damage fragile pieces or indent the sample by using too much pressure. If more detailed information is required, fibres and pigments can be analysed. When removal is not an option – perhaps joinery has to go back up or a new wallpaper is to be hung over the top – recording this information may be all that is practically possible and the records will become valuable reference material, of interest to householder and museum curator alike.

If the original piece is to be covered over, various methods to protect it should be considered. The replacement may be lined with a strong Japanese paper and attached to stretchers, or it may be given a false margin and attached to a stretcher or lightweight acid-free support panel. If new paper has to be applied directly onto the old, it may be possible first to face the latter with a thin Japanese paper, over which a layer of good quality lining paper should be hung. Above all, it is imperative to make sure that all the materials, including the paste, are of an approved conservation quality.

Cleaning and repair on the wall

Each paper requires careful assessment of its components and problems before a course of action is decided upon. Frequently conservation treatments have to be adapted to tackle each task according to its own requirements. There is also no point in embarking on any treatment until building works, rewiring, or redecorating are completed. Checks should be made of old sources of damage, such as blocked gutters, leaking roofs and dirty chimneys.

Where the paper is to remain visible on the wall it may only need some gentle dry-cleaning with soft-bristled brushes to remove dust and loose dirt, taking care not to dislodge loose pigments or lift areas of paper. (Powdery pigments on block-printed 18th- and 19th-century papers, for example, cannot withstand anything more vigorous.) Any treatment beyond this should be referred to a wallpaper conservator for examination, advice and care. The procedures described below and in the next two sections are the province of the professional.

356 Lifting areas can be stuck back down using a fine brush and pure starch paste or methyl cellulose. Where there are air bubbles behind the paper, tiny amounts of paste can be inserted with a syringe. If the surface is strong enough, the next stage would be mechanical cleaning using erasers. After that – again, if the surface allows – a hand-held vacuum cleaner with a fine muslin over the nozzle may be used.

Missing areas need to be infilled using a carefully matched paper, and all retouching must be kept firmly to the new repairs. Where large areas are missing or only a small fragment remains, but is to be used as a guide to re-paper the wall, there are specialist firms who are able to copy old patterns. A decision may have to be made whether to reproduce the faded colours of the fragment or the brighter shades it would have had when new.

Removal

Where a wall has been damp or the paste has degraded it is sometimes possible to lift a paper by easing it off gently with a spatula or scalpel. More often the old adhesives can be stubborn and it may be necessary to introduce some moisture to facilitate removal. A small area should always be tested first, as any treatment involving water or steam may result in loss of depth of colour and possible staining. A fine spray of water/alcohol mix may be
358 enough to introduce some flexibility into the paper. If not, steam may be effective, with its advantage of heating and dissolving the adhesive. In extreme cases a conservator may need to resort to enzymes to break down the adhesive. Flaking colours may have to be consolidated prior to removal as well as afterwards. Severely damaged pieces may need a temporary facing before any attempt can be made to detach them. This is frequently the case with those that have been stuck down on wood.

More than one person is needed to remove large areas of wallpaper. When dealing with long 'drops', the length should be supported to prevent the weight from tearing the paper at the point where it is still attached to the wall. The top edge can be attached to pulleys if strong enough. The paper may be supported on a large tube, or even on a suitably padded broomhead held by an assistant to take the weight of the drop. If there are several layers to be removed it is important to keep a clear record of the order in which they were hung.

Repair and storage after removal

Detached papers need to be transported safely to wherever they are going to be repaired. For small fragments this does not present a problem, but long drops should ideally be kept flat. After the front has been gently dry-cleaned and a check has been made for lifting paper or pigments in need of consolidation, the piece can be turned over to lie face down on clean blotters. Old adhesives, plaster, and any loose old linings are then removed from the back. It may be necessary further to consolidate loose pigments from behind by using a suction table in conjunction with steam to assist penetration. Washing may be possible in some cases of severe staining, or poultices may be used on local marks. Loose fragments should be reattached and tears supported prior to any relining.

Where rehanging is to be undertaken, relining is often necessary. Japanese paper is most suitable for this purpose because the long fibres give it great strength. It is important when rehanging a historic paper to remember that this process too should be easily reversible. Once relined, the paper may be mounted on stretchers or on lightweight acid-free supports. Where that is impossible (for example in conjunction with decorative cornicing), the wall may be faced with a three-layer 'sandwich' of lining paper/woven polyester textile/lining paper. The textile, which in an emergency acts as a release sheet, should be cut 2 inches (50 mm) shorter all the way round a good paper-to-paper bond.

Rescued samples that are not to be rehung need their future use to be considered when deciding how best to repair and store them. Are they to be part of a study collection, or stored? In both cases papers should be dry-cleaned. Dangerously fragile pieces may need lining, and flaking colours may need consolidating. No attempt should be made to brighten up the appearance with varnishes or fixatives. Always be alert to any markings on the back. Excepting museum 'house styles', identification marks should be done in 3B pencil.

Where there are no flaking colours and the fragment is strong, it may be quite satisfactory to place the paper 362 in a transparent melinex envelope to protect it from dust and allow easy handling and study. If storage is all that is required, it may be sufficient to place the pieces in an acid-free box, interleaved with acid-free tissue paper. Slightly weaker samples may need to be attached to an acid-free board with a melinex cover, though the static created by the melinex would make this unsuitable for flaking colours. In that case a window mount of acid-free mounting board is needed to avoid contact of any kind with the vulnerable surface. Larger pieces can be given lightweight supports such as a polyurethane foamcore board, first lined with an acid-free paper. Samples should be attached at two corners (to allow examination of the back), using Japanese paper hinges and a pure starch paste. Large pieces can be given a false margin and attached with this to the supporting board. Pressure-sensitive tapes should never be used to fix papers to supports.

Flat storage on shelves, in solander boxes, is always preferable: tightly rolled specimens crack and tear over time and cannot be unrolled easily for study or exhibition. Damaged or heavily embossed papers must be kept flat. If some pieces have to be stored rolled, it should be with the design outermost, on large-diameter tubes that have been covered in melinex and acid-free tissue as a barrier, with acid-free tissue interleaved in the rolling process. The tube should then be wrapped in a dust-cover and supported to avoid pressure on the paper. Unused rolls should be stored wrapped in acid-free tissue.

If the rescued papers are to be put on exhibition it is always preferable to show the whole sheet, damaged edges and all. Frames should have fillets to hold the ultra-violet-filtered glass or perspex away from the surface of the paper. The Cooper-Hewitt Museum in New York has designed an ingenious moulded perspex frame that allows the display of an unused roll of wallpaper with a length exposed to show the repeat; the roll is supported, and can be easily removed for return to storage.

Good housekeeping

Both stores that house rescued samples and rooms with wallpapers *in situ* should practise standard museum good housekeeping; strong sunlight can quickly fade a paper, and moisture will encourage mould and insects. There should be careful monitoring of the temperature and relative humidity (RH), ideally at levels suitable for paper (20°C and 50–55% RH). Light levels must be watched carefully (50 lux is recommended, though low for a work situation), and all windows should be ultra-violet-filtered (60–80 lumen) and have blinds. It is sometimes practical with rooms that are open to the public to put up perspex screens to protect the papers from wear, held at least ¾ inch (20 mm) away from the wall to allow air circulation. No furniture should be pushed up against the wallpaper. All polishes, cleaning fluids, wood preservatives and fungicidal agents must be kept well away. Regular checks should be made for areas lifting away from the wall, flaking colours, or insect attack. Buildings must be maintained in good order to prevent damage such as that from burst pipes or soot falls down chimneys.

As public interest in conservation grows, hopefully more people will be stimulated to keep records and/or samples of discoveries – and not to forget that today's papers will be the historic papers of tomorrow.

Notes

Full details of works given in short-title form will be found in the Bibliography, pp. 264–66.
BSIM = Bulletin de la Société Industrielle de Mulhouse
JDA = Journal of Decorative Art
JSA = Journal of the Society of Arts
MAD = Musée des Arts Décoratifs, Paris
MPP = Musée du Papier Peint, Rixheim
O&H = C. C. Oman and J. Hamilton, *Wallpapers: A History and Illustrated Catalogue of the Collection of the Victoria and Albert Museum*
V&A = Victoria & Albert Museum, London
WAG = Whitworth Art Gallery, Manchester

1 Manifold Beginnings:
Single-Sheet Papers

[1] For general help or information on specific points, my thanks go to the following: Jürgen Beyer, Herwig Colaert, Frank Daelemans, Philippe de Fabry, Lesley Hoskins, Bernard Jacqué, Marc-Henri Jordan, Andreas Schulze, Jacques and Françoise Subes, Friederike Wappenschmidt and Anthony Wells-Cole.
[2] See A. K. L. Thijs, 'Behangpapier Anno 1582', *Ons Heem*, XXV, no. 3, 1971, pp. 112–13.
[3] See H. Jenkinson, 'English Wall-Paper of the Sixteenth and Seventeenth Centuries', *Antiquaries Journal*, V, 1925, p. 240, n. 1; the paper was initially attributed to Hieronymus Cock (1510?–70), later to the English-based printer Hugo Goes. For the archaeological discussions see Appuhn and Heusinger, *Riesenholzschnitte*, pp. 89, 102.
[4] See Appuhn and Heusinger, cit.
[5] The doll's house, formerly in the Bodmer Collection, was sold at Sotheby's, London, 8–9 November 1989.
[6] Both historic and modern terminology for the papers is somewhat confusing. Umbrella terms used in the 20th century for printed and/or coloured papers that are not specifically *wallpaper* are *Buntpapier* in Germany, *domino* in France, *sierpapier* in Holland, *carte decorate*, *carte siliografate*, etc. in Italy, and in England 'decorative paper'.
[7] See Adhémar, *L'Imagerie populaire française*.
[8] *Encyclopédie*, V, Paris 1755, p. 35.
[9] Ibid., IX, Paris 1772, p. 860. Two sorts of English wallpaper decorated with spangles made of flaked isinglass are described by Robert Dossie in *The Handmaid to the Arts* (II, London 1758, pp. 426–27). In one – no longer fashionable by his day, he says – they were sprinkled loosely on a varnished coloured ground. In the other – itself rarely seen – they were applied in a pattern in the same way as flock, and served to imitate silver embroidery.
[10] Ibid., p. 861.

2 Flocks, Florals and Fancies:
English Manufacture 1680–1830

[1] Sugden and Edmondson, *English Wallpaper*, p. 32.
[2] John Houghton, in *A Collection of Letters for the Improvement of Husbandry and Trade*, London 1689–1703, 30 June 1699.
[3] See Wells-Cole, *Historic Paper Hangings*, nos 26–31.
[4] 'A straight stitch on canvas worked in zigzag lines, often in graduations of colour', Margaret Swain, *Historical Needlework: A Study of Influences in Scotland and Northern England*, London 1970, p. 122.
[5] Entwisle, *Book of Wallpaper*, pl. 25.
[6] Sugden and Edmondson, *English Wallpaper*, pl. 33.
[7] As at Ham House (Surrey), for instance, or the recently restored palace of Het Loo in Holland.
[8] As in a paper from South Street Cottage in Epsom: see Wells-Cole, *Historic Paper Hangings*, no. 31.
[9] Dossie's discussion of 'paper hangings', from which the following extracts are taken, appears in *Handmaid*, II, pp. 410–27.
[10] Although details of printed designs may often have been re-touched.
[11] The Act was 10 Anne c.18: see Dagnall, *Tax on Wallpaper*, fig. 1. Dagnall's booklet is the standard work on this subject in England.
[12] An early 18th-century paper with this stamp, from Rickerscote Hall, Stafford, is in the collection at Temple Newsam, Leeds, while another, from 29 Sackville Street, London, datable around 1730, is illustrated in Rosoman, *London Wallpapers*, pl. 12.
[13] Dagnall, *Tax on Wallpaper*, p. 5.
[14] At Hurlcote or Hulcote Manor, Easton Neston (Northamptonshire); the paper is in the V&A (O&H 48; col. pl. p. 106), and an example of a similar damask is at Temple Newsam, in the Roger Warner collection of textiles.
[15] This important early Tudor house, extensively remodelled throughout the 18th century, has yielded up many original wallpapers which have been added to by the gift of papers from other provenanced buildings; owned since 1922 by the City of Leeds, it has become a centre for the study of English wallpapers.
[16] Peter Thornton, *Baroque and Rococo Silks*, London 1965, pl. 114A.
[17] As at Temple Newsam.
[18] At Temple Newsam, for instance, the wall-height from dado to cornice is 13½ feet (4.1 m), so a paper with a 7-foot (2.1 m) pattern drop would have repeated just under twice, obviating waste.
[19] This pattern was revived in the second half of the 19th century by Watts & Co., London (the furnishing firm set up in 1868 by the architects Bodley and Garner) under the title 'Pear'.
[20] As in another example found in the Privy Council offices (V&A; O&H 59).
[21] For instance, at Ham House (Surrey), Skokloster Slott in Sweden, and elsewhere.
[22] One hung in a first-floor rear reception room at 17 Albemarle Street (Rosoman, *London Wallpapers*, pl. 22); another still hangs in a ground floor drawing room at Christchurch Mansion.
[23] Sugden and Edmondson, *English Wallpaper*, pl. 28, and John Cornforth in *Country Life*, 9 July 1992, pp. 46–49.
[24] Nylander et al., *Wallpaper in New England*, fig. 1.3 and cat. 1.3; the latter house was built in 1774 but the paper may only have been hung during the following decade.
[25] Dossie, *Handmaid*, p. 423.
[26] ibid., pp. 425–26.
[27] Chippendale may have supplied more of the same to Sir Rowland Winn for a bedroom at Nostell Priory (Yorkshire) some years later: his invoice of 4 March 1768 specifies '8 Pieces of Norfolk Crimson and Yellow Flock 9/– 3 12 0' (Blue Account Book, no ref. no.); see Lindsay Boynton and Nicholas Goodison, 'Thomas Chippendale at Nostell Priory', *Furniture History*, IV (1968), p. 47. The Soho Square example is illustrated in Rosoman, *London Wallpapers*, pl. 17. Papers could be invoiced either by the yard or by the piece.
[28] At 17 Albemarle Street, see Rosoman, *London Wallpapers*, pl. 19; this paper is a printed rather than a flocked version. The pattern was revived in the 19th century by Watts & Co. under the name 'Old English'.
[29] This was revived by Watts & Co. as 'Malmesbury'.
[30] Wells-Cole, *Historic Paper Hangings*, p. 8.
[31] The design of the flock paper, however, exactly matches that of a decorative paper printed in Bologna in the 1770s (V&A, Dept of Prints and Drawings).
[32] Cit. Entwisle, *Literary History*, p. 50.
[33] Nylander et al., *Wallpaper in New England*, cat. 1.2.
[34] These wallpapers are illustrated in Sugden and Edmondson, *English Wallpaper*, pls 30, 31. The present contributor may once have believed that the 'Pomegranate' pattern could have been earlier: see Wells-Cole, *Historic Paper Hangings*, no. 4.
[35] A magnificent example still hangs at Tyninghame near Edinburgh.
[36] Wheeley and Darly's trade-cards, in the Heal Collection, British Museum, London, are illustrated in Rosoman, *London Wallpapers*, pp. 10, 12.
[37] *Leeds Mercury*, 11 May 1773; for a more detailed look at the retailing of paper hangings in a provincial town, see Wells-Cole, *Historic Paper Hangings*, pp. 47–48.
[38] Dossie, *Handmaid*, p. 419.
[39] This is also true of another floral paper hung in a house in Sackville Street, London, after 1732 – although the final effect, achieved by a highly detailed outline print, is rather different: see Rosoman, *London Wallpapers*, pl. 12.
[40] In the collections of Temple Newsam and Wakefield Museum respectively.
[41] Rosoman, *London Wallpapers*, pl. 13. Pieces are also in the collection of the V&A (O&H 57).
[42] Another example is the abstract design of white festoons and feather shapes on a strong blue ground which was hung in a first-floor bedroom at Aston Hall near Birmingham: Wells-Cole, *Historic Paper Hangings*, no. 50.
[43] Another was used in the decoration of Osterley Park (Middlesex), c. 1775. See Christopher Gilbert and Anthony Wells-Cole, *The Fashionable Fire Place*, Leeds 1985, no. 63.
[44] See John Cornforth in *Country Life* (cit. at n. 23).
[45] Letter of 12 June 1753; *Letters of Horace Walpole, Earl of Orford, to Sir Horace Mann*, ed. Lord Dover, London 1833, III, p. 45.
[46] Other yellow-ground print-room designs were hung at the Old Manor, Bourton-on-the-Water (Gloucestershire), in 1769 (O&H 100) and near London in the Manor House, Crooms Hill, Greenwich (Rosoman, *London Wallpapers*, pl. 27). Exactly contemporary with these is a similar paper hung, rather surprisingly, in the hall, in the Lady Pepperrell House, Kittery Point (Maine), built c. 1760; some of the scenes were adapted from *The Ladies Amusement* published by Robert Sayer in London in 1762. Two further designs are based on large and small compartments alternating. In one the framework is 'Modern' and takes the form of decorative arbours of floral stalks, shells and scrolls with Classical caryatids; two pastoral scenes also alternate. The other paper is similar in type but 'Gothic' in character: a decidedly romantic design hung in the house of John Langdon in Portsmouth (New Hampshire) in 1785, it falls almost mid-way between the earliest Gothic Revival paper hangings of the 1750s and 1760s and those of the early 19th century. See Nylander et al., *Wallpaper in New England*, cats 6.1, 6.2.
[47] For instance in the V&A (O&H 1018, 1019); in the same collection is an album containing drawings of flowers etc. as working material for his wallpaper designs (O&H 1020).
[48] Dossie, *Handmaid*, p. 410.
[49] *Letters* (cit at n. 45), pp. 44–45.
[50] Not at Markenfield Hall, as once believed, see Wells-Cole, *Historic Paper Hangings*, no. 21; a fragment of the same design survives in the Oxford Museum.
[51] For the Stafford paper see Wells-Cole, *Historic Paper Hangings*, no. 39. A small fragment of the paper hung at Temple Newsam was recovered in 1991; it was too small to reconstruct, and the room was rehung with an experimental reprint of the Amen Court paper, printed from hand-cut blocks on rolls made up of individual sheets: see John Cornforth in *Country Life*, 23 Sept. 1993, pp. 72–75.
[52] In America, English pillar-and-arch papers hung in houses in Kittery Point (Maine), Marblehead and North Andover (Massachusetts): see Nylander et al., *Wallpaper in New England*, cats 4.1, 4.2, 4-b.
[53] West Yorkshire Archives Service, Leeds.
[54] V&A (O&H 117). Another example of this pattern, at Clandon Park, was also thought to be a copy, but Bernard Jacqué considers it to be a later version, in flock, by Réveillon himself.

3 The China Trade:
Oriental Painted Panels

[1] In 1695 an auction of 66 pieces or lengths of 'Japan paper' for hangings was held at the Marine Coffee House, Birchin Lane, in the City of London. Quoted in Teynac, Nolot and Vivien, *Wallpaper*, p. 61.
[2] Madame du Bocage, *Letters on England, Holland and Italy*, 1750.
[3] See Lynn, *Wallpaper in America*.
[4] For a full gazetteer of Chinese wallpapers see Wappenschmidt, *Chinesische Tapeten*.
[5] The flock paper was supplied by Chippendale for Nostell Priory in 1768: see above, chapter 2, n. 27. Lady Mary Coke in 1766 noticed in His Majesty's Lodge, Richmond Park, 'An Indian [i.e. Chinese] paper which cost three guineas the sheet', presumably a 4-yard (3.65 m) length: *Letters and Journals of Lady Mary Coke*, ed. J. A. Home. A letter in the archive at Dunster Castle (Somerset) describes an 'India paper representing the several stages of a Chinese manufacture . . . the figures very compleat and interspersed with romantick views' that could not be had for less than 7s. a yard; even the commoner papers

'representing trees, birds and flowers' cost 4s. a yard.
6 Memoirs and Observations . . . Made in a late journey through the Empire of China, London 1697, p. 160.
7 For a more detailed history of this motif, see J. Irwin and K. B. Brett, Origins of Chintz, London 1970.
8 Quoted in Country Life, LXXX, 1936, p. liv.
9 There are two examples in the V&A where printing has been used for the outlines only: E.412, 413–1924, early 18th century, wood-engraving with tempera; E.2286–1966, mid-18th century, print from woodblock with tempera.
10 I am indebted to Merryl Huxtable and Craig Clunas for this information.
11 I am grateful to Joosje van Dam for this information.
12 Cowtan and Sons was a London firm of decorators, serving a largely upper-class clientèle throughout Britain. Its order books, dating from 1824–1938, include cuttings of wallpapers and other material for interior decoration. They are now held in the V&A (E.1862–1885–1946).
13 Cowtan order book (V&A, E.1864–1946), Jan. 1838.
14 Oliver Brackett, Accounts of Chippendale Haig & Co. for the Furnishing of David Garrick's House in the Adelphi, London 1920.
15 As in the paper supplied by Cowtan and Sons for Sandringham House (Norfolk) in the early 19th century, or that hung at Fawley Court (Buckinghamshire) in the billiard room, described in the Diaries of Mrs Philip Lybbe Powys of Hardwicke House, Oxon, ed. Emily J. Climenson, London 1899, Oct. 1771.
16 Lady Mary Coke (cit. at n. 5).
17 Leeds Art Calendar, 61, 1968, pp. 14–17.
18 Journal of the Rt Hon. Sir Joseph Banks, 1768–71.
19 See Clunas, Chinese Export Watercolours.
20 V&A (E.3587–3593–1922), late 18th century, from Archdeaconry House, Peterborough.
21 Ibid.
22 Spink & Son Ltd, London, The Art of Textiles (sale), Dec. 1989, cat. 6. Such silk panels were also used as wallcoverings; indeed the 'paper' in the Chinese Chippendale Bedroom at Saltram is actually a painted silk on a paper support.
23 See Susan Lambert, ed., Pattern and Design: Designs for the Decorative Arts 1480–1980, London 1983, pp. 64–67.
24 J. B. Jackson, An Essay on the Invention of Engraving and Printing in Chiaro Oscuro, London 1754, p. 8.
25 Journal of Eugène Delacroix, under 9 Oct. 1847.

4 Luxury Perfected: The Ascendancy of French Wallpaper 1770–1870

1 The essential work for the study of wallpaper in France remains the classic publication by Clouzot and Follot, Histoire du Papier peint. On German manufacturers, see especially Olligs, Tapeten; on England, Entwisle, Book of Wallpaper; on the United States, Lynn, Wallpaper in America, and Nylander et al., Wallpaper in New England. The Musée du Papier Peint at Rixheim has since 1990 issued an annual bibliography of publications.
2 On the technical aspects, see Jacqué, 'Technique et papier peint'.
3 See especially the situation of the American market, considered in Lynn, Wallpaper in America, and Nylander et al., Wallpaper in New England.
4 Jean-Baptiste Réveillon, Relation historique et très intéressante des malheurs arrivés au Sr Réveillon, entrepreneur de la manufacture royale de Papiers Peints, Faubourg saint Antoine à Paris, écrite par lui même avec le détail de tout ce qu'on lui a saccagé et volé, Paris 1789.
5 The partnerships were Arthur & Grenard until 1789, Arthur & Robert 1789–94, and Robert & Cie after 1794, following the execution of Arthur, an Englishman, who was a revolutionary and friend of Robespierre.
6 This point is considered in Jacqué, ed., Papiers peints en arabesques.
7 Archives of Nicolas Dollfus & Cie, in the MPP (Z 94).
8 French wallpapers of the period 1800–1850 are the subject of an anthology by Nouvel, Wallpapers of France.
9 See Nouvel-Kammerer, 'Les Inventions techniques', pp. 107ff. The first papers using the new technique were issued in 1822.
10 This type of motif has not yet been studied systematically. In the meantime, see e.g. Bernard Jacqué,

'Les Roses du papier peint', in Rosa, rosa, rosae, exh. cat., Grasse 1991.
11 See e.g. Fabry, 'Dessins et dessinateurs', pp. 101–6.
12 See Jacqué and Nouvel-Kammerer, Papier peint.
13 Several instances are documented in England. Horace Walpole, for example, in a letter of 12 June 1753 describing the new furnishings of Strawberry Hill, his house near London, mentions a sitting room 'hung with a blue and white paper in stripes adorned with festoons, and a thousand plump chairs, couches, and luxurious settees covered with linen of the same pattern'. The letter incidentally shows that Walpole, an English aristocrat, had wallpaper in almost every room. See Letters of Horace Walpole, Earl of Orford, to Sir Horace Mann, ed. Lord Dover, London 1833, III, pp. 44–45.
14 See Stuart Durant, Ornament, a Survey of Decoration since 1830, London 1986; L'Age d'or des arts décoratifs 1800–1851, exh. cat., Paris 1991; and L'Art en France sous le Second Empire, Paris 1799.
15 See Jacqué and Nouvel-Kammerer, Papier peint, pp. 9–11.
16 Bernard Jacqué and Geert Wisse, 'Note sur un ensemble de papiers peints imprimés en taille-douce à Paris à la fin du XVIIIᵉ siècle', Nouvelles de l'estampe, Paris, Oct. 1992, pp. 5–29.
17 Now in the MPP.
18 See MPP, Mirage du luxe.
19 The story of the designers is complex, and yet to be written. Some worked alone; others worked in studios where each specialized in a particular area. The ornemaniste Zipélius, for instance, was in partnership with the flower designer Joseph Fuchs, and their studio, which may have included more than a hundred designers, was one of the leading ones in France during the Second Empire.
20 Nouvel-Kammerer, 'De la créativité technique', pp. 101–6.

5 Arabesques and Allegories: French Decorative Panels

1 Madame de Genlis, Discours moraux sur différents sujets et particulièrement sur l'éducation, 1802.
2 Ibid.
3 Several examples of this set with a green ground survive: one is mounted in a Louis XVI folding screen (MAD); others extend further at the top (MAD); yet others are accompanied by intermediate panels (ill. Clouzot and Follot, Papier peint, p. 57). The variety is indicative of the range of ways in which this sort of paper could be used. See V. de Bruignac, 'Des papiers peints en arabesque de la manufacture Réveillon', BSIM, no. 793, 1984, pp. 117–28. Three little panels of sight, smell and hearing also exist on a blue ground, accompanied by lateral panels (ex coll. Charles Huard, now RISD Museum, Providence).
4 V&A (E.835–1980).
5 Figures of goddesses very similar in style to these herms appear in a paper panel in the MAD (988.611).
6 Olligs, Tapeten, I, p. 255.
7 Archives Nationales, Paris, F12 2281 (report of 1807).
8 Design no. 1080, MPP (985PP) and Musée de la Révolution Française, Vizille. The design corresponding to ill. 112 is MPP 982PP48. In the firm's album the gouache designs are dated 1789; however, there are 476 designs entered for 1789 and only 15 for the years 1789–93, so it would seem that the 1789 record date was given to papers printed both earlier and later, during the period when Jacquemart & Bénard first rented and then took over the Réveillon factory. Both the revolutionary papers cited were probably printed in 1793. Some revolutionary French papers were also exported to the United States; see above, p. 120.
9 BN (LI 15, 920–924). There is hope that it may be restored.
10 Le Normand, Annales, pp. 47–49.
11 MAD (29574).
12 Archives Nationales, Paris, F12/1659. The address of Deyrieu is given as 'rue Grenelle-honoré maison Languedoc, no. 27'.
13 MAD (10720).
14 Ill. in Clouzot and Follot, Papier peint, p. 151.
15 Details of these overdoors are reproduced in McClelland, Historic Wall-Papers, pp. 163–64, with the title 'Les Portiques d'Athènes'.

16 See McClelland, Historic Wall-Papers, p. 225, MAD (56838), V&A (E.737–1912), and Rhode Island School of Design, Providence (34.958). I now (2005) consider that the Mediterranean Seaport should be attributed to Jean-Gabriel Charvet rather than Horace Vernet.
17 Le Normand, Annales, p. 46.

6 Wide Horizons: French Scenic Papers

1 Le Normand, Annales, pp. 9–10.
2 The Expositions des Produits de l'Industrie had as their purpose to present to the public the best products of French industry. They were in a sense the forerunners, on a national scale, of the great international exhibitions which began in 1851 in London. The reports are an invaluable source of information on the development of wallpaper, particularly of scenic wallpaper.
3 For 1806, see Notices sur les objets envoyés à l'Exposition des Produits de l'Industrie française rédigées et imprimées par S.E. M. de Champagny, Paris 1806, pp. 91, 256. For 1819: Rapport du jury central sur les Produits de l'Industrie française . . . rédigé par M. L. Costaz, Paris 1819, pp. 152, 153. For 1834: Rapport du jury central sur les Produits de l'Industrie française exposés en 1834 par le baron Ch. Dupin, Paris 1834, vol. 1, p. 183. For 1851: Travaux de la commission française sur l'Industrie des Nations publié par l'ordre de l'Empereur, Paris 1851, 26th jury, pp. 21, 22.
4 On the rules of anonymity and the absence of artists' names in the case of scenic wallpapers, see Nouvel-Kammerer, Papiers peints panoramiques, pp. 26ff. and 105ff.
5 Letter from Joseph Dufour to M. le Curé Génillon, 27 Sept. 1819 (private collection).
6 Joseph Dufour, Livret explicatif sur les Sauvages de la mer Pacifique, Mâcon, an XIII [1804/5], p. 11.
7 See above, n. 3 (1851).

7 An Ocean Apart: Imports and the Beginning of American Manufacture

1 Walter Kendall Watkins, 'The Early Use and Manufacture of Paper-Hangings in Boston', Old-Time New England, 12, Jan. 1922, p. 109. See also Lynn, Wallpaper in America, p. 22.
2 All five almanacs are in the collection of the Peabody and Essex Museum in Salem, Mass.
3 The descriptions were gathered from the following compilations of newspaper advertisements: George Francis Dow, ed., The Arts and Crafts in New England, 1704–1775, Topsfield, Mass.; Rita Susswein Gottesman, ed., The Arts and Crafts in New York, 1726–1776, New York 1938; and Alfred Coxe Prime, comp., The Arts and Crafts in Philadelphia, Maryland, and South Carolina, 1721–1785, pt 1, Topsfield, Mass., 1929. The Bucktrout advertisement is quoted in Lynn, Wallpaper in America, p. 143.
4 John M. Dickey, Research and Planning Studies for the Restoration of the Proprietary House, Perth Amboy, New Jersey, Media, Pa., unpublished report, 1 July 1973.
5 The Lee papers and their print sources are discussed in Catherine Lynn Frangiamore, 'Landscape Wallpaper in the Jeremiah Lee Mansion', The Magazine Antiques, CXII, no. 6, Dec. 1977, pp. 1174–79. On the Van Rensselaer paper, now installed in the American Wing of the Metropolitan Museum of Art, New York, see E. B. Donnell, 'The Van Rensselaer Painted Wallpaper', Bull. of the Metropolitan Museum of Art, XXVI (suppl.), 1931, pp. 10–16.
6 Lynn, Wallpaper in America, p. 125.
7 John Welsh, Jr, Letter book, MS. 766, 1781–86, W462, p. 30, Baker Library, Harvard Business School, Cambridge, Mass.
8 Advertisement of John Colles, Daily Advertiser, 11 April 1787, as quoted in Rita Susswein Gottesman, ed., The Arts and Crafts in New York, 1777–1799, New York 1954, p. 153.
9 Independent Chronicle (Boston), 20 April 1795.
10 Eliza S. Quincy, Memoir of the Life of Eliza S. M. Quincy, Boston, 1861, p. 86.
11 Casey Papers, 22:317. Historic New England Archives, Boston.

[12] See above, n. 7.

[13] Ibid.

[14] *General Advertiser* (Charleston, S.C.), 18 Nov. 1790, as quoted in Alfred Coxe Prime, comp., *The Arts and Crafts in Philadelphia, Maryland, and South Carolina, 1786–1800*, ser. 2, Topsfield, Mass., 1932, p. 219.

[15] *Charleston City Gazette*, 10 Feb. 1795 (Prime 1932 [cit. at n. 14], p. 221).

[16] *Federal Gazette* (Philadelphia. Pa.), 9 Oct. 1792 (Prime 1932 [cit. at n. 14], pp. 283–84).

[17] Ibid., 11 March 1795 (Prime 1932 [cit. at n. 14], p. 284).

[18] William Strickland, *Journal of a Tour of the United States of America, 1794–1795*, ed. Rev. J. E. Strickland, New York (Lynn, *Wallpaper in America*, p. 93).

[19] *New York Mercury*, 13 Dec. 1756 (Lynn, *Wallpaper in America*, p. 107).

[20] Watkins (cit. at n. 1), p. 113.

[21] *New York Gazette*, 23–30 Nov. 1767 (Gottesman 1938, p. 237).

[22] *Pennsylvania Packet*, 29 May 1775 (Prime 1929 [cit. at n. 3], p. 277).

[23] Gottesman 1954, p. 155.

[24] *Pennsylvania Packet*, 18 Oct. 1785 (Prime 1929 [cit. at n. 3], p. 281).

[25] *Independent Gazetteer*, 26 Dec. 1786 (Prime 1932 [cit. at n. 14], p. 277).

[26] Norman B. Wilkinson, *Papermaking in America*, Greenville, Del., 1975, pp. 19–23.

[27] Nylander et al., *Wallpaper in New England*, pp. 19, 27.

[28] *Columbian Centinel* (Boston), 24 Sept. 1800.

[29] Gottesman 1954, p. 155.

[30] Skipwith Papers, Earl G. Swem Library, The College of William and Mary, Williamsburg, Va.

[31] Rundlet's wallpapers and the invoice are in the collection of Historic New England, Boston.

[32] *New-England Palladium* (Boston), 10 Aug. 1813 (Nylander et al., *Wallpaper in New England*, p. 13).

[33] See above, n. 31.

[34] *Pennsylvania Packet*, 4 Dec. 1797 (Prime 1932 [cit. at n. 14], p. 285).

[35] See Nylander et al., *Wallpaper in New England*, p. 12.

[36] Bureau of Census, Fourth Census, 1820, Census of Manufacturers, Rhode Island and Massachusetts respectively.

[37] Louis B. McLane, *Documents Relative to the Manufacturers in the United States, Collected and Transmitted to the House of Representatives . . . By the Secretary of the Treasury, House Executive Documents*, Washington, D.C., 1833, pp. 144–45.

[38] The label is dated 1833. The bandbox is in the collection of Old Sturbridge Village, Mass.

[39] *Massachusetts Spy* (Worcester, Mass.), 20 Aug. 1823 (Harris); 4 May 1836 (Nickels and Barrey).

[40] *Massachusetts Spy*, 10 May 1837.

[41] Lynn, *Wallpaper in America*, p. 312.

[42] Factory and Store Daily Memorandum, 1840–68, 10 vols. Privately owned. The Bumstead journals are discussed by Karen Guffey in an essay published in Nylander et al., *Wallpaper in New England*. They are explored further in Redmond, 'American Wallpaper'.

8 The English Response: Mechanization and Design Reform

[1] Sugden and Entwisle, *Crace Papers*, p. 36.

[2] Sugden and Edmondson, *English Wallpaper*, pp. 128–29.

[3] Bernard Jacqué, 'Petit vade-mecum technique à l'usage de l'amateur de papier peint ancien', *BSIM*, no. 823, 1991, p. 32.

[4] These figures and further details relating to the taxes on wallpaper are given in Dagnall, *Tax on Wallpaper*.

[5] Sugden and Entwisle, *Potters of Darwen*, pp. 115–16.

[6] Ibid., p. 100.

[7] Sugden and Edmondson, *English Wallpaper*, p. 52.

[8] Sugden and Entwisle, *Potters of Darwen*, p. 52.

[9] Nylander et al., *Wallpaper in New England*, p. 33.

[10] Sugden and Edmondson, *English Wallpaper*, p. 140.

[11] Lynn, *Wallpaper in America*.

[12] *Journal of Design and Manufactures*, 1, 1849, p. 169.

[13] *Art Union*, 6, 1844, p. 179.

[14] Redgrave, *Report on Design*, p. 27.

[15] Sugden and Edmondson, *English Wallpaper*, p. 139.

[16] *The Decorator's Assistant*, 1847, p. 117.

[17] Ibid.

[18] C. Thackrah, *The Effects of the Principal Arts, Trades and Professions etc. on Health and Longevity*, London 1832.

[19] Entwisle, *Victorian Era*, p. 27.

[20] Sugden and Entwisle, *Potters of Darwen*, p. 108.

[21] Greysmith, *Wallpaper*, p. 109. M. Digby Wyatt, *Industrial Arts of the 19th Century*, London 1852, text accompanying pl. 100, states that this incident took place at the Dauptain factory in Paris, where Clarke had installed the machine.

[22] H. W. & A. Arrowsmith, *The House Decorator and Painter's Guide*, London 1840, p. 111.

[23] *The Builder*, IX, 1851, p. 422.

[24] Sugden and Entwisle, *Crace Papers*, p. 47.

[25] See above, n. 12.

[26] *Select Committee Report on the Schools of Design*, London 1849, p. 141.

[27] *Catalogue of the Select Specimens of British Manufacture and Decorative Art*, London 1847, p. 4.

[28] Pugin, *True Principles*, p. 29.

[29] Ibid.

[30] Redgrave, *Report on Design*, p. 26.

[31] Pugin, *True Principles*, p. 1.

[32] C. Dickens, *Hard Times*, London 1854; repr. 1967, pp. 51–52.

[33] Redgrave, *Report on Design*, p. 25.

[34] Jones, *Grammar of Ornament*, p. 5.

[35] Ibid., p. 6.

[36] For example, *The Illustrated London News*, 1862, pp. 597–98.

[37] Quoted in S. Macdonald, *The History and Philosophy of Art Education*, London 1970, p. 240.

[38] L. Parry, *Willam Morris Textiles*, London 1983, p. 129.

[39] Harvey and Press, *William Morris*, p. 182.

[40] Morris's agents abroad included Samuel Bing in Paris; Walther in Frankfurt; Hirchwald in Berlin; Cowtan & Tout Inc. in New York; and Woodville & Co. in Philadelphia and Melbourne.

[41] Sugden and Entwisle, *Potters of Darwen*, p. 52.

[42] *The Builder*, 25, 1867, p. 362.

9 Proliferation: Late 19th-Century Papers, Markets and Manufacturers

England

[1] The statistical information in this section relies on W. Hamish Fraser, *The Coming of the Mass Market 1850–1914*, London 1981.

[2] Mrs Panton, *Nooks and Corners*, London 1889, p. 12.

[3] Mrs Panton, 'Artistic Homes and How to Make Them', *The Lady's World: a Magazine of Fashion and Society*, London 1887, p. 240.

[4] *JDA*, VII, 1887, pp. 33–35.

[5] Press cutting from the *European Mail*, 6 Jan. 1892, included in a volume of cuttings, pamphlets, etc., relating to Jeffrey & Co. (V&A, Dept of Prints and Drawings, E.42A 1–3).

[6] Elisabet Stavenow-Hidemark, *Sub Rosa*, Stockholm (Nordiska Museet) 1991, passim.

[7] *Kelly's Post Office Directory of Merchants and Manufacturers*, London 1900.

[8] *JDA*, III, 1883, pp. 368–72.

[9] John Walker in *JDA*, XI, 1891, April suppl., p. 1, quoted in Woods, 'Pedigree Papers', p. 249. On the subject of this section, in addition to the latter article, see also J. Banham, 'Outstanding Designs', *Traditional Homes*, June 1987.

[10] Sugden and Entwisle, *Potters of Darwen*, p. 65.

[11] *JDA*, IV, 1884, p. 472.

[12] *JDA*, XI, 1891, p. 66.

[13] *JDA*, XVII, 1897, p. 84.

[14] *JDA*, X, 1890, Feb. suppl., p. v.

[15] *JDA*, III, 1883, p. 403.

[16] *JDA*, X, 1890, Feb. suppl., pp. v–vii.

[17] For the discussion of pattern-drawers, in-house designers and freelancers which follows see Linda Parry, *Textiles of the Arts and Crafts Movement*, London 1988, rev. edn 2005.

[18] Frederick Aumonier (head of William Woollams & Co.), 'Wallpapers, their Manufacture and Design' (paper read before the Soc. of Architects, 1895), quoted in Christine Woods, 'A Marriage of Convenience: Walter Crane and the Wallpaper Industry', in Greg Smith and Sarah Hyde, eds, *Walter Crane: Artist, Designer, Socialist*, Manchester and London 1989, p. 59.

[19] Sugden and Entwisle, *Potters of Darwen*, p. 45.

[20] Turner, *Art Nouveau Designs from the Silver Studio Collection*, pp. 11–12.

[21] For what follows on artists and architects as designers see Woods in *Crane* (cit. at n. 18).

[22] See C. Woods, *The Magic Influence of Mr Kydd: Blocked and Stencilled Wallpapers 1900–1925*, Manchester 1989.

[23] For the Davenport and Cotterell examples that follow see *JDA*, VIII, 1888, Jan. suppl., p. iv.

[24] *The Clifton Book of Wallpapers*, WAG W.1967.1066.

[25] Mawer Cowtan, 'Reminiscences and Changes in Taste in Home Decoration' (paper read before the Incorporated Institute of British Decorators, 6 March 1914).

[26] Fraser (cit. at n. 1), p. 146.

[27] Walter Crane and Lewis F. Day, *Moot Points: Friendly Disputes on Art and Industry*, London 1903. Crane also produced designs for textiles and ceramics.

[28] A. S. Jennings, 'The Decoration of Small Houses', *JDA*, XXXIII, 1913. Mark Turner and Lesley Hoskins, *The Silver Studio of Design*, Newton Abbot (Devon) 1988, p. 42.

[29] Fraser (cit. at n. 1), p. 136.

[30] Monopolies Commission, *Report on the Supply of Wallpaper*, Jan. 1964, p. 6; and the Wall Paper Manufacturers Ltd, *Prospectus on the Issue of Stocks and Shares*, 1900.

[31] Woods, 'Pedigree Papers', p. 250.

[32] Jennings (cit. at n. 28), p. 52.

The United States

[1] *Furniture Gazette*, 30 Dec. 1876.

[2] *Philadelphia Trade Directory*, 1874, p. 17.

[3] 'The American Trade in Paper-Hangings', *Furniture Gazette*, 10 May 1879, p. 323.

[4] J. Leander Bishop, *A History of American Manufacturers from 1608 to 1868*, Philadelphia 1868, III, pp. 179–82.

[5] *Scientific American*, 31 Dec. 1881, p. 418; and *Frank Leslie's Illustrated Newspaper*, 27 May 1882, p. 219.

[6] Nylander et al., *Wallpaper in New England*, p. 233.

[7] See above, n. 3.

[8] The Metropolitan Museum of Art, *In Pursuit of Beauty: Americans and the Aesthetic Movement*, New York 1986, p. 69.

[9] 'The Frieze and the Dado', *Carpentry and Building*, no. 6, June 1884, pp. 106–7.

[10] Lynn, *Wallpaper in America*, p. 417.

[11] 'How Wallpaper is Sold', *New York Times*, 18 Sept. 1898.

[12] 'Wallpaper', *Decorator and Furnisher*, no. 6, Sept. 1890, p. 192.

[13] Lynn, *Wallpaper in America*, p. 464.

[14] *Decorator and Furnisher* (cit. at n. 12), p. 193.

France

[1] See the *livres d'échantillonnage* or sample books of Jean Zuber & Cie (in the MPP), which mention machine-printed papers copying motifs from block-printed papers.

[2] Charles Blanc, *Grammaire des arts décoratifs*, Paris 1881, p. 71.

[3] See L. Wolowski, *Dictionnaire universel théorique et pratique du commerce et de la navigation*, Paris 1863, pp. 971–76.

[4] See Bernard Jacqué, 'Petit vade-mecum technique à l'usage de l'amateur de papier peint ancien', *BSIM*, no. 823, 1991, pp. 35–39.

[5] See Bernard Jacqué, 'La Perfection dans l'illusion? Les techniques de fabrication de la manufacture Balin (1863–1898)', *BSIM*, no. 823, 1991, pp. 107–17.

[6] See Lynn, *Wallpaper in America*, pp. 367ff.

[7] MPP (PC).

10 Unsteady Progress: From the Turn of the Century to the Second World War

The Continent of Europe

[1] The wallpaper was used in the Bloemenwerf house at Uccle (Belgium) in 1895 and shown in the 'Study' at the Secession Exhibition in Munich in 1899. See, e.g., K. J.

Sembach, *Henry van de Velde*, London 1989, p. 53.
2 *Die Tapete*, V, 1908, p. 8.
3 Similar associations were founded in Switzerland, Austria, England and France, and later in the United States.
4 This was the Grand Salon in the 'Hôtel du Collectionneur', Ruhlmann's pavilion in the exhibition.
5 See Tilmann Buddensieg, *Keramik in der Weimarer Republik*, exh. cat., Nuremberg 1985.
6 See Josef Leiss in Olligs, *Tapeten*, II, p. 182.
7 *Tapeten-Zeitung*, LIX, 18, 1950, p. 471.

Britain and the United States
1 Katzenbach, *American Wallpaper*, p. 82.
2 H. S. Goodhart-Rendel (reviewing the 'Exhibition of Historical and British Wallpapers' held at the Suffolk Galleries, London, in May 1945), *The Architect and Building News*, 1 June 1945, p. 123.
3 Sugden and Edmondson, *English Wallpaper*, pp. 185–86.
4 Allen-Higgins Co. of Worcester (Mass.), in *Carpets, Wallpapers and Curtains* (New York), 26 Aug. 1905, p. 7.
5 Ogden Codman, Jr, and Edith Wharton, *The Decoration of Houses*, New York 1897, p. 27.
6 *London Journal of Commerce*, XVI, no. 406, 1901.
7 Ackerman, *Wallpaper*, p. 80.
8 Montgomery Ward & Co., *Decorator Approved Wallpapers*, 1939, p. 37.
9 Hapgood, *Wallpaper and the Artist*, p. 183.
10 For a full discussion of Edward Bawden's contribution to wallpaper design see Mark Pinney, 'The Rediscovery of Wallpaper', in Turner et al., *A Popular Art*.
11 Paul Nash, 'New Draughtsman', *Signature No. 1*, 1935, p. 27.
12 J. M. Richards, *Edward Bawden*, 1946, p. 8.
13 F. R. S. Yorke, 'Modern Wallcoverings', *Architectural Review*, Feb. 1932, pp. 71–80.
14 The leading figure in this was R. V. M. Busby, director of Lightbown Aspinall. See Lesley Hoskins, 'The Industry', in Turner et al., *A Popular Art*, p. 51.

11 Post-War Promise: Pattern and Technology up to 1970

The United States
I owe thanks to John Quilter, Victor Scotese, Martin Johnson, Lanette Scheeline, Louis Bowen, Abraham Edelman and SueEllen Appleman.
On output, manufactures and products of the 1950s, the best overall source of information is Ronald White, 'A Thesis on the Wallpaper Industry', *Wallpaper and Wallcoverings*, Jan., Feb., March and Nov. 1958.
1 Donald Fitzhugh, 'Wallcoverings Essay: Keep the Home Walls Smiling', *Wallpaper and Wallcoverings*, Dec. 1969, p. 18.
2 'The Wallcoverings Newsreel, Fifty Years of Headlines', *Wallpaper and Wallcoverings*, May 1969, pp. 15–16.
3 Ten Years of Allman Awards', *Wallpaper and Wallcoverings*, Nov. 1956, p. 27.
4 *Interior Design and Decoration*, Aug. 1950, p. 35. On Plattsburg, see 'From Logs on the River to Finished Wallpaper at America's Only Fully Integrated Mill', *Wallpaper and Wallcoverings*, Sept. 1962, pp. 168–75.
5 *The Wallpaper Magazine*, Oct. 1952, p. 27.
6 Warren B. Nelson, 'The Design and Manufacture of Wallpaper', *Empire State Architect*, Dec. 1944, p. 8.
7 *Craft Horizons*, Winter 1949, pp. 12–14.
8 *Wallpaper and Wallcoverings*, Jan. 1966, p. 21.
9 Mary Roche, 'Wallpapers Show Distinctive Design', *New York Times*, 3 Jan. 1949.
10 *Interiors*, April 1955, p. 113.
11 Mary Roche, 'Papers for Today's Walls', *New York Times Magazine*, 31 Oct. 1948.
12 George Nelson in *Interiors*, Nov. 1949, pp. 68–75.
13 *New York Times*, 10 Oct. 1950.
14 William Yeo, 'The Designer's Viewpoint', *Wallpaper and Wallcoverings*, May 1958, p. 60.
15 *Interiors*, Nov. 1967.
16 Ibid.
17 'Jack Denst Accepts the Justin P. Allman Award', *Wallpaper and Wallcoverings*, July 1967, p. 11.

Britain and the Continent of Europe
1 I would like to thank the following for their generous provision of information: Duncan Burton of Crown

Wallcoverings, Sam Chorlton, Brian Day, Ullrich Eitel of Marburger Tapetenfabrik, Eddie Heath, J. H. P. Heesters, Osborne & Little, Gerrit Rasch, Tom Smail of Vymura, Sabine Thümmler, the Wallcovering, Fabric and Retailers Association, and Jean-Claude Zerapha of essef.
2 In France, post-war reconstruction had renewed 70 per cent of the wallpaper industry by 1958, giving production of 44,000,000 rolls a year; by 1966 that had almost doubled. Britain reached pre-war levels of output (100,000,000 rolls p.a.) in 1954 and by 1964 had taken that to almost 130,000,000. German output rose from 43,000,000 rolls in 1950 to 122,700,000 in 1968.
3 For discussion of the relationship between wallpaper and the post-war 'good design movement' in Britain, see Mark Pinney, 'The Rediscovery of Wallpaper', in Turner et al., *A Popular Art*.
4 Organized by the Verband Deutscher Tapeten-fabrikanten (Association of German Wallpaper Manufacturers) and the International Wallcovering Manufacturers Association (IGI).
5 A survey indicated that in 1967 they accounted for almost a quarter of the market. Reported in *Decorating Contractor*, April 1968, p. 20.
6 Published by Föreningen Svensk Form (Swedish Society of Industrial Design).
7 In the case of very expensive artists, Rasch would offer a royalty rather than outright purchase.
8 For example, the architect H. Salomonson (former member of De 8) and E. Elffers-Andriesse.
9 For a full discussion of post-war wallpaper in the Netherlands see E. G. M. Adriaansz and M. J. T. Knuijt, 'Industrieel vervaardigde behangsels 1945–1990', in Koldeweij et al., *Achter het Behang*.
10 *Souvenir Book of Crystal Designs: the fascinating story in colour of the Festival Pattern Group*, HMSO for the CoID, 1951.
11 'Palladio' was frequently featured in the magazine *Design*, published by the Design Council. Individual papers regularly won Design Centre awards. See, for example, *Design*, no. 162, June 1962, p. 60.
12 Pinney (cit. at n. 3).
13 It was estimated that in 1954 about 75 per cent of all British households did at least some of their own decorating, whereas the figures for Germany and Belgium in 1961 were 40 per cent and 60 per cent respectively. *Economist*, 26 June 1954, and *The Decorator*, June 1961, p. 57.
14 Reported in *Design*, no. 215, Nov. 1966, p. 25.

12 Off the Shelf: Design and Consumer Trends since 1970
1 There are few secondary sources for this period, and I am grateful to the following individuals for help and information: Hank Bolhuis, Duncan Burton, Jackie Calavitta, Sam Chorlton, John Dixon, Ullrich Eitel, Guy Evans, Norman Gibbon, Michael Levete, H. J. Morgan, Tom Newcomb, Tom Olsen, Felicity Osborne, Gerrit Rasch, John Robinson, Helen Sheane, Tom Smail, John Wilman, George Zacal and Jean-Claude Zerapha.
2 Lee Taylor in *Campaign*, 3 Dec. 1982.
3 In response to such issues, the National Guild of Professional Paperhangers was established in the USA in 1974.

13 Limited Editions: 1995 to Today
1 GenCorp had become the worldwide market leader in 1998, with the acquisition of the UK-based Muraspec and Brymor from Walker Greenbank. Walker Greenbank – with the Circa, Harlequin and Zoffany brands and Anstey, the manufacturing unit – bought and sold Coles, and more recently acquired the Sanderson plant and brand, which had gone into receivership in 2003. Although removed to new locations, the Coles and Sanderson block-printing continued.
2 Coloroll had been bought out of receivership by John Wilman Ltd in 1990; in 1999 the company was restructured and, with Gleadway's purchase of Vymura, these three brands were brought together. Through Crown, IHDG (UK) maintained the well-known English brands Shand Kydd and Storey, and their acquired French brand, Decorene. Lincrusta and Anaglypta, registered trademarks of Akzo Nobel Decorative Coatings Ltd (an amalgam of

Akzo Coatings, Nobel, Crown Berger and Sadolin UK in 1993–94), were licensed by IHDG (UK and USA), as they are by CWV today. Other brands from the former Imperial/IHDG stable, such as Katzenbach & Warren, Sterling, Sunworthy, Imperial Fine Interiors and Albert Van Luit, are among those now issued by Blue Mountain. For an account of the principal changes in the UK, see 'A Look Back at 26 Years of *Home Decor* Reporting', *Home Decor* July/Aug. 2004, pp. 12–15; this reference courtesy of George Zacal. For other information my thanks go to George, and to Lesley Hoskins, Donald Kang, Sue Kerry, Michael Parry, Judith Straeten, Bruce Vinocur and Jocelyn Warner.
3 H-A is itself a division of Germany's Langbein-Pfanhauser Werke AG, which elected to develop its market share of interior decoration products in 1997.
4 Japanese wallcoverings are wider, being based on the traditional width of a *tatami* mat, 36¼–36⅝ in. (92–93 cm). Japan's wallcoverings consumption is predominantly of vinyls and specified by building contractors; both DIY installation and imports account for only a few per cent of the market. Among imports, most papers come from Belgium and Finland; Belgium also leads in the supply of woven wallcoverings. Vinyls come (in declining amounts) from the Republic of Korea and (in rapidly increasing volumes) from China, which has cut the import of Taiwanese and American vinyls. See JETRO, *Marketing Guideline for Major Imported Products IV: Wall Coverings*, Tokyo, 2003.
5 By 2003 when, within months of each other, printed non-wovens were finally introduced by the American firms Eisenhart and IHDG, the former cited its liaison with the adhesive maker Roman Decorative Products, while the latter credited the non-woven EasyLife, made by the German Ahlstrom Corporation. Ahlstrom pioneered the non-woven process in 1930 for textile-related applications.
6 Acousticals are generally made of polyester and olefin fibres. Increasingly stringent health and safety parameters prompted the addition of antimicrobial agents, which inhibit the growth of bacteria as well as mould and mildew. Among medical wallcoverings are vinyls integrated with Bio-Pruf (a Morton International vinyzene), available since 1999 from the Netherlands-based Vescom group (whose distributors include its acquisition, Helen Sheane), and patented bacteriostatic Resinflex vinyls from Italy, especially for operating theatres and laboratories. The first breathable woven vinyl wallcovering was introduced in 2004 by Omnova. Meanwhile German firms such as Marburg and the specialists in glass-fibre products, Vitrulan, led in the provision of electromagnetic shielding wallcoverings.
7 See, for example, *Vinyl Performance Everyday. Environmental Profile: Vinyl Wallcovering*, produced by the Vinyl Institute, the Wallcoverings Association, and the Chemical Films and Fabrics Association, Chicago, c. 2004.
8 The printable version is a latex-saturated nylon-reinforced paper and the dry transfer substrate has an integral or laminated polymer protective medium.
9 A useful guide to manufacturers' sites can be found at www.wallpaperinstaller.com, although beware the term 'maker', which covers producers but also editeurs. The same caveat applies to www.thepaperhangers.com/greatlinks/manufacturers.html (National Guild of Professional Paperhangers, Inc.). For mainly North American news and views, including aspects of the industry's struggle to produce a joint promotional campaign, see www.wallpapernewsonline.com.
10 Glasgow's artists included David Shrigley, Martin Boyce and Hayley Tomkins; see Gill Saunders, *Wallpaper in Interior Decoration*, London/New York 2002, pp. 148–50. For 'On the Wall', see http://www.risd.edu/museum_exhibitions.cfm?type=past and http://www.fabricworkshop.org/exhibitions/on_the_wall.php. Japan's Murakami designed the first 'art paper' produced by Studio Printworks, New York; see http://www.studioprintworks.com/portfolio.html.
11 'No More White Walls': first annual Wallpaper Council contest for students from design schools, judged by Todd Oldham, April 2003.

Bibliography

BSIM = Bulletin de la Société industrielle de Mulhouse

I. This section lists books and articles which offer a wide coverage of the history of wallpapers. It includes the standard works which themselves provide bibliographies.

Ackerman, P., Wallpaper: Its History, Design, and Use, 2nd edn, New York 1938

Banham, J., ed., Encyclopedia of Interior Design, London 1997

Bibliothèque Forney (Paris), Le bon motif, Papiers peints et tissus, Les trésors de la bibliothèque Forney, Paris 2004

Borchers, W., Alte und neue Bildtapeten: Papiertapeten mit Landschafts- und Figurendekor 1800–1951, Städtisches Museum Osnabrück in association with the Verband Deutscher Tapetenfabrikanten 1951

Bruignac, V. de, Le Papier peint, Paris 1995

Clouzot, H., Le Papier peint en France du XVIIe au XIXe siècle, Paris 1931

— and C. Follot, Histoire du Papier peint en France, Paris 1935

Cooper-Hewitt Museum (New York), Wallpapers in the Collection of the Cooper-Hewitt Museum, Washington, D.C., 1981

Entwisle, E. A., The Book of Wallpaper, London 1954

—, A Literary History of Wallpaper, London 1960

Frangiamore, C. Lynn, Wallpapers in Historic Preservation, Washington, D.C., 1977

—, 'Wallpaper: Technological Innovation and Changes in Design and Use', Technological Innovation and the Decorative Arts: Winterthur Conference Report 1973, Charlottesville, Va., 1974

Greysmith, B., Wallpaper, London/New York 1976

Hamilton, J., An Introduction to Wallpaper, London 1983

Hapgood, M. Oliver, Wallpaper and the Artist: From Dürer to Warhol, New York 1992

Heesters, J. H. P., Vier eeuwen behang. De geschiedenis van de wandbespanning in Nederland, Delft 1988

Jacqué, B., ed., 'Technique et papier peint', BSIM, no. 823, 1991

—, De la manufacture au mur: pour une histoire matérielle du papier peint 1770–1914, doctoral thesis, Univ. of Lyon 2, 2003

— and O. Nouvel-Kammerer, Le Papier peint, décor d'illusion, Barembach 1987

— and G. Wisse, Le Murmure des murs: Quatre Siècles d'histoire du papier peint, Brussels 1997

Kiselev, I., 'Russian and European Wallpaper in the Eighteenth through Twentieth Centuries', Antiques & Collecting (Chicago), April 1995, pp. 47–50

Koldeweij, E. F., E. G. M. Adriaansz and M. J. T. Knuijt, Achter het Behang: 400 jaar wanddecoratie in het Nederlandse binnenhuis, Amsterdam 1991

Lassen, H., Tapetes Historie, Faaborg 1947

Lynn, C., Wallpaper in America from the Seventeenth Century to World War I, New York 1980

McClelland, N., Historic Wall-Papers from their Inception to the Introduction of Machinery, Philadelphia/London 1924

Mick, E. W., Deutsches Tapetenmuseum Kassel, Kassel-Wilhelmshöhe n.d.

Murphy, P., comp., The Decorated Wall: Eighty Years of Wallpaper in Australia, c. 1850–1930, Elizabeth Bay, N.S.W., 1981

Musée des Arts Décoratifs (Paris), Trois siècles de papiers peints, 1967

'Musée du Papier Peint' (Rixheim), BSIM, no. 793, 1984

Nylander, R. C., Wallpapers for Historic Buildings: A Guide to Selecting Reproduction Wallpapers, Washington, D.C., 1983, rev. edn 1992

—, E. Redmond and P. J. Sander, Wallpaper in New England, Boston 1986

Olligs, H., Tapeten – Ihre Geschichte bis zur Gegenwart, Brunswick 1969–70

Oman, C. C., Catalogue of Wallpapers, Victoria and Albert Museum, London 1929

— and J. Hamilton, Wallpapers: A History and Illustrated Catalogue of the Collection of the Victoria and Albert Museum, London/New York 1982

Sanborn, K., Old Time Wall Papers, Greenwich, Conn., 1905

Saunders, G., Ornate Wallpapers, Exeter, Devon, 1985

—, Wallpaper in Interior Decoration, London/New York 2002

Sugden, A. V., and J. L. Edmondson, A History of English Wallpaper, 1509–1914, New York 1925/London 1926

Taylor, C., Wallpaper, Princes Risborough, Bucks., 1991

Teynac, F., P. Nolot and J. D. Vivien, Wallpaper: A History, London/New York 1982

Thümmler, S., Die Geschichte der Tapete, Eurasburg 1998

—, Tapetenkunst: französische Raumgestaltung und Innendekoration von 1730 bis 1960, Wolfrathausen 2000

Tunander, I., Tapeter, Stockholm 1955

—, Tapeter i Sverige, Västerås 1984

Turner, M., The Silver Studio Collection: A London Design Studio 1880–1963, London 1980

— and L. Hoskins, Silver Studio of Design: A Design and Source Book for Home Decoration, Exeter, Devon, 1988

The Wallpaper History Review, Manchester, 1993/94, 1995, 1996/97, 2001, 2004/5

Webb, V., et al., Les Sauvages de la Mer Pacifique, Sydney 2000

Whitworth Art Gallery (Manchester), Historic Wallpapers in the Whitworth Art Gallery, 1972

Woods, C., ed., Sanderson 1860–1985, London 1985

II. The following sections offer additional, more specialized material relating to individual chapters or groups of chapters. Further sources are given in the notes.

Chapters 1 and 2 (single-sheet papers and English wallpapers before 1830)

Adhémar, J., Imagerie populaire française, Milan 1968

Appuhn, H., and C. von Heusinger, Riesenholzschnitte und Papiertapeten der Renaissance, Unterschneidheim 1976

Bakker, I. C., 'Een Zestiende eeuws plafond behang te Middelburg', Monumenten, 7, no. 1, 1986, pp. 4–8

Baroli, G., Mostra di Remondini, Calcographie stampatori bassanesi, Bassano 1958

Closson, E., 'L'Ornementation en papier imprimé des clavecins anversois', Revue belge d'archéologie et d'histoire d'art, II, 1932, pp. 105–12

Clouzot, H., 'La Tradition du papier peint en France au XVIIe et au XVIIIe siècle', Gazette des beaux-arts, 1912, pp. 131–43

Cordonnier-Detrie, P., 'Jacques Gaugain: maître cartier-dominotier-imagier en la ville du Mans au XVIIIème siècle', Bull. de la Soc. d'Agriculture, Sciences et Arts de la Sarthe, 3rd ser., II, 1927–28, 2nd fasc., pp. 236–59

—, 'Trois papiers-dominos de Jacques Gaugain et de sa veuve', Bull. de la Soc. d'Agriculture, Sciences et Arts de la Sarthe, 3rd ser., III, 1929–30, pp. 193–202

Dagnall, H., The Tax on Wallpaper: An Account of the Excise Duty on Stained Paper 1712–1836, Edgware, Mx., 1990

Doizy, M. A., and S. Ippert, Le Papier marbré, Paris 1985

Dossie, R., The Handmaid to the Arts, II, London 1758

Entwisle, E. A., 'Early Black and White Papers', Connoisseur, XCVII, Jan. 1936, pp. 16–17

—, 'Early Wallpapers', Country Life, CXIV, July 1953, pp. 212–13

Fabry, P. de, 'La Fabrication des papiers de tapisserie: un exemple particulier: Papillon', BSIM, no. 823, 1991

Fichtemberg, M., Nouveau manuel complet du fabricant de papier fantaisie, papiers marbrés, jaspés, maroquinés, gaufrés, dorés…, Paris 1852

Finck-Haelffig, M., Die Herstellung von Buntpapier: Kleisterpapieren, Stempel-, Tusch-, Oel- und Schablonen-papieren, Ravensburg 1926

Fischer, H. von, 'Bemalte bernische Decke und Wandtafeln', Bemalte Holzdecken und Täfelungen, Bern 1987, pp. 9–11

Foot, M. M., 'The Olga Hirsch Collection of Decorated Papers', British Library Journal, VII, no. 1, Spring 1981, pp. 12–38

Franklin, A., Dictionnaire historique des arts, métiers, professions exercés à Paris depuis le XIIIe siècle, Paris 1906

Grunebaum, G., Buntpapier: Geschichte – Herstellung – Verwendung, Cologne 1982

Gusman, P., 'J. B. Papillon et ses papiers de tenture (1698–1776)', Byblis, IX, 1924, pp. 18–23

Haemmerle, A., Buntpapier: Herkommen, Geschichte, Techniken, Beziehungen zur Kunst, Munich 1961

Hamilton, J., 'Early English Wallpaper', Connoisseur, July 1977, pp. 201–6

Heal, A., 'Paper Stainers of the 17th and 18th Centuries', Country Life, CVI, July 1949, pp. 258–60

Heijbroek, J. F., and T. C. Greven, Sierpapier, Amsterdam 1994

Heusinger, C. von, 'Ein neuentdecktes Exemplar der Dürer-Tapete auf schwarzen Grund', Jb. der Berliner Museen, XXV, 1983, pp. 143–59

Ionides, B., 'Old Wallpapers in a Sixteenth-Century House', Architectural Review, 56, 1924, pp. 194–95

Jenkinson, H., 'English Wall-Paper of the Sixteenth and Seventeenth Centuries', Antiquaries Journal, V, 1925, pp. 237–53

Lengler, J. M., 'Eine Deckentapete der Spätrenaissance aus Chur', Jahresbericht 1982 des Rätischen Museums Chur, pp. 229–41

Maclot, P., 'De Polychrome interieurafwerking van het renaissance burgerinterieur in Antwerpen', in J. van Cleven, Het historisch interieur in Vlaanderen, 227, jg. 38, Sept. – Oct. 1989, pp. 22–24

— and P. van de Wee, 'Plafondbehang en beschildering ontdekt in der Reynderstraat no. 5', Bull. van de Antwerpse Vereniging voor Grot- en Bodemonderzoek, 1–2, 1982, pp. 4–30

—, 'Wat er ons allemaal boven het hoofd hangt te Antwerpen. Papier "troef" in de Bergstraat no. 1', Bull. van de Antwerpse Vereniging voor Grot- en Bodemonderzoek, 1, 1986, pp. 4–8

Mick, E. W., Altes Buntpapier, Dortmund 1979

Niemeyer, J. W., 'De Collectie sierpapieren', Bull. van het Rijksmuseum, no. 3, 1984, pp. 141–45

Oman, C. C., 'Old Wall-Papers in England', Old Furniture, I, 1927, pp. 272–76

—, 'Wall-Papers of Early England: 1495–1770', Fine Arts, XVIII, March 1932, pp. 25–29

Papillon, J. M., Traité historique et pratique de la gravure en bois, Paris 1766

Petitjean, M., 'Négoce et fabrication du papier peint en province: l'example de Besançon (1750– 1830)', BSIM, no. 793, 1984, pp. 129–36

Piguet, C., and N. Froidevaux, eds, Copier-coller: Papiers peints du XVIIIème siècle, Neuchâtel 1998

Potrzebnicka, E., and J. Charytoniuk, 'Die Restaurierung einer Papiertapete in einem Krakauer Bürgerhaus', Restauro, 1990, no. 3, pp. 213–17

Quilici, P., Carte decorate nella legatoria del '700: dalle raccolte della Biblioteca Casanatense, Rome 1988

Remondini, Un Editore del Settecento, exh. cat., Milan 1990

Renfer, C., 'Eine neuentdeckte Papierdekoration der Spätrenaissance aus Zürich', Unsere Kunstdenkmäler, XXIX, no. 3, 1978, pp. 345–49

Rijksmuseum Meermanno-Westreenianum (The Hague), Sier-papier, 1975

Rosoman, T., London Wallpapers: their Manufacture and Use, 1690–1840, London 1992

Saulnier, R., 'Un Gentilhomme dominotier à Besançon au XVIIIe siècle', L'Art populaire en France, 1933, pp. 74–82

—, 'Une Lignée de cartiers-dominotiers bisontins', L'Art populaire en France, 1934–35, pp. 74–82

Schöpfer, H., 'Papiertapeten aus der Mitte des 18. Jahrhunderts mit grossformatigen Landschaften', Revue suisse d'art et d'archéologie, no. 47, 1990, pp. 327–40

——, Un Paysage de dominos du milieu du 18ème siècle, Rixheim 1997

Seguin, J. P., Dominos: papiers imprimés, Paris 1991

Thijs, A. K. L., 'Behangpapier anno 1582', Ons Heem, XXV, no. 3, 1971, pp. 112–13

Thornton, P., Seventeenth-Century Interior Decoration in England, France and Holland, London 1978

'Tussen plafond en plint, Cultuurgeschiedenis van het behang', Volkscultuur, tijdschrift over tradities en tijdsverschijnselen, jg. 9, no. 1, 1992

Van Heurck, E., and G. J. Boekenoogen, Histoire de

l'imagerie populaire flamande, Brussels 1910

Wace, A. J. B., 'Lining Papers from Corpus Christi College', *Oxoniensa*, 1937, pp. 166–70

Wells-Cole, A., *Historic Paper Hangings from Temple Newsam and other English Houses*, Leeds 1983

Wisse, G., 'Meubelpapieren', *Gentse wooncultuur in Mozarts tijd: een remarquabel ambelissement*, Ghent 1991, pp. 92–95

—, 'Contribution à l'étude des techniques de fabrication des papiers peints des Pays-Bas autrichiens: l'importance des archives', *BSIM*, no. 823, 1991, pp. 79–86

Wojtzak, M., 'Conservation and Restoration of Early Wallpapers from Kraków', *Conference on Book and Paper Conservation (Budapest 4–7 Sept. 1990)*, Budapest 1992, pp. 257–70

Wood, S., *Paper Chase: an exhibition of decorated papers from the Schmoller Collection*, Edinburgh 1987

Chapter 3 (Chinese wallpapers)

Clunas, C., *Chinese Export Watercolours*, London 1984

Coleridge, A., 'Hanging Chinese Wallpaper', *Furniture History*, 1966

Entwisle, E. A., 'Painted Chinese Wallpapers', *Connoisseur*, XCIII, June 1934, pp. 367–74

Impey, O., *Chinoiserie: The Impact of Oriental Styles on Western Art and Decoration*, London 1977

Oman, C. C., 'English Chinoiserie Wallpapers', *Country Life*, LXXIII, 11 Feb. 1933, pp. 150–51

Saunders, G., '"Painted Paper of Pekin": Chinese Wallpapers in England', *V&A Album*, London 1983, pp. 306–11

Wappenschmidt, F., *Chinesische Tapeten für Europa*, Berlin 1989

Chapters 4, 5, 6 (France 1770–1870)

Baumer-Müller, V., *Schweizer Landschaftstapeten des frühen 19. Jhdts*, Bern 1991

Clouzot, H., *Tableaux-tentures de Dufour & Leroy*, Paris n.d.

Entwisle, E. A., *French Scenic Wallpapers 1800–1860*, Leigh-on-Sea, Essex, 1972

Fabry, P. de, 'Dessins et dessinateurs de la manufacture Jean Zuber & Cie 1790–1870', *BSIM*, no. 793, 1984, pp. 101–6

Guibert, M., *Papiers Peints, 1800–1875*, Paris (Bibliothèque Forney) 1980

Gusman, P., *Panneaux décoratifs et tentures murales du XVIIIème et du commencement du XIXème siècle*, Paris 1900

Jacqué, B., ed., *Les Papiers peints en arabesques de la fin du 18ème siècle*, Paris 1995

—, *Un Tournant du goût: le papier peint autour de 1797*, Rixheim 1997

Jordan, M., 'L'Étude d'un domaine méconnu du papier peint en France sous l'Ancien Régime: les livraisons pour le département du garde-meuble de la couronne de 1764 à 1792', in F. Daelamans and G. Wisse, eds, *Pour l'histoire du papier peint*, Brussels 2001, pp. 81–104

Kosuda-Warner, J., with E. Johnson, eds, *Landscape Wallcoverings*, New York 2001

La Hougue, V., O. Nouvel and B. Ottinger, *Thomas Couture – Jules Desfossé. Souper à la maison d'o*, Senlis 1998

Le Normand, S., *Annales de l'Industrie nationale et étrangère*, Oct. 1822

Musée du Papier Peint (Rixheim), *Le Mirage du luxe: les décors de papier peint*, exh. cat., 1988

—, *Papier Peint et Révolution*, exh. cat., 1989

Nouvel, O., *Wallpapers of France 1800–1850*, New York 1981

Nouvel-Kammerer, O., 'Les inventions techniques chez Jean Zuber & Cie', *BSIM*, no. 793, 1984, pp. 107ff.

—, ed., *Papiers peints panoramiques*, Paris 1990

—, 'De la créativité technique des fabricants de papier peint en France au XIXe siècle', *BSIM*, no. 823, 1991, pp. 101–6

—, ed., *French Scenic Wallpaper 1795–1865*, Paris 2000

Les Papiers peints du château d'Allaman, Lausanne 1995

Polk Douglas, E., *French Panoramic Wallpaper, Historical background, characteristic development and architectural application*, MA thesis, Univ. of Virginia, 1976

'Rich paperhangings just received: French panoramic

wallpaper and its American archival resources', in F. Daelamans and G. Wisse, eds, *Pour l'histoire du papier peint*, Brussels 2001, pp. 35–52

Thümmler, S., 'Wallpaper at about 1800 – Diversity and Spreading of a New Product', *PapierRestaurierung*, V, June 2004, pp. 18–24

Velut, C., *Décors de papier: production, commercialisation et usages des papiers peints à Paris, 1750–1820*, doctoral thesis, Univ. of Paris I, 2001

Witt-Döring, C., 'Die Wiener Tapetenfabrikation der ersten Hälfte des 19. Jhdts am Beispiel der Fabrik Michael Spörlin & Heinrich Rahn', *Das k.k. National-Fabriksprodukten-Kabinett, Technik und Design des Biedermeier*, Munich 1995, pp. 162–71

Chapter 7 (America before 1870)

Hotchkiss, H., 'Wallpaper Used in America, 1700–1850', in *The Concise Encyclopedia of American Antiques*, ed. Helen Comstock, II, New York 1958, pp. 488ff.

Redmond, E., 'American Wallpaper, 1840–1860: The Limited Impact of Early Machine Printing', master's thesis, Univ. of Delaware, 1987

Watkins, W. Kendall, 'The Early Use and Manufacture of Paper-Hangings in Boston', *Old-Time New England*, 12, Jan. 1922, pp. 109–19

Chapters 8 and 9 (1870–1900)

Archer, M., 'Gothic Wallpapers – An Aspect of the Gothic Revival', *Apollo*, 78, 1963, pp. 109–16

Banham, J., 'Outstanding Designs', *Traditional Homes*, June 1987

—, S. Macdonald and J. Porter, *Victorian Interior Design*, London 1991

Briggs, A., *Victorian Things*, 1988

Burnett, J., *A Social History of Housing 1815–1935*, 2nd edn, London 1986

Eastlake, C. L., *Hints on Household Taste*, London 1868

Entwisle, E. A., *Wallpapers of the Victorian Era*, Leigh-on-Sea, Essex, 1964

Floud, P., 'Dating Morris Patterns', *Architectural Review*, 126, 1959, pp. 14–20

Forge, S., *Victorian Splendour: Australian Interior Decoration 1837–1901*, Oxford 1981

Fraser, H., *The Coming of the Mass Market 1850–1914*, London 1981

The Great Exhibition. Reports by the Juries, III, London 1852

Harvey, C., and J. Press, *William Morris, Design and Enterprise in Victorian Britain*, London 1991

Hoskins, L., 'Wallpaper', in L. Parry, *William Morris*, London 1996

Illustrated Catalogue of the Great Exhibition, London 1851

International Exhibition: Illustrated Catalogue, II, London 1862

Jervis, S., *High Victorian Design*, London 1983

Jones, O., *Grammar of Ornament*, London 1856

Journal of Design and Manufactures, London 1849–53

Lynn, C., 'Surface Ornament', in *In Pursuit of Beauty: Americans and the Aesthetic Movement*, New York 1986

Morris, W., *Some Hints on Pattern Designing*, London 1899

Peel, D., *The New Home*, London 1898

Pugin, A. W. N., *The True Principles of Pointed or Christian Architecture*, London 1841, repr. 1973

Redgrave, R., *Report on Design*, London 1852

Smith, G., and S. Hyde, eds, *Walter Crane: Artist, Designer, Socialist*, Manchester/London 1989

Stavenow-Hidemark, E., *Sub Rosa*, Stockholm 1991

Sugden, A. V., and E. A. Entwisle, *The Crace Papers: Two Lectures on the History of Paperhangings delivered by John Gregory Crace to the Royal Institute of British Architects on 4th and 18th February 1839*, Birmingham 1939

—, *Potters of Darwen. A Century of Wallpaper Printing by Machinery*, Manchester 1939

Turner, M., ed., *Art Nouveau Designs from the Silver Studio Collection*, London 1986

Whitworth Art Gallery (Manchester), *A Decorative Art: 19th Century Wallpapers in the Whitworth Art Gallery*, exh. cat., 1985

Woods, C., 'Pedigree Papers or Popular Patterns', *Apollo*, Oct. 1989

—, 'Those hideous sanitaries: tracing the development of washable wallcoverings', *The Quarterly, Journal of the British Association of Paper Historians*, (pt 1) no. 26, April 1998, pp. 1–5, (pt 2) no. 27, July 1988, pp. 17–18

—, 'An Object Lesson to a Philistine Age: The Wall Paper Manufacturers Museum & the formation of the National Collections', *Journal of Design History* (Oxford), XII, no. 2, 1999, pp. 159–71

Whiteway, M., ed., *Christopher Dresser: a Design Revolutionary*, London/New York 2004

Wyatt, M. Digby, *The Industrial Arts of the 19th Century*, London 1852

Chapters 10, 11, 12, 13 (1900–today)

Andral, C., 'Mutations technologiques contemporaines: causes et conséquences de l'impression héliographique dans l'évolution des revêtements muraux', *BSIM*, no. 823, 1991

Ausstellung der österreichischen Tapetenindustrie, exh. cat., Vienna 1913

Bayer, H., W. Gropius and I. Gropius, eds, *Bauhaus. 1919–1928*, Stuttgart 1955

Bayer, P., *Art Deco Interieur*, Munich 1990

'Berliner Kunst. Otto Eckmann', *Berliner Architekturwelt*, special issue, Oct. 1901

Bie, O., *Die Wand und ihre künstlerische Behandlung*, Berlin 1928

Bosker, G., and L. Lencek, *Off the Wall: Wonderful Wall Coverings of the Twentieth Century*, San Francisco, 2004

Brunhammer, Y., *Art Deco Style*, New York 1984

Chambre Syndicale des Fabricants de Papiers Peints de France, *Le Papier Peint*, 1958

Clouzot, H., *Le Style moderne dans la décoration moderne*, Paris 1921

Cooper-Hewitt National Design Museum (New York), *Kitsch to Corbusier: Wallpapers from the 1950s*, New York 1995

DeSalvo, D., A. Massie and G. Saunders, *Apocalyptic Wallpaper: Robert Gober, Abigail Lane, Virgil Marti, and Andy Warhol*, Columbus, O., 1997

Design Council, *Svensk Form. A Conference about Swedish Design*, London 1981

'Deutsche Form im Kriegsjahr. Die Ausstellung Köln 1914', *Jahrbuch des Deutschen Werkbundes*, Munich 1915

Eisler, M., *Dagobert Peche*, Vienna 1925

Feuss, A., *Wenzel Hablik. 1881–1934. Auf dem Weg in die Utopie. Architekturphantasien, Innenräume, Kunsthandwerk*, diss., Hamburg 1994

Fuchs, H., and F. Burckhardt, *Produkt Form Geschichte. 150 Jahre deutsches Design vom Jugendstil bis zur Gegenwart*, Munich 1980

Garner, P., ed., *The Encyclopedia of Decorative Arts 1890–1940*, London 1978

Gordon Clark, J., *Wallpaper in Decoration*, 2nd edn, London/New York 2001

Hastra Tapeten, *100 Jahre*, Bonn (H. Strauven K.G. Tapetenfabrik) 1961

Jackson, L., *The New Look: Design in the Fifties*, London 1991

—, *20th Century Pattern Design: textile and wallpaper pioneers*, London/New York 2002

Jacqué, B., *Versailles chez soi, les décors de papier peint*, Rixheim 2000

—, *Papiers peints du XXe siècle*, Rixheim 2003

—, 'Papiers peints du Bauhaus au musée de Rixheim: la collection 1934', *La Revue du Louvre et des Musées de France*, no. 5, 2003, pp. 79–81

— and H. Bieri, eds., *Papiers peints Art Nouveau*, Milan 1997

Katzenbach, L. and W., *The Practical Book of American Wallpaper*, Philadelphia 1951

Kieselbach, B., and R. Spilker, eds, *Rasch Buch/book 1897–1997*, Bramsche 1998

Koch, A., *Das neue Kunsthandwerk*, Darmstadt 1923

Kölnischer Kunstverein (Cologne), *Der westdeutsche Impuls*, exh. cat., 1984

Lisker, R., 'Über Tapete und Stoff in der Wohnung', in W. Gräff, ed., *Innenräume*, Stuttgart 1928

McClelland, C., *The Practical Book of Decorative Wall Treatments*, Philadelphia/London 1926

Menschen, Muster und Maschinen. Wissenwertes von der

Marburg-Tapete, Marburg c. 1960

Monopolies Commission, *Report on the Supply of Wallpaper*, Jan. 1964, repr. 1969

Nerdinger, W., *Richard Riemerschmid. Vom Jugendstil zum Werkbund*, Munich 1982

Neuwirth, W., *Wiener Werkstätte. Avantgarde, Art Deco...*, Vienna 1984

Österreichisches Museum für Angewandte Kunst (Vienna), *Die Wiener Werkstätte. Modernes Kunsthandwerk von 1903–1932*, exh. cat., 1967

Rasch, E., 'Die Tapete seit 1900', *Zeitschrift Architektur und Wohnform/Innendekoration*, 7, 1960

Schmutzler, Robert, *Art Nouveau*, London 1979

Schoeser, M., *Fabrics and Wallpapers* (Twentieth Century Design), London/New York 1986

—, *More is More: an antidote to minimalism*, London 2001

Seling, H., *Jugendstil. Der Weg ins 20. Jahrhundert*, Heidelberg 1959

Selle, G., *Design-Geschichte in Deutschland*, Cologne 1987

Sembach, K.-J., *Henry van de Velde*, London/New York 1989

Städtisches Museum Osnabrück, *Künstlerisches Schaffen – Industrielles Gestalten*, 1956

Taut, B., *Die neue Wohnung*, Leipzig 1924

Thümmler, S., 'Bauhaus Wallcoverings' and 'Historische Aspekte der Designentwicklung der Tapetenfabrik Rasch', in *Zeitwände*, cat., Bramsche 1992

—, 'Les Papiers peints Bauhaus, noblesse et sobriété', in J. Fiedler and P. Feierabend, eds, *Bauhaus*, Cologne 2000, pp. 462–65

Turner, M., M. Pinney and L. Hoskins, *A Popular Art: British Wallpapers 1930–1960*, London 1989

Usines Peters-Lacroix, *UPL*, 1973

Verband Deutscher Tapetenfabrikanten mit dem Internationalen Verein der Tapetenfabrikanten, *ITA 60*, Munich 1960

Whately, A., *Modern Wallpaper & Wallcoverings: introducing color, pattern, & texture into your living space*, New York 2002

Wichmann, H., *Aufbruch zum neuen Wohnen. Deutsche Werkstätten und WK-Verband 1898–1970*, Basel 1978

—, *Jugendstil – Floral und Funktional*, Munich 1984

Wingler, Hans M., *Das Bauhaus*, Bramsche 1962

Wood, S., *Paper Chase: an exhibition of decorated papers from the Schmoller Collection*, Edinburgh 1987

Woods, C., *The Magic Influence of Mr Kydd: Blocked and Stencilled Wallpapers 1900–1925*, Manchester 1989

—, 'A Semi-Private Enterprise', in M. Salisbury, ed., *Artists at the Fry: Art and Design in The North West Essex Collection*, Cambridge 2003, pp. 84–94

Postscript

Clapp, A. F., 'Examination of the Winterthur Wallpapers', *Journal of the American Institute for Conservation*, no. 20, 1981, pp. 63–71

—, *Curatorial Care of Works of Art on Paper*, New York 1987

'Conservation of Historic Wallpaper', *Journal of the American Institute for the Conservation of Historic and Artistic Works*, special issue, Spring 1981

Dante, C., N. Ravanel, A. Paolucci and R. Signorini, *Il Restauro delle carte da Pariti*, Mantua 1988

Georgian Group, *Wallpaper* (Guide no. 6), London c. 1990

Hunter, D., *Papermaking: The History and Technique of an Ancient Craft*, New York 1978

Huxtable, M., and P. Webber, 'The Conservation of Eighteenth Century Chinese Wallpapers in the United Kingdom', *Preprints of the IIC 1988 Kyoto Conference on the Conservation of Far Eastern Art*, 1988, pp. 52–58

Kosel, B., et al., 'Marburger Salzbaende – Reducing High Salt Concentrations in Books', *PapierRestaurierung*, V, June 2004, pp. 11–17

McDermott, A., 'Decorative Discoveries', *Traditional Homes Magazine*, I, no. 2, Nov. 1984, pp. 66–71

Phillips, M. W., 'Wallpaper on Walls: Problems of Climate and Substrate', *Journal of the American Institute for Conservation*, no. 20, 1981, pp. 83–90

Rickman, C. 'Wallpaper Conservation', *Preprints of UKIC 20th Anniversary Conference*, 1988, pp. 64–70

Sandwith, H., and S. Stainton, *The National Trust Manual of Housekeeping*, London 1985

Solomons, O., 'Conservation of Historic Wallpapers', in T. Rosoman, *London Wallpapers, their Manufacture and Use*, London 1992, pp. 52–53

Thompson, J. M. A., *Manual of Curatorship*, London 1986

Thomson, G. *The Museum Environment*, London 1986

Turner, S., *Which Paper?*, 1991

Victorian Society, 'Wallcoverings', by K. Wedd (Care for Victorian Houses no. 5), London 1993

The Wallpaper History Society Review, 1989–92

Weston, R., 'Paper Trace', *Traditional Homes Magazine*, I, no. 2, Nov. 1984

Glossary

block-printing   Method of decorating paper using wooden blocks (usually one for each colour component of the pattern) bearing a design in relief. Each block is furnished with pigment by being dipped onto a **colour tray** and is placed face down on the paper which, with the application of pressure to the back of the block, receives the impression. One colour is printed along the full length of the roll or piece and allowed to dry before the next block is brought into play. The complete pattern is thus built up block by block. Marker or 'pitch' pins at the corners of the block face act as **register** guides for the printer.

blown vinyl   Relief wallcovering made by printing with a **vinyl** ink containing a catalyst that expands when heated.

collection   Set of patterns issued by a manufacturer or distributor usually identified by name or number.

colour tray   Container for pigment in the **block-printing** process. A solid but elastic base covered with sturdy cloth is evenly spread with colour (by hand or machine) in preparation for furnishing the face of a block.

colour trough   Receptacle for pigment, used in **machine-printing**. A roller-fed or endless blanket carries colour from the trough to the printing roller.

companion paper   Pattern, usually unobtrusive, intended for use in conjunction with a more demonstrative design.

counterproof   Transfer pattern produced by facing a newly made print with a clean, dampened sheet of paper and passing the pair through a rolling press. The result is a mirror image of the original print. Large repeating designs can be built up in this way.

crown hanging   Type of decoration in which a frieze or wide border is an integral part of the main wall covering or filling.

cylinder-printing   Interchangeable with **roller-printing**.

digital printing   Processes utilizing a digital file, whether scanned, photographed or digitally generated, and printed by various digital means, including inkjet, laserjet, electrostatic, thermal transfer and **dry transfer printing**. All colours are printed simultaneously.

distemper colour   Opaque printing medium with pigments carried in a water-based glue or size.

domino   French term for single-sheet decorative papers with a variety of uses, precursors of wallpaper proper. Superseded in quality and prestige in the early 18th century by **papier de tapisserie**.

double flock   Using a repetition of the **flocking** process, two or more layers are applied. The colour of the fabric shearings can be varied in each application.

dry-erase surfaces   Wallcoverings developed in the early 1990s to provide chalkboard-like surfaces that can be plain, metallic or patterned and are used for erasable writing, projection or as a magnetic surface. Thermoplastic film is laminated to a vinyl substrate and backed with scrim or **vlies.**

dry transfer printing   The design is electrostatically printed onto a donor medium, which through heat and pressure is transferred to a wallpaper, usually a latex-saturated, nylon-reinforced composite paper.

duplex embossing   Two papers are laminated together during the **embossing** process to give additional depth and strength to relief.

easy-strip paper   Laminated wallpaper allowing for quick removal of the top, patterned, layer.

embossing   Wide-ranging term for a variety of techniques which produce relief finishes. It can be used to describe **flocking** but more commonly refers to stamping paper under pressure using plates, blocks or rollers. Often, pairs of male and female dies are used, the paper passing between the two. Embossing can be shallow, hardly noticeable, and used to give overall texture to a printed pattern, or it can provide the main feature of the design. See also **duplex embossing**, **in-register embossing and ink-embossing**.

engraved-roller-printing Form of **roller-printing** where the cylinders, usually metal, carry the design etched or engraved in stipples and lines. The fineness of the **intaglio** makes it unsuitable for printing with thick **distemper** colours and it is mostly used for oil-based inks.

flexographic printing Employing the same principle as traditional **surface-printing**, this process, introduced in the 1960s, uses solvent-based inks and rubber rollers cut in shallow relief.

flocking Technique for achieving a fabric-like effect and dense colouring. The pattern is printed in adhesive. Chopped wool, silk, or, later, nylon or acrylic, fibres are sprinkled on and stick to the glued areas only. See also **double flock; mock flock; raised flock**.

grasscloth Fabric of loosely woven grasses laminated to a paper backing.

gravure see **photogravure**.

ground Overall colour applied to the paper before printing. See also **satin ground**.

half-drop see **repeat**.

in-register embossing and ink-embossing Techniques for registering the printed colours exactly with the relief pattern.

in-register vinyl **Vinyl**-coated paper with an additional relief exactly matching the printed pattern.

intaglio printing Processes (hand- and machine-) in which the printing pigment is transferred to the paper from plates, blocks or rollers bearing an etched or engraved design. Dots and fine lines are usually employed to make up the pattern. See also **engraved-roller-printing; 'sanitary' wallpaper**.

irisé, also known as **rainbow effect** Subtle shaded effect of grounding or printing. For the former, a box holding pigment is divided into compartments, each containing a different colour. A wide, long-bristled brush is dipped into the tray to take up the various colours and is then (re-charged as necessary) dragged along the whole surface of a roll of paper laid out on a table. The colours are then smoothed and blended using clean brushes. Varying the direction of the brush strokes achieves different effects. *Irisé* printing uses the same principle, charging one block with a variety of hues.

machine-printing Term covering all types of mechanical printing methods but often used as a synonym for **surface-** or **engraved-roller-printing**.

mica Crystalline mineral, more or less finely powdered, added to the printing or grounding medium to give a shiny effect.

mock flock, also known as **counterfeit flock** A cheaper effect where powdered dry colour is substituted for fabric shearings.

non-woven see **vlies**.

offset printing A high-speed rotary method based on the lithographic principle that water repels ink. With pattern areas made receptive to ink through exposure to film negatives, photo-sensitive dampened paper or metal cylinders transfer the design to a rubber roller, which in turn transfers, or offsets, the design to the paper. Also called four-colour printing because it utilizes black, cyan (blue), magenta and yellow to produce all colours.

on demand printing Term used both for **digital printing**, emphasizing that this method does not require manufacturers to hold a stock of patterned rollers, and for custom hand printing by means such as **block-printing** and **screen-printing**.

papier de tapisserie French term for patterned paper intended for use on walls, produced as **single sheets** to be joined in hanging.

papier peint French term introduced in the mid-18th century denoting paper pasted into rolls before printing with **distemper**.

paste-the-wall Hung by pasting the wall rather than the wallcovering, which must be backed or entirely composed of **vlies**.

photogravure printing **Intaglio** machine-printing method using metal rollers photochemically engraved with tiny dots varying in depth. Each roller is furnished with a different colour solvent-based ink which is scraped away leaving pigment only in the engraved cells. The paper is fed between this and a rubber cylinder which presses the surface into the engraved cells to take up the colour. Up to twelve colours can be printed. A modern version of **engraved-roller-printing** much used since the 1970s.

plastic printing A form of **roller-printing** using a plaster-like printing medium to produce a raised surface.

print Old or trade term for a woodblock.

print-cutter Block-cutter or engraver. The term 'engraving' is used whether the design is intaglio, in relief or flat (as in screen-printing).

printing see **block-printing; cylinder-printing; digital printing; dry transfer printing; flexographic printing; intaglio printing; machine-printing; offset printing; on demand printing; plastic printing; photogravure printing; roller-printing; 'sanitary' wallpaper; screen-printing**.

private printing Arrangement whereby patterns are printed for a company or individual by another company.

rainbow effect American term for *irisé*.

raised flock Repeated applications of adhesive and flock increase the depth of relief. Pressure applied to the surface gives the flock more solidity and sharpness. Some raised flocks were produced in off-white with the intention that they should be painted.

ready-pasted Wallpaper issued with an adhesive backing that needs only wetting (not pasting) before hanging.

register Accurate fitting together of the separately printed parts that make up a total pattern.

repeat Complete single unit of a pattern that, by repetition, makes up the whole design. In a half-drop repeat, the horizontal match between drops is stepped by half the vertical repeat dimension.

repiquage Overprinting a flock pattern with **distemper** colour.

roller-printing Rotary technique whereby continuous paper is drawn between the surface of a large central drum and a number of smaller rollers bearing the pattern which turn against the drum. Each roller is fed by a continuous cloth belt passing through a trough of pigment. With separate rollers printing each colour element in the design, the pattern is complete when the paper has passed all of the rollers and leaves the machine. The term includes both **surface-** and **engraved-** or **intaglio** methods. The first attempts at roller-printing used engraved rollers but were generally unsatisfactory and gave way to **surface-printing**. Later the engraved process was re-adopted with great success for **'sanitary' wallpapers** and is now used in **photogravure printing**.

rotogravure see **photogravure**.

'sanitary' wallpaper Type of paper produced by the **engraved-roller** method. The small amount of thin oil-based ink deposited gives a very smooth surface, somewhat resistant to water. It can be readily varnished, rendering it washable and thus "sanitary". The printing process builds up the design from small dots, giving the impression of shaded and blended colour very different from the solid masses of **surface-printing**. It can also produce much finer detailing than surface methods. Although cutting the rollers is expensive, the technique economizes on printing inks.

satin ground Shiny finish produced using short-bristled brushes and talc to polish a **distemper** ground.

screen-printing Process which uses a fine mesh stretched taut across a rectangular frame to form a kind of **stencil**. One screen is required for each colour element in the design. Areas which are to print are left clear, the rest of the screen being blocked out. The roll of paper is stretched out on a long table, the screen is laid on top, and colour is drawn across the screen and pushed down through the holes in the mesh using a squeegee. One screen at a time is printed along the length of the paper, the pattern being built up by the subsequent addition of further colours. Initially a hand process; various elements of the method are now mechanized.

Rotary screen-printing is a high-speed adaptation of flat screen-printing, using rollers made of rigid metal mesh. The printing medium is pushed through the clear areas from the inside of the roller. As in most fully mechanized methods all of the colours are printed, one after the other, as the paper passes through the machine.

selvedge Unprinted margin on both sides of a roll of wallpaper. **Register** marks and production information such as the manufacturer's name are sometimes found there. At least one of the selvedges has to be removed before hanging.

semi-trimming Before the introduction of trimmed papers, the **selvedge** was left on for protection of the edge of the roll during transport and handling but was perforated for easier removal.

single-sheet papers Small, individual sheets of hand-made patterned paper which either stand alone or form a repeating or continuous design when pasted together on the wall. They were superseded first by rolls made up of a number of sheets stuck together before printing and then by rolls of continuous machine-made paper.

site-specific Wallcovering tailor-made for a specific interior.

stamp 18th-century term meaning to print.

stencil Technique for reproducing patterns by cutting the area to be printed out of a sheet of resistant material such as leather, card or thin metal. This is laid over the paper and colour is brushed or sprayed through the cut-away parts. Relatively cheap to prepare and easy to apply, it is sometimes found in conjunction with **block-printing**.

stick-ons A range of pre-cut decorative appliques made of various media including paper, vinyl and rubber. These may be self-adhesive, pre-pasted, requiring paste, or applied by pasting the receiving surface.

surface-printing Form of **roller-printing** where the cylinders bear the design to be printed in relief. The raised surface of the (usually wooden) roller can be formed from wood, metal strips and pins, or metal outlines packed with a compressible material such as felt.

techno wallcoverings A wide range of engineered wallcoverings including those designed to meet anti-bacterial or acoustic criteria, to provide electromagnetic shielding or damp barriers, and to replace slate, melamine and porcelain **dry-erase surfaces**.

trimming Process of removing selvedges prior to hanging. Originally done by the paper-hanger, it is now (except in the case of some hand-prints) standardly done by machine before sale. See also **semi-trimming**.

uni Paper of a single colour (sometimes shaded) and no pattern.

velvet paper Early term for **flock paper**.

vinyls Range of wallcoverings employing polyvinyls in several ways: as a coating for traditional papers, as a printing surface with a paper or fabric backing, or as a relief medium. They have a washable, hard-wearing, plastic surface. See also **blown vinyl; in-register vinyl**.

vlies German for 'fleece'. Wallcovering or backing made like paper but with textile fibres and binders added to the long-fibre cellulose pulp, and reinforced with acrylates and pigments for opacity. Vlies are dimensionally stable when wet and therefore allow for easy repositioning and thus **paste-the-wall** treatment. Because the technology was derived from machines making needle-punched and abraded textiles, vlies are also called non-wovens.

woodchip Paper with a rough surface produced by the inclusion of shards of wood in the pulp.

Wallpaper Reference Collections Accessible to the Public

The wallpaper collections listed here vary greatly in size and content. Some are general, covering a wide time span and a range of products. Others are small, many of them specializing in papers of a particular type, provenance or period. Most of the major collections show their holdings from time to time and some maintain permanent exhibitions. But frequently, especially in the smaller museums and archives, there are only limited facilities for display. In these cases material held 'behind the scenes' is often available for personal consultation. Intending visitors are advised to write or telephone in advance to check accessibility, details of the holdings, opening hours, and to make an appointment if necessary.

AUSTRALIA

Caroline Simpson Library & Research Collection, Historic Houses Trust of NSW
The Mint, 10 Macquarie Street, NSW 2000.
Tel. +61 (2)8239 2233. www.hht.nsw.gov.au
Powerhouse Museum 500 Harris Street, Ultimo,
P.O. Box K346, Haymarket, Sydney, NSW 1238.
Tel. +61 (2)9217 0111. www.phm.gov.au

AUSTRIA

MAK – Österreichisches Museum für angewandte Kunst Stubenring 5, 1010 Vienna.
Tel +43 (0)1 711 360. www.mak.at

BELGIUM

Musées Royaux d'Art et d'Histoire
10 Parc du Cinquantenaire, 1000 Brussels.
Tel. +32 (0)2 741 7348. www.kmkg-mrah.be

ENGLAND

English Heritage Architectural Study Collection
Kenwood House, London NW3 7JR.
Tel. +44 (0)20 7973 3492
MoDA (Museum of Domestic Design & Architecture) Middlesex University, Cat Hill, Barnet,
Herts, EN4 8HT. Tel. +44 (0)20 8411 5244.
www.moda.mdx.ac.uk
Olga Hirsch Collection of Decorated Papers
British Library, 96 Euston Road, London NW1 2DB.
Tel. +44 (0)20 7412 7767.
www.bl.uk/collections/early/holdingbindings
Temple Newsam House Leeds LS15 0AE
Tel. +44 (0)113 264 7321.
www.leeds.gov.uk/templenewsam
Victoria & Albert Museum Cromwell Road, London
SW7 2RL. Tel. +44 (0)20 7942 2000. www.vam.ac.uk
Whitworth Art Gallery Oxford Road, Manchester
M15 6ER Tel. +44 (0)161 275 7450.
www.whitworth.man.ac.uk

FRANCE

Bibliothèque Forney Hôtel de Sens,
1 rue du Figuier, 75004 Paris.Tel. +33 (0)1 42 78 14 60
Bibliothèque Nationale 58, rue de Richelieu,
75002 Paris. Tel. +33 (0)1 47 03 81 26. www.bnf.fr
Grantil (company archive) Archives départementales de
la Marne, 129 avenue de l'Yser, 51100 Reims.
Tel. +33 (0)3 26 85 17 58
Musée des Arts Décoratifs 107 rue de Rivoli,
75001 Paris. Tel. +33 (0)1 44 55 57 50. www.ucad.fr
Musée du Papier Peint La Commanderie,
28 rue Zuber, B.P. 41, 68171 Rixheim.
Tel. +33 (0)3 89 64 24 56. www.museepapierpeint.org

GERMANY

Bayerisches Nationalmuseum Prinzregentenstrasse
3, 80538 Munich. Tel. +49 (0)89 211 2401.
www.bayerisches-nationalmuseum.de

Deutsches Buch- und Schriftmuseum
Deutscher Platz 1, 04103 Leipzig.
Tel: +49 (0)341 227 1250. www.ddb.de
Deutsches Museum Museumsinsel 1,
80538 Munich. Tel. +49 (0)89 21791.
www.deutsches-museum.de
Deutsches Tapetenmuseum Kassel
Brüder-Grimm-Platz 5, 34117 Kassel.
Tel. +49 (0)561 31680 300. www.tapeten-institut.de
Germanisches Nationalmuseum
Kartäusergasse 1, 90402 Nuremberg.
Tel. +49 (0)911 13310. www.gnm.de
Kunstbibliothek, Staatliche Museen zu Berlin
Matthäikirchplatz 6, 10785 Berlin-Tiergarten.
Tel. +49 (0)30 266 2029.
www.smb.spk-berlin.de
Schlossmuseum Schlossplatz 4, Aschaffenburg,
63739. Tel. +49 (0)6021 386 740.
www.aschaffenburg.de/wDeutsch/tourismus/museum
Stiftung Weimarer Klassik
Frauentorstrasse 4, 99423 Weimar.
Tel. +49 (0)3643 545 102. www.weimar-klassik.de

ITALY

Biblioteca Casanatense Via S. Ignazio 52,
00186 Rome. Tel. +39 (0)66 976 031.
www.biblioroma.sbn.it/casanat
Museo Civico di Bassano del Grappa
Piazza Garibaldi 34, Bassano del Grappa.
Tel. +39 (0)42 4519 450. www.museobassano.it
Raccolta Stampe Achille Bertarelli
Castello Sforzesco, 20121 Milan.
Tel. +39 (0)28 0509 189. www.bertarelli.org

THE NETHERLANDS

Koninklijke Bibliotheek
Prins Willem-Alexanderhof 5, 2595 BE, The Hague.
Tel. +33 (0)70 314 0911. www.kb.nl
Rijksmuseum Stadhouderskade 42,
1071 ZD Amsterdam. Tel. +33 (0)20 674 7047.
www.rijksmuseum.nl
Sikkens Schildersmuseum
Wilhelminalaan 1, 2171 CS Sassenheim.
Tel. +33 (0)25 222 1089.
www.sikkens.nl/nl/about/museum
Stichting Historische Behangsels en Wanddecorations in Nederland
Achter Clarenburg 2, 3511 JJ Utrecht.
Tel. +33 (0)70 345 8224

NEW ZEALAND

Hawke's Bay Cultural Trust Office, Museum and Century Theatre 65 Marine Parade,
P.O. Box 248, Napier. Tel. +64 (0)6 835 7781.
www.hawkesbaymuseum.co.nz
Northcote-Bade Collection
New Zealand Historic Places Trust, Private Box 105-291,
Auckland. Tel. +64 (0)9 307 8896.
www.historic.org.nz

UNITED STATES

Athenæum of Philadelphia
219 South 6th Street, Philadelphia, PA 19106.
Tel. +1 215 925 2688. www.philaathenaeum.org
Brooklyn Museum
200 Eastern Parkway, Brooklyn, NY 11238-6052.
Tel. +1 718 638 5000. www.brooklynmuseum.org
Butler Library, Columbia University
535 West 114th Street, New York, NY 10027.
Tel. +1 212 854 2271.
www.columbia.edu/cu/lweb/indiv/butler
Colonial Williamsburg Foundation
P.O. Box 1776, Williamsburg, VA 23187-1776.
Tel. +1 757 229 1000. www.history.org
Connecticut Historical Society
1 Elizabeth Street, Hartford, CT 06105.
Tel. +1 860 236 5621. www.chs.org
Cooper-Hewitt, National Design Museum, Smithsonian Institution
2 East 91st Street, New York, NY 10128-9990.
Tel. +1 212 849 8472. www.ndm.si.edu

Harry Ransom Humanities Research Center, University of Texas, 21st and Guadalupe,
P.O. Box 7219, Austin, TE 78713-7219.
Tel. +1 512 471 8944. www.hrc.utexas.edu
Historic New England (formerly Society for the
Preservation of New England Antiquities)
141 Cambridge Street, Boston, MA 02114.
Tel. +1 617 227 3956. www.historicnewengland.org
Houghton Library, Harvard University,
Cambridge, MA 02138. Tel. +1 617 495 2441.
www.hcl.harvard.edu/houghton
Metropolitan Museum of Art 1000 Fifth Avenue
at 82nd Street, New York, NY 10028-0198.
Tel. +1 212 535 7710. www.metmuseum.org
Museum of Fine Arts, Boston Avenue of the Arts,
465 Huntington Avenue, Boston, MA 02115-5523.
Tel. +1 617 267 9300. www.mfa.org
**National Trust for Historic Preservation Library
Collection** Hornbake Library, University of Maryland,
College Park, MD 20742. Tel. +1 301 405 6320.
www.lib.umd.edu/NTL/kithomes
Old Sturbridge Village 1 Old Sturbridge
Village Road, Sturbridge, MA 01566.
Tel. +1 508 347 3362. www.osv.org
Peabody-Essex Museum East India Square, Salem,
MA 01970-3783. Tel. +1 978 745 9500.
www.pem.org
Philadelphia Museum of Art
P.O. Box 7646, Philadelphia, PA 19101-7646.
Tel. +1 215 763 8100. www.philamuseum.org
Rhode Island School of Design Museum
224 Benefit Street, Providence, RI 02903.
Tel. +1 401 454 6500. www.risd.edu/museum.cfm
**Society for the Preservation of New England
Antiquities** see **Historic New England**
Stowe Center Library & Museum Harriet Beecher
Stowe Center, 77 Forest Street, Hartford, CT 06105.
Tel. +1 860 522 9258.
www.harrietbeecherstowe.org/collections
**Valentine Museum – Museum of Life & History
of Richmond** 1015 East Clay Street, Richmond,
VA 23219. Tel. +1 804 649 0711

Additional Sources of Information

In addition to societies and museums, the Internet offers a very rich resource for information about all aspects of wallpaper and its history. Websites often provide useful links to other organizations, manufacturers and sources. But care needs to be taken – addresses and sites change frequently and information is unregulated.

The Antiquarian and Landmarks Society 255 Main Street, Hartford, CT 06106, USA. Tel. +1 860 247 8996. www.hartnet.org

Deutsches Tapeten-Institut GmbH Langer Weg 18, 60489 Frankfurt a. M., Germany. Tel. +49 (0)69 520 035. www.tapeten-institut.de

Historic Charleston Society P.O. Box 1120, Charleston SC 29402, USA. Tel. +1 843 723 1623. www.historiccharleston.org

Historic Deerfield Box 32, Deerfield, MA 01342-0321, USA. Tel. +1 413 774 5581. www.historic-deerfield.org

Historic Wallpaper, A Guide to Resources www.web.simmons.edu/~olsons/520

Historic Wallpaper Specialties Tel. +1 423 929 8552. www.historicwallpapering.com

The Museum of Early Southern Decorative Arts Old Salem, P.O. Box F, Salem Station, Winston-Salem, NC 27108-0346, USA. Tel. +1 336 721 7300. www.oldsalem.org

The Strawbery Banke Museum P.O. Box 300, Portsmouth, NH 03802, USA. Tel. +1 603 422 7526. www.strawberybanke.org

Wallpaper History Society c/o Victoria & Albert Museum, Cromwell Road, London SW7 2RL, England

Winterthur Museum, Garden & Library Route 52, Winterthur DE 19735, USA. Tel. +1 302 888 4600. www.winterthur.org

WRN Associates 65 South Prospect Street, P.O. Box 187, Lee, MA 01238, USA. Tel. +1 413 243 3489. www.paper-hangings.com

www.esplinters.net/Museum/Wallpaper *Information about Russian and American wallpapers* **www.historicnewengland.org/wallpaper/ reading/** **www.wallpapers-uk.com/historydownloads** Tel. +44 (0)125 422 2800. *History section on the CWV Ltd website.* www.wallpapers-uk.com

http://directory.google.com/Top/Business/ Construction_and_Maintenance/Materials_ and_Supplies/Wall,_Floor_and_Decorative_ Finishes/Wallpaper_and_Coverings/

Suppliers of Historic Patterns

Reproductions of historic wallpapers vary considerably. Some are made using the original printing method, materials and colours. At the other extreme are designs based on old models but adapted to new production techniques, rescaled and recoloured. There is also an increasing number of dealers in old wallcoverings – often called 'vintage'. The suppliers here all offer some papers that are closely related to identifiable historic examples. Information about the pedigree of a pattern can often be obtained from websites, pattern books, brochures or from the manufacturer or distributor. The collections and institutions listed in the previous sections are another source of advice. Suppliers' main offices are listed below. They or their websites will be able to provide details of local distributors and retailers.

Adelphi Paper Hangings P.O. Box 494, The Plains, VA 20198-0494, USA. Tel. +1 540 253 5367. www.adelphipaperhangings.com

Alexander Beauchamp Appleby Business Centre, Appleby Street, Blackburn, Lancs BB1 3BL, England. Tel. +44 (0)1254 691 133. www.alexanderbeauchamp.com

Laura Ashley Freepost SY1225, P.O. Box 19, Newtown, Powys SY16 1DZ, Wales. Tel. +44 (0)871 9835 999. www.lauraashley.com

Authentic Interiors 40 Gurner Street, Paddington, NSW 2021, Australia. Tel. +61 (2)9360 9893. www.authenticinteriors.com.au

Blue Mountain Wallcoverings Inc., Anaglypta and Lincrusta 15 Akron Road, Toronto, Ont. M8W 1T3, Canada. Tel. +1 800 219 2424. www.ihdg.com

Cynthia Bogart English Print Rooms P.O. Box 65, East Norwich, NY 11732, USA. Tel. +1 516 624 6979. www.printrooms.com

Bradbury & Bradbury P.O. Box 155, Benicia, CA 94510, USA. Tel. +1 707 746 1900. www.bradbury.com

Brunschwig & Fils Inc. 75 Virginia Road, North White Plains, NY 10603, USA. Tel. +1 914 684 5800. www.brunschwig.com

J. R. Burrows & Co. P.O. Box 522, Rockland, MA 02370, USA. Tel. +1 781 982 1812. www.burrows.com

Cole and Son Lifford House, Lifford Road, 199 Eade Road, London N4 1DN, England. Tel. +44 (0)20 8442 8844. www.cole-and-son.com

Colefax & Fowler 39 Brook Street, London W1K 4JE, England. Tel. +44 (0)20 7493 2231

Cowtan & Tout 979 Third Avenue, New York, NY 10022, USA. Tel. +1 212 753 4488

CWV Group Ltd, Anaglypta and Lincrusta Number One@The Beehive, Shadsworth Business Park, Lions Drive, Blackburn BB1 2QS, England. Tel. +44 (0)1254 222 800. www.wallpapers-uk.com

De Gournay 112 Old Church Street, Chelsea, London SW3 6EP, England. Tel. +44 (0)20 7823 7316. www.degournay.com

Design For Delight vintage wallpapers 1950s–1970s Jonkerplantsoen 2c, 1508 EE Zaandam, The Netherlands. Tel. +31 (0)75 655 5420. www.designfordelight.nl

Farrow & Ball Ltd Uddens Estate, Wimborne, Dor. BH21 7NL, England. Tel. +44 (0)120 287 6141. www.farrow-ball.com

Galacar & Co. Essex, MA 01929, USA. Tel. +1 978 768 6118

Gracie Inc. 419 Lafayette Street, New York, NY 10003, USA. Tel. +1 212 924 6816. www.graciestudio.com

Griffen Mill handmade papers www.griffenmill.com

Hamilton Weston Wallpapers 18 St Mary's Grove, Richmond, Sy TW9 1UY, England. Tel. +44 (0)20 8940 4850. www.hamiltonweston.com

Hannah's Treasures vintage wallpapers 1920–1960 P.O. Box 326, Harlan, IA 51537, USA. Tel. +1 712 755 3173. www.hannahstreasures.com

Fa. Julius Hembus Palleskestrasse 3, 65929 Frankfurt a. M., Germany. Tel. +49 (0)69 23 20 60. www.historische-tapeten.de

Christopher Hyland Inc. D&D Building, 979 Third Avenue, Suite 1710, New York, NY 10022, USA. Tel. +1 212 688 6121. www.christopherhyland.net

Interior1900 vintage wallpapers internet boutique www.interior1900.com

Johnny-Tapete vintage wallpapers Simone Schäfer & Falco Kleinschmidt GbR, Steeler Strasse 270, 45138 Essen, Germany. Tel. +49 (0)201 282 292. www.johnny-tapete.de

K. G. Designs 6 Hinkler Street, Brighton le Sands, NSW 2216, Australia. Tel. +61 (2)9597 5430. www.vandykes.com

Katzenbach & Warren 23645 Mercantile Rd, Cleveland, OH 44122-5901, USA. Tel. +1 216 464 3700.

Lutson Goudleder embossed and gilded leather hangings www.lutson.com

Laura McCoy Designs Inc. Stratford, CT 06614, USA. Tel. +1 203 386 1233. www.lauramccoydesigns.com

Mauny c/o Zuber & Cie: see below

Carol Mead Design www.carolmead.com

E. W. Moore & Son vintage wallcoverings 39–43 Plashet Grove, London E6 1AD, England. Tel. +44 (0)20 8471 9392. www.ewmoore.com

Mt Diablo Handprints 451 Ryder Street, Vallejo, CA 94590, USA. Tel. +1 707 554 2682. www.carterandco.com

Nobilis 29 rue Bonaparte, Paris 75006, France. Tel. +33 (0)1 43 29 21 50. www.nobilis.fr

Paperhangings 463 Whitehorse Road, Balwyn, VIC 3103, Australia. Tel. +61 (3)9888 4063

Sanderson Sanderson House, Oxford Road, Denham, Bucks. UB9 4DX, England. Tel. +44 (0)1895 830 044. www.sanderson-online.co.uk

Scalamandre 300 Trade Zone Drive, Ronkonkoma, NY 11779, USA. Tel. +1 631 467 8800. www.scalamandre.com

F. Schumacher & Co. 79 Madison Avenue, New York, NY 10016, USA. Tel. +1 212 213 7900. www.fschumacher.com

Secondhand Rose vintage 138 Duane Street, New York, NY 10013, USA. Tel. +1 212 393 9002. www.secondhandrose.com

David Skinner & Sons The Mill, Celbridge, Co. Kildare, Ireland. Tel. +353 (0)1 627 2913. www.skinnerwallpaper.com

George Spencer Designs 33 Elystan Street, London SW3 3NT, England. Tel. +44 (0)20 7584 3003. www.georgespencer.com

Françoise and Marie-F. Subes Château des Evêques, St Pandelon, 40180 Dax, France. Tel. +33 (0)5 58 98 72 19

Tapetorama vintage wallpapers Rädmansgatan 5, 211 46 Malmö, Sweden. Tel. + 46 (0)40 50 55 85. www.tapetorama.se

Thibaut 480 Frelinghuysen Avenue, Newark, NJ 07114, USA. Tel. +1 973 643 1118. www.thibautdesign.com

Victorian Collectibles 845 East Glenbrook Road, Milwaukee, WI 53217, USA. Tel. +1 800 783 3829. www.victorianwallpaper.com

Waterhouse Wallhangings 260 Maple Street, Chelsea, MA 02150, USA. Tel. +1 617 884 8222. www.wallpaperinstaller.com/waterhouse

Watts of Westminster 3/14 Third Floor, Centre Dome, Chelsea Harbour Design Centre, London SW10 0XE, England. Tel. +44 (0)20 7376 4486. www.wattsofwestminster.com

Wolff House Wallpapers 133 South Main Street, Mt Vernon, OH 43050, USA. Tel. +1 740 397 9466. www.wolffhouseartpapers.com

Geert Wisse Meubelpapieren/Papiers à meubler D'Heuverhove te Wijlegem, 9630 Zwalm, Belgium. Tel./fax. +32 (0)55 49 68 92. geertwisse@skynet.be

Zoffany Chalfont House, Oxford Road, Denham, Bucks. UB9 4DX, England. Tel. +44 (0)8708 300 350. www.zoffany.co.uk

Zuber & Cie 28 rue Zuber, BP 1, 68171 Rixheim, France. Tel. +33 (0)3 89 44 13 88. www.zuber.fr

Index

Numerals in *italic* type refer to illustrations and captions. An asterisk * indicates that a concept will also be found in the Glossary, pp. 266–67.

Acknowledgments for Illustrations

Sources of photographs and locations of images illustrated, in addition to those mentioned in the captions, are as follows:

Abbotsford, Melrose 66 ● Courtesy American Antiquarian Society, Worcester, Mass. 175 ● G. P. & J. Baker 322 ● Blue Mountain Wallcoverings, Inc., Toronto 336, 337 ● Society for the Preservation of New England Antiquities, Boston 167, 176, 205, photo David Bohl 33, 60, 155, 158, 162, 163, 165, 166, 168, 171, 177 ● Courtesy Deborah Bowness 347 ● Bradbury & Bradbury 329 ● Brewster Wallcovering Company 346 ● Royal Pavilion, Art Gallery and Museums, Brighton 63 ● Brunschwig & Fils, New York 350 ● Koninklijke Musea voor Kunst en Geschiedenis, Brussels, photo Geert Wisse 12 ● Collection of the Burchfield Art Center, Buffalo State College, Buffalo, N.Y., Buffalo Foundation Fund (1973:39) 272 ● Collection Carlhian 131 ● 'Orange Lily' by Jane Gordon Clark for Ornamenta, London 333 ● Prestwould Foundation, Clarksville, Va. 169 ● colourEverything, Sydney, www.coloureverything.com 349 ● Photo courtesy Concord Museum, Concord, Mass. 173 ● Photo Country Life Picture Library 32, 58, 83 ● Coutts & Co., London 61 ● Crown Wallcoverings 303, 304, 306, 323, 330 ● Jack Denst Designs, Chicago 313 ● Photo DRAC Rhône-Alpes, CRMH, Lyons 129 ● in Dresden: Landesamt für Denkmalpflege 2, 3; Stadtmuseum 8 ● National Gallery of Ireland, Dublin 154 ● English Heritage Photographic Library 35, 37, 48, 49 ● Epsom & Ewell Borough Council, photo Anthony Wells-Cole 23, photo Temple Newsam House, Leeds City Art Galleries 24, 25, 26 ● Guy Evans Ltd 324 ● Photo Flammarion 132, 138, 139, 143, 144, 148, 151, 152 ● Musée d'Art et d'Histoire, Fribourg 17 ● Front, Stockholm. Photo Anna Lonnerstam 352, 353 ● Graham & Brown, Blackburn 345 ● Lesley Hoskins 183, 200, 295 ● IdeaStix Inc., Torrance, Calif., 'Tropical Pairs' © 2000. Image Karoline Daly KDSF 338 ● Imperial Wallcoverings, Inc. 318 ● Photo courtesy Imperial Wallcoverings 327 (wallpapers from left to right, © 1989 Mario Buatta/© Katzenbach & Warren, Inc./© Louis W. Bowen Fine Wallcoverings MCMLXXXX/ © Sterling Prints/© Imperial Wallcoverings/© Katzenbach & Warren, Inc./© Imperial Wallcoverings/a Gear design by Raymond Waites © 1990 Gear Holdings, Inc.) ● Imperial Wallcoverings/© Sterling Prints ● Innovations in Wallcoverings, Inc., New York 342 ● Photo J. C. Jacques © 1976, Inventaire Général 109 ● Mr and Mrs Antony Jarvis, photo Temple Newsam House, Leeds City Art Galleries 34, 51 ● Deutsches Tapeten-museum, Kassel 21, 82, 84, 85, 93, 134, 251–255, 257–264 ● Interactive Wallpaper™ by Rachel Kelly, London 340, 341 ● Tracy Kendall, London 351 ● Photo A. F. Kersting 59 ● Kings Lynn Museum, photo Temple Newsam House, Leeds City Art Galleries 28 ● Temple Newsam House, Leeds City Art Galleries 36, 38, 40, 43, 47, 50, 52, 53, 65 ● in London: Heal Collection, Trustees of the British Museum 27; © Central Saint Martins Art and Design Archive, The London Institute 314; Tate Gallery 179; Courtesy of the Board of Trustees of the Victoria & Albert Museum 6, 29, 41, 44, 55, 62, 67–72, 127, 141, 185, 193, 196–198 ● Lydiard Park, Borough of Thamesdown 39 ● in Manchester: Manchester City Art Galleries 208; Whitworth Art Gallery, University of Manchester 22, 182, 184, 187, 189, 199, 204, 206, 209–213, 217, 220–222, 224–229, 231, 239 ● The Jeremiah Lee Mansion/The Marblehead Historical Society, Marblehead, Mass., photo David Bohl 156, 160 ● Marburger Tapetenfabrik, J. B. Schaefer GmbH & Co. KG 305, 307, 311, 325, 328, 332, 344 ● Photo Georgina Masson 54 ● Mauny 308 ● © Copyright 1993 Wittelsbacher Ausgleichsfonds München, Munich 130 ● © National Trust Photographic Library, photo John Bethell 30, photo Erik Pelham 31 ● Maître Néret-Minet, photo Flammarion 143 ● New Bedford Whaling Museum, Mass. 170 ● in New York: Courtesy of Cooper Hewitt, National Design Museum, Smithsonian Institution–Art Resource, NY (1943-54-1, Gift of Misa Myrta Mason) 181, (1937-57-3; Gift of John D. Rockefeller, Jr) 215, (1972-51-13, Gift of Deerfield Academy) 232, (1970-26-4cdd, Gift of Jones and Erwin) 235, (1979-91-8, Gift of Victorian Collectibles) 237, (1972-50-2, Gift of Municipal Wallpaper, Greeley, Colorado) 238, (1959-130-1, Gift of Denst and Soderlund) 281, (1959-134-1, Gift of Katzenbach and Warren, Inc) 282, (1949-25-1, Gift of Edward F. McGuiness) 283, (1954-21-6, Gift of B.H. Hellman) 285 (1947-92-1, Gift of United Wallpaper) 286, (1953-198-3c, Gift of The Wallpaper Magazine) 288, (1969-55-1, Gift of Laverne International) 289, (1992-129-1, Gift of Kathleen Paton) 290, (1969-52-1, Gift of United Wallpaper) 291, (1969-54-1, Gift of Woodson Wall-papers, Inc) 292, (1969-70-3, Gift of William Justema) 293, (Libraries, photo Ken Pelka) 236, (Picture Collection) 280, (Wallpaper Research Files) 234, 287, 361; The Byron Collection, Museum of The City of New York 240 ● Old Sturbridge Village, Sturbridge, Mass. 174 ● ÖNCÜ GRUP A.S., Istanbul 334 ● Ashmolean Museum, Oxford 7 ● Pacific Wallcoverings Limited, NZ. 'Looking East' cover design Bernadette Breen of Imago Design, Wellington, NZ 335 ● in Paris: Bibliothèque Forney 89, 94, 256; Bibliothèque Nationale de France 19, 124, 241; Musée des Arts Décoratifs 80, photo L. Sully-Jaulmes 10, 20, 73, 74, 78, 87, 95–101, 105, 106, 113–123, 125, 126, 128, 137, 140, 149, 150, on deposit from Musée Carnavalet, Paris 102, photo Flammarion 138, 139, 144, 151, 152 ● PGC Promotions Ltd 321 ● Collection Bernard Poteau 108 ● Photo Francis de Richemont/Photodéco 107 ● Private Collection 1, 11, 15, 103, photo Flammarion 132, 148 ● Gebr. Rasch GmbH & Co., Bramsche 298, 300, 319, 331, 339 ● Musée du Papier Peint, Rixheim 9, 16, 64, 75–77, 79, 81, 90, 92, 112, 135, 136, 146, 147, 180, 242–249 ● 'Beadazzled™ Flexible Glass Bead Wallcovering. © 2004 The Maya Romanoff Corporation. Patent Pending. Photo © Darrin Haddad 343 ● Photo Rost, Courtesy Landesamt für Denkmalpflege, Mainz 110 ● Photo Royal Commission on the Historical Monuments of England 192 ● Arthur Sanderson & Sons Ltd 186, 188, 190, 194, 201–203, 214, 216, 230, 294, 296, 297, 301, 302, 316, 320 ● Mary Schoeser 326 ● MoDA (formerly Silver Studio Collection), Middlesex University 218, 219, 265–271, 273–279, 354–360, 362, 363 ● © 1984 Sotheby's, Inc. (New York) 91 ● Stafford Borough Council, photo Temple Newsam House, Leeds City Art Galleries 42 ● in Stockholm: Nordiska Museet 223; The Royal Collections 88 ● Stonor Park, Henley-on-Thames, Oxon 153 ● Photo L. Sully-Jaulmes 250 ● Courtesy Peter Topp Wall-coverings Ltd, London 207 ● Courtesy Ingemar Tunander 299 ● Turner Wallcoverings Ltd 315 ● The Mark Twain House, Hartford, Conn. 233 ● Photo Centraal Museum, Utrecht 56 ● Musée de la Révolution Française, Vizille, photo P. Fillioley 111 ● Vymura International Ltd 309, 310 ● Dr Friederike Wappenschmidt 57 ● in Washington, D.C.: Library of Congress, Prints and Photo-graphs Division 172; © 1983 National Gallery of Art, Washington: gift of Edgar William and Bernice Chrysler Garbisch 157, 161 ● Watts & Co. Furnishings Ltd, London 195 ● Stiftung Weimar-er Klassik, Weimar 18 ● Kloster Wienhausen 4 ● Colonial Williamsburg Foundation 159 ● Winfield Design Associates, Inc. 312 ● Photo Geert Wisse 12, 13, 14, 86, 104 ● York City Art Gallery 178 ● York Wallcoverings, York, Pa. 348 ● © Zoffany Ltd, Wakefield Museums, Galleries and Castles 45, 46 ● Zuber & Cie 142, 145, 317 ● Swiss National Museum, Zürich (LM 2654. Co-2963) 1.